A Landscape Photographer's Guide to
Glacier National Park

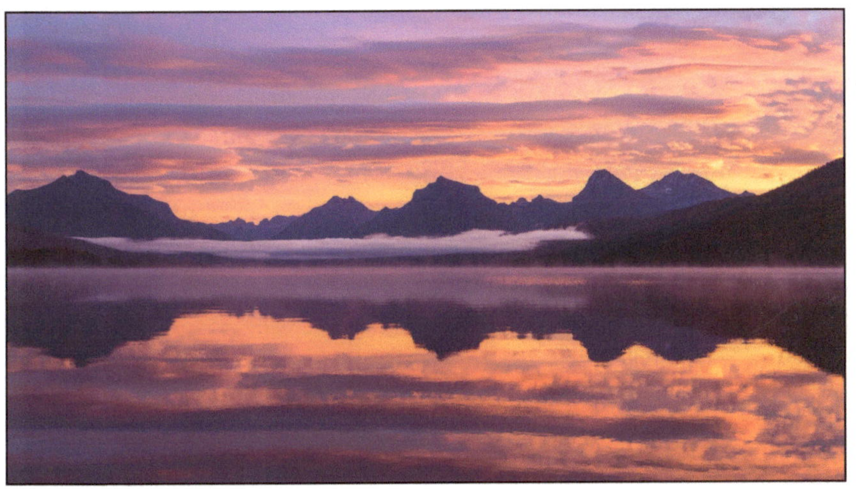

Anthony Jones

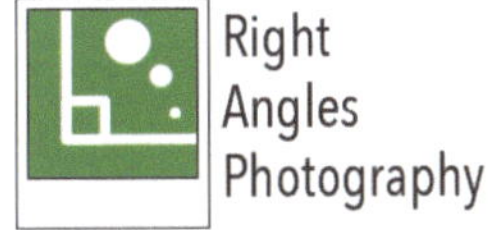

To Taryn, my daughter.

I'm proud of you.

MAPS PRINTED IN THIS BOOK ARE FOR ORIENTATION ONLY AND SHOULD NOT BE USED FOR NAVIGATION.

Media Sources:

Park Maps, pp. 4-6, 8, 10, 12-14, 31, 35, National Park Service, public domain.

Webcam Image, p. 49, National Park Service, public domain.

All other images by the author.

Contents

MONTANA
BOUNDARY MOUNTAINS
Boundary Creek
Kintla Creek
Lake Nooney
Lake Wurdeman
Mount Custer 8883ft 2702m
Campbell Mountain 8245ft 2513m
Upper Kintla Lake
Carcajou Lake
Goat Overlook
(closed: no border crossing)
Boulder Pass
Brown Pass
Brown Lake
Lake Janet
Rainbow Falls
Kintla Lake
Kintla Peak 10101ft 3079m
Agassiz Glacier
Thunderbird Glacier
Lake Francis
Olson Creek
Kootenai Lakes
Kintla Glacier
Numa Ridge
Thunderbird Mountain 8790ft 2679m
Dixon Glacier
LIVINGSTON
Akokala Lake
Mount Carter 9843ft 3000m
Weasel Collar Glacier
Kootenai Peak 8542ft 2603m
Stoney Indian Pass
Rainbow Glacier
Cerulean Lake
Valentine Creek
Round Prairie
vi
a
Big Prairie
Bowman Creek
Bowman Lake
Lower Quartz Lake
Middle Quartz Lake
Quartz Lake
GLACIER
Continental Divide
Vulture Peak 9638ft 2937m
Vulture Glacier
RANGE
FLATHEAD MOUNTAIN
Moose Creek
Hawk Creek
Road (closed in winter)
North Fork
6mi 10km
Mount Geduhn 8375ft 2552m
Grace Lake
FLATHEAD NATIONAL FOREST
0.3mi 0.5km
1mi 2km
Polebridge
Polebridge
Logging Lake
Longfellow Peak 8904ft 2714m
Lake Evangeline
Ruger Lake
NAT
Hay Creek
Flathead River
Winona Lake
Quartz Creek
Quartz Creek
Logging Creek
Dutch Lake
Arrow Lake
Coal Creek
Logging Creek
13mi 21km
Anaconda Creek
Inside North Fork Road
i
Trout Lake
Av
Stanton Mountain 7750ft 2362m
Rogers Lake
Lake McDonald
Camas Creek Entrance
Camas Creek
Camas Road
Lake McDonald
Outside North Fork Road
b
Road
Forest and Fire Trail
Huckleberry Mtn 6593ft 2009m
11mi 18km
29mi km
HOWE RIDGE
Big Creek Outdoor Education Center
Big Creek U.S. Forest Service
Big Creek
Fish Creek
LAKE McDONALD
315ft 961m
SNYDER RIDGE
32mi 51km
Fish Creek
Going-to-the-Sun Road
APGAR
13mi 21km
Fern Creek
Apgar
Apgar Visitor Center
To Eureka
WHITEFISH RANGE
Glacier Institute Field Camp
2mi 3km
West Entrance Park Headquarters
West Glacier Railroad Depot
APGAR MOUNTAINS
WHITEFISH LAKE
Lake Five
10mi 16km
Blankenship Bridge
5km
FLATHEAD NATIONAL
Whitefish Lake State Park
93
Whitefish
Burlington Northern and Santa Fe Railway
2
Coram
Teakettle Mountain 5936ft 1809m
Hungry Horse U.S. Forest Service
South Fork Flathead River
40
Columbia Falls
93
Flathead River
2
206
SWAN RANGE
Glacier Park International Airport
To Kalispell
To Kalispell

Legend

Unpaved road
Trail
Distance indicator 3mi 5km
Continental Divide
Glacier
Warden/Ranger station
Warden/Ranger station (infrequently staffed)
Food service and lodging
Picnic area
Riding stable
Boat tour/rentals
Campground
Primitive campground
Backcountry campground
Self-guiding trail
Wheelchair-accessible trail
Lookout tower

4

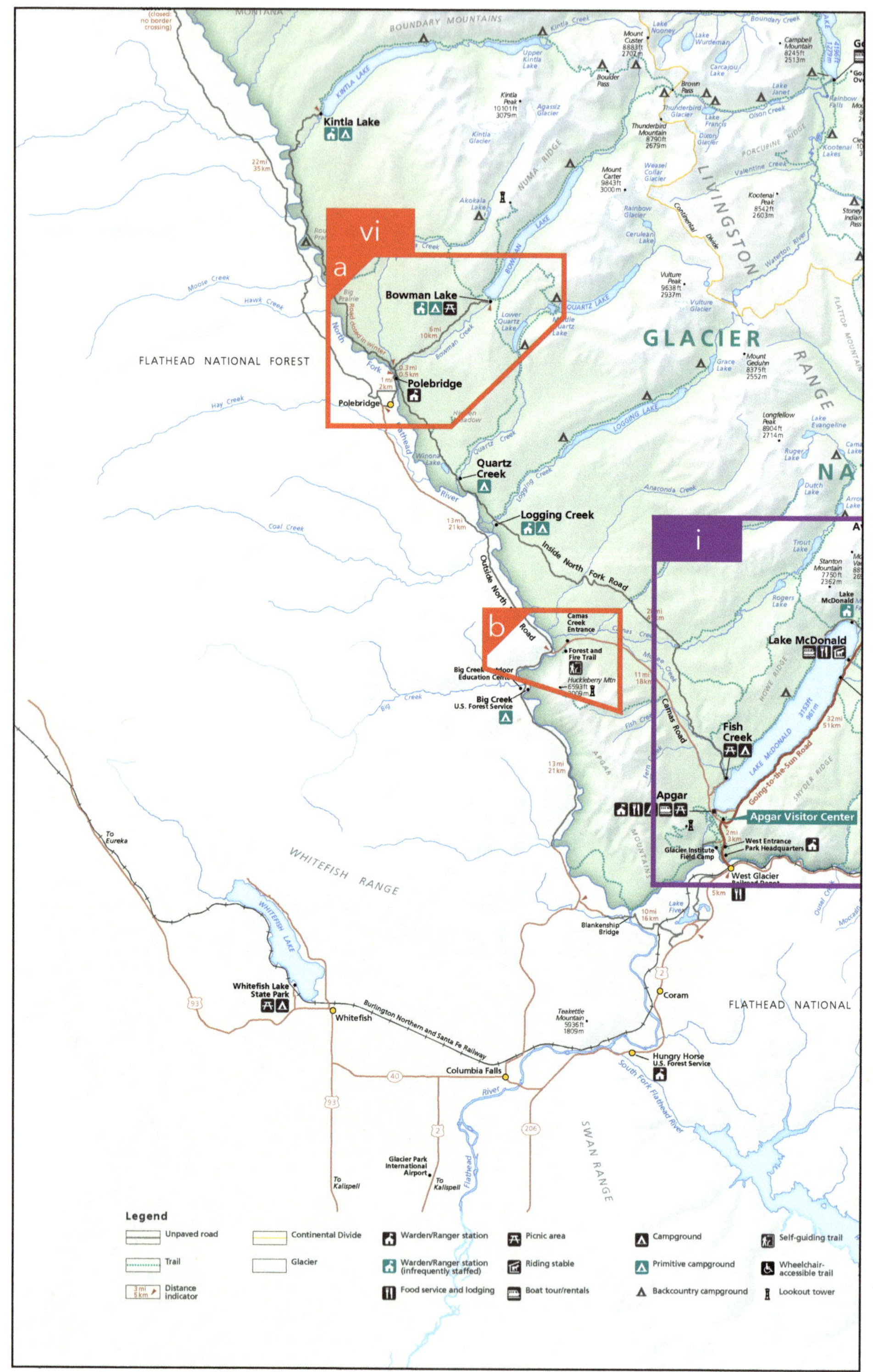

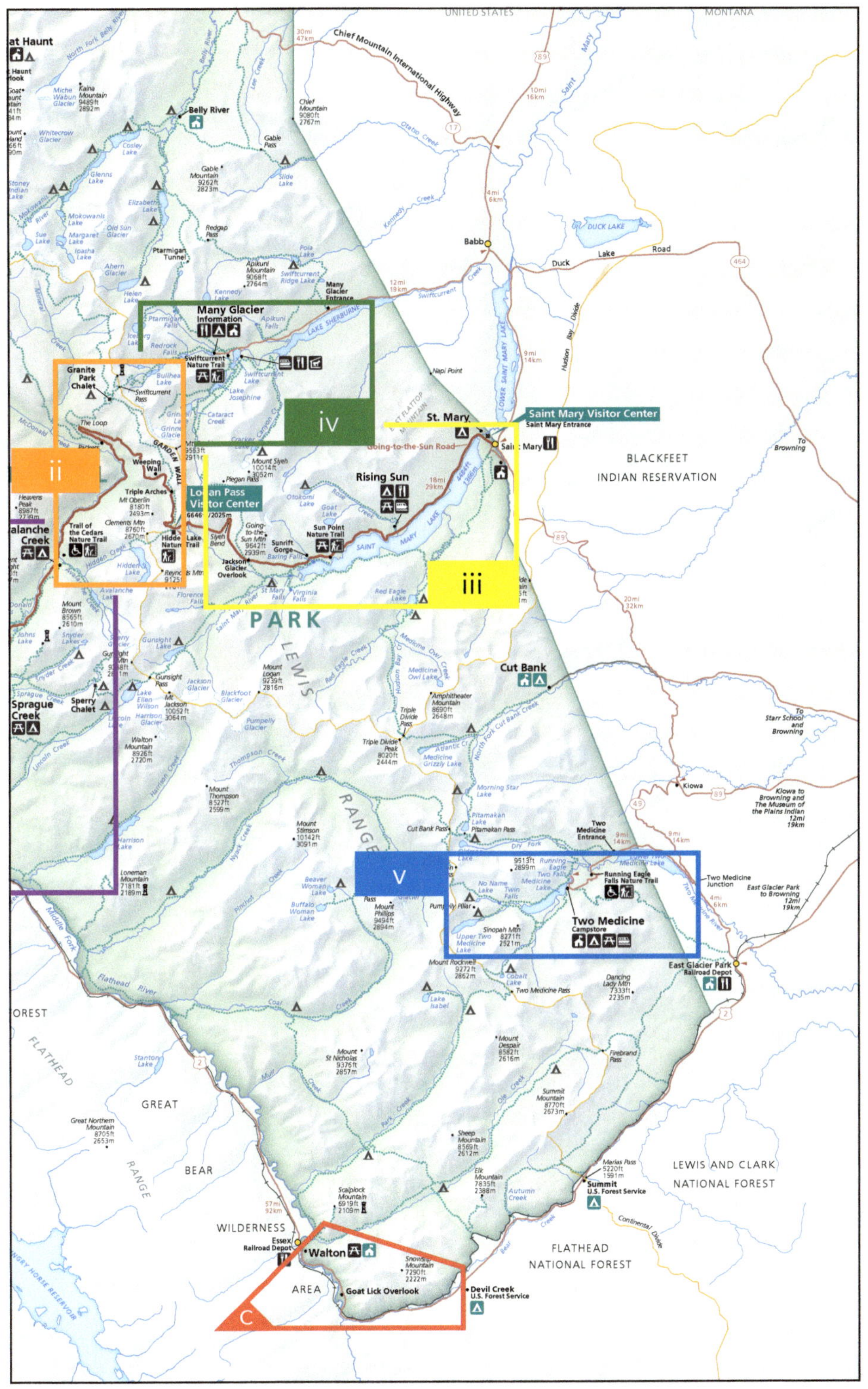

UNITED STATES
MONTANA
Chief Mountain International Highway
North Fork Belly River
Goat Haunt
Goat Haunt Overlook
Kaina Mountain 9489ft 2892m
Miche Wabun Glacier
Whitecrow Glacier
Mount Cleveland 10466ft 3190m
Cosley Lake
Glenns Lake
Belly River
Chief Mountain 9080ft 2767m
Gable Pass
Gable Mountain 9262ft 2823m
Slide Lake
Otatso Creek
Babb
DUCK LAKE
Duck Lake Road
Stoney Indian Lake
Mokowanis River
Elizabeth Lake
Redgap Pass
Kennedy Creek
Sue Lake
Margaret Lake
Old Sun Glacier
Ipasha Lake
Ahern Glacier
Ptarmigan Tunnel
Apikuni Mountain 9068ft 2764m
Poia Lake
Swiftcurrent
LAKE SHERBURNE
LOWER SAINT MARY LAKE
Hudson Bay Divide
Helen Lake
Ptarmigan Falls
Redrock Falls
Iceberg Lake
Many Glacier Information
Swiftcurrent Nature Trail
Many Glacier Entrance
Apikuni Falls
Kennedy Lake
iv
Napi Point
Granite Park Chalet
Bullhead Lake
Swiftcurrent Pass
The Loop
Weeping Wall
GARDEN WALL
Grinnell Lake Grinnell Glacier
Lake Josephine
Swiftcurrent Lake
Cataract Creek
Cracker Lake
Cracker Canyon Creek
EAST FLATTOP MOUNTAIN
St. Mary
Saint Mary Visitor Center
Saint Mary Entrance
ii
Mount Gould 9553ft 2911m
Going-to-the-Sun Road
Saint Mary
BLACKFEET INDIAN RESERVATION
To Browning
Heavens Peak 8987ft 2739m
Triple Arches
Mt Oberlin 8180ft 2493m
Mount Siyeh 10014ft 3052m
Piegan Pass
Logan Pass Visitor Center
Rising Sun
Avalanche Creek
Trail of the Cedars Nature Trail
Clements Mtn 8760ft 2670m
Hidden Lake Nature Trail
Lake Trail
6646ft 2025m
Otokomi Lake
Going-to-the-Sun Mtn 9642ft 2939m
Goat Lake
Sun Point Nature Trail
SAINT MARY LAKE
Rose Creek
iii
Reynolds Mtn 9125m
Hidden Lake
Sunrift Gorge
Baring Falls
Siyeh Bend
Jackson Glacier Overlook
Florence Falls
St Mary Falls
Virginia Falls
PARK
Red Eagle Lake
Mount Brown 8565ft 2610m
Avalanche Lake
Sperry Glacier
Gunsight Lake
Red Eagle Creek
Hudson Bay Creek
Medicine Owl Creek
Cut Bank
Johns Lake
Snyder Lakes
Gunsight Mtn 9258ft 2821m
Mount Logan 9239ft 2816m
Gunsight Pass
Jackson Glacier
Blackfoot Glacier
Medicine Owl Lake
Sprague Creek
Sperry Chalet
Lake Ellen Wilson
Mt Jackson 10052ft 3064m
Harrison Lincoln Creek
Pumpelly Glacier
Amphitheater Mountain 8690ft 2648m
Triple Divide Pass
Kiowa
To Starr School and Browning
LEWIS
Walton Mountain 8926ft 2720m
Thompson Creek
Triple Divide Peak 8020ft 2444m
Medicine Grizzly Lake
North Fork Cut Bank Creek
Kiowa to Browning and The Museum of the Plains Indian 12mi 19km
Harrison Lake
Mount Thompson 8527ft 2599m
RANGE
Morning Star Lake
Nyack Creek
Loneman Mountain 7181ft 2189m
Mount Stimson 10142ft 3091m
Cut Bank Pass
Pitamakan Lake
Pitamakan Pass
Two Medicine Entrance
Two Medicine Junction
East Glacier Park to Browning 12mi 19km
Beaver Woman Lake
Pinchot Creek
Cut Bank Creek
V
No Name Lake
Running Eagle Two Falls
Twin Falls
Running Eagle Falls Nature Trail
Pass
Mount Phillips 9494ft 2894m
Buffalo Woman Lake
Pumpelly Pillar
LOWER TWO MEDICINE LAKE
MIDDLE FORK FLATHEAD RIVER
Flathead River
Upper Two Medicine Lake
Sinopah Mtn 8271ft 2521m
Two Medicine Campstore
East Glacier Park Railroad Depot
Mount Rockwell 9272ft 2852m
Cobalt Lake
Two Medicine Pass
Dancing Lady Mtn 7333ft 2235m
FOREST
FLATHEAD
Lake Isabel
Mount St Nicholas 9376ft 2857m
Mount Despair 8582ft 2616m
Firebrand Pass
GREAT
Stanton Lake
Park Creek
RANGE
BEAR
Great Northern Mountain 8705ft 2653m
Sheep Mountain 8569ft 2612m
Summit Mountain 8770ft 2673m
LEWIS AND CLARK NATIONAL FOREST
Elk Mountain 7835ft 2388m
Marias Pass 5220ft 1591m
Summit U.S. Forest Service
Continental Divide
WILDERNESS
Scalplock Mountain 6919ft 2109m
Essex Railroad Depot
Walton
Autumn Creek
Ole Creek
Bear Creek
FLATHEAD NATIONAL FOREST
AREA
Snowslip Mountain 7290ft 2222m
Goat Lick Overlook
Devil Creek U.S. Forest Service
C
HUNGRY HORSE RESERVOIR
30mi 47km
17
89
Saint Mary River
10mi 16km
464
4mi 6km
12mi 19km
9mi 14km
18mi 29km
89
20mi 32km
49
9mi 14km
4mi 6km
2
57mi 92km
2

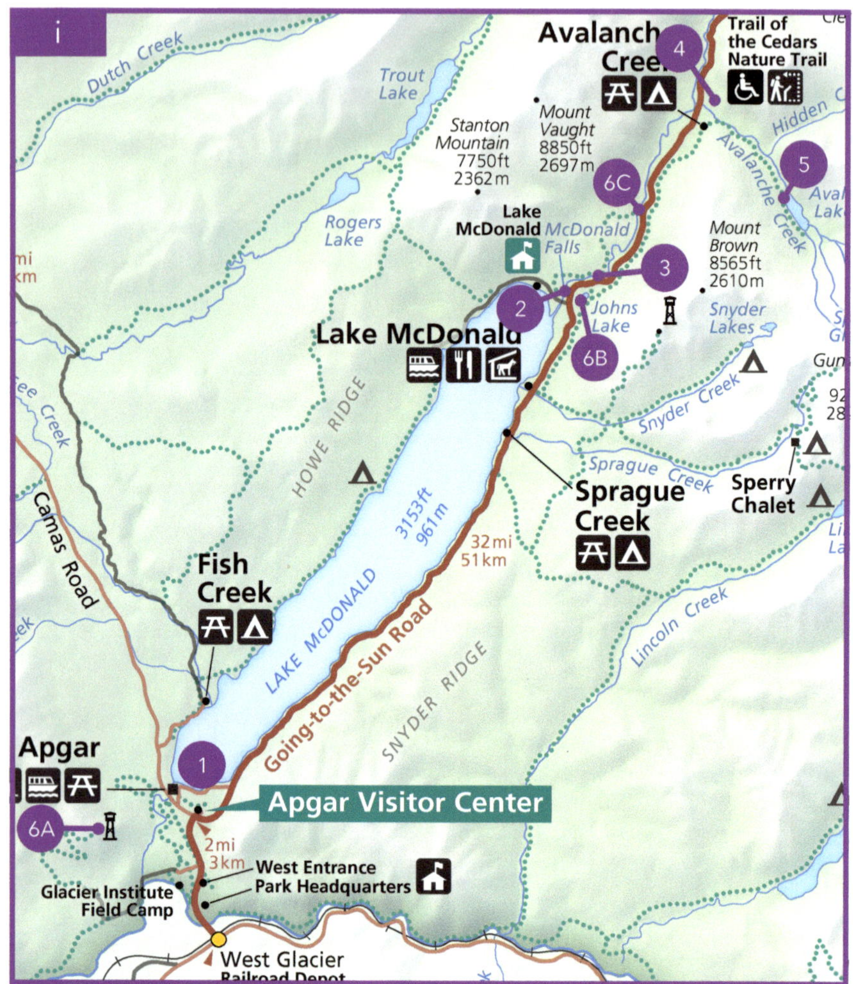

1. Lake McDonald 46

Sunrise photography at Lake McDonald can be extraordinary. Several lakeshore sites are presented as options for your pursuit. During the daytime, captain a small motor boat (available for rental) or provide the power yourself in a canoe or kayak or on a stand-up paddleboard.

2. McDonald Falls 50

Find the "hidden" trail and descend through the forest to McDonald Falls. A variety of compositions are possible here, and small pools of water make for an interesting foreground.

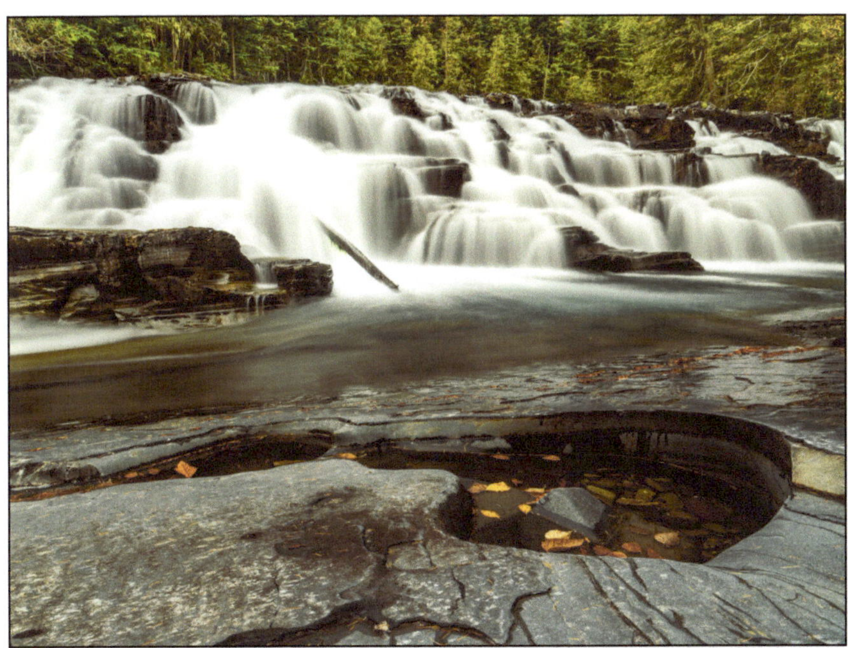

McDonald Falls   24mm f/16 2s ISO50

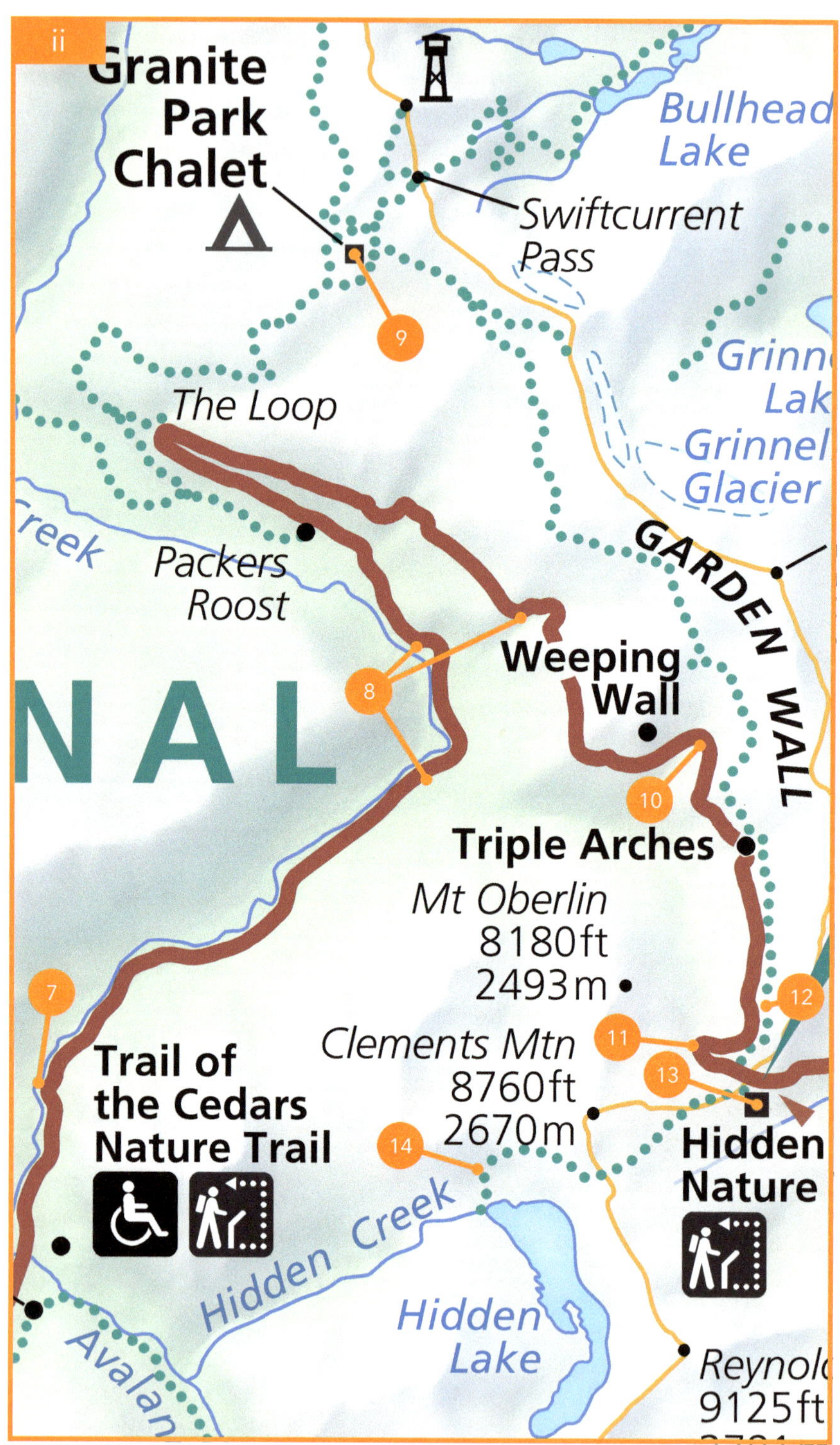

ii
Granite Park Chalet
Bullhead Lake
Swiftcurrent Pass
9
The Loop
Grinne
Lak
Grinnel
Glacier
Creek
Packers Roost
GARDEN WALL
NAL
Weeping Wall
8
10
Triple Arches
Mt Oberlin
8180ft
2493m
7
Clements Mtn
8760ft
2670m
11
12
13
Trail of
the Cedars
Nature Trail
14
Hidden
Nature
Hidden Creek
Hidden Lake
Avalan
Reynol
9125ft

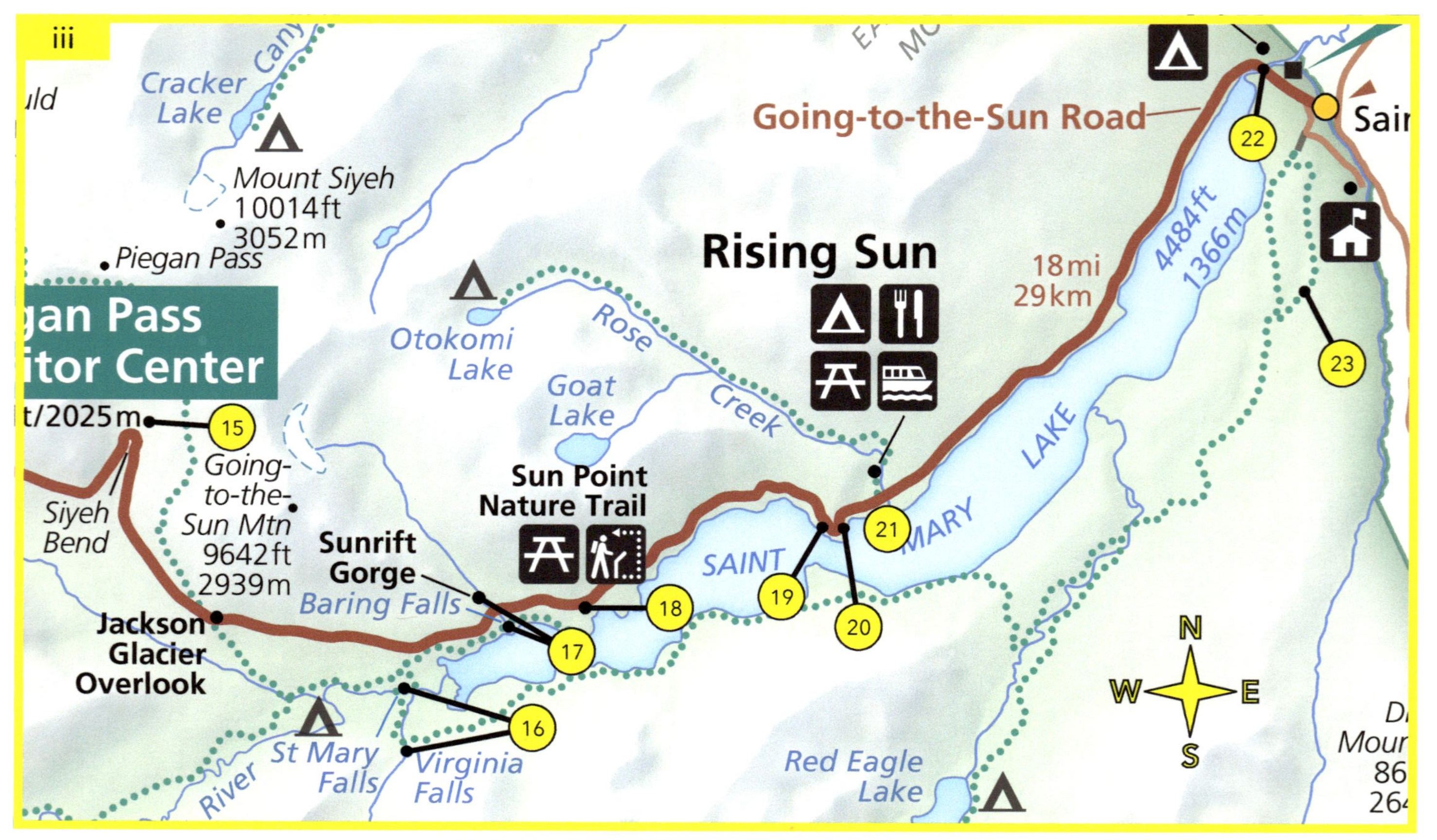

Going-to-the-Sun Road
Rising Sun
Cracker Lake
Canyon
Mount Siyeh
10014ft
3052m
Piegan Pass
gan Pass
itor Center
t/2025m
15
Going-to-the-Sun Mtn
9642ft
2939m
Siyeh Bend
Sunrift Gorge
Baring Falls
Otokomi Lake
Goat Lake
Rose Creek
Sun Point Nature Trail
Jackson Glacier Overlook
St Mary Falls
Virginia Falls
River
16
17
18
19
20
21
SAINT
MARY
LAKE
4484ft
1366m
18mi
29km
22
23
Sair
Red Eagle Lake
N
E
S
W
D
Mour
86
264
iii
10

Discover an optical illusion along Siyeh Creek, where the water appears to flow against gravity.

Crowded midday, arrive early for these two popular waterfalls. The water flow can be vigorous.

Challenge your composition talent at Sunrift Gorge and then follow Baring Creek under Sun Road to the gushing waterfall below.

Stunning views east and west, and satisfactorily high above Saint Mary Lake, Sun Point provides weather-beaten trees as an appropriate Glacier National Park foreground.

Along Sun Road, consider this the favorite for sunrise. A renovated overlook provides multiple viewing options of this renowned park feature.

A fun exercise in nighttime photography. An alternative location is presented, as well as sites for capturing the Milky Way.

Climb aboard and depart from Rising Sun, meandering past Wild Goose Island. All but the final tour of the day dock at Baring Falls, allowing passengers to visit after a short hike.

Built in 1935 and featured in the film "Forrest Gump," this stone bridge, covered in part by bright orange lichen, sits neatly below the majestic, distant peaks of Glacier National Park.

Start at a historic ranger station and barn, situated among Aspen that are a vibrant yellow in the fall. The loop provides variety in your hike experience, and near the far end is a pond and beaver habitat to admire.

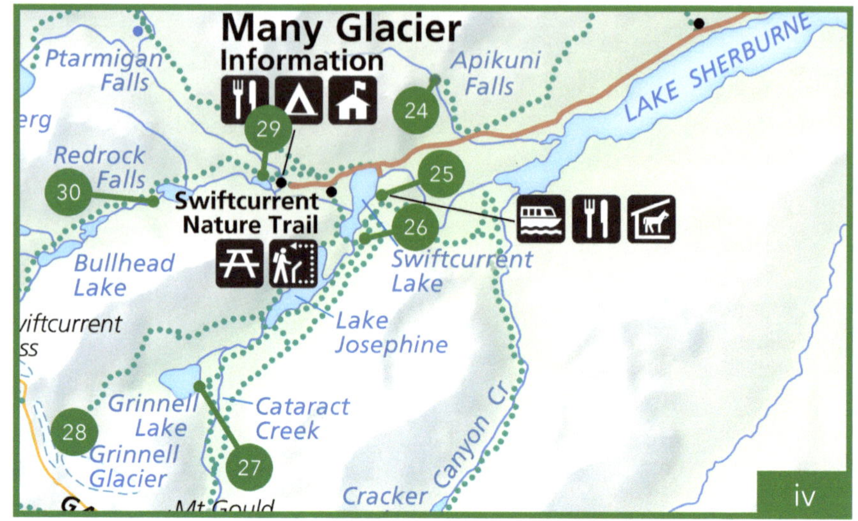

24. Apikuni Falls   102

Ascend through the woods to discover this multi-tiered waterfall, just beyond your line of sight from the road.

25. Many Glacier Boat Tour   104

Two tours in one: glide along both Swiftcurrent Lake and Lake Josephine while learning about the history and ecosystem of Many Glacier. Keep an eye out for wildlife in the distance.

26. Swiftcurrent Nature Trail   106

An easy route around Swiftcurrent Lake. My recommendation is to begin and end at Many Glacier Hotel for easier parking.

27. Grinnell Lake   107

A round-trip hike of about 7 miles, Grinnell Lake is an area favorite with its teal-colored water under neighboring peaks. The route is mostly level and popular with families.

28. Grinnell Glacier   109

Beyond Grinnell Lake, though not accessible on the same trail approach, Upper Grinnell Lake sits some 1,500 ft higher in elevation and holds water (and ice!) from Grinnell Glacier and the even higher Salamander Glacier. The effort is worth it – the site is marvelous for photography!

29. Fishercap Lake   112

Take a short hike, or couple with Redrock Falls, to this "reflection" lake. Moose and deer frequent the lakeshore.

30. Redrock Falls   114

In color theory, the plentiful orange and red rocks here make for a perfect complementary pairing to the aqua water and green trees. This could be a case study in an art class!

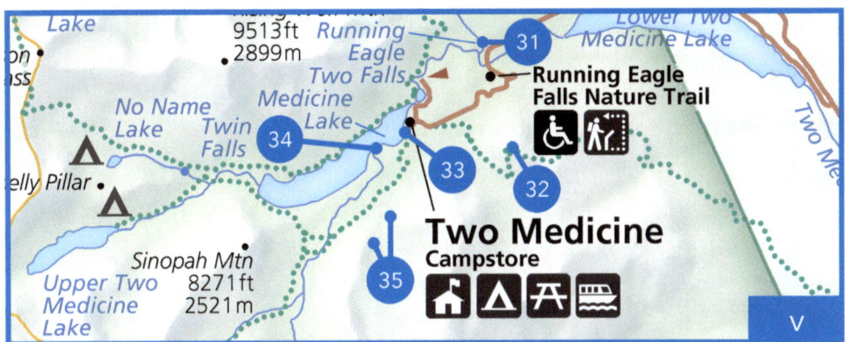

31. Running Eagle Falls   116

The most fascinating waterfall you may have ever seen!

32. Scenic Point Trail   118

Elect the entire distance to Scenic Point or to about the 2-mile point, where the Two Medicine Lake vista becomes excellent.

33. Two Medicine Lake   122

Unsettled clouds often occupy Two Medicine's west back-drop, providing a colorful sunrise that's hard to beat.

34. Paradise Point   123

If limited on time, the short hike to Paradise Point provides an additional perspective on Two Medicine Lake and Rising Wolf Mountain to its north.

35. Aster Falls & Aster Park   124

Venture southwest and climb to Aster Park, where windswept trees become less dense for improved views. Either going or while coming back, detour to gentle Aster Falls.

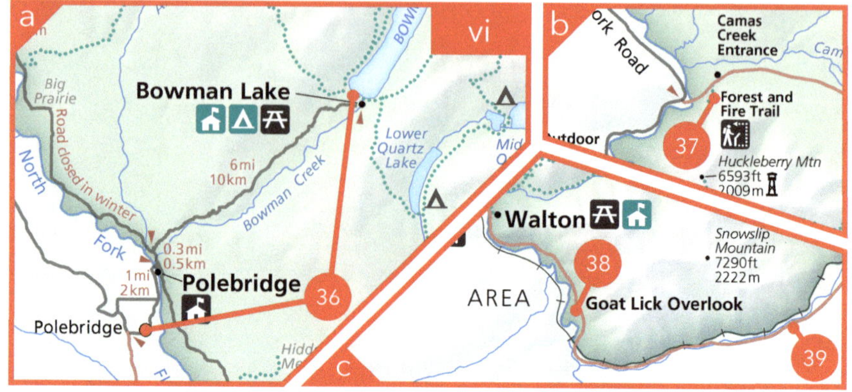

36. Polebridge & Bowman Lake 128

Visit the Polebridge Mercantile for delicious baked treats and navigate a bumpy dirt road back into the national park, continuing to picturesque Bowman Lake.

37. Forest and Fire Nature Trail 131

Perhaps more educational than photogenic, this short loop trail provides compositions highlighting the juxtaposition of rapid forest regrowth around larger fire-charred trees.

38. Goat Lick Overlook 132

Goat sightings are unfortunately rare at this stop along the highway between West Glacier and East Glacier Park, but there is still photography potential. It's worth a brief stop.

39. Silver Staircase Waterfall 133

A seasonal waterfall, at its best in spring. When Sun Road is closed and driving this route is necessary, it fits the bill nicely.

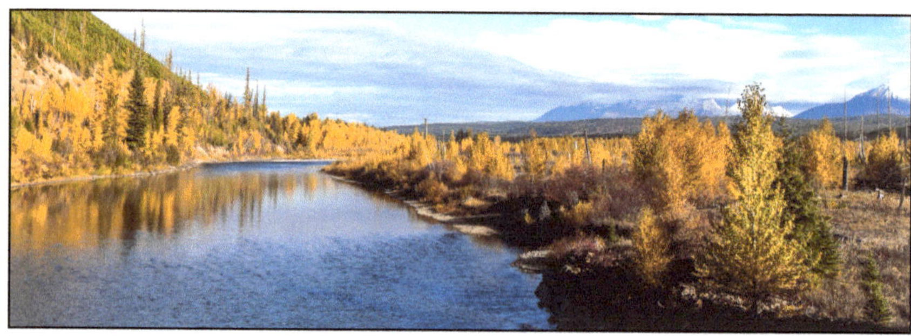

North Fork Flathead River in Late September 28mm f/11 1/125s ISO100

Introduction

Welcome to Glacier National Park, the "Crown of the Continent." Its name embodies a park not only *with* glaciers but also its unique mountainscape *carved by* glaciers.

Photography in Glacier National Park is incredibly rewarding, thanks to the razor-sharp shapes of its mountain peaks, the variety of forest colors each season provides, the quickly-moving and ever-changing clouds, and of course the abundance of interesting wildlife present. Traverse Going-to-the-Sun Road (or "Sun Road," as locals call it), the park's main corridor, for awe-inspiring views. Visit Many Glacier and Two Medicine to easily extend your reach further into the wilderness.

Pre-trip planning is a must to make the most of a visit. Seasonal road closures, trail closures due to wildlife, and frequently-changing weather add to the challenge. Nowhere else have I traveled where I've not only needed a Plan A and B, but also a Plan C and D.

This book's purpose:

Its core intent is to guide you **-the photographer-** throughout the park, to minimize "blind exploration" for sites, and to maximize the number of praiseworthy images you take home.

This book is especially catered towards those who I like to call "weekend photographers." Those who may visit the park only for 2-5 days — and for some people what may be their *only* visit to this national park. As such, the sites presented herein are more likely to be roadside or very short hikes, in order to maximize experiences, when time is limited. (There are some longer treks on the list, for those who do have the time.)

My style is also to provide honest information. Not every site is a "must see" / ★★★★. So sometimes the news is great; sometimes not so great. The idea is that you're armed with enough information to create a daily itinerary that meets or exceeds your goals as a landscape photographer on travel. My own philosophy as a traveling photographer, is that I seek destinations where the reward matches or exceeds the effort to get there. This is one of the governing philosophies of this book.

How to Use this Book

I have divided the park, for the photographer's needs, into 6 areas. For quick reference, please see that each area's color is consistent throughout the book. (This is for quickly finding maps, sections, etc.)

While a lot of literature you will come across may speak to the park's history, geology, flora, fauna, and so on, this book will focus mostly entirely on elements useful to the photographer. I'm no historian, geologist, or botanist, and it would be wasteful to reproduce a lot of that information in here, as it would only add to the volume's heft. I sincerely hope that you have room for this book in your camera bag, and that you take it along with you every step of the way.

I've also omitted the most basic "general" photography lessons in here as well. There are many excellent resources on that topic. I will, however, provide some key details in the Tips & Techniques section that I think are relevant to making the most of your visit to Glacier National Park.

So let's dissect the information presented for each of these sites. The following is a sample, taken from Running Eagle Falls (31):

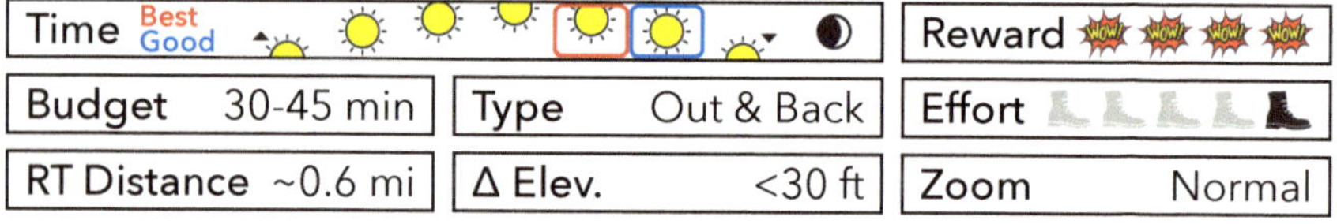

Time: The icons represent sunrise, early AM, late AM, midday, early PM, late PM, sunset, and nighttime. The red box(es) represent the best time(s) of day to be there. The blue box(es) represent good time(s). Ideally you are visiting during the "best" times, but itineraries do not always allow this, hence providing multiple options. The above site is best in the early afternoon. *One major caveat here: Clouds can change everything (and normally for the better!), offering softer, more accommodating light during other times of the day. Make impromptu adjustments, accordingly.*

Reward: One to 4 "Wow's." Now honestly, if it warrants printing in the book, then it's got merit, right? So a 1-Wow here isn't like a 1-star motel. It's just relative! This site receives the highest honor of 4 Wow's.

Budget: Your time is valuable, and this is how much time you might expect to spend at this site (including getting there, if it is a hike). For the sample site, plan for between 30-45 minutes.

Type: This is the circuit that you will cover. "Roadside" involves some walking (but not hiking); you likely will work near the side of the road or from a nearby overlook. "Meandering" means that there's not really a prescribed route, and so you should expect to explore the area via your own path. "Out & Back" is a route that you hike out one way, and then you turn around and hike back on the return. "Loop" begins and ends at the same place, though you mostly will not retrace your own steps. "Lollipop Loop" is an out & back with a loop at the far end.

Effort: This is the physical effort required while on the hike. Here, we are using the "Boots" scale. Zero Boots highlighted is typical for walks (most often on paved paths), then 1-5 Boots reflect a hike's effort, similar to using the Easy-Moderate-Strenuous scale, but here with a 2-Boot representing Easy-Moderate and a 4-Boot representing Moderate-Strenuous. For the sample site, as you will read about on pages 116-117, the route is easy, hence the 1-Boot rating.

RT Distance: "RT" is Round-Trip. This is the total hiking distance. Our sample site's round-trip distance is approximately ("~") 0.6 mile.

Δ Elev.: Change in Elevation. I need to be careful here. There are many ways to talk elevation and how it is recorded on a hike. For this book and this purpose, what is presented is simply the difference between your lowest elevation and your highest elevation. Some trails go up-and-down, and up-and-down, and so on. This value does not capture the summation of all those ascents and descents; it is merely the difference between the highest and the lowest points, while on the trail. For the sample site, the change in elevation is less than ("<") 30 feet.

Zoom: I'm a firm believer in "less is more." Taking every lens on every hike can be backbreaking. And being weighed down is no fun. So, in this box I'll suggest the key lens(es) you will want to take. Adding more is up to you. Using 35mm (full frame-equivalent) focal lengths, please consider "Wide" = Wide Angle (14-35mm), "Norm" = Normal (24-100mm), and "Tele" = Telephoto (70-200mm+).

Finally, each section will have photos of *hopefully* what you can expect to see and photograph – or do better than I could! Below most of these pictures are the camera settings that I used for the shot. Example:

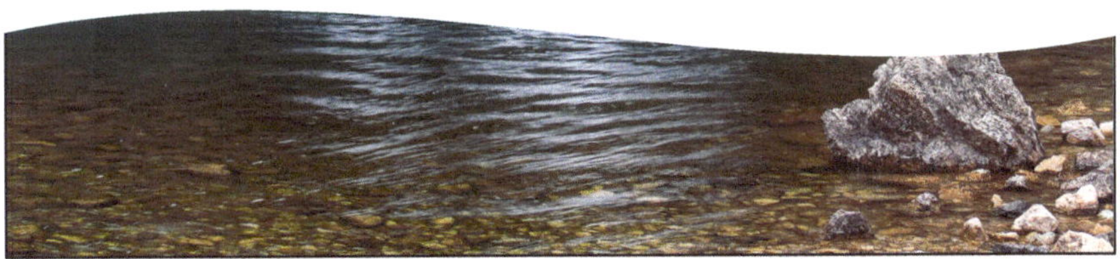

"Trick Falls"

50mm f/11 1s ISO100

The Six Park Areas

Note: Going-to-the-Sun Road is at times abbreviated as "GTTSR" or simply "Sun Road." The National Park Service sometimes uses "GTSR."

For your orientation and planning purposes, this book defines six geographic areas within and around the park – Lake McDonald, Sun Road West, Sun Road East, Many Glacier, Two Medicine, and finally "On the Outskirts." The National Park Service arranges the heart of Glacier somewhat differently... This nuance is explored on page 31.

I'd like to address the elephant in the room (or the library, perhaps)... **Glacier National Park has *many* more sites with serious photography potential beyond the 39 listed in this book.** I have captured the best of the most accessible sites, along with some requiring moderate effort and time, and a handful of more lengthy / strenuous pursuits. Those not listed here are typically of the more strenuous or remote variety. I am confident though, if you pursue any of them you will capture many sensational photos, without my guidance.

As you peruse this book I imagine you'll begin to make note of areas and sites of interest, and in turn these notes will evolve into various planning strategies for your itinerary. (This is my hope, at least.)

This is a large park, and because so its maps can be deceptive with their diminutive scale. For example, the drive from Apgar to St. Mary along Sun Road is approximately 50 miles and takes upwards of 2 hours to complete. The Driving Information section on page 32 will aid in your planning, as you consider which area(s) to pursue on a given day.

I learned a hard lesson in my early visits to Glacier National Park that demonstrated my existing method for park planning was inadequate. **Nowhere else have I traveled where I've been more impacted by closures due to weather and wildlife than at Glacier.** This is simply a reflection of the degree of extreme wilderness that this park is. I was accustomed to planning my time throughout each day with a Plan A and a contingency Plan B. **In Glacier, I learned that having a Plan C and a Plan D were wise to have, and regularly I found myself pursuing one of these alternatives.** More planning thoughtfulness is required, but when faced with any of the typical obstacles (including parking availability) you will be poised to pivot quickly to another site and minimize any lost time.

Now, let's take a look at each area...

Lake McDonald

The **West Entrance**, just north of West Glacier, is the most heavily used portal into Glacier National Park, immediately serving the Apgar area as well as the beginning of the eastbound route on Sun Road. The **Camas Creek Entrance** is another option on this side of the park, but I will wait to detail it on page 28 in the On the Outskirts section.

Southwest of West Glacier lie many communities in the Flathead Valley of northwest Montana. The cities of Kalispel, Whitefish, and Columbia Falls offer all the amenities travelers need. The communities of Coram, Hungry Horse, and West Glacier (and still others) offer less than "everything," but lodging, gas, and groceries are covered (or at least close by). **No gas stations are present within the park**, so be sure to arrive with enough fuel for the entire day's travel.

Apgar, the area to the south of Lake McDonald, includes a visitor center, a village, and a large campground.

The Apgar Visitor Center is more of a "hub" for information and transportation connections than an interior space to explore. See pages 35-36 regarding the shuttle service and Red Bus tours.

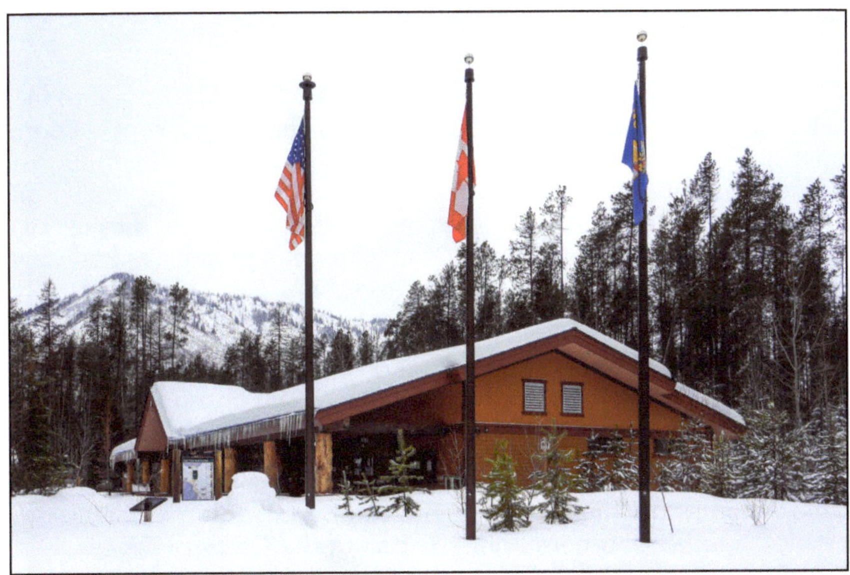

Apgar Visitor Center in the Cold of Winter   35mm f/11 1/400s ISO100

Apgar Village is a quaint row of facilities with businesses, including a restaurant, gift shops, equipment rentals, and an inn. Glacier Outfitters offers kayaks and bicycles for rental, among other things – including **bear spray rental**. Rather than buying new bear spray and then having to contend with discarding it later, rental here is a great option.

Apgar also has useful trails, connecting the visitor center, campground, and village. There is a larger network of trails in the area, to the south and southwest, but most of these are purposed for commuting cyclists and for horseback riding. (There's not a lot to photograph here.) An information board in front of the Apgar Education Center (opposite Eddie's Cafe) has a detailed map of the Apgar area, if curious. The walk between the visitor center and village takes less than 15 minutes.

Access to the rocky, south shore of Lake McDonald is convenient. Here, if visiting in the summer you'll see many visitors taking watercraft out onto the water. This is also one of the best places for **sunrise**, as outlined on pages 46-48.

One final point of interest in Apgar is the **Camas Road Bridge over McDonald Creek**. Views of the creek from here can be great. (See page 39.) A parking pullout is located on the west side of the bridge.

Back on Going-to-the-Sun Road, we head north along the east shore of the lake. Several pullouts exist on the lake side of the road... The noteworthy ones are explored on page 46. The others may simply be for the purpose of offering information about Lake McDonald, its history and ecosystem, or additional options for lake access. The west side of Lake McDonald is Howe Ridge, and evidence of a 2018 fire dominates vistas looking this direction across the lake.

After traveling approximately 8 miles up the lake, find a turnoff to the **Lake McDonald Lodge**. The lodge is a Swiss chalet-style construction, built in 1913. It is smaller than some of the others in the park, though if lodges and rustic interiors are of interest, consider a visit. The challenge with the Lake McDonald Lodge on the outside is its close proximity to the lakeshore and adjacent trees. I've yet to get a broad, head-on view that I like of its formal entrance, which faces the lake.

Our area of "Lake McDonald" continues north along Sun Road past four more sites with water features and concludes at **Avalanche**, with its picnic area, shuttle transfer, campground, and hiking trails. Trail of the Cedars (4) is noteworthy among the ones here, as it's considered the most hiked trail within Glacier National Park.

Unfortunately, **parking at Avalanche can be incredibly challenging**. Do not take parking here lightly. If Trail of the Cedars or Avalanche Lake (5) is of interest, planning for an early or late arrival is wise. Consider *early* if only interested in Trail of the Cedars, followed by a continuation up-mountain on Sun Road to other sites, or *late* if Avalanche Lake is desired. The recommended times of day to visit these two sites, based on preferred lighting, align with this strategy. Alternatively, consider parking elsewhere and utilizing the shuttle system for access here.

Sun Road - West

For both this section and the next (Sun Road East) I'll be covering a handful of honorable mentions – locations that didn't quite make the cut as stand-alone sites but are noteworthy, nonetheless.

The drive resumes much the same just beyond Avalanche... On the approach to **The Loop**, the **West Side Tunnel** is an interesting feature. Parking is available on both ends (along the down-mountain side of the road). Two tunnel "windows" are present, allowing visitors to walk to viewing areas. Please be careful when walking in the tunnel; the elevated walkways along the sides of the road are narrow. The window on the right provides a better vista – it's fascinating from here to see Sun Road as it makes its way towards Logan Pass. A "framed" photo of **Heaven's Peak** is also possible from the opposite walkway, though managing your exposure properly is challenging. Multiple exposures may help sort out which works best, once back home.

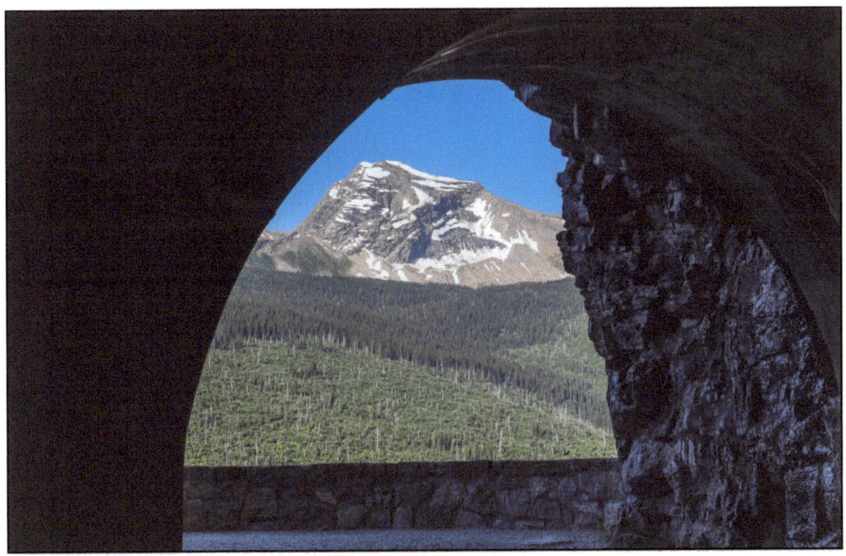

Heaven's Peak from Inside the West Side Tunnel   55mm f/8 1/400s ISO100

The Loop is where the real ascent begins. This is also where the mileage table begins on page 33. Once on this section of Sun Road, options to safely turn around are limited.

Stop at the *formal* **Bird Woman Falls Viewpoint** (see narrative on page 61) for a view of the falls in the distance, as well as Haystack Creek and **Haystack Falls** on your left. If your journey is up-mountain, take note of your odometer once passing by Haystack Falls – another 0.5 mile towards Logan Pass is a pair of long pullouts with a pleasant view of the valley below.

Back on the road, **Weeping Wall** is the next of-interest feature. I've provided some insight on the photography aspect of Weeping Wall in the Big Bend (10) narrative... Now I'll add some color to hopefully temper expectations. Weeping Wall's most extreme water flow occurs when snow is melting from above. Imagine abundant snow feeding it and also abundant snow the National Park Service is contending with trying to clear this upper section of Going-to-the-Sun Road. The issue becomes timing. In order to witness Weeping Wall in all its glory, Sun Road must be open to access it. But if it takes additional weeks to clear the road, by the time Weeping Wall is accessible the show may be over. I have not had good fortune here. I hope yours is better.

Big Bend is up next, and it's the location of a truly unique comfort station that was designed to look as though it was built into the side of the mountain. It's a neat sight, especially for what it is!

The remaining, interesting feature not otherwise covered is **Triple Arches**. If driving down-mountain, you won't even notice this stone structure, but when heading up-mountain you can see it clearly. My recommendation is to monitor your mileage (according to page 33) and have your passenger take a picture from within the car. It may be acceptable to slow down a little for the activity, but stopping on the road could be hazardous to those behind you. The shot below was taken on a wet and cloud-filled day in September.

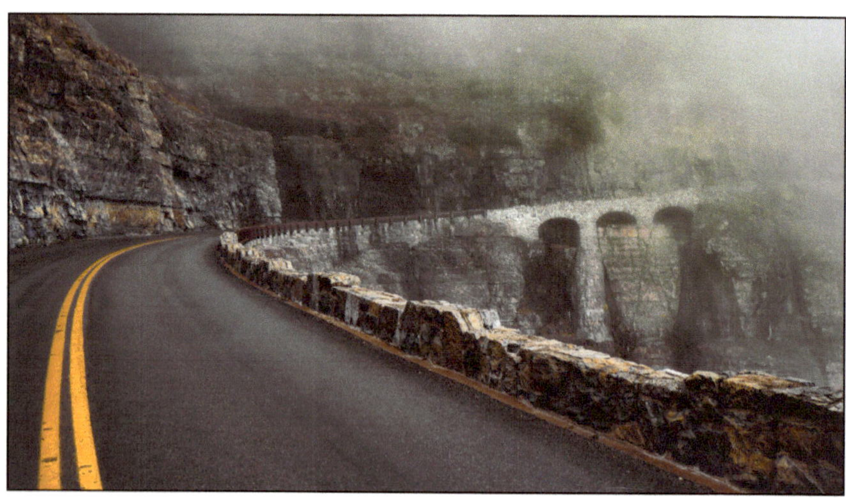

Cloudy Approach to Triple Arches   40mm f/11 1/60s ISO400

Sun Road – East

We're going to change directions here and explore this section as though traveling from St. Mary to Logan Pass (westbound).

As we began with Lake McDonald, let's first consider what's just outside the park from St. Mary, and then we'll make our way in. I want to be careful though not to duplicate thoughts here for the sake of saving space... Browning is the closest large town to this entrance, but we'll review its access and features in the Two Medicine section.

South of St. Mary, approximately 1.8 miles up the hill on Highway 89, is a large pullout with multiple **Blackfeet steel sculptures**. This location provides a sensational vista of the distant mountains with the valley below. Wayside boards provide insight on the Blackfeet and also the **Red Eagle Fire of 2006**. A visit here is highly recommended.

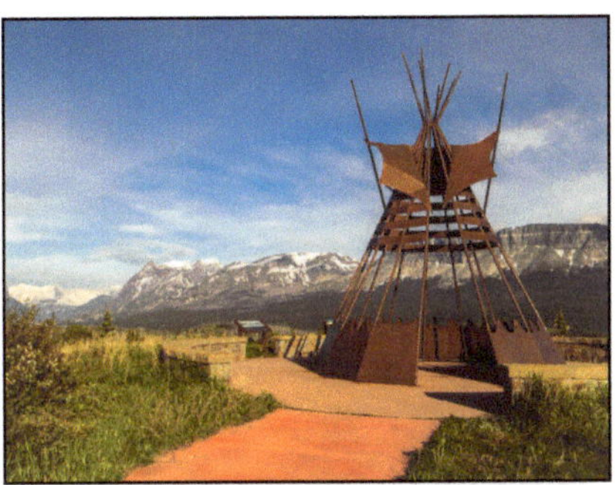

35mm f/5.6 1/160s ISO100

Back in the small community of St. Mary we have a few lodging options, the largest being the accommodations at St. Mary Village. A handful of restaurants is in this area, as well as groceries and two gas stations. One of my go-to's when traditional accommodations are found to be booked is the adjacent St. Mary KOA. They offer camping sites as well as cabins, though a cabin stay will require you to bring your own linens.

Heading into the park find a Glacier National Park sign on the right with easy, on-asphalt parking on both sides of the road. Lighting at this park sign can be challenging, and the scenery behind the sign is unfortunately somewhat lacking. Still, a compulsory photo of yourself or your group in front of at least one park sign can work well here. *My favorite sign, however, is covered on page 28.*

The St. Mary Entrance and Visitor Center is grand. This visitor center provides historical information on the Salish & Pend d'Oreille, Kootenai, and Blackfeet people, a theater, topographical map, gift shop, and one sensational panorama from the big windows. **Ranger-led astronomy programs** are offered here as well.

Back on the road, cross the St. Mary River Bridge (22) to travel along the northwest side of St. Mary Lake. The journey remains level for a while, passing multiple meadows to the right (if westbound). I have been along this stretch countless times and always expected to see wildlife in these open spaces, but to my surprise none was ever present.

There is one often-overlooked stop that I do find interesting, and that is a viewpoint for the distant **Triple Divide Peak**. Falling rain above this peak may finally drain not only into the Atlantic and Pacific Oceans, but also to Hudson Bay, north through Canada. Wow!

The peak is about 9 miles in the distance, and many days its visibility can be difficult with lighting and clouds. Still, if of interest make a brief stop and have a look. This pullout's location is captured in the table on page 33. In the photo below, Triple Divide Peak is the small tip on the left lit by early morning light. The larger feature is Norris Mountain.

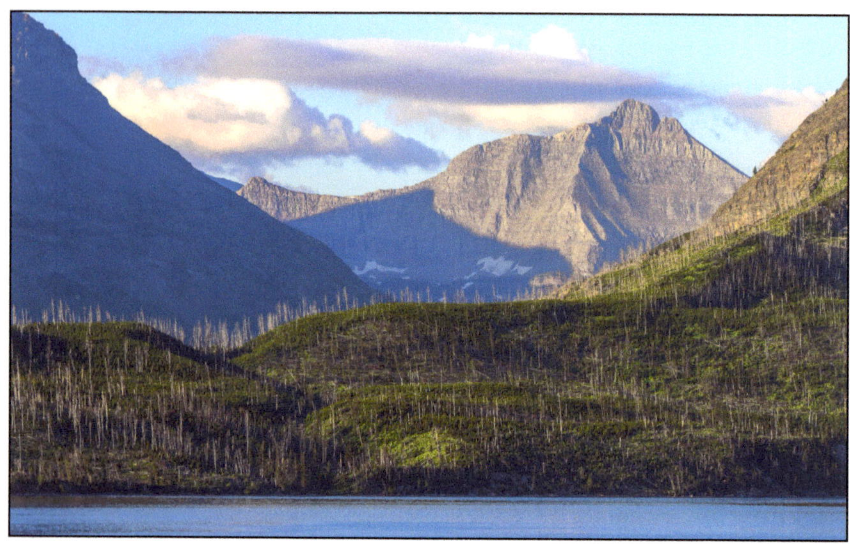

Triple Divide Peak and Norris Mountain   200mm f/8 1/250s ISO100

Rising Sun marks the transition along Sun Road from a level drive to climbing towards Logan Pass. The **Golden Staircase** is the next of-interest feature, with its retaining wall "steps" cut from the adjacent Altyn Limestone. (See page 96 for more information.) The road sharply bends; Wild Goose Island Overlook (19) comes up next.

In Stanley Kubrick's 1980 "The Shining," the movie begins with a head-on view of Wild Goose Island. An aerial sequence follows the family's yellow Volkswagen Beetle along Going-to-the-Sun Road, though the film's editing reorders sections of the road. Of note, when they arrive to the lodge, this building is not in Glacier National Park. It is the Timberline Lodge at Mt. Hood, in Oregon.

Between Wild Goose Island and Sun Point, evidence of the **Reynolds Creek Fire of 2015** is overwhelming. Dead trees remain standing, seemingly defiant of their experience and the decades ahead when they once again will yield to providing nutrients for a next generation's

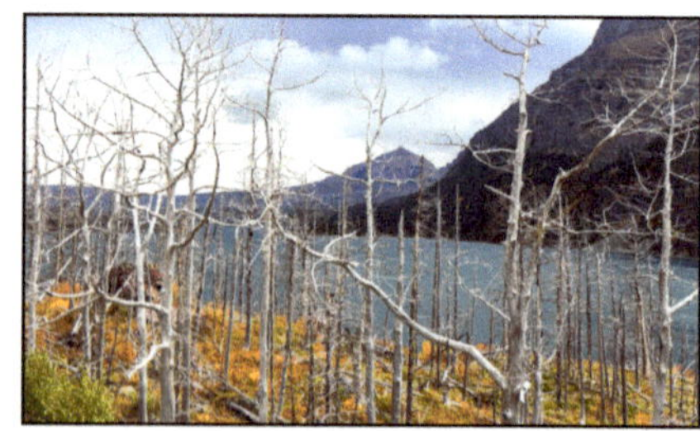

40mm f/5.6 1/400s ISO100

growth on the forest floor. The trees are captivating from a roadside vantage... At first glance they appear white, but under direct lighting they have a unique glimmer of silver.

Pass Sunrift Gorge (17) and see Virginia Falls (16) in the distance. On further, the **Jackson Glacier Overlook** is another interesting stop. A short telephoto focal length of about 100mm provides good framing of the glacier ~6 miles away. (Interestingly, it doesn't seem this far.)

Next, continue up-mountain around Siyeh Bend to an open stretch with **Heavy Runner Mountain** opposite the valley below, through the **East Tunnel** to **Lunch Creek**. This last spot is aptly-named – a nice place for a picnic lunch. I have seen **bighorn sheep** along the creek here.

Finally reach Logan Pass, where we finished the Sun Road West section.

Many Glacier

Follow signage to Many Glacier onto an unmarked road near the tiny community of Babb. If in need to refill provisions, Babb has a wonderful little general store. The drive into Many Glacier begins on pavement, and once adjacent to Lake Sherburne it changes to gravel. *I sure hope that one day this is an outdated statement, and the entire route is paved.* The 2.5-mile gravel section is a bumpy one. Asphalt returns near the entrance station.

Along this entire drive, keep an eye out for wildlife – especially bears. Pass the trailhead to Apikuni Falls (24) and briefly drive next to a mountainside, below Altyn Peak. Swiftcurrent Creek is to the left, with **Swiftcurrent Falls** ahead. A pullout is on the creek side of the road with short, informal paths leading down off the road for an improved view of the water below. Be careful here; the dropoff in places is sudden.

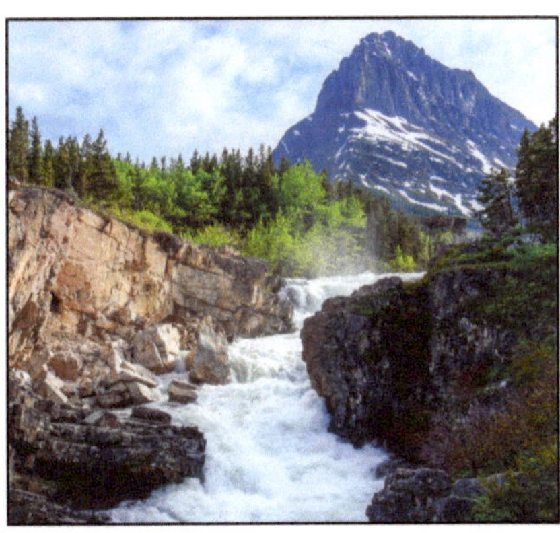

50mm f/8 1/200s ISO200

Left at the intersection is to the Many Glacier Hotel; straight is towards the Swiftcurrent Motor Inn. Many Glacier's one, *large* parking area is at the hotel. (You do not need to be staying at the hotel to park here.) Two additional parking areas remain – a small semicircle one, especially well-suited for hiking to Grinnell Lake (27) and Grinnell Glacier (28), and a second parking area in front of the motor inn, serving trails to the west. Both the hotel and motor inn have dining options.

From the lawn of the Many Glacier Hotel a view across Swiftcurrent Lake with Grinnell Point is an obligatory composition. A stitched panorama (or in-phone panorama) seems to often best a single composition here. Another nearby location suitable for photography is in front of the lakeside Stream Gaging Station (sic) near the bridge. The photo on page 101 was taken from here one evening after dinner.

Two Medicine

As with elsewhere, let's take a moment and first explore what's outside this area. The closest community is East Glacier Park Village with its historic **Glacier Park Lodge**. Also known as the "Big Tree Lodge," it was constructed in 1913 by the Great Northern Railway to promote tourism in the west. Its construction is marvelous. Even if not staying here, it is worth visiting its interior.

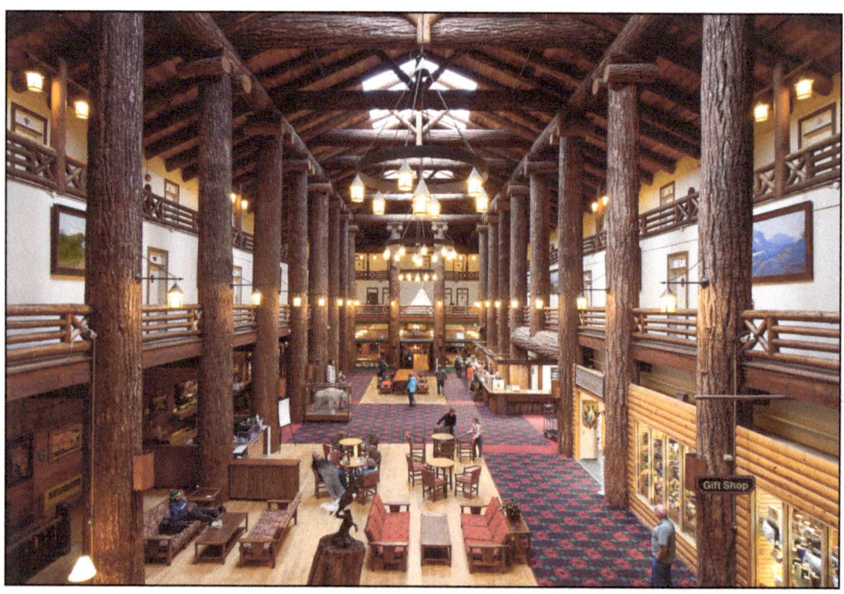

Glacier Park Lodge   18mm f/8 0.6s ISO400

East Glacier Park offers some dining and groceries options, but they are limited. A gas station is on the north end along Highway 2.

For a full variety of services, the town of Browning is about a 15 minute drive northeast. If traveling from East Glacier Park or Two Medicine to St. Mary or Many Glacier a drive into Browning may be required for some travelers... **Montana Highway 49 has a vehicle length restriction of 21 feet due to sharp curves from the Two Medicine entrance to its junction with Highway 89 to the north.** The alternative route is through Browning, where Highways 2 and 89 meet.

The Two Medicine area has abundant Aspen. This is a great side of the park to explore during the fall when they're aglow. (See page 38.)

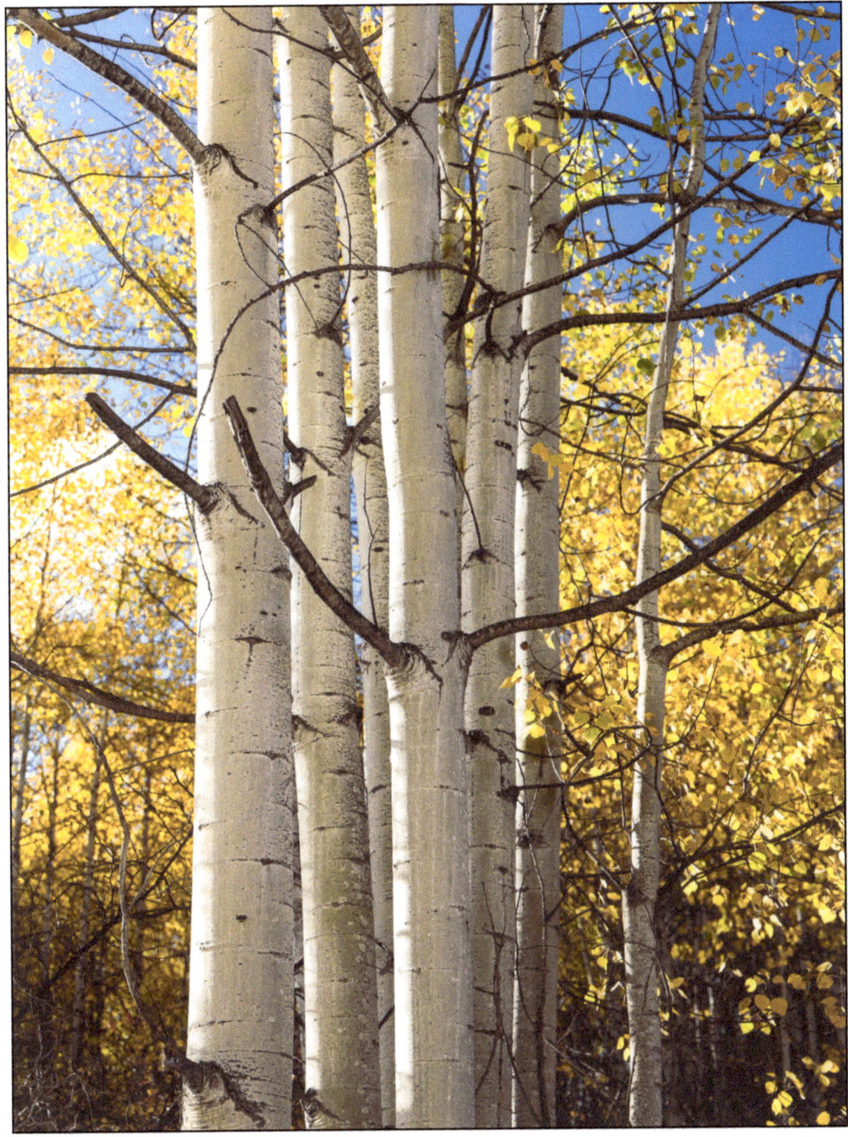

Aspen Gold   50mm f/5.6 1/160s ISO100

Two Medicine Lake is the highest elevation lake accessible by road, at ~5,160 feet. I suspect that's one reason it's **windy** here so often.

One route I recommend skipping is the Two Medicine Lake North Shore Trail. It's uninteresting. A brief narrative regarding other trails in this area may be found on page 124.

On the Outskirts

Finally, here we have a selection of sites along the perimeter of Glacier. Please note: Silver Staircase Waterfall (39) and a part of Polebridge (36) are outside the national park boundary.

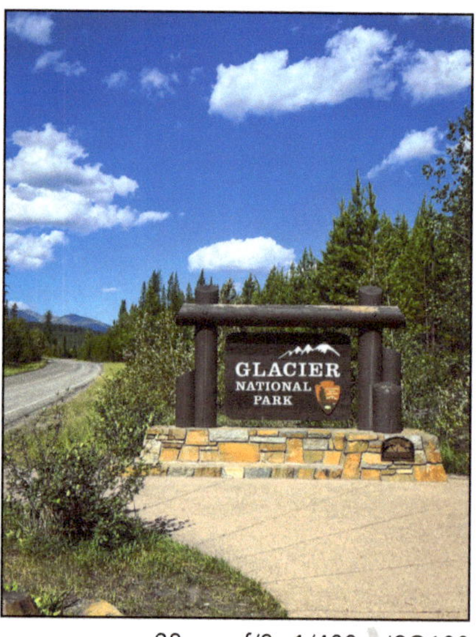

28mm f/8 1/400s ISO100

Let's begin at the **Camas Creek Entrance**, northwest of Apgar. I'll get right to the point on its access from the south via Columbia Falls, if you're sizing it up as an alternative to the West Entrance. About 10 miles of this route is along a gravel road that is incredibly bumpy at times. I would think twice on driving this instead of to the West Entrance. Once here, no matter your route, it does have what I believe is the best Glacier National Park entrance sign of the lot. They're all good, but I feel this one is the best because it offers more features in the background.

A pilgrimage to the small community of **Polebridge** and its famous mercantile makes a lot of sense if looking to explore beyond the usual park areas. Of note, Polebridge (the community) and Polebridge (the Ranger Station) are on opposite sides of the North Fork Flathead River. See important commentary about the roads on pages 128-129.

One honorable mention is **Chief Mountain**, along the northeast park boundary. Montana Highway 17 heads northwest from Highway 89 towards a US-Canada border crossing, and ~4.8 miles into this drive is an elevated pullout that provides this vantage below.

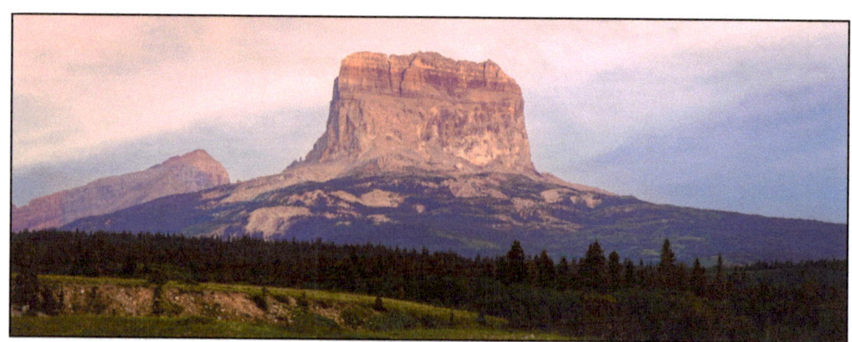

Chief Mountain Sunrise

100mm f/5.6 1/20s ISO100

Tips & Techniques

As briefly mentioned in the "How to Use this Book" section, I want to share with you what I think are some of the more unique pieces of advice for your trip to Glacier National Park. Some of this information is park-specific (logistics and planning, mostly), while other details and thoughts are photography-related.

Let's get straight to it...

Additional Resources
Please do not skip this!

My goal, in writing this book, is to minimize the resources that you must seek-out, purchase or print, and ultimately rely on in order to enjoy *photography* at Glacier National Park. So, along with this book in hand you need access to three additional resources:

1. The Glacier National Park Website (www.nps.gov/glac/index.htm),

2. A printed copy of the National Park Service map of Glacier National Park, and

3. Printed copies of the main park areas' trails (which are in more detail than the main park map).

The Website...

I'm not going to guide you through the whole website – that would be silly. Though, it is in your best interest to make some time and explore it completely, or very close to. Also, a disclaimer – some of these subcategories listed here may change names over time, as the website evolves, so if you cannot find what you're looking for based on my guidance here, try finding it outside the website with your favorite search engine. Just be sure that when you follow the results, you're staying within the www.nps.gov domain. It is the most reliable.

Alerts

On the top banner there is a link to park alerts. This could be abnormal weather or road conditions, or any upcoming or emergency activities that visitors need to be aware of. Check this ahead of your trip, and as connectivity allows, check it regularly during your trip.

Weather

Links to multiple resources are available on the Alerts page. Weather conditions can change rapidly throughout this region. Again, as connectivity allows, check this regularly during your trip.

Semi-related to weather are forest fires, insomuch that even when none are ablaze in or near Glacier smoke from them migrates throughout the region because of weather patterns. Poor visibility and unhealthy air are the result. This can *really* impact a visit to the park. **If the region is affected by wildfire smoke, study the reports carefully.** It is not uncommon for the west and east sides of the park to have different conditions. It may be possible to concentrate your visit to areas that are less impacted.

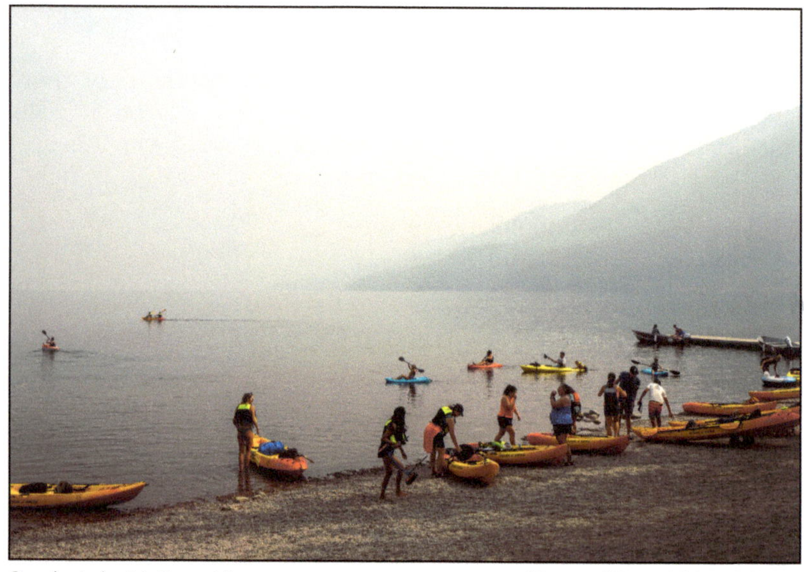

Smoky Lake McDonald   35mm f/8 1/320s ISO100

Trail Status

Trail closures due to wildlife activity are not uncommon in Glacier National Park, and planning around these closures is a typical activity for many visitors. **As suggested on page 18, having multiple contingency plans for your day's itinerary is recommended to minimize valuable downtime in the event of an unexpected closure.** At time of writing, to access the website's trail status report find a link to the "Hiking the Trails" page on the Alerts page. Once there, another click on the "Trail Status" pull-down will provide a final link to the "Trail and Area Closure" page. I recommend creating a bookmark to this page for easier access going forward.

Maps

Again on the top banner, follow the maps link to a page with an interactive park map. Your first task is to find and download the PDF of the park map that you will be provided once you arrive at a park entrance pay station. These maps are worth their weight in gold. I advise to print in color your downloaded copy on the largest paper possible. The copy you will receive at the park, unfolded, is approximately 24 x 16 inches. This is the same map used on pages 4-14 of this book, and the same map that I listed as Item 2 on page 28 for you to carry during your visit. At time of writing, the Glacier National Park map in PDF format is found using the National Park Service Cartography page. (Search for available maps in Montana on the interactive map of the United States.)

You're not done printing yet. Unlike the large park maps and the website, the National Park Service has yet to standardize across the parks on how they provide detailed maps and information for trails. At Glacier National Park they are called "Area Trail Maps." Printed versions of these maps are available throughout the park, most always front and back on letter size paper.

Return to the "Hiking the Trails" page (as noted on the prior page) and find a pull-down titled "Area Trail Maps." Here you will see links for Lake McDonald, Many Glacier, North Fork & Goat Haunt, St. Mary, and Two Medicine. Eureka!.. Here is the deviation I mentioned on page 18. These areas do not exactly align with the ones in this book. Regardless, orientation between this book and these maps is straightforward. I recommend to print them all for reference, as your planning and visit requires. These cover Item 3 on page 28.

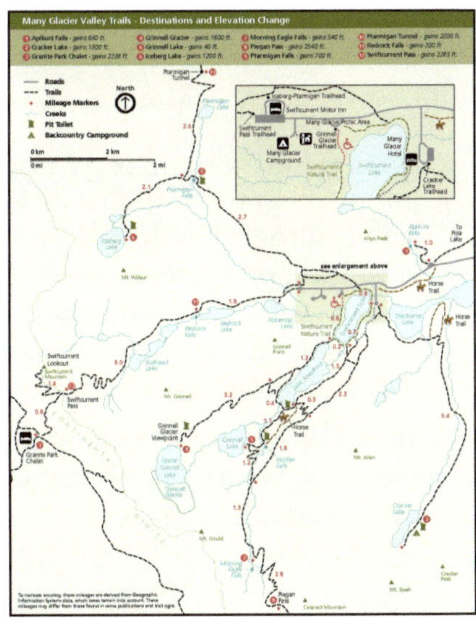

One final comment regarding maps, in general... When beginning a hike most all trailheads have an information board with details about the hike and features ahead. I recommend at the start of your hike to take a photo of the map on this board. Its details may be useful while on the trail.

Driving Information

When studying these maps, the driving distances do not seem that long, and therefore the driving times may surprise you. Here are some typical figures, where VC = Visitor Center:

Apgar VC to Logan Pass	30 mi	1 hr 15 min
Logan Pass to St. Mary VC	18 mi	45 min
St. Mary VC to Many Glacier (Hotel)	21 mi	40 min
St. Mary VC to Two Medicine (Lake)	34 mi	55 min
St. Mary VC to East Glacier Park	31 mi	50 min
East Glacier Park to Two Medicine (Lake)	11 mi	25 min
Apgar VC to East Glacier Park	57 mi	1 hr 15 min
Apgar VC to Polebridge (Mercantile)	25 mi	55 min
Polebridge (Mercantile) to Bowman Lake	7 mi	40 min

Vehicle Reservation System

Among the plethora of byproducts from the year 2020, prominent parks within the National Park System were entirely overwhelmed with a surge of visitors. As a result, in 2021 Glacier implemented a vehicle reservation system to combat this overcrowding. Its implementation continues to evolve, and I would be remiss to outline its present characteristics here, as I have not doubt it will continue to be updated in the years to come.

This is a hot topic because traveling throughout the park in a personal vehicle is what most visitors intend to do. Securing reservations to access areas of interest on a preferred day can be challenging and not always with desirable results. **Impromptu travel to certain areas of the park may not be possible.**

The best advice that I can provide is to study the vehicle reservation system webpage closely. At time of writing, it is found under "Plan Your Visit" on the Glacier homepage, and then "Vehicle Reservations." Gain a clear understanding of when and how passes are made available (paying close attention to the time zone when released). Assess if there are times of the day when passes are not required (such as very early morning or in the evening).

Going-to-the-Sun Road

Driving along (and riding along) Going-to-the-Sun Road is a truly enchanting experience. It traverses the continental divide, connecting the West Entrance near Apgar with the St. Mary Entrance. This is the only thoroughfare in the park.

The following table will help to gauge mileage along the more eastern half of this 50-mile route, where points of interest can sneak up on you.

The Loop	**0.0 mi**	25.0 mi
Bird Woman Falls Viewpoint	2.8 mi	22.2 mi
Haystack Falls Viewpoint	3.0 mi	22.0 mi
Weeping Wall	4.7 mi	20.3 mi
Big Bend	4.9 mi	20.1 mi
Triple Arches	5.8 mi	19.2 mi
Oberlin Bend	7.3 mi	17.7 mi
Logan Pass	7.7 mi	17.3 mi
East Tunnel	8.9 mi	16.1 mi
Siyeh Bend	10.5 mi	14.5 mi
Jackson Glacier Overlook	12.5 mi	12.5 mi
St. Mary & Virginia Falls	14.7 mi	10.3 mi
Sunrift Gorge & Baring Falls	15.3 mi	9.7 mi
Sun Point (Turnoff)	15.9 mi	9.1 mi
Wild Goose Island Overlook	18.7 mi	6.3 mi
Golden Staircase	19.1 mi	5.9 mi
Rising Sun	19.6 mi	5.4 mi
Triple Divide Peak Viewpoint	21.4 mi	3.6 mi
St. Mary River Bridge	25.0 mi	**0.0 mi**

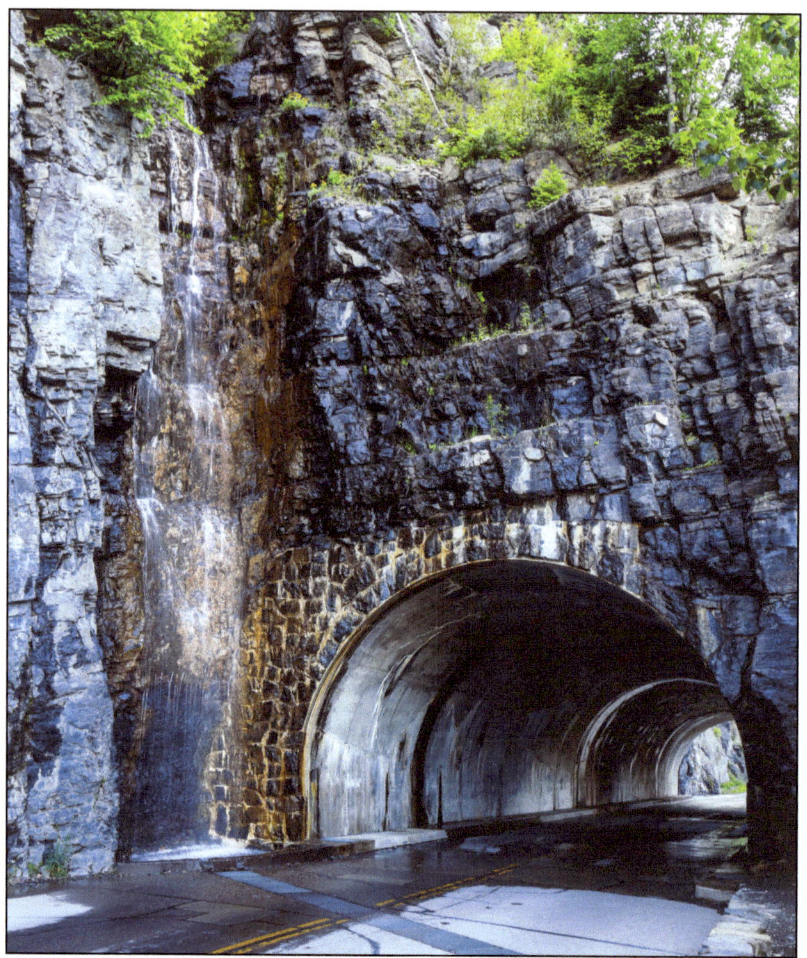

West Side Tunnel along Going-to-the-Sun Road   35mm f/5.6 1/20s ISO200

The most sensational section is between The Loop and Rising Sun, covering approximately 20 miles of the entire 50-mile length. Here the road relentlessly climbs and descends, with tight curves and minimal lane clearances at times. **Drive within the speed limit and use lower gears to preserve your vehicle's brakes. Vehicle size restrictions are enforced.**

Seasonally, Sun Road may be closed intermittently for snow removal, and once the snow depth reaches an unmanageable threshold the road closes for the winter, though "winter" here can be misleading. Permanent snow closures may happen as early as October and last until July! November through mid-June is more typical.

Search for "Going-to-the-Sun Road General Info" on the Glacier website for more details.

Going-to-the-Sun Road Shuttle Service

A free shuttle service is provided between Apgar and St. Mary from **July 1 through Labor Day**. The route has 4 sections with 3 mandatory transfers at Avalanche Creek, Logan Pass, and Rising Sun. The transfers allow for the use of larger bus sizes, where possible. The smaller buses are necessary for the mountainous section of Sun Road. Apgar to Avalanche Creek and Rising Sun to St. Mary use 28-passenger buses, while 15-passenger buses (or "vans") are used in between.

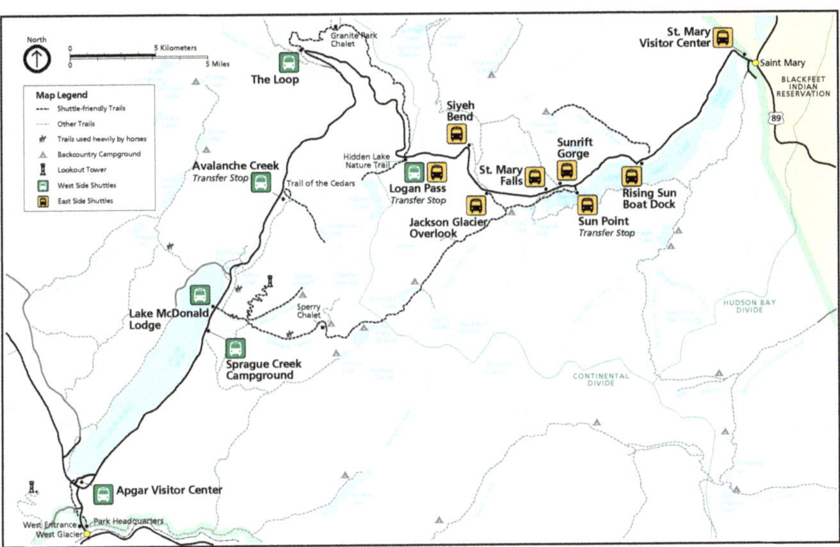

The shuttles are handy when parking along the route becomes problematic. Bonus — if you're otherwise the driver of your own vehicle they offer an opportunity to take a break and lazily gaze out the windows, when you otherwise wouldn't be able to.

Since they seem to run at or near capacity throughout the day, loading and unloading them is at the mercy of the passengers' pace, and so a strict schedule of arrival and departure times is not possible. The drivers do communicate frequently with each other over radio and have a good idea of where visitors are bunched up. If at a crowded stop and curious of an approximate loading time for your party, be courteous and inquire — I've found the drivers friendly and insightful.

If you are traveling alone and at a crowded bus stop pay close attention to the driver as a bus is loaded. They generally ask for any "singles," and you need to be ready to raise your hand with an index finger raised, representing that you're traveling alone. Occasionally this will get you onto an earlier bus and perhaps in the front passenger seat alongside the driver.

Red Bus Tours

I must be mindful here – I could write *pages* about the intriguing history of the Red Buses in Glacier National Park and the tours now offered on them. Rather, I'll leave it to you to research if you think of interest. The tours are managed by a concessioner, Glacier National Park Lodges. Search online for "Glacier Red Bus Tours."

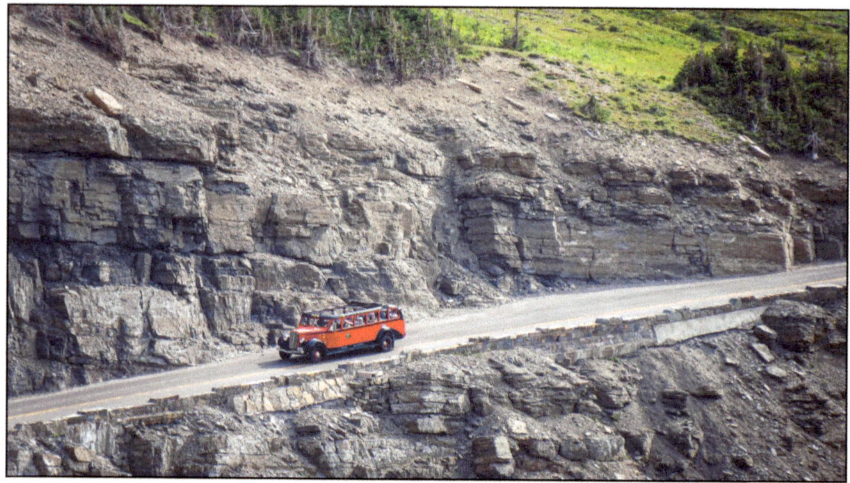

Red Bus from the Highline Trail   400mm f/8 1/500s ISO400

Tours are offered in a variety of lengths and locations... I have done the "Eastern Alpine" tour between St. Mary and Logan Pass and thoroughly enjoyed it. A tour may serve as an alternative to driving your personal vehicle on Sun Road, though reservations for these can fill early.

Seasons

Is Glacier National Park open year-round? Yes.

However... Accessibility to much of the park is impractical during the winter and spring due to snow. If interested in exploring most or all of what this book suggests, summer through early fall is the best bet.

Spring

Early springtime in Glacier is more like a continuation of winter. Temperatures may begin to show signs of warming and days become longer, but snow keeps long sections of roads closed. The fervent visitor monitors road conditions for hiking and cycling access... These options are made available before vehicular traffic, especially in May and June.

The most noteworthy attribute during the early months of snowmelt is **extreme water flow** and **high water levels in lakes** throughout the park. Access to these features remains challenging in April, so plan a May or early June visit if this is of interest.

Snow showers remain a possibility. Below is a June photo along the Beaver Pond Loop (23) route. Early wildflowers were abloom, and I was also rewarded with intermittent snowfall.

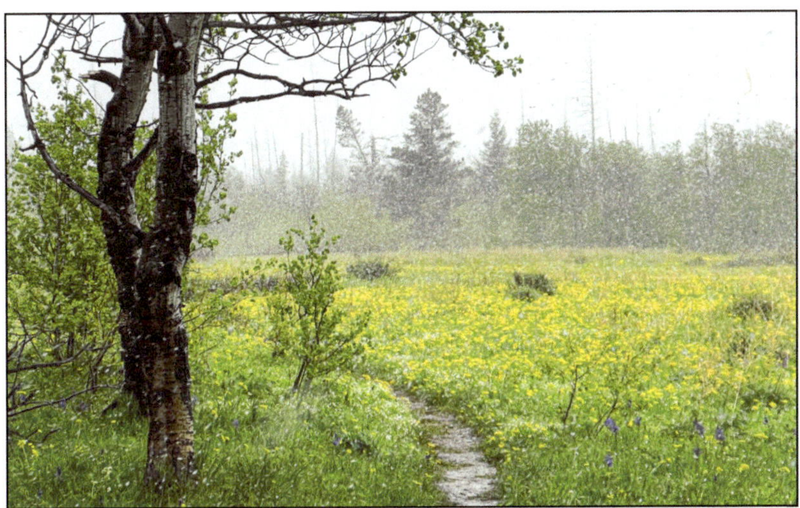

Wildflowers and Wild Weather in June   70mm f/5.6 1/160s ISO100

Summer

As would be expected, visitation numbers peak in the summer months (especially July and August). Weekends, week days — it does not matter. Once the entire length of Going-to-the-Sun Road opens, the park gets busy.

Summer temperatures may warm to "shorts weather" comfortable, especially in the lower elevations, but once you venture into the mountains it can still be cool to cold. I have seen too many summer travelers shivering at Logan Pass in shorts and sandals. It is best to pack for temperature swings and to dress in layers.

Most of the photos in the book were taken between mid-June and mid-September. This is when the park was most accessible for me, and I expect your experience will reflect my own.

Wildflowers seem to peak in late July, but I've also seen an incredible show in mid-August. It varies year by year. The hike to Hidden Lake Overlook (14) is a marvelous place to see them.

The one "gotcha" with summer is the higher probability of wildfire smoke (page 30). Keep an eye on this as your trip approaches.

Fall

Isn't fall awesome just about everywhere? Well, nowhere comes to mind that it's not, and Glacier is no exception here. In fact, Glacier has a trick up its sleeve — it doesn't have one showing of fall colors but instead has two showings! I'll do my very best here at forecasting *when* and what to expect...

Color seems to peak among the deciduous trees the last week in September. These include Aspen, Cottonwood, and others. If you were to err on the safe side, plan early (mid-September) for partial color. This is magnificent as well. If arriving late, the leaves will have fallen and the mission may be unsuccessful. All roads typically remain open, though an occasional, as-needed clearing of snow may be necessary at higher elevations.

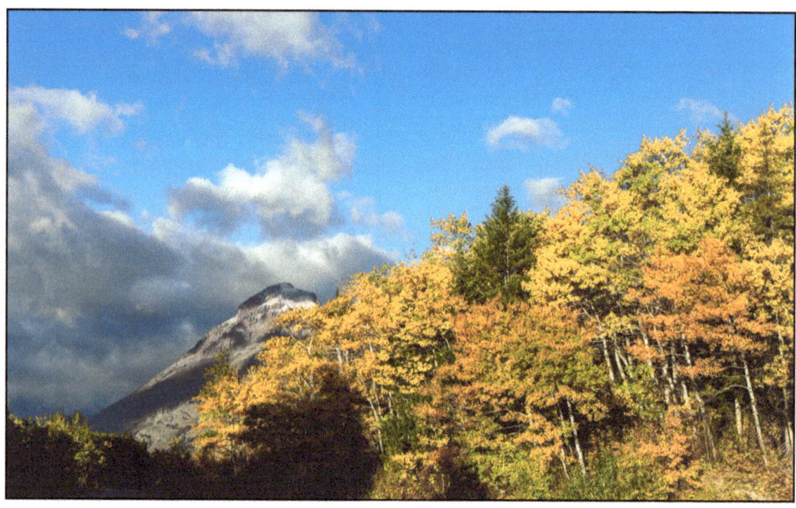

Aspens in Two Medicine   50mm f/8 1/200s ISO100

Then in about the third week of October, well after the afor-mentioned leaves have fallen, the Western Larch's needles change from their apparent evergreen (they're not an "evergreen") to a chartreuse and then a golden yellow. These trees are truly unique and make for pleasant, sweeping compositions. They are found primarily on the west side of the park. Of note, by this time it is not uncommon for snowfall to more often interrupt travel into higher elevations, if not entirely for the winter ahead. Also, the "gray" overcast of winter is also more likely in play... Excursions in pursuit of Western Larch will feel more "winter-like" on the whole.

If only one trip to Glacier is possible in the fall, I recommend the September version. Abundant color, especially with Aspen, and a higher probability of broader accessibility is simply the better bet.

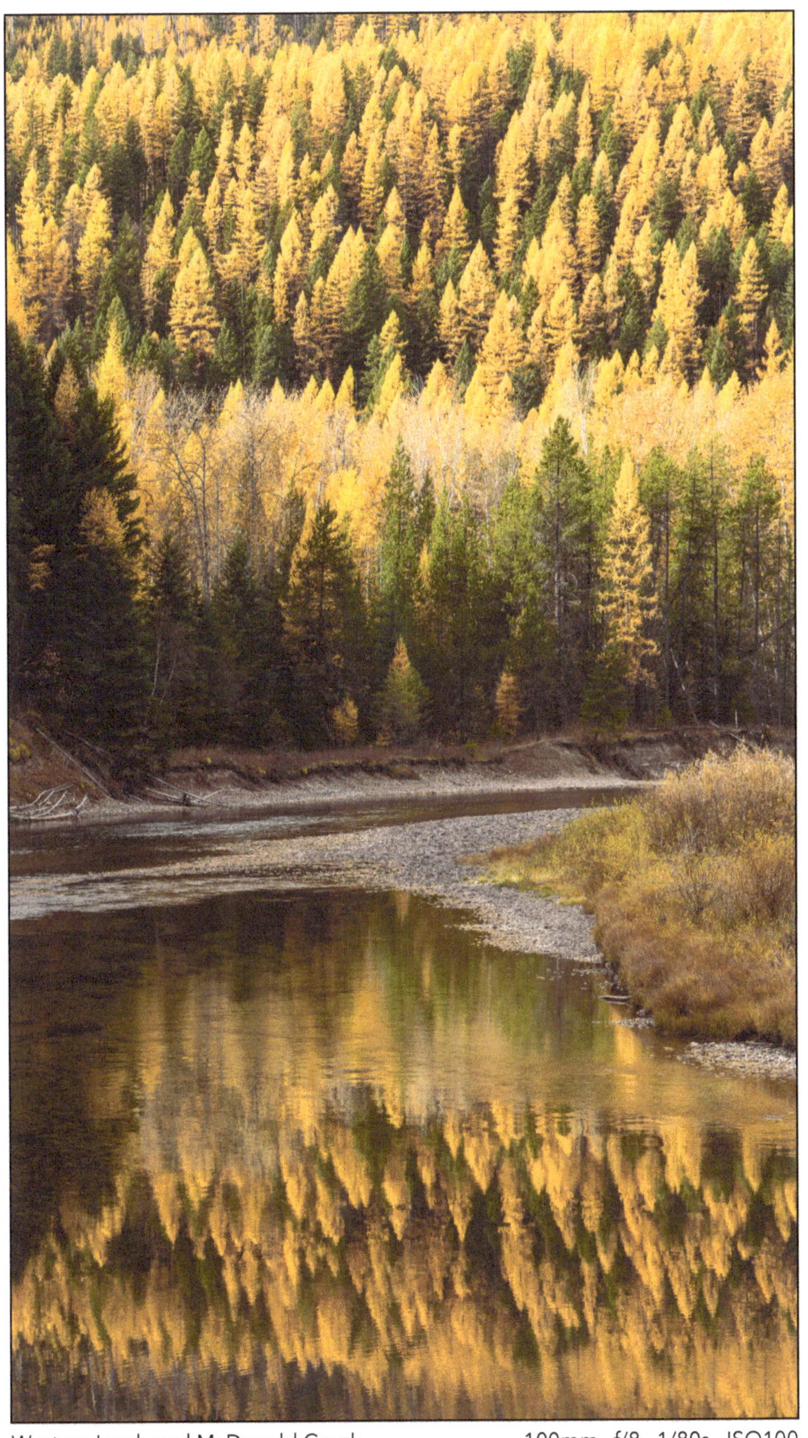

Western Larch and McDonald Creek   100mm f/8 1/80s ISO100

Winter

You might already have a vision of what Glacier is like in the winter, and you're probably right. It's nearly entirely engulfed in snow.

The National Park Service works to keep the West Entrance to Apgar and Sun Road to the Lake McDonald Lodge plowed. A small network of cross-country skiing and snowshoeing trails exist at the lower elevations. If of interest, on the Glacier homepage follow "Plan Your Visit" to "Things to Do" and finally onto "Cross-country Skiing" for information on this series of trails.

I have visited Apgar via the West Entrance in February. The road had been plowed but an additional ~10 inches of snow had re-accumulated. Our high-clearance 4WD vehicle was adequate. (Had there not been other vehicles' tracks already on the road, I would have abandoned the journey in.) The woods around the Apgar Visitor Center provided a few snowy compositions with beams of sunlight and trees' shadows, but the most sensational sight was the frozen shoreline of Lake McDonald and the snowy mountains in the distance.

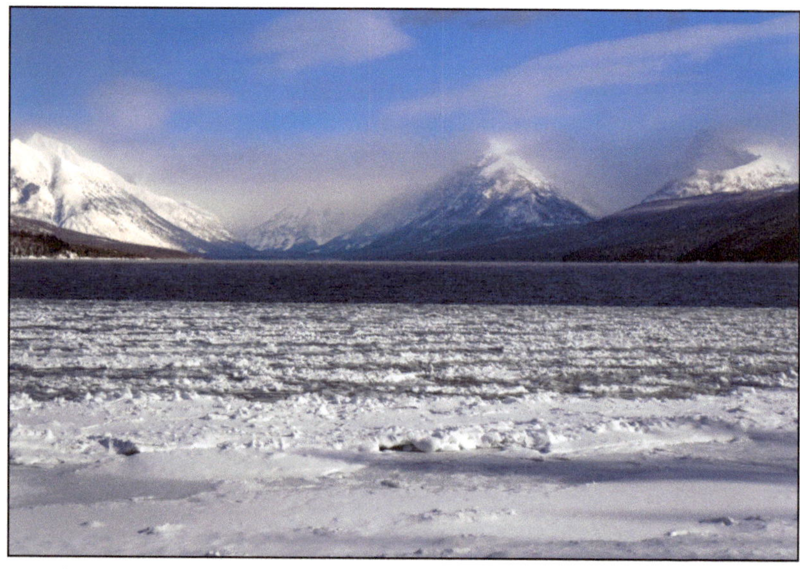

Icy Lake McDonald   50mm f/16 1/320s ISO200

I had the luxury of having visited Lake McDonald many times before, so I had a good idea about where the rocky shore ended and the water below began. Still, I did not venture far onto the snowy, icy surface. **Exercise extreme caution here** – what may appear to be a solid, frozen surface may give way under your weight. A plunge into the icy water would be incredibly dangerous.

Wildlife

Of interest to many Glacier National Park visitors is to see some of the remarkable wildlife throughout the park. Wildlife is certainly part of the appeal here.

The National Park Service provides visitors with guidelines for do's and don'ts regarding safety, as well as for preservation of the animals' environment. Please do read through the information provided, and if not provided then seek what the National Park Service makes available. I will save space here and not reiterate this critical information, but I will add some additional elements that I have learned along the way.

Grizzly Bears & Black Bears

I'll begin with this regarding bears – **your objective should be to discover a bear or bears from the safety of your vehicle and not while on a trail**. The photos on the next page were taken one morning as I exited Many Glacier, in a meadow near Apikuni Falls (24). I rolled down my window and snapped these photos from inside my car. Once the two Grizzly Bears were finished wrestling here, they *sprinted* across the road towards Lake Sherburne to continue their shenanigans. In a matter of seconds, they passed by within 100 feet of the stopped vehicles. They're fast.

I've had three undesirable, on-trail encounters with bears – twice with grizzlies and once with a black bear. Each of these encounters was within 20 feet of the bear. Each time the bear paid me little attention and carried on. I was fortunate.

OK, enough storytelling and onto some advice...

Both grizzly bears and black bears are found throughout the entire park, though for what it's worth the majority of my sightings have been in Many Glacier.

Carrying bear spray is promoted. Montana Fish, Wildlife & Parks has an easy-to-find, online video demonstrating how to most effectively deploy it if needed. I highly recommend watching this.

Bears saunter at a pace sometimes faster than we walk – especially if we are climbing and therefore walking more slowly. Look over your shoulder regularly to see if one is coming upon you from behind, as they often use hiking trails for their own travel.

Finally, my own method for more easily identifying these two bears... When a black bear is on all fours, you will notice that its rump (or butt, if you don't mind) sits noticeably higher than its front shoulders. A grizzly bear's rump tends to sit more even with the front shoulders, if not somewhat below the front shoulders.

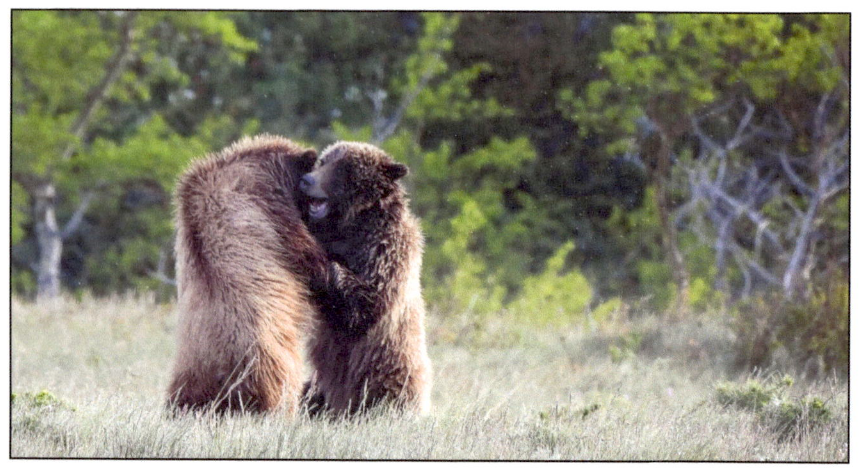

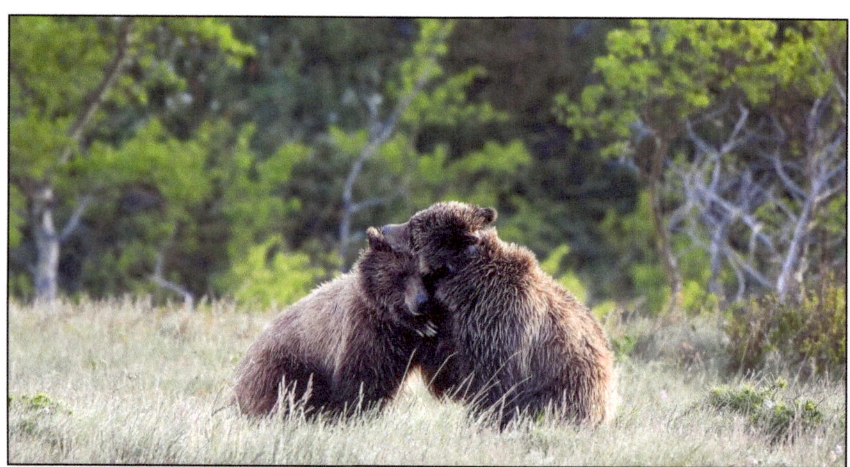

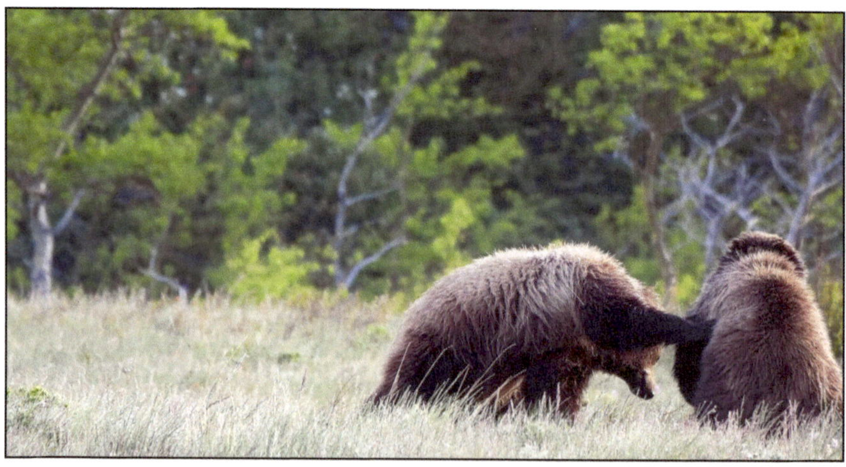

Brotherly Love   400mm   f/5.6   1/400s   ISO1600   (then 2:1 digital crop)

Mountain Goats & Bighorn Sheep

Behold the mountain goat – the symbol of Glacier National Park. Oberlin Bend (11) seems to be most easily-accessible place to repeatedly spot them. If you see a crowd of people near the parking area or on the viewing platform here, odds are they're watching goats in the area.

Mountain goats do shed their winter coat in the spring. Admittedly, they're a bit unsightly during this process. By midsummer a full, fresh white coat adorns them once again.

Bighorn sheep share nearly the same habitat as mountain goats, but they seem a bit more reclusive. I have experienced multiple sightings looking up-mountain while on the Highline Trail (12).

Moose

The "giant of the forest," moose tend to habitat near water features, especially bogs with grasses and willows for nourishment. They are easily startled and can be unpredictable when alarmed.

I have seen moose in Many Glacier and on the Beaver Pond Loop (23) trail. The Many Glacier Boat Tour (25) provides an insightful narrative on moose, as they're fairly common throughout that area. See also Fishercap Lake (29) – a Many Glacier location with perhaps as high a probability as anywhere for a sighting.

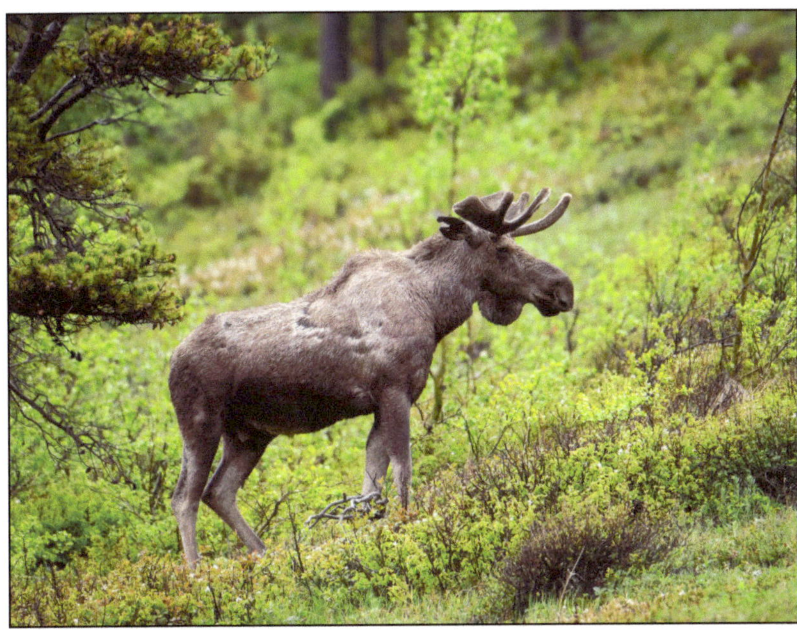

Bull Moose in Many Glacier

400mm f/8 1/250s ISO1600

Filters

Polarizing Filter

On a water scene, look to the polarizing filter to reduce glare, to see "into" the water, and sometimes enhance the reflections on the water's surface that you do want. A circular polarizer has a rotating front element, that when turned (and while you're looking through it – either by itself or through the camera) reduces glare and reflection of light. It also tends to enrich colors. And while colors' "pop" may be simulated using saturation and hue adjustments during post-processing, I have yet to find a computer program to date that can easily simulate a polarizer's effect on water. This is where it really shines.

Two caveats to polarizing filters… First, they really only work when the light source (the sun) is at a substantial angle, relative to the lens. At sunrise and sunset, its effect will be negligible. Second, be careful if choosing to use one with an ultra-wide angle focal length (such as 20mm and wider) – they can cause a strange gradation in the corners of the frame, especially with the color of the sky.

Neutral Density Filter

A neutral density (ND) filter is like a pair of sunglasses for your lens. It allows you to apply longer shutter speeds while allowing ISO and f-stop settings closer to your liking.

For the landscape photographer the most common application is for use with flowing water. If your desire is to create that silky-looking flow of water, you need to really slow your shutter speed down. Take a look at the shutter speeds used on waterfalls throughout this book. For the look I'm describing, my rule of thumb is 0.5 to 2 seconds. Conversely, if your goal is to capture the more natural "tumble" of water, try between 1/60-1/100 second. See page 60 for the cascade of McDonald Creek at Red Rock Point, which was taken at 1/100s.

I recommend either a 3-stop (0.9) or a 4-stop (1.2) ND filter.

Capture vs. Final

When capturing an image, I pay close attention to its histogram, and I encourage you to as well. (Go research this topic if necessary.) None of the photographs in this book are "straight from the camera." But then again, none have what some might call "voodoo" applied either. Just basic adjustments to shadows, highlights, saturation, contrast, etc. – to mimic, as best I can, what I remember seeing.

Lake McDonald

Apgar to Avalanche

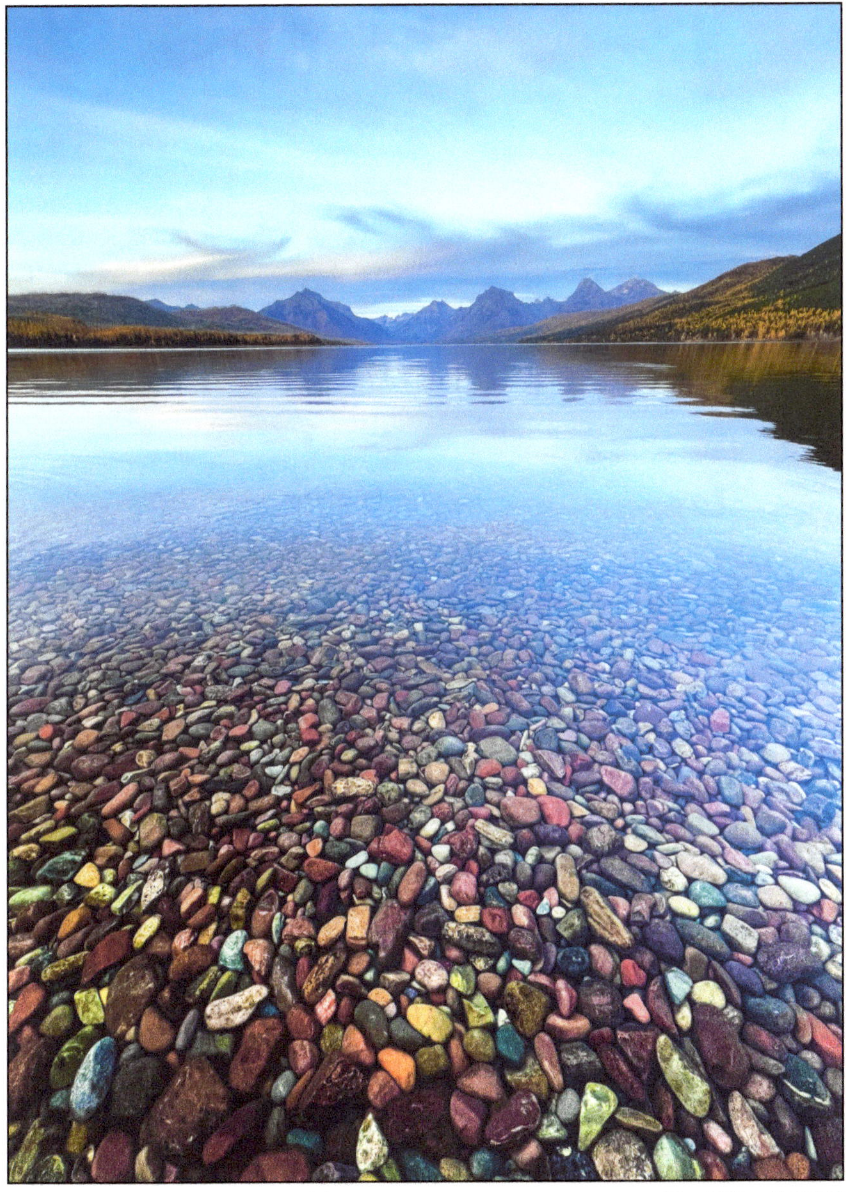

Colorful Rocks at Lake McDonald   14mm f/8 1/30s ISO200

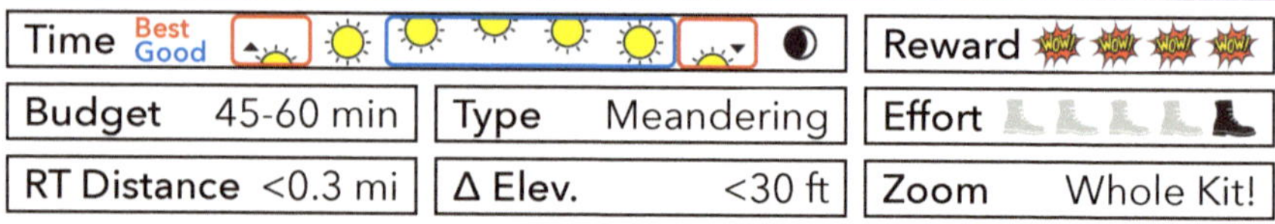

Time	Best Good		Reward	
Budget	45-60 min	Type	Meandering	Effort
RT Distance	<0.3 mi	Δ Elev.	<30 ft	Zoom	Whole Kit!

Lake McDonald is a number of things: the largest lake within Glacier National Park, your "wow I've arrived" gateway feature if entering from West Glacier, and an easy and fun way to pursue on-water recreation. But be careful — it is also a location that can inadvertently soak up too much of your limited time if you allow. (Pun intended.)

Having said this, and before we explore its best photography potential, I would like to share that one of my most enjoyable experiences in Glacier was in a rented motorboat, mid-morning, through Glacier Park Boat Company. I highly recommended it if your schedule allows.

The rocks along the *long* shoreline perform the role as foreground, as seen on the prior page and additional photos on the next two pages. Much of the rest of the scene is evident, but I do want to explore what I've learned on when, where, and how to capture images here.

When... For the underwater rocks to be visible the lake's waterline must be close to its nominal height. When is it not at nominal? During intense snowmelt. This, as expected, is based on snowpack and the pace of warming spring temperatures. Conclusion: some years, from late spring into the early summer, Lake McDonald will not have a workable shoreline to capture these interesting rocks. If a sunrise excursion is planned, I recommend to gauge the lake level a day or two before, to see if the gently-sloping shore is visible and accessible.

Where... Four locations that I can confidently recommend:

★**Apgar.** Facing the lake, to the right of both docks, walk east along the south shore until you find shallow rocks suitable to your liking. This location is straightforward and is capable of producing great results.

For the next two spots along the east shore, zero your odometer where Sun Road passes Apgar Loop Road (near the campground).

Sun Road Pullout at 1.4 miles. Unlike the next location, the route to the rocky beach here is informal and can be particularly challenging in the dark. Please be careful if pursuing this option. This stretch of beach offers larger rocks and can be better at sunset.

★**Sun Road Pullout at 2.8 miles.** Here we have a pullout with formal steps and a wide path to a large, rocky beach. This location works well for facing both directions along the length of the lake.

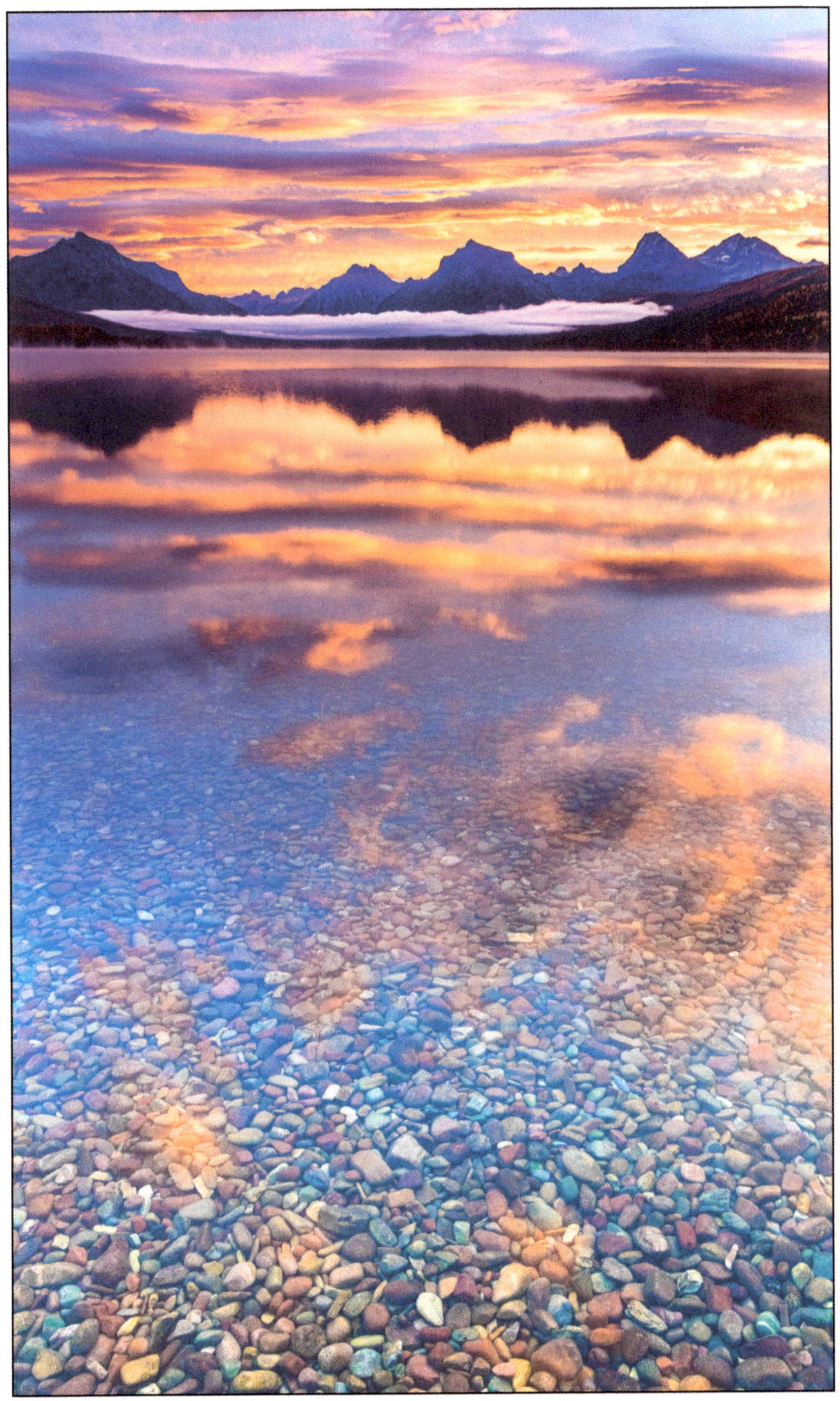

Lake McDonald Sunrise

24mm f/16 0.8s ISO400

Fish Creek. The shore adjacent to the Fish Creek Campground offers a view northeast with Rocky Point in the left of the frame. Plan to walk through the shallow water of Fish Creek where it exits into the lake.

Finally, the how... First though, I may need to temper your expectations somewhat. If you have not seen the "rainbow rocks" photos elsewhere before, then you'll be delighted in its genuine magnificence in person. However, if like me you have seen others' work here with out-of-this-world colors among the rocks and up-close mountains, you may be left wondering, "what the heck?" The rocks are colorful, but in person are quite muted. Photos in circulation have varying degrees of saturation applied – sometimes quite extreme. And when the mountains appear incredibly close, the only viable explanation is that the composition is a merging of two photos, one of the rocks with a wide-to-normal focal length and one of the mountains with a telephoto focal length. No one is right or wrong; photography is art. But what you and your camera are able to capture in one composure may not be as you expected.

My preference is to set my tripod on the waterline and to experiment with different working heights. Since the rocks in the foreground are very close relative to the distant mountains, depth of field is an issue (if not focus-stacking with multiple exposures). A wider angle lens helps resolve this issue, though the mountains appear "pushed" even further away. Depending on your lighting, a polarizer may help to better see the rocks below the surface, but be careful with its impact to the sky in the top corners of the frame with any ultra-wide angle focal lengths.

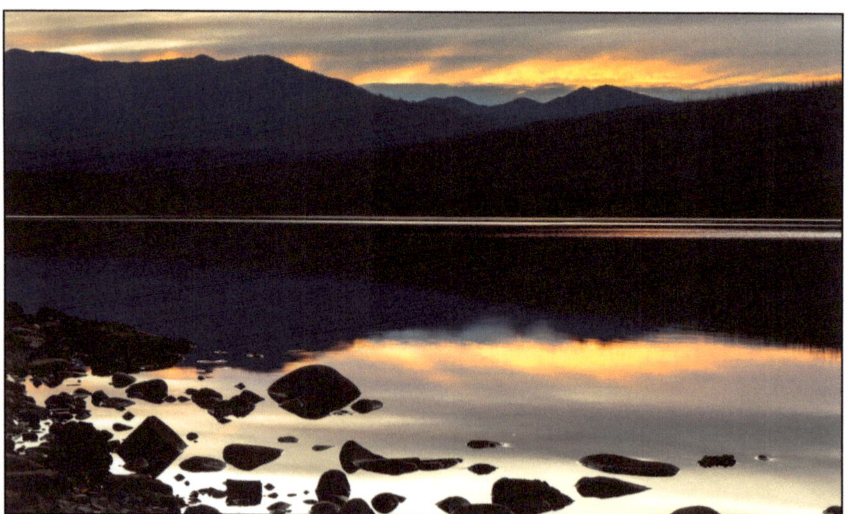

Lake McDonald Sunset from along Sun Road · · · · · · · · 70mm f/16 0.6s ISO50

The distant mountains make for a pleasing, single capture with a telephoto lens. Or, use to merge multiple images as noted above.

Wait, what's this? This wasn't in the Table of Contents!

I scatter these throughout my books, usually two or three per volume... Offbeat topics, usually that can apply anywhere – maybe even beyond this national park. They're "just for fun."

Glacier has a family of webcams throughout the park, and I'm grateful for them. I would regularly use their real-time snapshots to monitor current conditions, for help with trip planning and to better understand seasonal changes.

On the Glacier National Park homepage the webcams are located under the "Learn About the Park" pull-down, then "Photos & Multimedia," and finally "Webcams." (If ever relocated, an online search on "NPS GLAC webcams" will likely take you to the right place.)

During a visit in October 2021 I was exploring Apgar Village and came upon the webcam in front of the Apgar Education Center. I thought to myself, "this would be a neat trick to send back home."

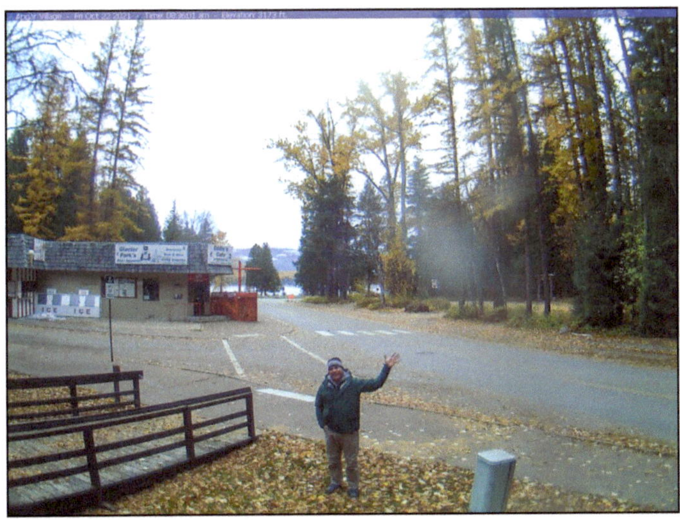

Enthusiastic in Apgar Village

The webcams capture a new still image about once/minute. It's arguably necessary to have cellular connectivity and the webcams page loaded on your smartphone, so that once your image appears you can capture a screenshot with you in the photo.

The thin banner at the top of this image reads:

Apgar Village - Fri Oct 22 2021 - Time: 08:36:01am - Elevation: 3173 ft.

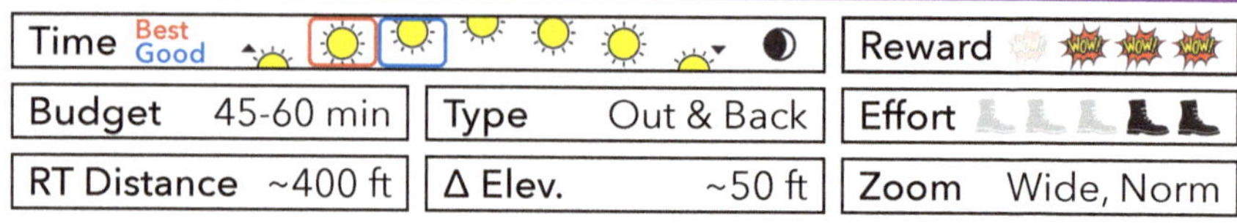

Among the handful of waterfalls west of Logan Pass, McDonald Falls is in my opinion the most photogenic — or at least the one waterfall with the *most abundant* potential for a variety of compositions.

Parking for the falls is available at an overlook approximately 0.3 mile north of North Lake McDonald Road. Unfortunately, there is not a clear line of sight from the overlook down to the falls; a downhill hike on an unmarked, well-trafficked trail is required for clear visibility. The entrance into the woods is at the far north end of the parking strip.

Please exercise caution on this trail and once on the rocks near the water — the ground and rocks can be slippery, and perhaps when least expected. (Remember your shoes may be muddy or wet from the short hike, so dry rocks may not yield the traction you might expect.) **Always maintain a safe distance from the water's edge.**

This eastern, rocky bank of the creek has multiple tiers to explore and work upon. Near the top are several pools of water, which make for a pleasing foreground near the bottom of the wide falls (as seen on page 7). From this vantage, with the exception of the pools in the foreground, McDonald Falls does appear similar to Sacred Dancing Cascade (3) with the water's broad cascade.

Walking down this staircase of rocks will allow for different perspectives of the water as it channels more powerfully to the creek's new elevation. From these additional locations along the bank is where McDonald Falls' various personalities really shine, adjacent to the textured rock.

With the near foreground elements I routinely find myself stopping down to f/16-f/22. This also helps slow the shutter speed along with a low ISO for a silky waterfall look. When the sky is brighter a ND filter may also be required.

Downstream of the falls is the vehicle bridge for North Lake McDonald Road. Depending on foliage color and sky conditions, this view is suitable for photography as well. (I have one good photo from here looking towards the lake, and I have many poor ones!)

One final comment, to round-out your knowledge about this site... There is a trail on the west side of McDonald Creek that allows for access to the brink of the falls, but with the off-angle spill of water the photography from that side isn't nearly as good as we see here.

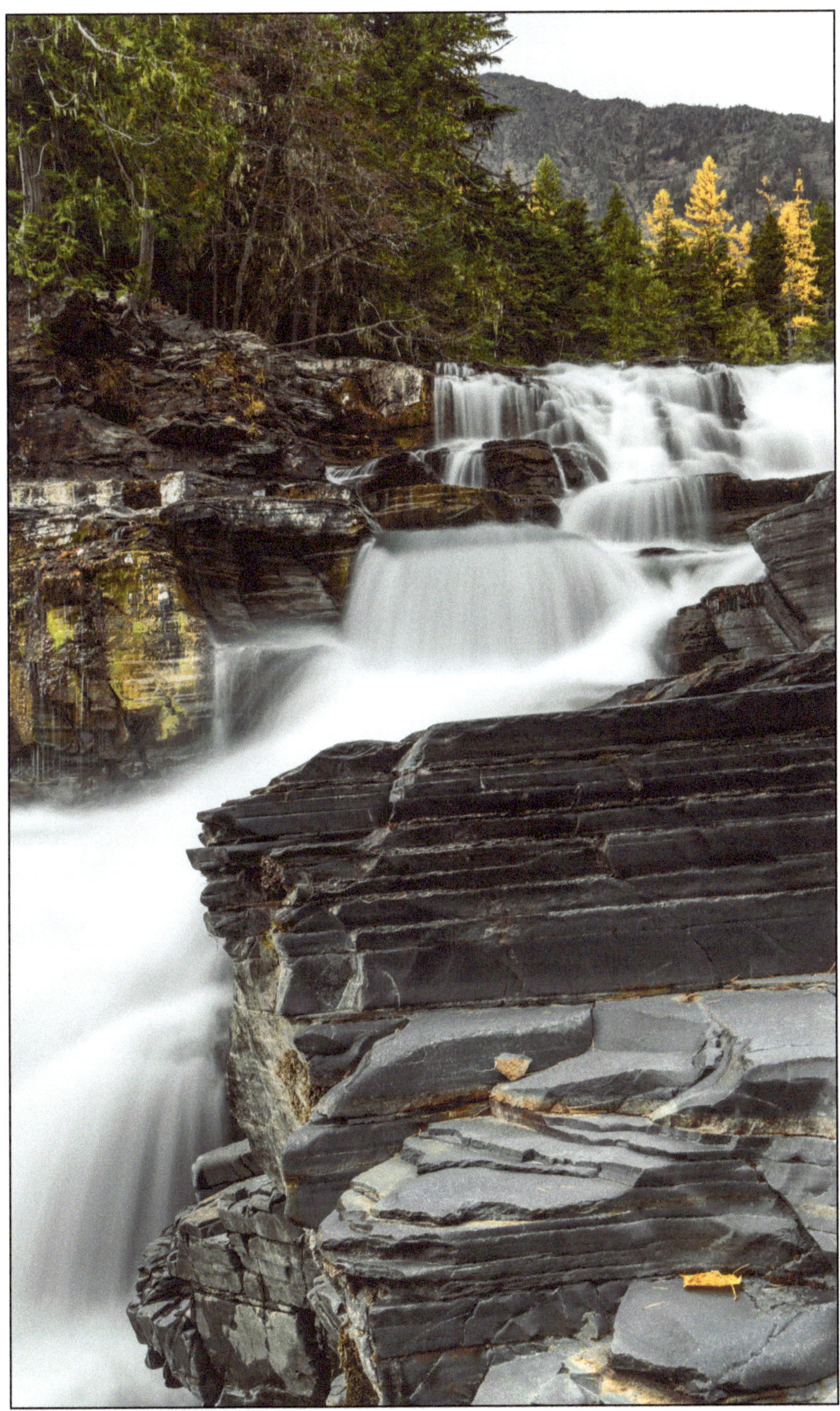

Tiers and Textures of McDonald Falls   35mm f/16 1.6s ISO50

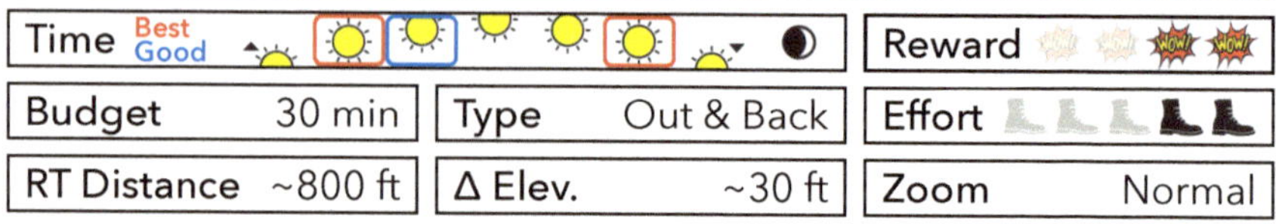

Time	Best / Good		Reward	
Budget	30 min	Type	Out & Back	Effort
RT Distance	~800 ft	Δ Elev.	~30 ft	Zoom	Normal

Sacred Dancing Cascade is a *wide* cascade of the McDonald Creek flow and without as much drop as McDonald Falls (2). The result is a particularly delicate waterfall. The challenge is framing it all within one frame and still capturing the desired amount of detail.

If your itinerary is short I recommend to choose only one of these two waterfalls, or alternatively save the second for another day (and hopefully a different-looking sky). The main difference with Sacred Dancing Cascade is that in spite of its same 2-Boot rating, it is easier to access. Though, in real contrast to McDonald Falls, it offers much less in terms of composition opportunities.

Parking for Sacred Dancing Cascade is another 0.4 mile up Going-to-the-Sun Road. A wide trail leads down to the bank of the river and a bridge for opposite side access (which goes unused for us here).

Carefully make your way over the abundant, large rocks as far as you comfortably can... In general, the further you trek, the more you will be able to capture the falls' width. A wide angle is not necessary, as the falls are still far enough away from where you must stop due to water.

This section along McDonald Creek, to the left and right of the bridge, is a marvelous location for a picnic lunch or an afternoon break.

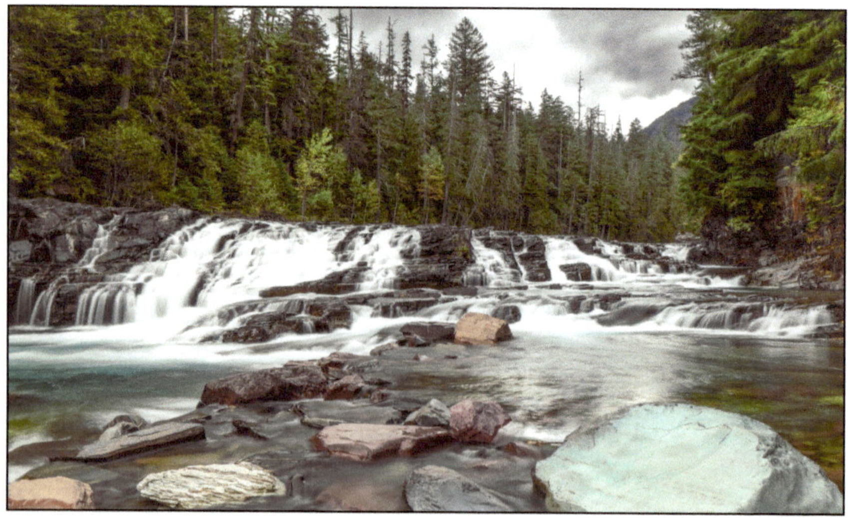

Sacred Dancing Cascade   28mm f/16 0.8s ISO100

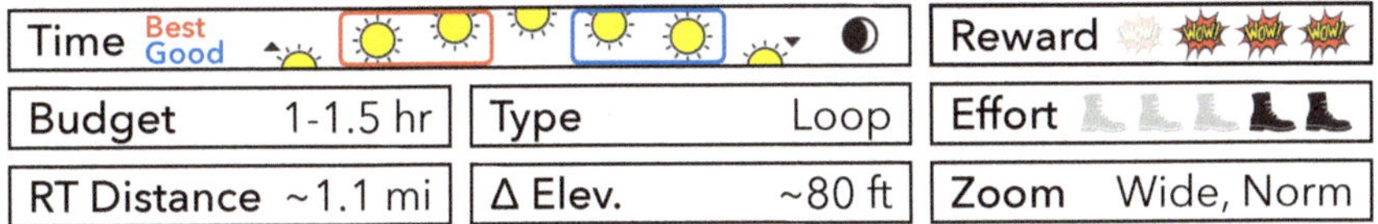

Time	Best Good	☀ ☀ ☀ ☀ ◑	Reward	💥 💥 💥 💥
Budget	1-1.5 hr	Type	Loop	Effort 👢👢👢👢**👢👢**
RT Distance	~1.1 mi	Δ Elev.	~80 ft	Zoom	Wide, Norm

The "formal" Trail of the Cedars loop is an easy 0.8-mile walk through an old growth forest dense with Western Red Cedar, Western Hemlock, Black Cottonwood, and Mountain Maple. Straddling Avalanche Creek, the north side of the loop is along a boardwalk, and the south side is a wide dirt trail. This route has minimal elevation gain.

The "plus" (+) component adds a short ascent along the trail serving Avalanche Lake (5), to experience a more photogenic section of Avalanche Gorge than otherwise seen along the main route.

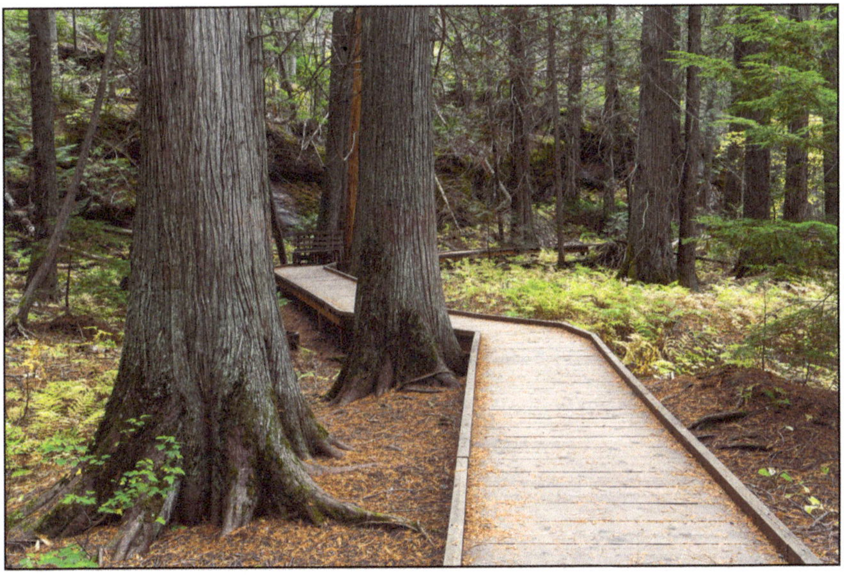

Boardwalk and Cedars   35mm f/8 1/25s ISO800

Parking is available along the road, in the picnic area west of the road, and in another small lot east of the road, adjacent to the campground.

I recommend a clockwise route, beginning on the boardwalk side. Not only is this the prescribed route, but I believe you'll find the boardwalk side more interesting, so why not start there. Before you head into the forest, survey the area closely – once near the end again it can be easy to get turned around with the multiple bridges and parking areas.

This forest is at its best either in the morning or when wet (including during light rain). Lighting can be sparse... A tripod is recommended.

With a morning start or with rain there will likely be fewer visitors on the route, so if your preference is to capture images without people these times are your best bet. That said, I cannot imagine you will find yourself alone – this is a popular trail. When the opportunity presents itself for a composition with people in it, their presence can be helpful in the picture to help portray the scale of these large trees.

I find myself without any specific recommendations for compositions along the boardwalk... What I can advise is to walk slowly (perhaps especially if the boardwalk is wet!) and to survey the forest not only in front of you and to your left and right, but also from time to time turn around and consider a composition behind you. (This could be accomplished with an out-and-back along the boardwalk, but I think a bit unnecessary; just remember to turn around occasionally.)

At the end of the boardwalk is a bridge over Avalanche Creek. Very many people enjoy this peekaboo view of the gorge upstream, but the very best views of the gorge are ahead, up the hill. OK to capture a shot or two here, but I promise you will be more thrilled with what's next.

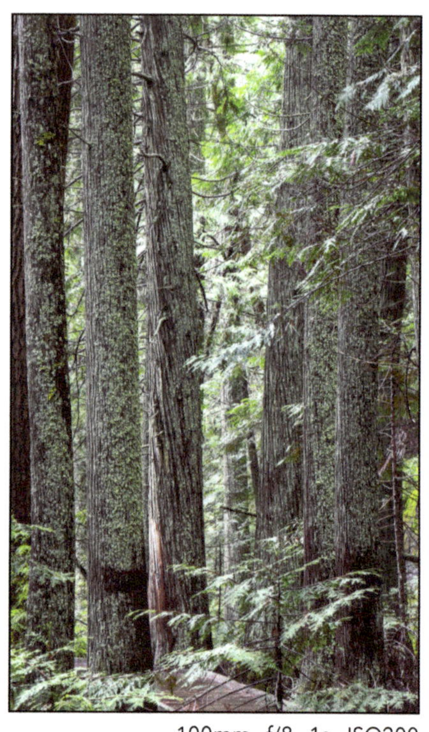

100mm f/8 1s ISO200

Once having cleared the bridge and after a short walk on the dirt path you will see to your left the well-marked trail to Avalanche Lake. This is the "+" part of this site, and as noted before I highly recommend it. The trail ascends immediately, but the climb is short.

You will find yourself near the "edge" of the gorge with a number of places to look down upon its features and the rushing water of Avalanche Creek. The area is well-trafficked, and a number of viewpoints are accessible. Where ever you choose to explore, **maintain a safe distance from the edge, and always be mindful of loose rocks and soil.**

With running water features, I prefer to compose images facing upstream when possible. My theory is that we tend to enjoy the sight of flowing water as though we're facing the direction of its source, rather than the direction of its destination.

Once finished along this short stretch, head back down and reconnect with the Trail of the Cedars loop. The dirt path ahead does offer a few new subjects along the way, but they tend to not be as sensational as what you have already seen. No less, have a look.

A restroom is located along this section of trail.

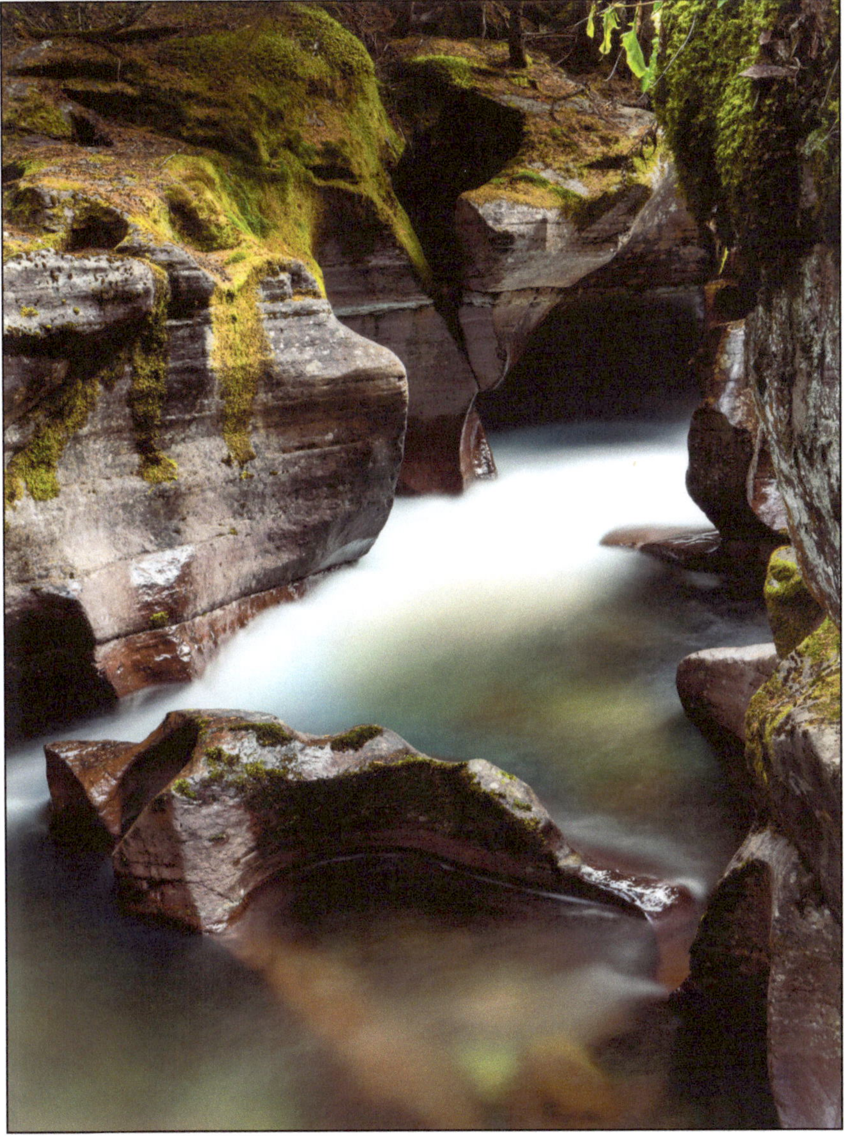

Avalanche Gorge

50mm f/22 20s ISO50

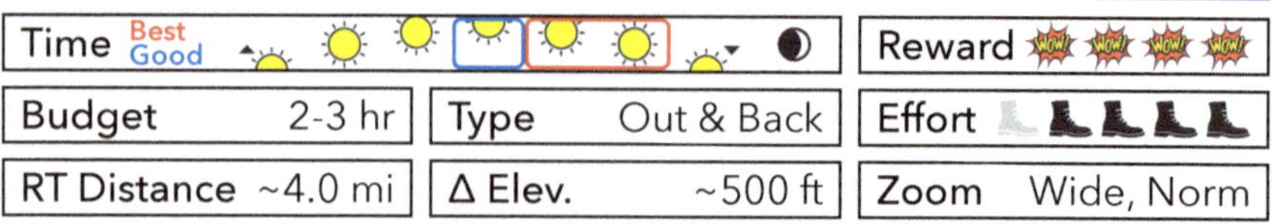

Time	Best Good									Reward	WOW! WOW! WOW! WOW!

Budget	2-3 hr	Type	Out & Back	Effort	
RT Distance	~4.0 mi	Δ Elev.	~500 ft	Zoom	Wide, Norm

Avalanche Lake is an incredibly popular hike. Its round-trip distance is palatable for many, the elevation change is quite manageable, and the payoff at the end is divine. A crowded trail is the trade-off.

Picking up where "Trail of the Cedars +" (4) left off along the gorge, the remainder of the route is reminiscent of many trails found in the Pacific Northwest. I feel at home here. The route is straightforward, and there are photogenic subjects along the way (namely abundant ferns), but the real goods are at Avalanche Lake.

Once at the lake you will find a long shoreline. This is a good thing, because it should allow you to easily find an unoccupied space to stop at and take it all in. If possible, find an area with partially-submerged, large rocks for a foreground (as below).

The one recommendation I can offer here is to experiment with various working heights. When set up lower, your foreground becomes more interesting even if sacrificing some of the lake's vibrant green color. The reflection on the water really pops.

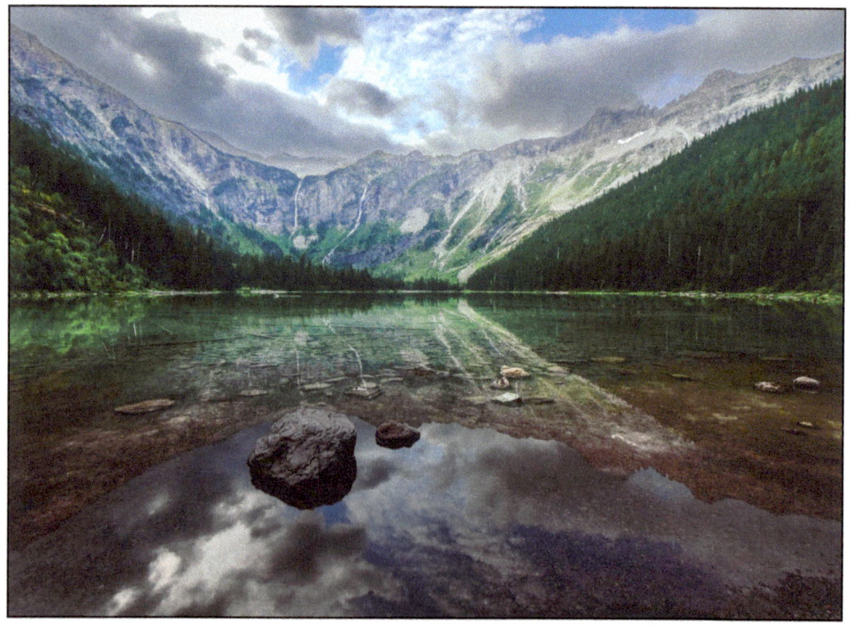

Avalanche Lake　　　　　　　　　　　16mm f/11 1/30s ISO200

In the spirit of saving a bit of space here, I do want to acknowledge three additional sites in this area that you're sure to either come across or hear about, but I'll do so in a more concise way.

Apgar Lookout: For those seeking a leg-burning hike in this area, the route to Apgar Lookout has you covered. Alternatively, Swan Mountain Outfitters offers a guided horseback ride to the top. I have done the in-saddle option and was happy with the experience and my decision.

From a dedicated parking area at the end of Quarter Circle Bridge Road, the 3.6-mile (one way) route climbs over 1,900 ft to a fire lookout tower just southwest of Lake McDonald.

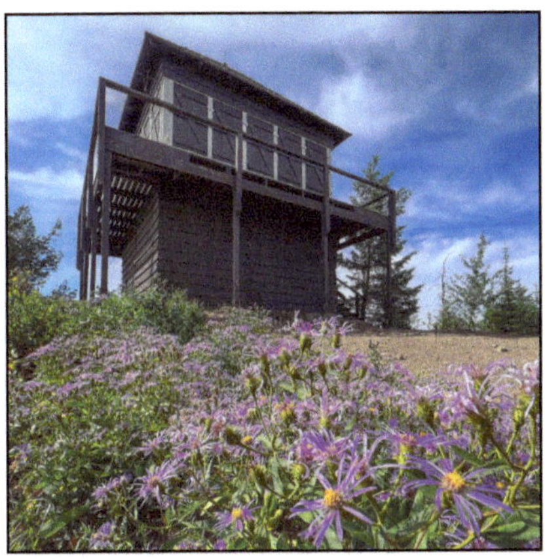

15mm f/8 1/250s ISO100

The views are good, but not great once at the top. Trees obstruct the views somewhat in nearly every direction. The **fire tower lookout** is the typical construction with a wraparound balcony accessible by stairs. The door to the interior is locked, so what's inside is left a mystery.

Photography is limited to some peekaboo shots of Lake McDonald through the trees and clever compositions of the fire tower lookout.

Johns Lake: In stark contrast to the above, Johns Lake is a short hike with mild elevation gain. A route named "Johns Lake Loop" is promoted in places, but having hiked that longer trek I would spend time elsewhere. If you are interested in visiting Johns Lake, I recommend making it a simple out-and-back.

The trailhead (with parking) is located along GTTSR, approximately 0.1 mile south of North Lake McDonald Road. An information board with a map of the area is at the trailhead. I recommend taking a picture of the map... There is a myriad of trails here, and it can be easy to become disoriented with the intersections once in the forest. From the trailhead to the lake is ~0.5 mile and gains ~100 ft in elevation.

At about 0.2 mile find a zigzag intersection with the horse trail. Notice on the horse trail to your right an abundance of **moss-covered trees**. I recommend a detour here on your way back after visiting the lake. The moss covering the trees is dense and photogenic.

The trail closes in on the lake, and a path to its boggy shore is evident. I have explored the shoreline and found this initial position most favorable for access and photography. Lilies are scattered about on the water surface, adding interest to the scene.

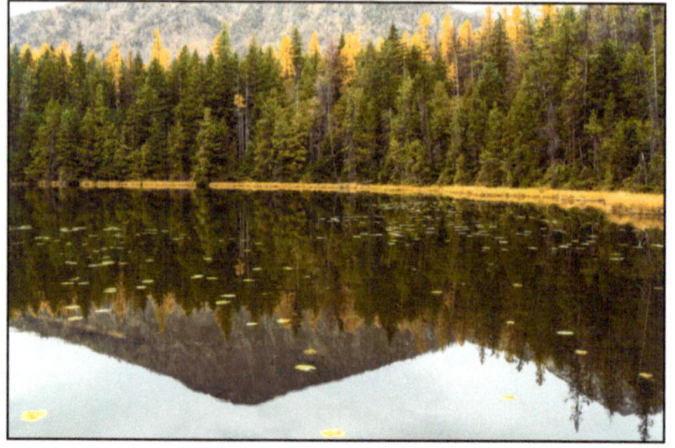

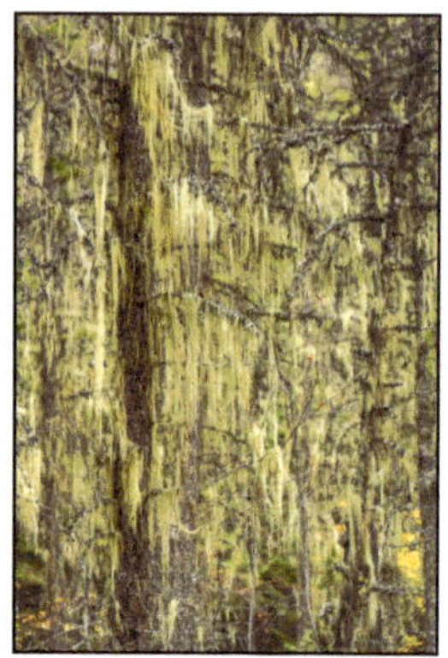

Johns Lake   35mm f/11 0.3s ISO100   100mm f/4

★**McDonald Creek Viewpoint:** This is the easiest of the three here and perhaps the best for photography. Look for a barely-visible, off-white set of wooden handrails leading down from an unmarked viewpoint and parking area about 1.4 miles up-mountain from Sacred Dancing Cascade (3). *This sounds like a scavenger hunt!*

The stairs lead down to a viewing platform where McDonald Creek rushes through a short-run gorge. A midday visit helps combat shadows and provides for more vibrant colors in the churning water.

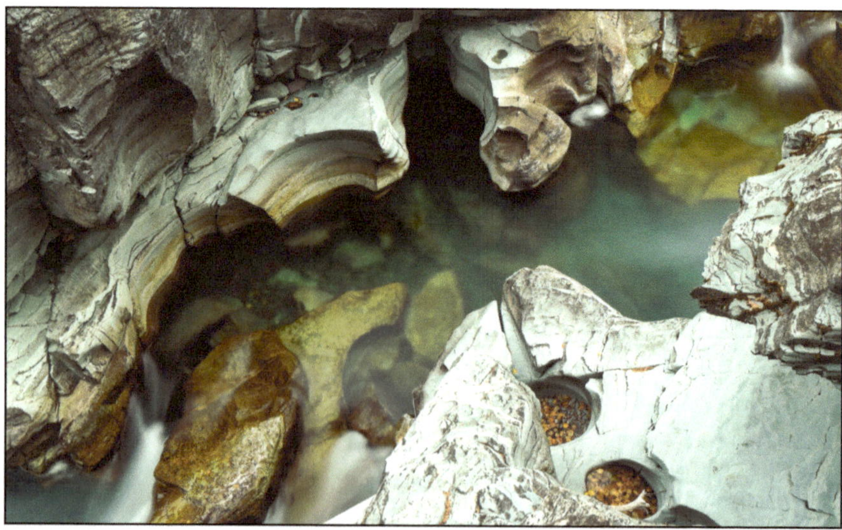

Polished Gorge of McDonald Creek   28mm f/16 6s ISO50

Sun Road – West

Red Rock Point to Logan Pass

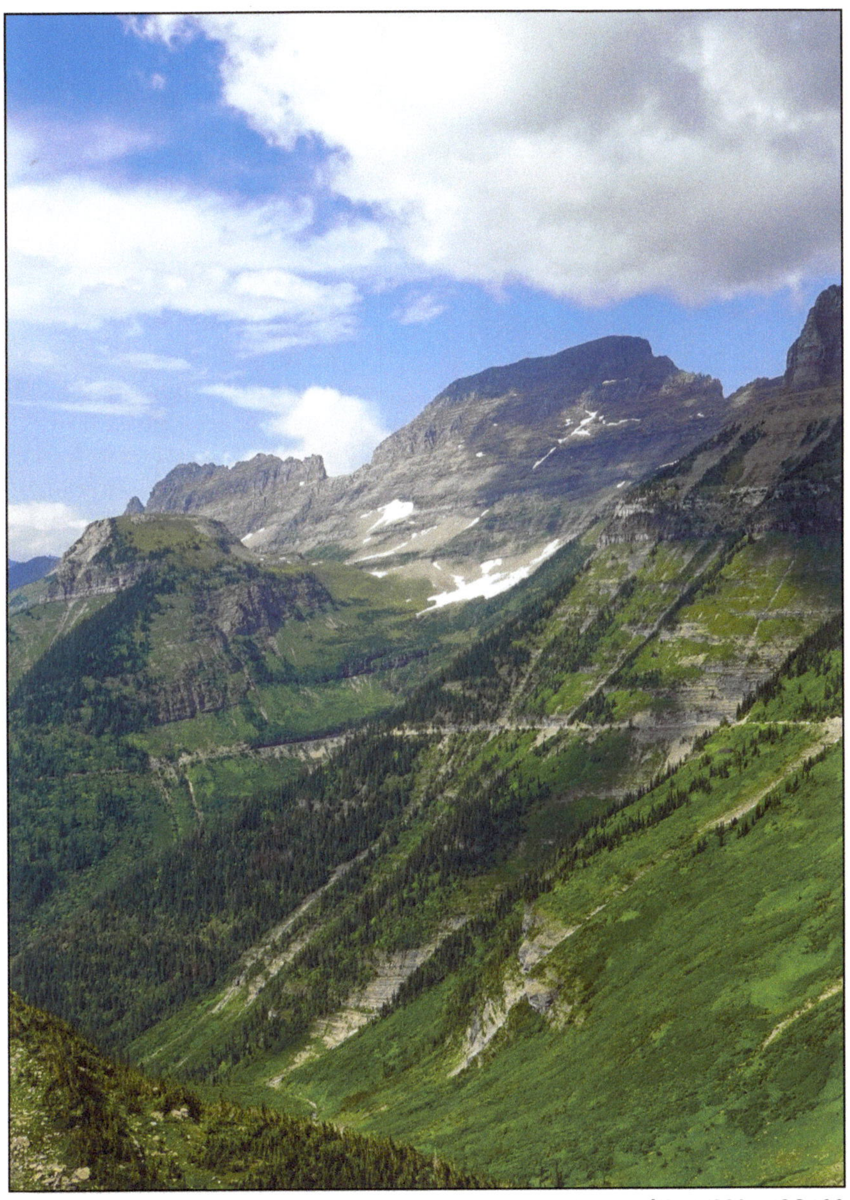

The Garden Wall from Oberlin Bend   35mm f/8 1/200s ISO100

Time	Best Good	Reward
Budget	15 min	Type	Roadside	Effort
RT Distance	~250 ft	Δ Elev.	~20 ft	Zoom	Wide Angle

About 1.0 mile north of Avalanche, and ~3.3 miles south of the small bridge over Logan Creek is Red Rock Point. Signage is sparse, but the parking area is obvious on this bend along Sun Road. A short path heads beneath the trees to a viewing platform of this McDonald Creek cascade amidst – you guessed it – a strata of red rocks.

My recommended time of day may seem atypical, but here the deep water has a marvelous teal color to it, and the best time of day most anywhere to highlight vivid colors in water is midday when the sun is directly overhead. The teal water entirely compliments the surrounding red rocks.

The view from the platform is sufficient, so as long as the sky and clouds are agreeable. I would like to assume as much when you visit, and so the 0-Boot rating and 15 minute budget are adequate. However... If you find that during your visit the sky is lackluster, I have found that a trek down upon the rocks in front of and below the height of the viewing platform offer an improved, close-up view that helps to highlight the water and mostly eliminate the sky. This would quickly add another 15-30 minutes and depending on your route elevate the journey to a 2-Boot rating. If you choose this option, please be careful.

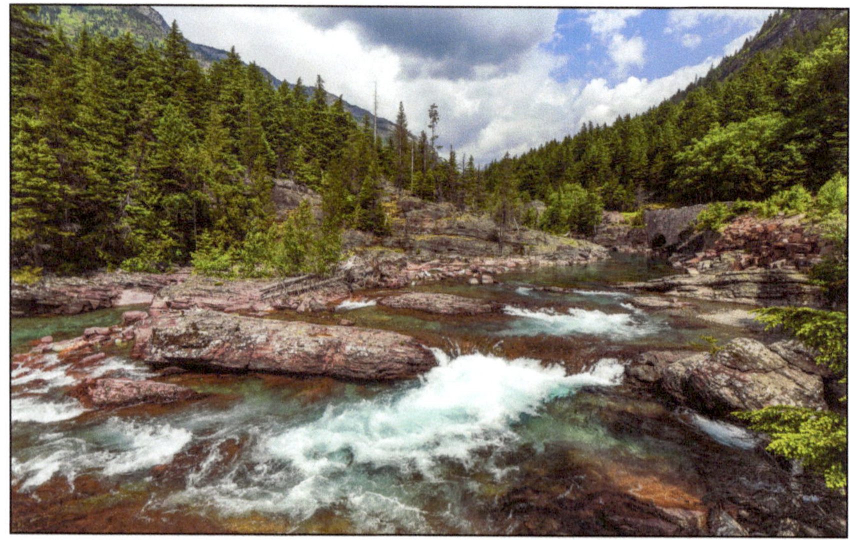

Red Rock Rapids

15mm f/8 1/100s ISO100

Time	Best Good		Reward			
Budget	15 min	**Type**	Roadside	**Effort**		
RT Distance	<200 ft	**Δ Elev.**	<10 ft	**Zoom**	Norm, Tele	

If you're already familiar with Glacier National Park and the typical viewpoints along Going-to-the-Sun Road, this site may seem out of order here. I intended this to be so — not misleading, but interesting rather.

Today's single, *formal* viewpoint of the 492 feet tall Bird Woman Falls is further up-mountain along Sun Road about 3 miles from The Loop. The turnout is large with ample parking for many vehicles. This is a great vantage of the falls, and of course do stop and take some pictures there. Its issue is that there is no foreground, and while the image can be good it tends to be void of any depth to lead the eye. The following photo was taken from this location on an overcast day in October when foliage color was abundant:

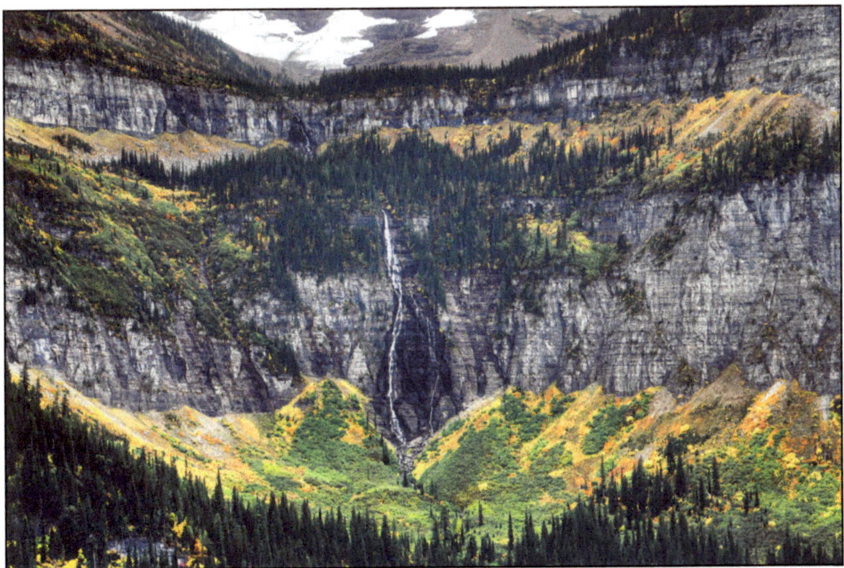

Bird Woman Falls - From Formal Viewpoint   200mm f/4 1/250s ISO100

I've already jumped ahead. Let's return to our previous journey up-mountain, beyond Red Rock Point (7). After ~3.3 miles (past Red Rock Point) find the well-marked **Logan Creek Bridge** built between 1926-1927. Parking is available near the bridge. A clear line of sight is available of Bird Woman Falls with Logan Creek in the foreground. In fact, the water flow of Logan Creek in part arrives from the falls!

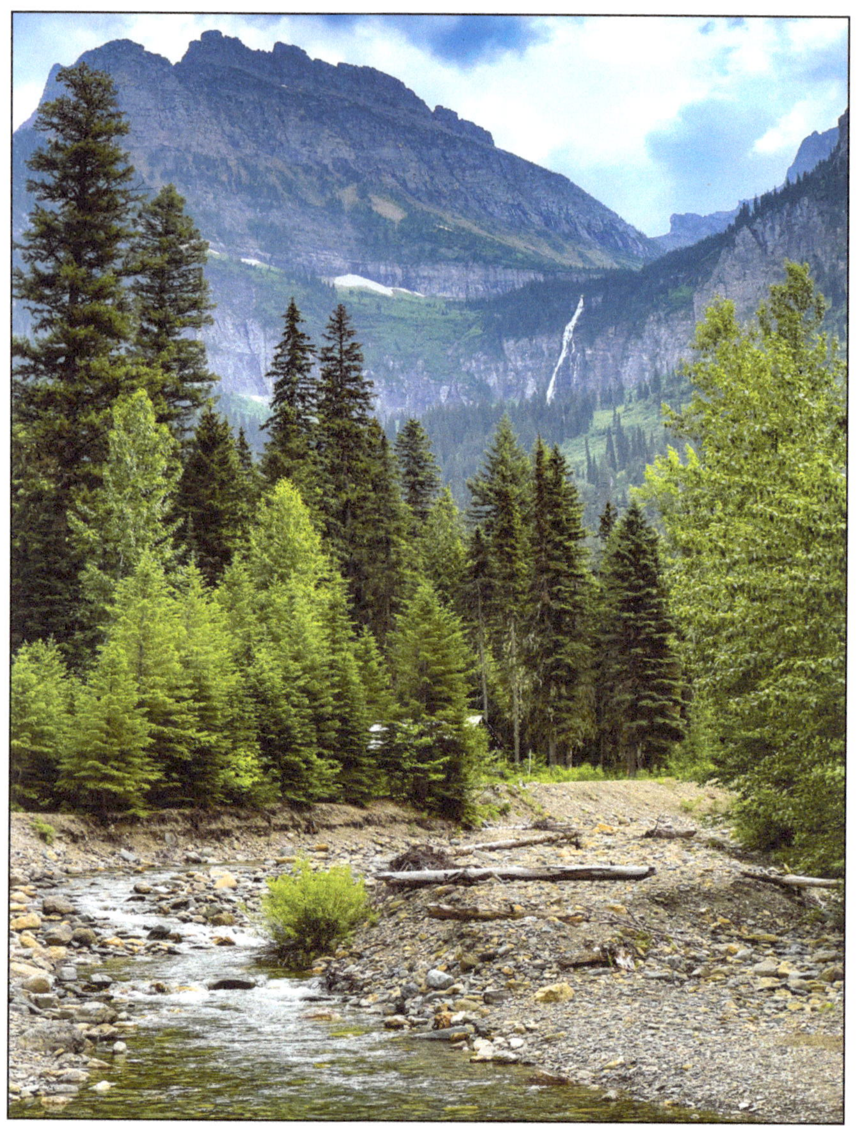

Bird Woman Falls - From Logan Creek Bridge   50mm f/8 1/80s ISO200

Among the options here, I like this one the best. It's nowhere near sensational, but it does the best job in storytelling the water's journey. There is a caveat... Midsummer the creek dries up due to decreased snowmelt, and I would argue that the composition then becomes the least interesting of these three.

Back on Sun Road, again heading up-mountain, after ~1.1 miles locate a pullout with stones arranged in a semicircle with a single stone in the middle. (This will be on your left if heading up-mountain.)

This was once the site of another formal viewpoint of Bird Woman Falls, with the wide McDonald Creek visible below. As you can see, the trees have once again taken over, and visibility of McDonald Creek is limited. Still, the stop is an easy one and worth a look.

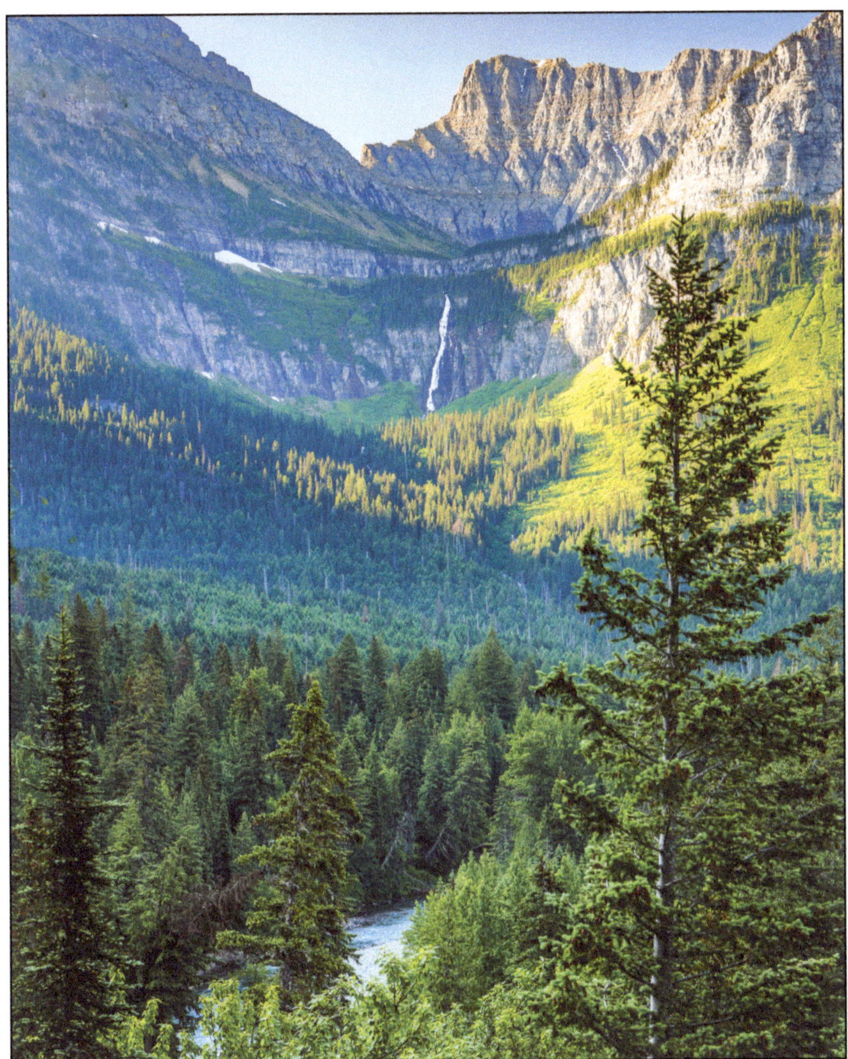

Bird Woman Falls - From Semicircle Viewpoint   70mm f/5.6 1/60s ISO200

With any of these three viewpoints, lighting conditions (including the brightness of the sky) seems to either be entirely favorable or entirely unfavorable. Sadly, the latter seems to more often be the case. So, if of interest, since all are an easy stop typically without parking challenges, as you drive by each time survey the lighting and consider a stop or simply rather to carry on.

Time	Best Good	Reward	WOW WOW WOW WOW
Budget	5-7 hr	**Type**	Out & Back	**Effort**
RT Distance	~8.4 mi	**Δ Elev.**	~2,400 ft	**Zoom**	Wide, Tele

Imagine a young Glacier Park in the early 20th century, without reliable roads and an influx of adventurous travelers. Navigation to the park's trails, as we know them today, was primarily on horseback. Now take a moment and study today's park map... Granite Park and its 1915 chalet aren't simply a destination, but rather at a **major junction** of trails to the north, northeast to Many Glacier, and southeast to Logan Pass. Look south past Sun Road, and see that Granite Park served the area towards Lake McDonald also.

Our route to Granite Park will be the most direct, starting at The Loop. Here, we can assess the elevations (and gain); The Loop is at 4,278 feet, and Granite Park is at 6,646 feet. This route may be the most direct, but the gain is significant.

Logan Pass, at 6,660 feet, is at nearly the same elevation as Granite Park. The **Highline Trail**, beginning at Logan Pass, is an alternate route, albeit longer at ~7.6 miles *one-way*. It does climb on the route somewhat (~600 feet), but given its length feels somewhat mild. A through-hike from Logan Pass to The Loop via Granite Park (with a subsequent shuttle ride, perhaps) is a popular option.

Onto the prescribed route... Starting at The Loop parking area (there are two, small lots – one lower, and one upper), find an information board at the upper parking section outlining the two conceived routes for Going-to-the-Sun Road. The illustration and history is fascinating. Carefully cross the road and begin on the "Loop Trail."

Almost immediately come to a bridge, crossing an unnamed creek. Depending on the amount of water flow, it can make an interesting composition, but many downed trees tend to challenge its appeal.

The hike climbs, switching at times between a forest experience and one with open, sweeping views. If possible, I recommend to hike with your telephoto lens on the ready, though probably stored for efficiency. This area seems to have a concentration of interesting birds and other wildlife, attested by the books to help with identification at the chalet. My strengths are not in birding, but on one ascent I spotted a bright-colored **Western Tanager** in the trees along the trail.

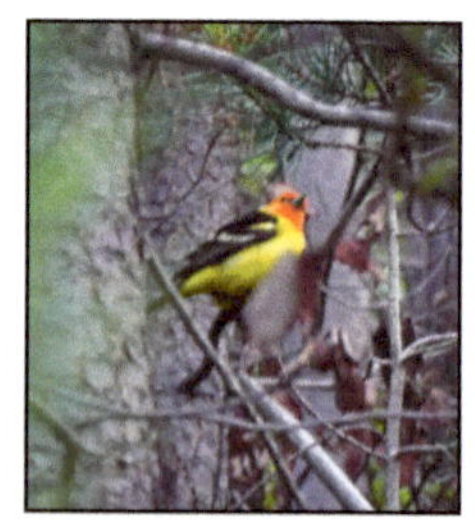

f/4 1/50s ISO800
200mm

Heaven's Peak feels as though it's monitoring your progress upward. Like elsewhere in the park, it remains difficult to capture anything in the foreground to go along with this shapely, standalone mountain.

Reach a switchback at about 2.5 miles and a southeast view rewards you with a good reason to take a break and a photo. Mount Oberlin juts into view, with Bird Woman Falls to its right. Sun Road is visible to the left, as it closes in on Oberlin Bend and Logan Pass.

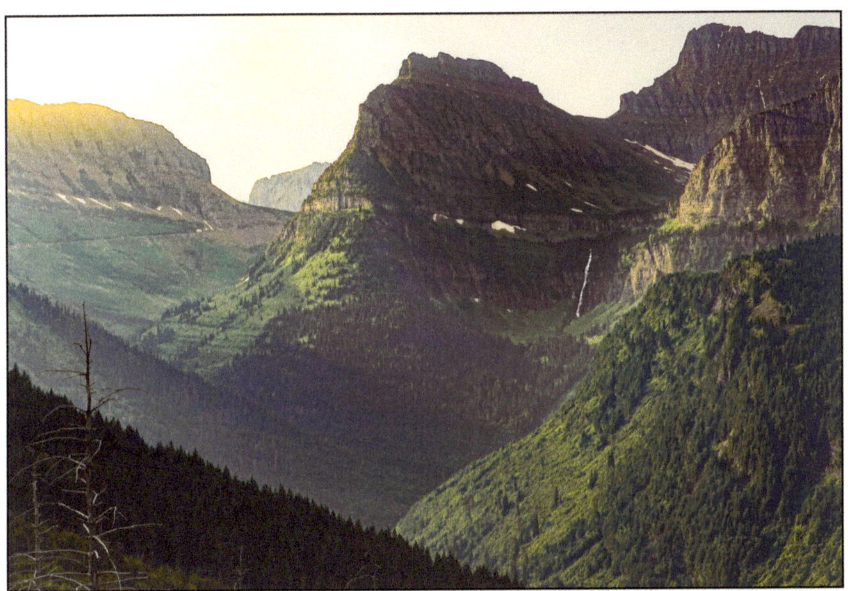

Mount Oberlin and Early Morning Light   100mm   f/8   1/200s   ISO100

The climb continues... At about 3.4 miles an informal viewpoint to the right is marked by a downed tree and trampled ground. While this is another good place for a breather, the view towards the mountains is mostly obstructed by treetops.

Finally, at about 3.8 miles the route presses forward over slanted, pink-colored rocks. Glance up and to the left, and you may sight the chalet's roof and chimney. You're closing in! But the final approach is not direct; you will continue straight and seemingly pass the chalet and accompanying buildings as you continue to ascend to their elevation.

Turn left at the intersection with the Highline Trail, and the buildings come into view. Wooden benches along the path up provide a great place for a break, as well as a wonderful panoramic view. Here it is easy to spot the trail that climbs to the **Grinnell Glacier Overlook**. If of interest and you still have fuel in the tank, this out-and-back route is ~1.6 miles *one-way* and gains ~860 feet in elevation. From here you can peer down onto the distant Grinnell Glacier (28).

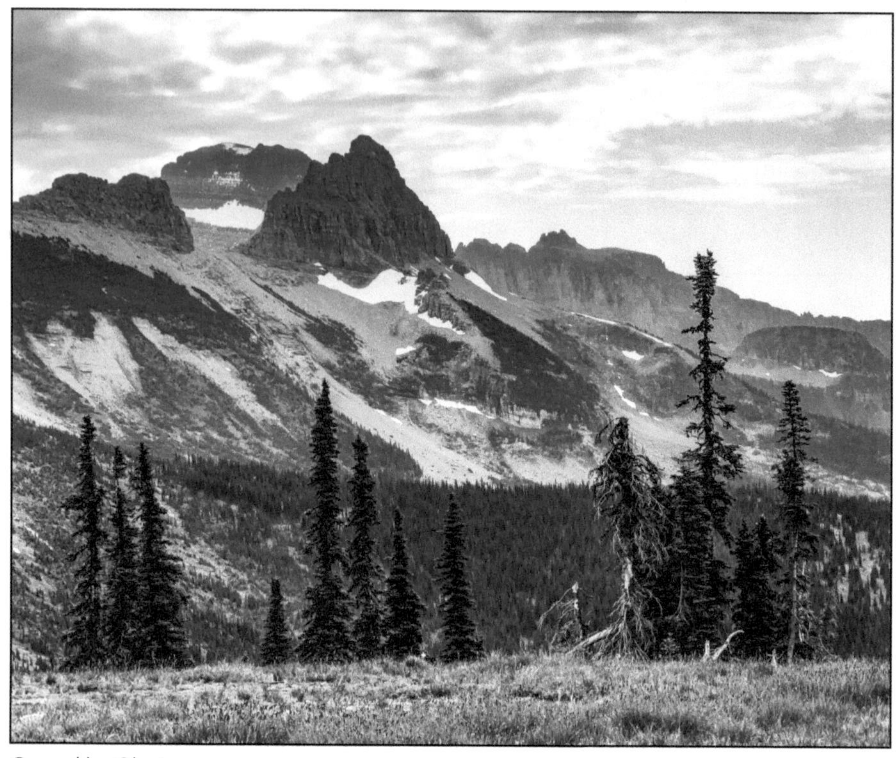

Carved by Glaciers

Make your way to the Granite Park Chalet, with its front porch and balcony facing southwest to Heaven's Peak. It's a magnificent, two story stone construction. Walk inside and enjoy the spacious dining hall with fun bits of resources and information throughout. Imagine embracing its warmth within, while visiting during a stormy day or night.

Rooms are available upstairs in the chalet and across the courtyard. If unoccupied, take a peek through the windows in the ground level accommodations for a sense of what this overnight experience might be like. The communal kitchen is open to registered guests; a variety of food options are available. For information on an overnight stay, check the website www.graniteparkchalet.com. ...The **Sperry Chalet**, east of Lake McDonald and accessing Gunsight Pass, is the second backcountry chalet in Glacier National Park. It is managed by the same company but on a different website, www.sperrychalet.com.

Enjoy exploration here, have a snack or meal, and head back the way you came. **One important note: at about 0.5 mile from the end is a fork in the trail easily missed during the hike up.** Stay left to return to The Loop. The trail to the right is the Packer's Roost Trail, and it will take you to a much lower elevation than where you started.

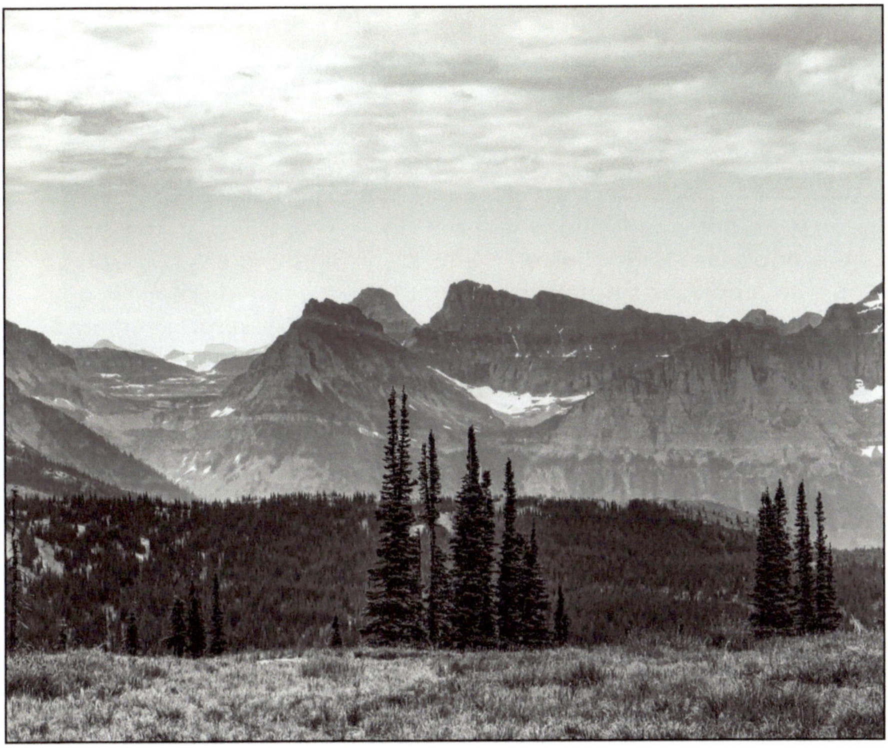

35mm f/8 1/500s ISO100

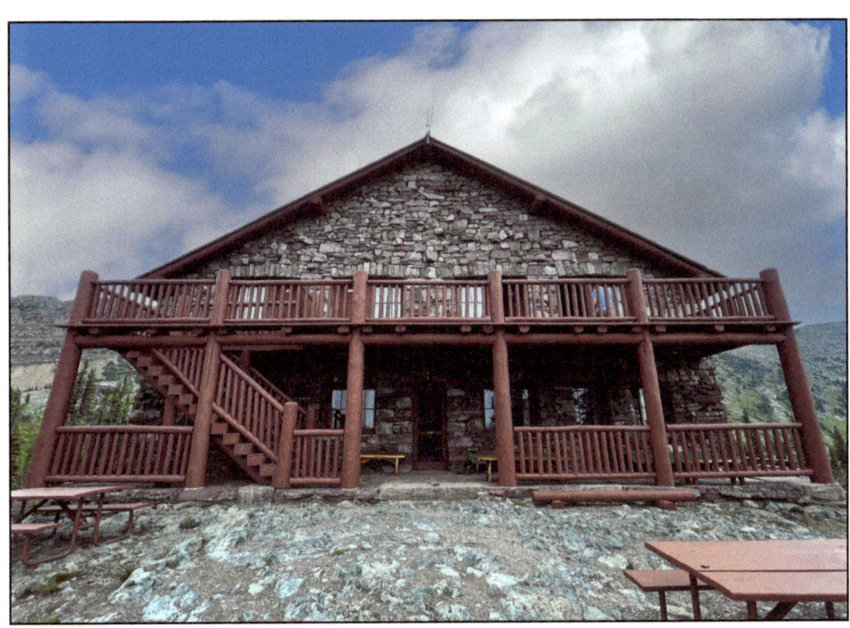

Granite Park Chalet

14mm f/5.6 1/320s ISO100

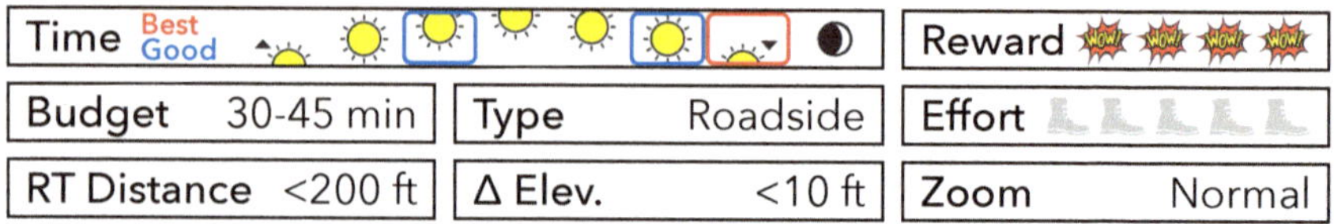

Time	Best / Good		Reward
Budget	30-45 min	Type	Roadside	Effort
RT Distance	<200 ft	Δ Elev.	<10 ft	Zoom	Normal

If you were left wondering where the photo was taken on the cover of this book, we've now solved the mystery. Big Bend is a convenient stop with ample parking along the mountainous section of Sun Road (there aren't many!), and the view is dynamite. It is approximately 5 miles east of The Loop and 3 miles west of Logan Pass. Please see page 33 for further mileage guidance along this drive.

Big Bend is well-known as a sunset destination and a favorite location for wedding photographers... I can all but guarantee you'll see a bride and groom to-be down the hill posing on the boulder for a portrait photographer. Some days there is a *line* of couples and photographers waiting their turn.

This activity is relevant for us, because unless you would also like a bride and groom (and photographer) in your landscape photograph, you'll likely do as I have and stay at the parking area elevation and frame *above* where they are standing below. This tends to work out, as more of the colorful sky is allowed to fill the frame.

Back to the logistics... In spite of its sunset popularity, and probably entirely due to the amount of parking available, I haven't ever run into so many visitors that parking became an issue. The view is more or less the same along the parking area, but to get as much of the west sky in the composition as possible I have found that I prefer the east end. This is a pleasant arrangement, because you can typically "work" from near your vehicle while you wait for the setting sunlight.

Beyond sunset, mid- to late morning tends to work well, and the lighting can be good in the late afternoon (if your schedule won't allow a sunset appointment). Admittedly, the 30-45 minutes of budgeted time is relevant for the act of capturing photos... It does not include an early arrival and waiting for conditions to change.

My recommendation for sunrise and sunset captures is to adjust your exposure compensation *down* 1-2 stops. I can go on and on here, having experimented with ETTR (exposing to the right), but no matter how much light I try and maximize on the digital sensor, the colors become lost. Exposing down helps to maintain the vibrant colors, even if it is at the expense of some noise later when boosting shadows. If concerned, consider bracketing multiple shots at various exposures so that you have an even better chance of returning home with "the one."

I do primarily shoot digital, but occasionally I will carry along a 6x6 medium format film camera. This shot below was with Kodak Ektar 100. I "squeezed" as much in as possible with the lens I had on me, with **Mount Cannon** on the left and **Heaven's Peak** entirely bathed in light on the far right. A more conventional 2x3 or 3x4 format will allow for more of both mountains to be captured. A focal length of 28-35mm is where I more typically work. The grade at right with Sun Road along its edge does limit just how much further west can be framed.

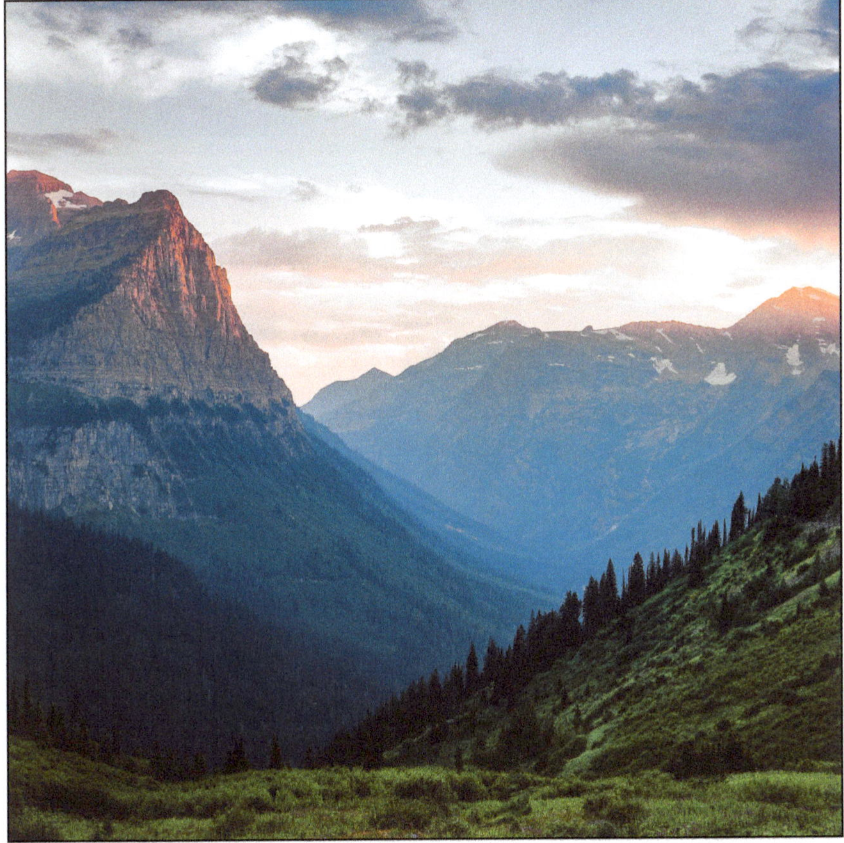

Mount Cannon by Sunset   45mm f/5.6 1/60s Ektar100

Of note, **Weeping Wall** (along Sun Road) is adjacent to Big Bend, just west of the parking area approximately 1,000 feet away. The parking area at Big Bend can be a great place to photograph it. Vehicles driving through the wet spectacle can add to the photo, adding scale to the feature. A short telephoto focal length between 70-100mm can capture the full width of the wall, and focal lengths of 200mm and beyond allow for a more detailed view of the cascade and potentially wet vehicles. See page 22 for additional thoughts on Weeping Wall.

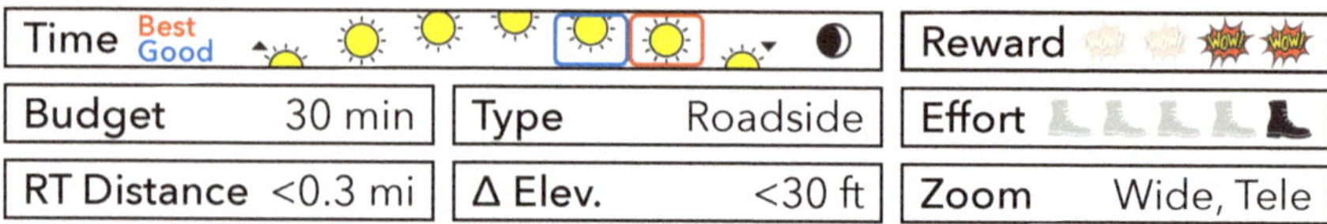

Time	Best / Good		Reward	
Budget	30 min	Type	Roadside	Effort
RT Distance	<0.3 mi	Δ Elev.	<30 ft	Zoom	Wide, Tele

Oberlin Bend is a sweet little stop with up to 3 items of interest... The location has a short boardwalk with a **viewing platform** looking north to the Logan Creek Valley and Sun Road. A nearby **waterfall**, also feeding Logan Creek, is alongside the road and flows vigorously in the early summer. But perhaps the main attraction, when present (which is often), are **mountain goats**.

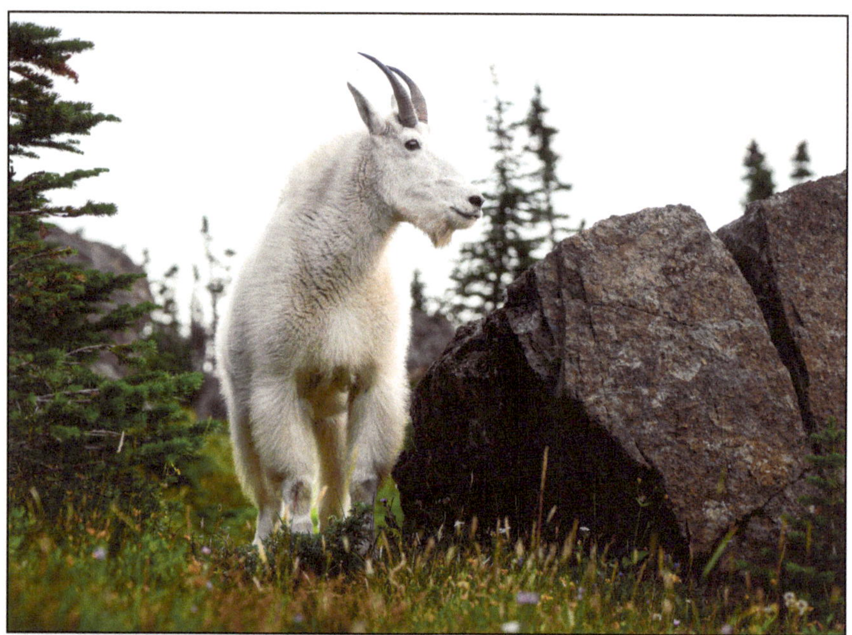

Meandering about Oberlin Bend　　　　　　　　200mm f/5.6 1/320s ISO400

This has been the one location where I have spotted the most mountain goats. **Bighorn sheep** are also around at times. When coming upon Oberlin Bend, whether making your way uphill or down, if you see visitors grouped together there's probably wildlife within sight. Parking may be the next challenge, but if you see a spot open then pull on in.

Working backwards now through the short list above, the waterfall is up the road about 300 feet. Its flow is seasonal, but as you can see to the right, it makes for a nice composition when wildflowers are blooming alongside it. Carefully walk along the rocks, off the road, to access it. A little climbing (<10 feet) may be required for the best view.

70

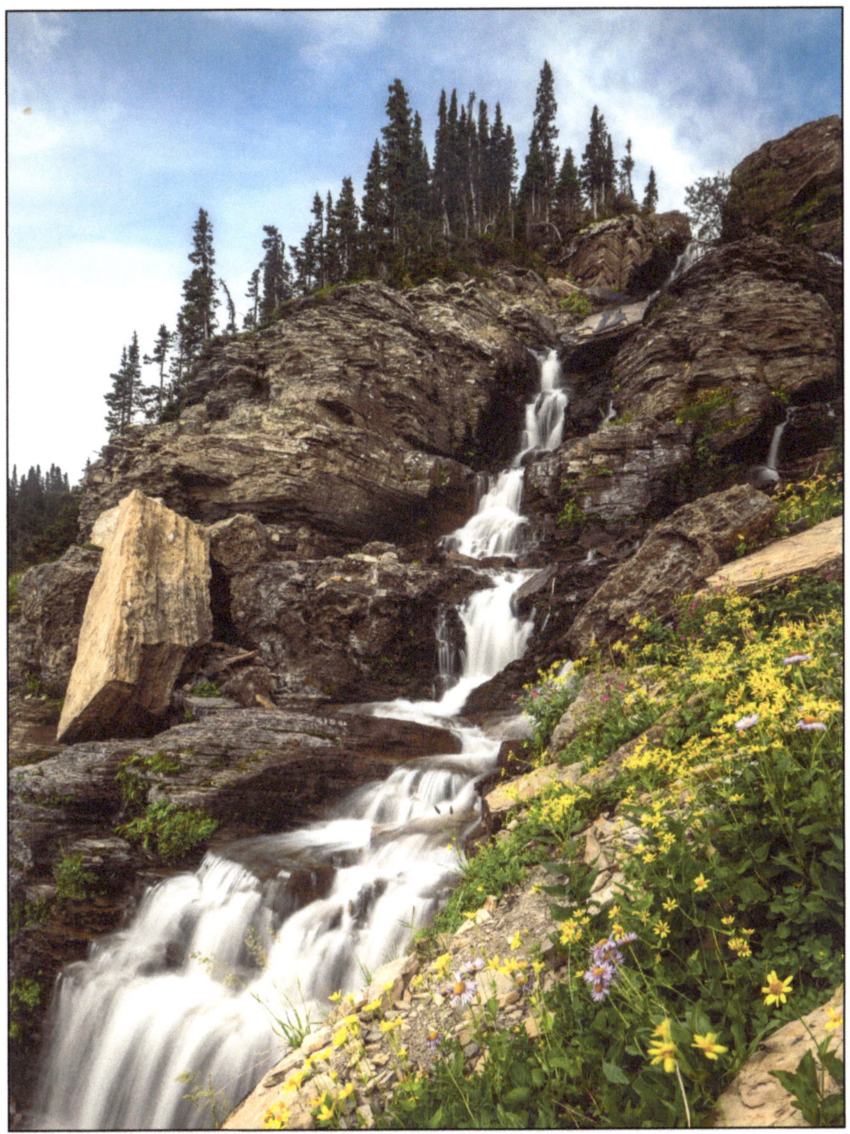

Logan Creek Waterfall near Oberlin Bend   20mm f/16 0.6s ISO50

Finally, the one "guarantee" at Oberlin Bend – the boardwalk and viewing platform. See page 59 for a composition from the viewing platform. A landscape orientation works as well, if not better. Here we can see the Garden Wall, Going-to-the-Sun Road, and Weeping Wall. Logan Creek's features on the valley floor are also interesting, but many bland rocks to the left consume too much of the same frame if this wider view is pursued. I'll often attach my telephoto, seeking wildlife in this valley, but so far I have come up empty-handed.

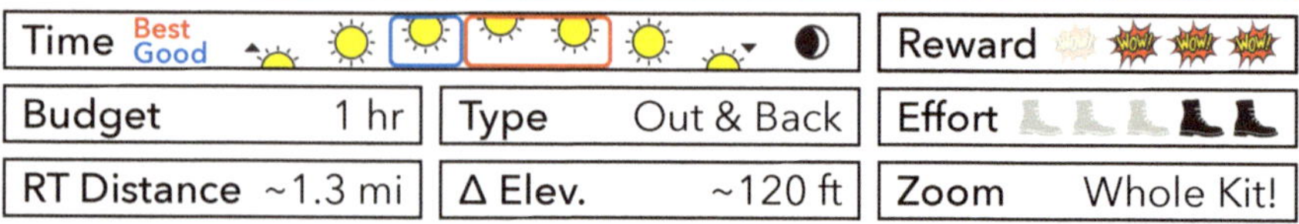

Time	Best Good	Budget	1 hr	RT Distance	~1.3 mi
		Type	Out & Back	Δ Elev.	~120 ft
Reward		Effort		Zoom	Whole Kit!

Here we're going to explore only the *beginning* of the Highline Trail, just beyond its first ½ mile from the Logan Pass end (east trailhead). The Highline Trail in its entirety is ~7.6 miles long, connecting Logan Pass to Granite Park (9). It's a marvelous trail, and I recommend it to anyone with the time and energy to pursue, but I was afraid simply listing it with its full length might have some visitors pass it by. This first segment is fantastic and adds a great "short hike" option while at Logan Pass, without the incredible amount of time to complete it from beginning to end.

Along this trail "outset" (beginning) we have another trifecta of photography opportunities, riding on the coattails of Oberlin Bend (11). Enjoy a unique hike along a **ledge with cables** to hold on to, peer upward along the rocky slopes for **bighorn sheep**, and find a path to **another great view of the Logan Creek Valley**. (See Oberlin Bend for the other.)

The hike begins near the Continental Divide sign at Logan Pass, across the crosswalk on Going-to-the-Sun Road. The majority of the work with the legs is here, as the trail immediately descends, with one switchback, before curving to align with the rock face below the south end of the **Garden Wall**.

This next ~¼ mile section is not extreme, but it also may not be for everybody. It is about 6 feet in width in its most narrow sections, and the dropoff towards Sun Road below is in excess of 100 feet. Cables are anchored into the wall of the rock side of the trail, but no fencing or rail is provided on the "road side" (below). If alone on the route or in single file with your party it is a straightforward hike, but once you meet oncoming hikers some careful shuffling may be required in places. ...Really, it is not extreme, and I imagine most visitors will feel comfortable, but if you have a strong fear of heights you may want to think twice or ask for further insight from a Park Ranger.

The views from the ledge are interesting, but they are only mildly photogenic. I believe the best photos from this section are of the route itself, to share with friends and family once back home. Of course be careful when taking photos from along here.

The photos at right illustrate the "interest" in the route and the features' scale with hikers present. (The latter is to help with your assessment.)

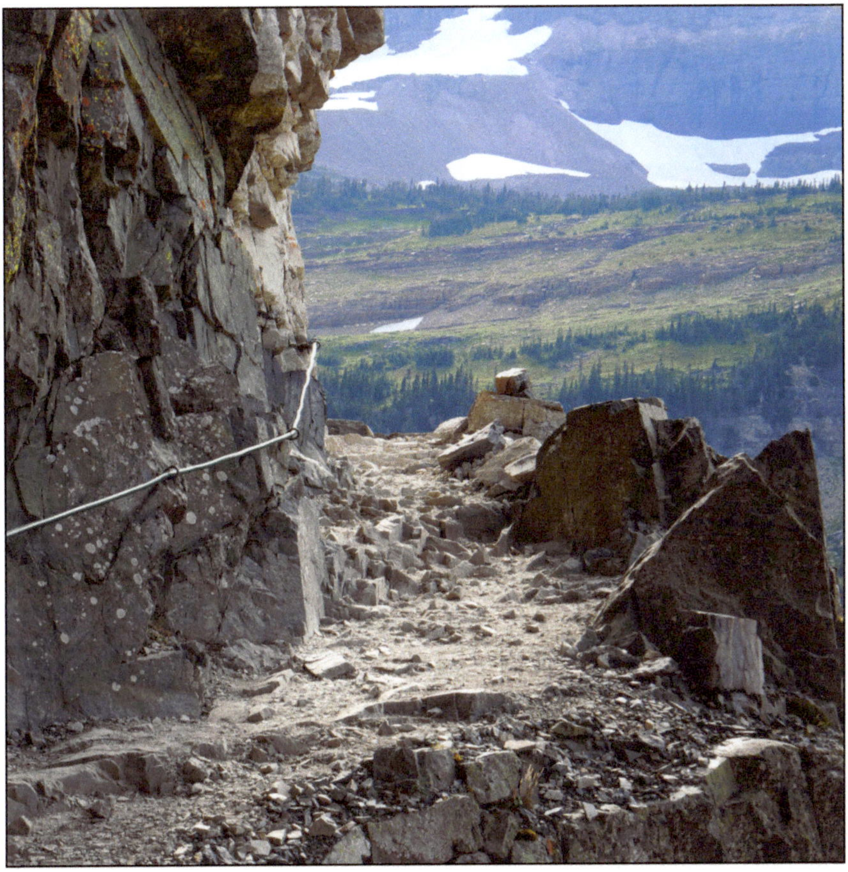

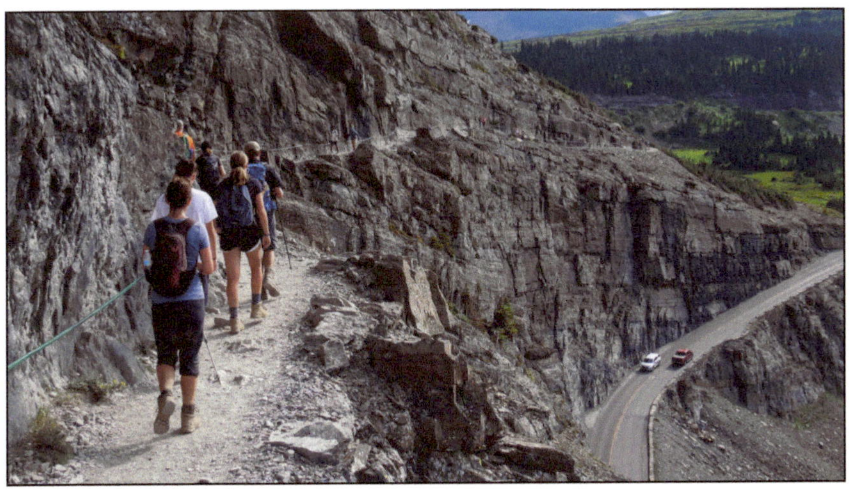

Highline Trail Ledge   85mm f/11 1/50s ISO100

Hiking along the Highline Trail   50mm f/16 1/80s ISO200

Following this section the trail opens up to a more typically comfortable route. Search the rocky grade above for bighorn sheep – they peruse this area often.

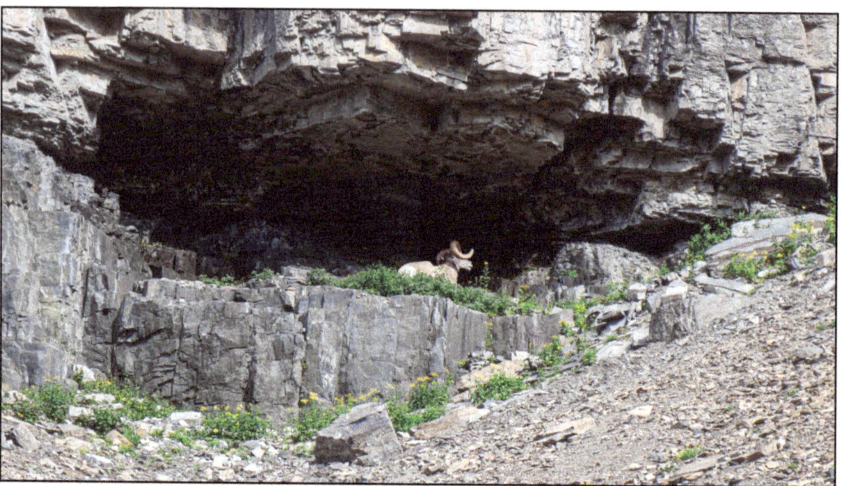

Bighorn Sheep below the Garden Wall — 400mm f/8 1/320s ISO200

At ~0.6 mile from the beginning there is a rock outcrop near the trail, and an evident path to the left leads to a panoramic view of the valley below. Please be careful with each step.

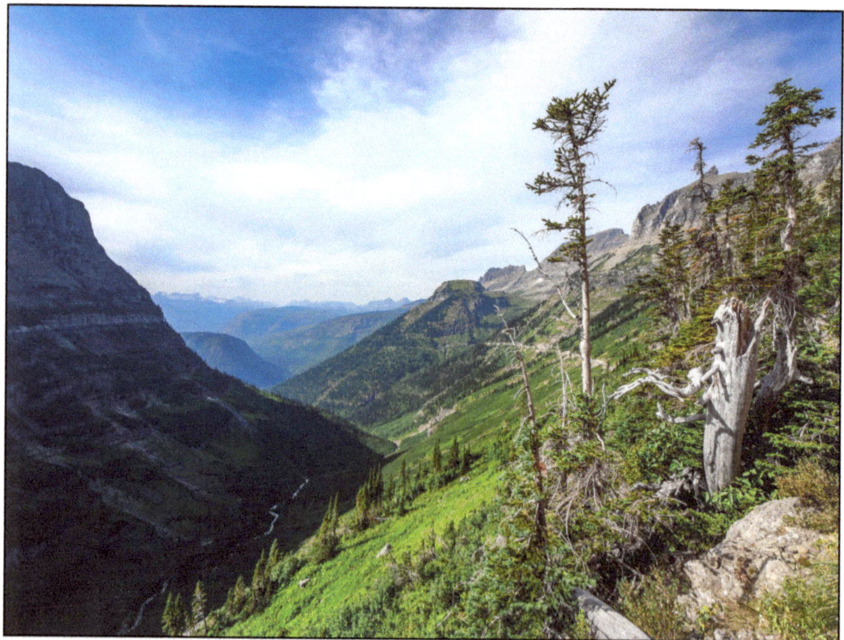

Logan Creek Valley — 14mm f/11 1/80s ISO100

As I'm sure you have already surmised, Going-to-the-Sun Road has many vistas to its valleys below. A fun technique to employ, if your camera has this feature (and many do), it its "miniature effect" filter.

This filter simulates the use of a perspective control lens, also known as a tilt-shift lens.

This effect creates sort of an optical illusion. With a narrow plane of focus and all above and below that plane severely out of focus, it gives the impression of looking at a toy or scale model of your composed scene.

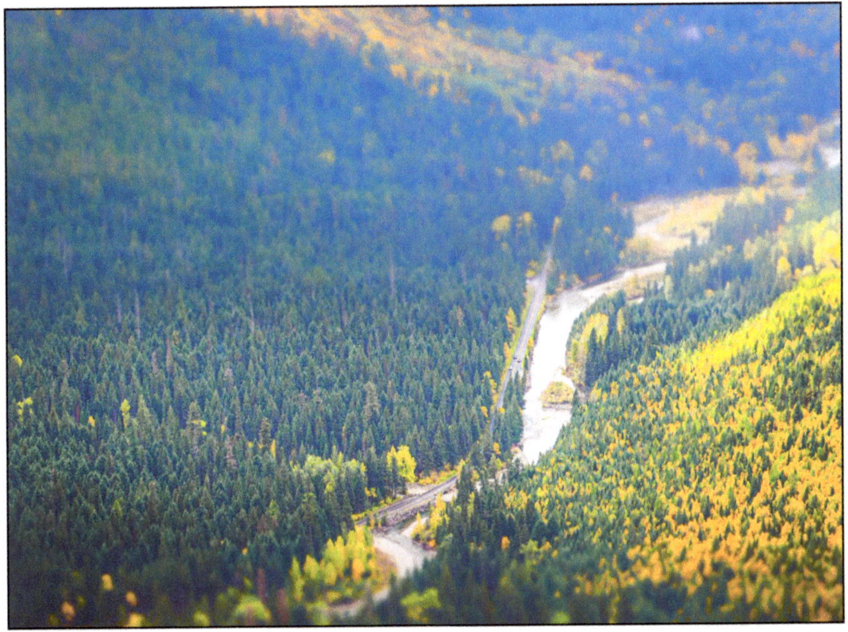

"Miniature" Version of Sun Road at Logan Creek   100mm "f/4" 1/400s ISO200

For those of you with perspective control or tilt-shift lenses, set tilt to maximum and see the results. Some experimentation here may be required.

In the photograph above I am at a small pullout and viewing area just before the formal Bird Woman Falls Viewpoint on the up-mountain side of Sun Road. The view is southwest with the Logan Creek Bridge barely within view. Roads and vehicles work well with this technique.

One final hint: Since this is intended to look like a scale model, applying extra saturation helps to convey the look even more so.

Time	Best Good ☀ ☀ ☀ ☀ ☀ ◑		Reward 💥 💥 💥 💥
Budget	30-45 min	Type	Meandering	Effort 👢 👢 👢 👢 👢
RT Distance	<0.4 mi	Δ Elev.	~50 ft	Zoom	Norm, Tele

Logan Pass is a quintessential stop in Glacier National Park. (As it should be.) Here we have a chance to park and explore a part of the Continental Divide and the highest elevation visitor center in Glacier.

Its large parking lot fills quickly in the morning. Throughout the day vehicles leave, but more arrive at a pace well in excess of spaces available. It really becomes a matter of luck if a spot becomes available when in search for one. It does happen though. Otherwise, the lot also serves the fleet of Red Buses along this route. If interested in seeing the subtle configuration differences among Red Buses, this is the place.

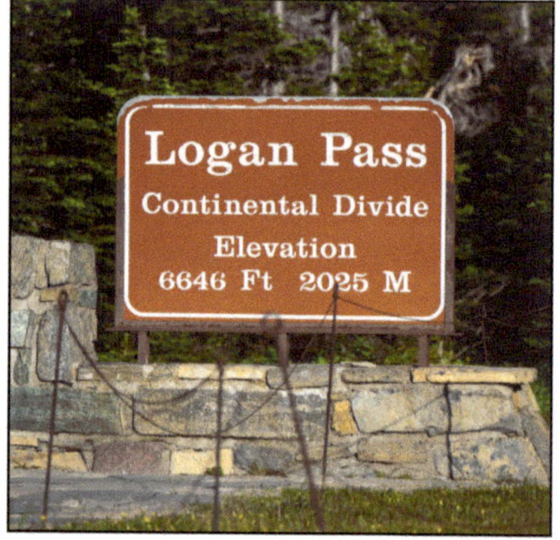

300mm f/5.6 1/640s ISO100

The visitor center, constructed in 1966, has a marvelous exterior shape that clearly was designed to mimic the surrounding mountains. Its footprint follows the stone foundation upon which it was built, making its way from above to below, in the same fashion mountains do. Inside is a grand fireplace and large windows with sweeping views.

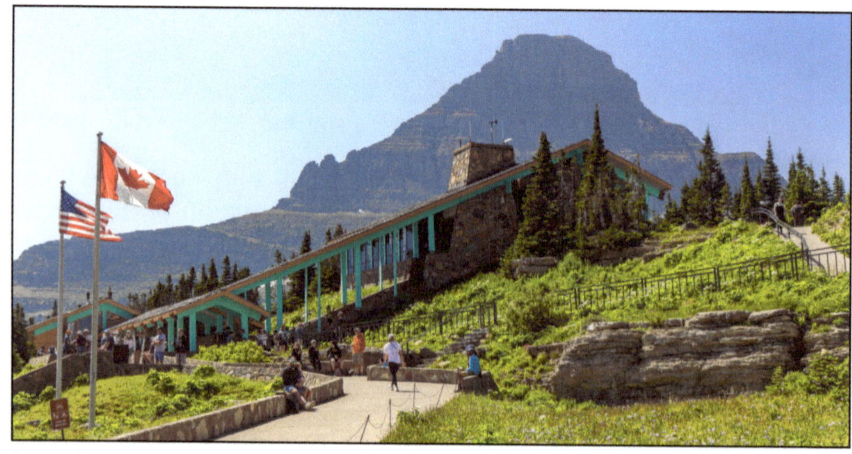

Logan Pass Visitor Center

55mm f/8 1/80s ISO100

Somewhat surprisingly, the area around the visitor center has only a handful of trails to explore. The Highline Trail (12) begins across the road, the Hidden Lake Trail boardwalk (see page 78) vanishes west, and the discreet route to Oberlin Mountain heads northwest (not covered in this book). All that remains is **a very small network of paved paths immediately adjacent to the visitor center**, which in total are captured in the table at left.

These paths really whet the appetite to explore more... I recommend checking out the aforementioned Highline Trail and to also consider some, if not all, of the route to the Hidden Lake Overlook. Be sure to read the latter in its entirety; the boardwalk is mighty inviting and lures the unaware. I've heard many on the route proclaiming something along the line of, "wow, how far does this go?"

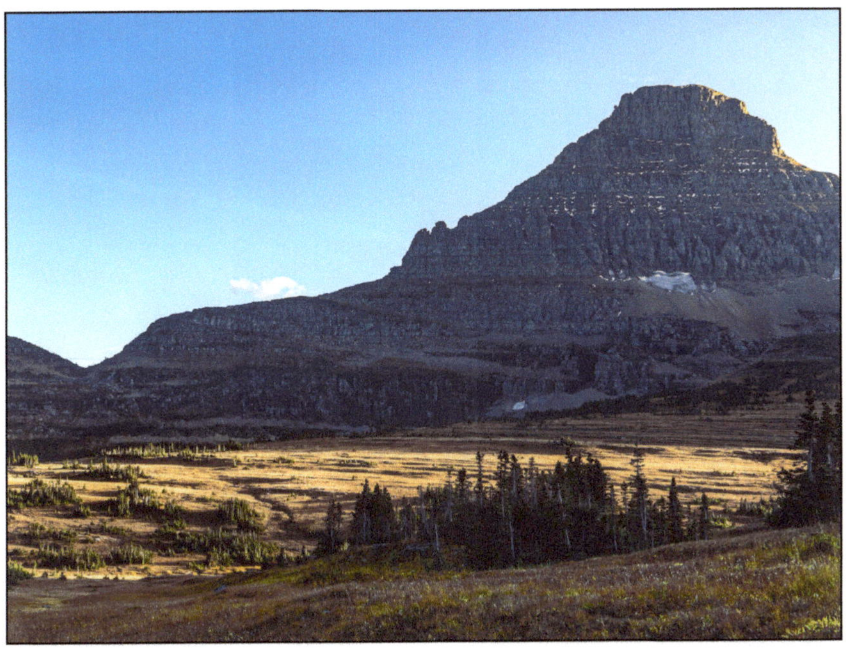

Reynolds Mountain and the Hanging Gardens   50mm f/11 1/100s ISO200

Ground squirrels regularly pose for pictures around the paved pathways near the visitor center. The printed level of detail in the photo of the visitor center at left is lacking, but one is standing on the rock below the tree adjacent to the chimney. They're fun to photograph.

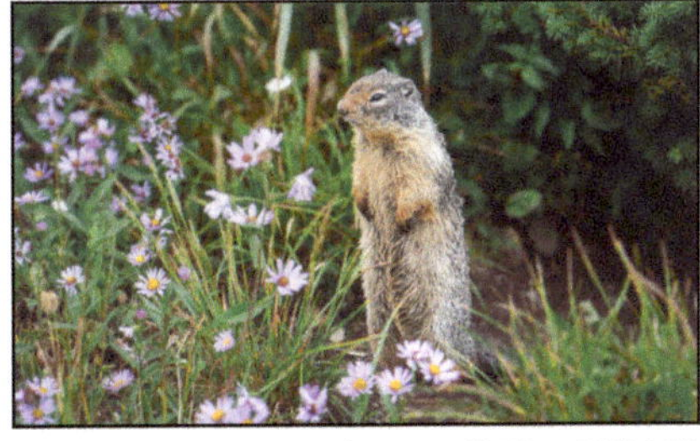

150mm f/5.6 1/250s ISO400

Time	Best Good ☀ ☀ ☀ ☀ ☀ ☀ ◑	Reward 💥 💥 💥 💥
Budget 1.5-2.5 hr	**Type** Out & Back	**Effort** 👢👢👢👢👢
RT Distance ~2.8 mi	**Δ Elev.** ~460 ft	**Zoom** Whole Kit!

The hike to Hidden Lake Overlook is superb. I recommend it whole-heartedly if your time *and legs* will allow.

I commented in the Logan Pass (13) narrative on the boardwalk leading west and away from the paved trails in the area... The route is incredibly inviting, though having talked with several visitors along the way here I believe many people set out on it as a way to explore more of the area without comprehension of the trail's length and elevation gain. Some turn around, and some aren't entirely outfitted to make it comfortably to the end. Exploring some and turning around is OK, but if interested in hiking its entirety... Well, I'm sure you won't be surprised now because you have the critical information above.

The boardwalk that we see is about 0.2 mile of its ~0.5 mile total length. Then the route changes to dirt for the final ~0.9 mile.

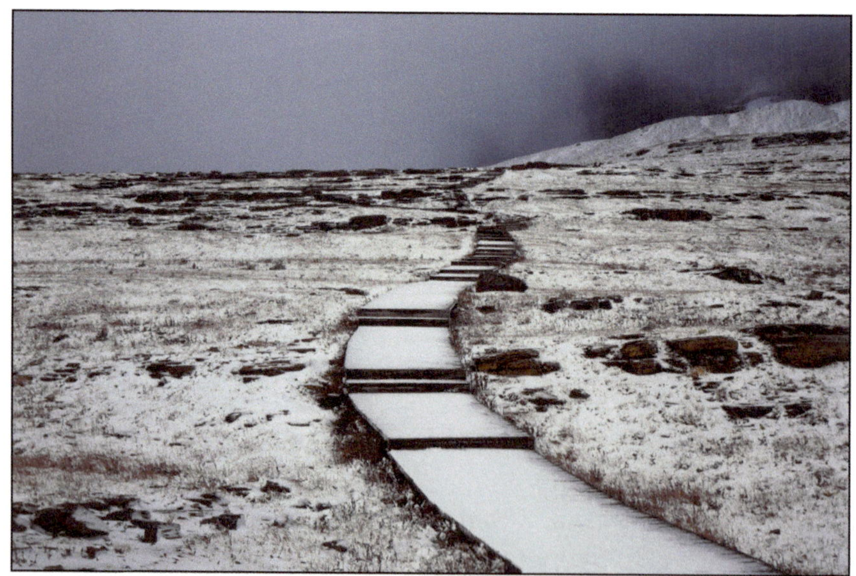

Snowy Boardwalk towards Hidden Lake   50mm f/8 1/400s ISO100

As you can see above, I have hiked this with the boardwalk covered in snow and ice. **It can be incredibly slippery.** I recommend wearing micro-spikes or similar strapped to the soles of your shoes. It may also be slippery when wet. Again, micro-spikes can help. Please be careful.

Now for some seasonal contrast, this route in the summer can really be abundant with wildflowers. I have found that the best flowers are concentrated in the area where the boardwalk ends, so if you're early in your hike and feeling like the flowers are already great, keep moving forward – the best may still be yet to come.

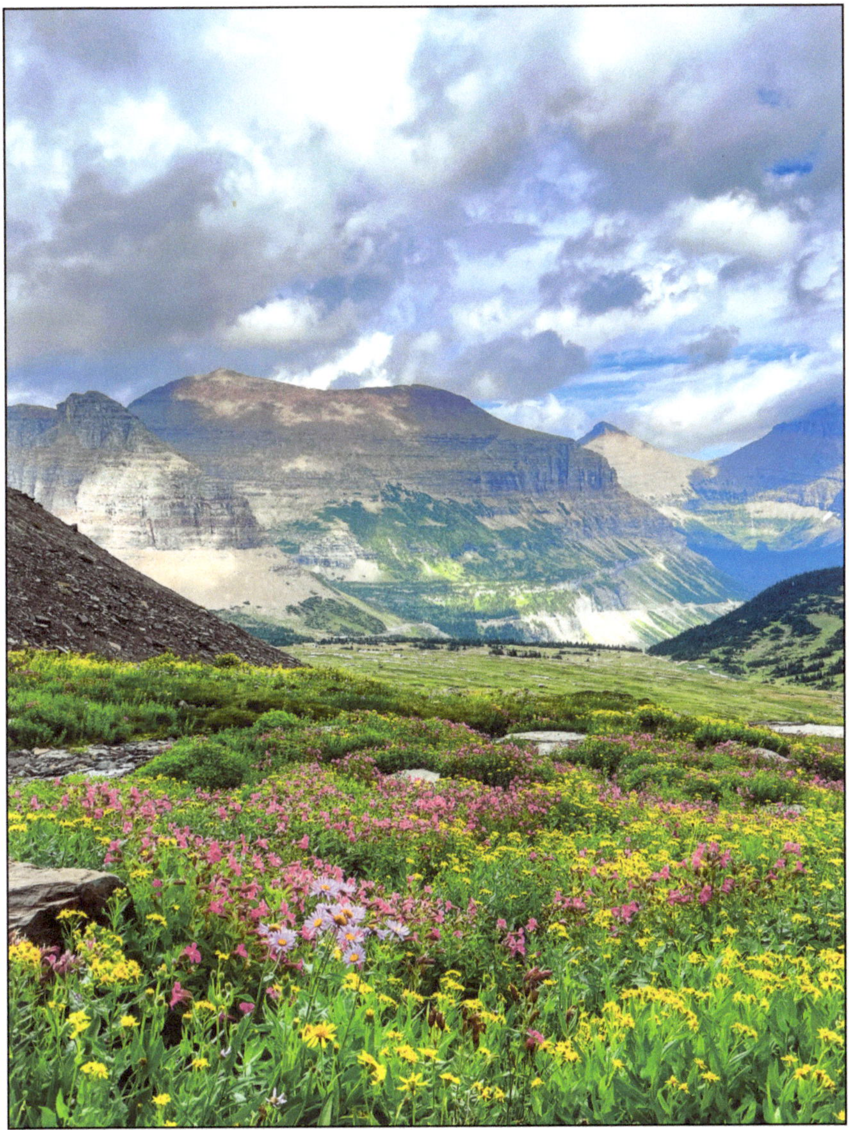

Logan Pass in Full Bloom   28mm f/8 1/160s ISO100

The views along this route are sensational. Sweeping vistas are in abundance, as well as opportunities for ground-level closeups.

Hoary marmots frequent rock piles near the trail. A telephoto lens will be required to best capture them.

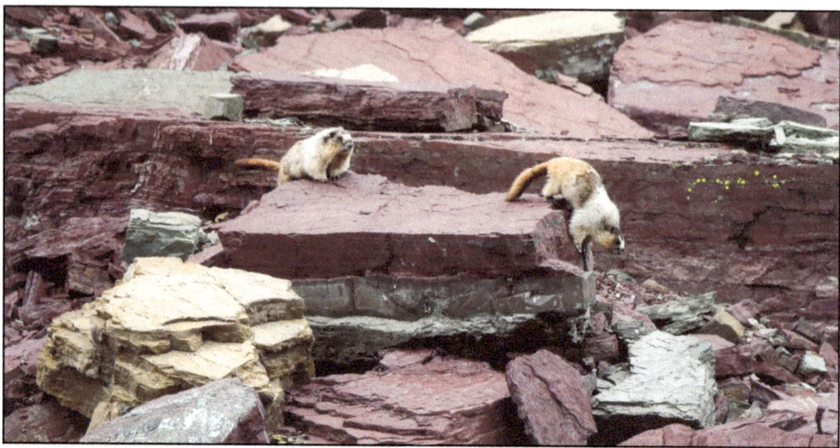

Hoary Marmots on the Prowl   400mm f/8 1/320s ISO800 (then 2:1 digital crop)

Finally, reach the viewing platform for the Hidden Lake Overlook. The lake stretches north to south, with Bearhat Mountain behind it to the southwest. A focal length of 18mm or wider is required to capture its full length, or alternatively a stitched panorama will do. I tend to steer clear of stitching photos with the typically fast-moving clouds here.

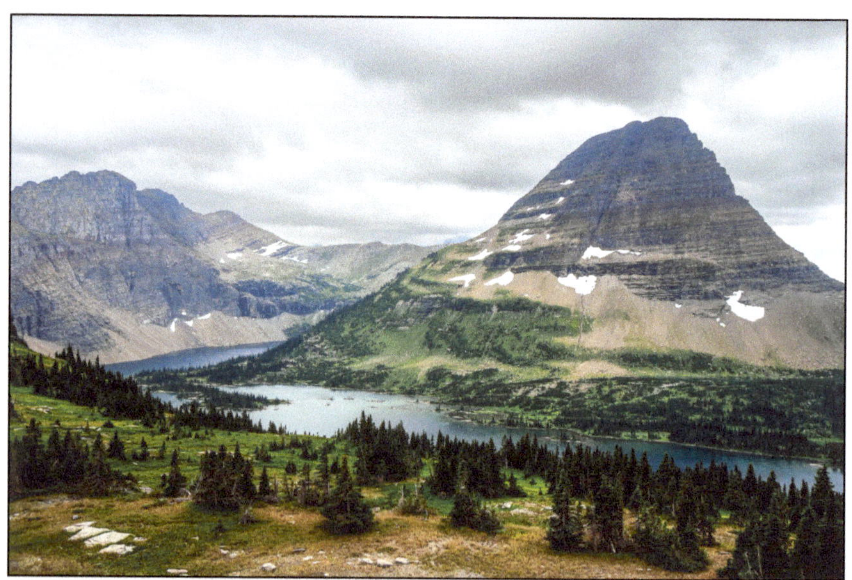

Hidden Lake and Bearhat Mountain   28mm f/11 1/60s ISO100

If interested, the route from here to the lake below is a strenuous one over loose terrain, losing 780 feet of elevation over ~1.5 miles.

Sun Road - East

Siyeh Bend to Saint Mary

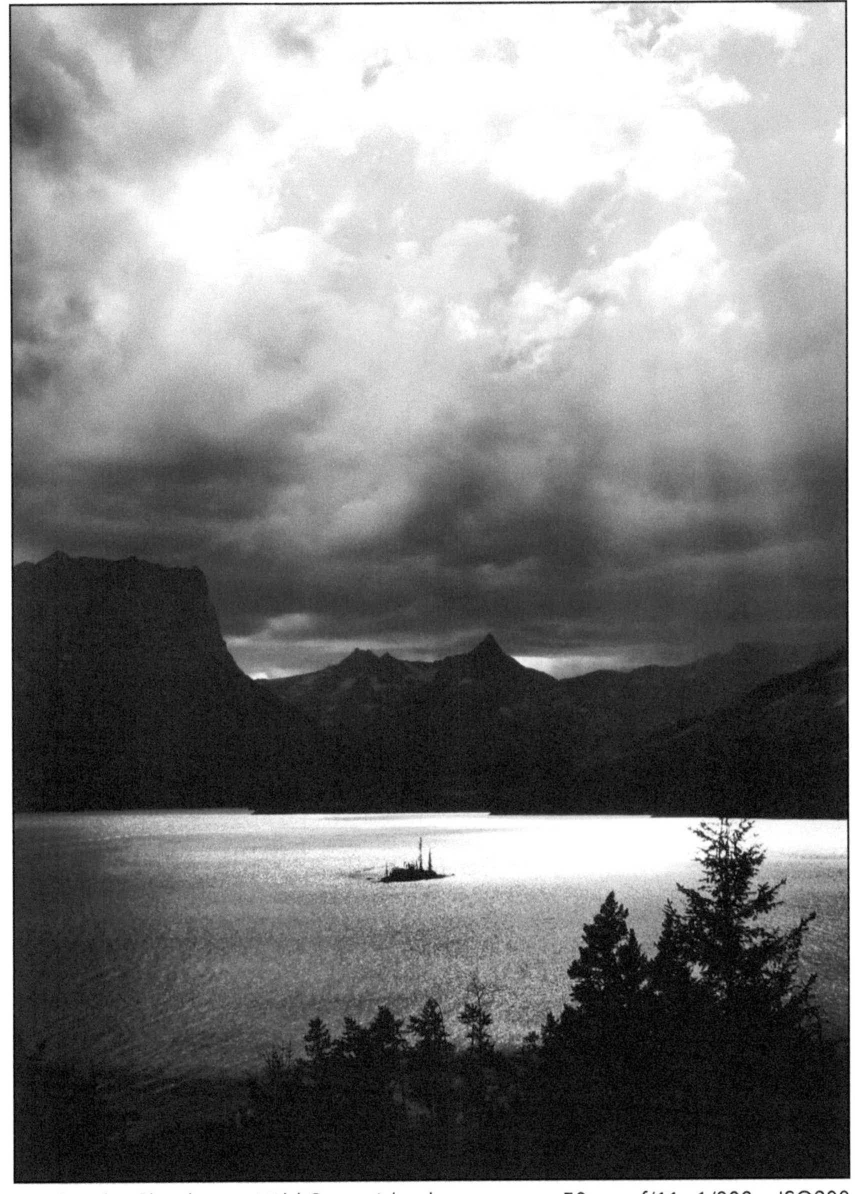

Break in the Clouds over Wild Goose Island   50mm   f/11   1/800s   ISO200

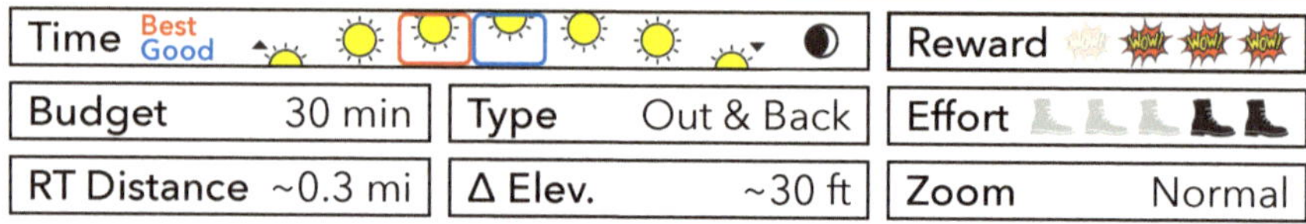

Time	Best / Good		Reward	
Budget	30 min	Type	Out & Back	Effort
RT Distance	~0.3 mi	Δ Elev.	~30 ft	Zoom	Normal

To my delight, I have just learned that the naming convention for this creek is as unique as the optical illusion of its water flowing upward. **Siyeh Creek** is the formal name. I had thought for years now that it was Piegan Creek because one of the sources of its flow is the Piegan Glacier, situated atop Piegan Mountain (in the left of the photo on the opposite page). But no. Instead the name Siyeh Creek is used, even though the Siyeh Glacier does not provide runoff here. Northwest of Helena there is already a Piegan Creek in Montana. Perhaps this is why.

Siyeh Bend, one of the few hairpin turns along Going-to-the-Sun Road, has a certain "je ne sais quoi" appeal from within a vehicle, and after many times around it one day I finally stopped to better explore the area. That day is pictured here. I remember noticing the peekaboo sky in particular. On a cloudless day, or an entirely socked-in day, the overall lighting and the view we see to the north is less remarkable. You'll be able to assess this on your approach. If still motivated to try for a photograph, a landscape orientation will allow elimination of a bright sky. A combination of a neutral density filter and a polarizing filter helps subdue the cascade and surrounding reflections.

The Piegan Pass trailhead is well-worn and easy to spot on the east side of Siyeh Creek. Descend initially and then follow the trail with the creek to your left. After the descent you will walk about 450 feet and find an accommodating path to the rocky creek edge. At this same point the initial trail veers away from the creek slightly, and after another 100 feet the trail turns sharply right. If you reach this sharp turn you'll know that you've gone too far.

Meander along the rocks on the east bank of Siyeh Creek upstream a bit. **Tread cautiously – some of the rocks may be slippery and/or loose.** The cascade is only 30-40 feet upstream from where you peeled off the main trail.

I do remember stacking filters here – one 3-stop ND and one circular polarizer. Regardless of orientation (vertical or horizontal), focal lengths between 28-50mm seem to work well. A tool to help ensure your camera is level helps, because nothing here seems so! So whether it be a bubble level or an in-camera level, I do recommend using.

Otherwise, as I often suggest, try various working heights to see which perspective matches your vision the best.

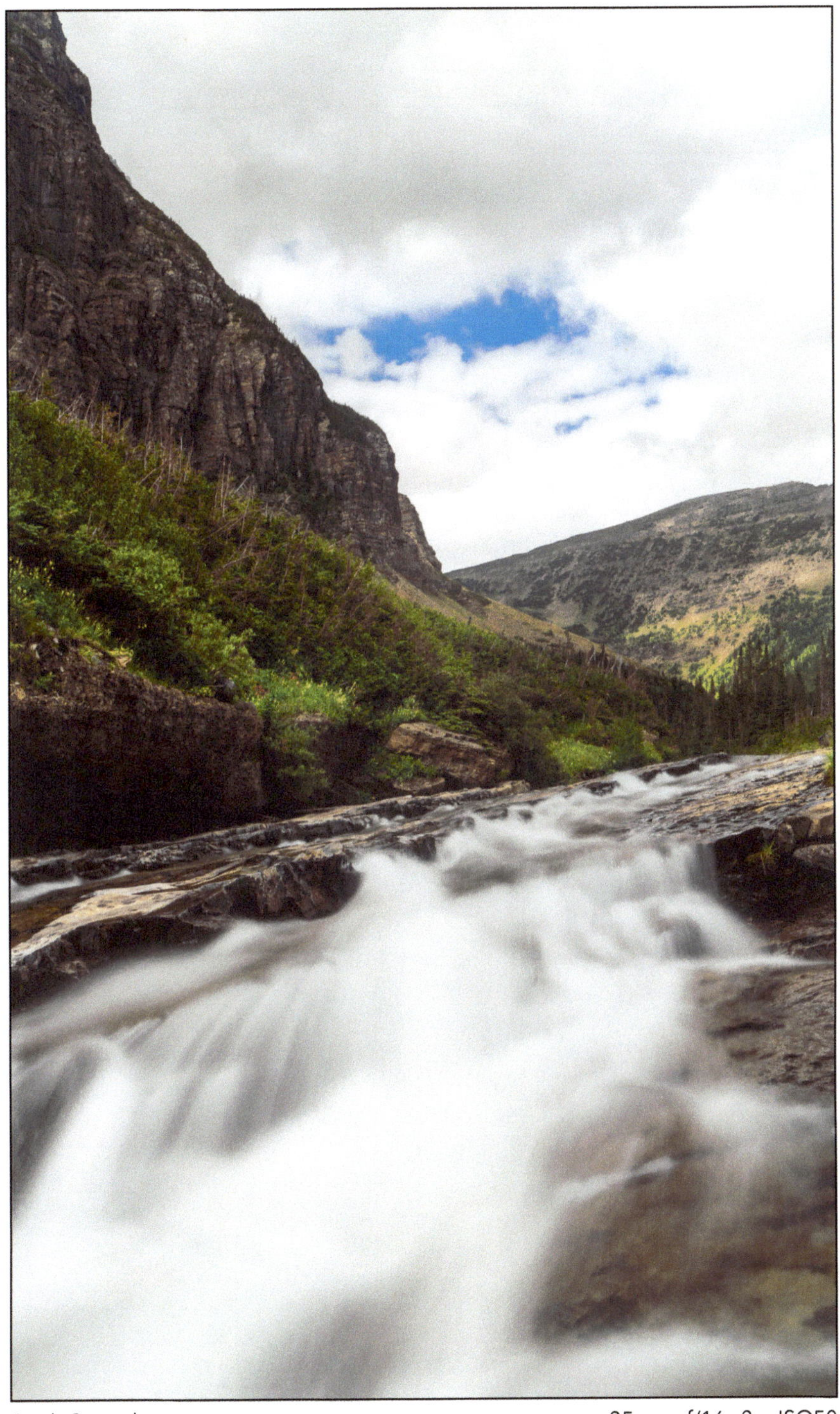

Siyeh Cascade

35mm f/16 2s ISO50

Time	Best Good	☀ ☀ ☀ ☀ ☀ 🌙	Reward	💥 💥 💥 💥
Budget	2-3 hr	**Type** Out & Back	**Effort** 👢 👢 👢 👢 👢	
RT Distance ~3.2 mi		**Δ Elev.** ~190 ft	**Zoom** Wide, Norm	

If waterfalls are your thing, this hike is not to be missed.

St. Mary Falls is the first along this route, after a 0.8-mile hike *downhill* from Sun Road to near the elevation of St. Mary Lake, where the St. Mary River thunders down from the mountains above. Virginia Falls is the final destination, after an *uphill* hike from St. Mary Falls. Virginia Falls is visible from along Sun Road, whereas St. Mary Falls is not.

Along the trail between St. Mary Falls and Virginia Falls, Virginia Creek has a handful of large unnamed falls and cascades. This is where the waterfall aficionados will continue to have some real fun. For the rest of us, the challenge becomes time management. It can be easy to spend 1-2 more hours here if pursuing these additional water features. Reading between the lines, I have not accounted for this extra time in the table above.

Of relevant noteworthiness: There are two hiking trails from along Sun Road towards St. Mary Falls. One is located at the shuttle stop; the other is located at the vehicle parking area. The hike duration, in the table above, is via the trail from the shuttle stop. Unfortunately, at time of writing, there are some discrepancies among some of the posted and circulated maps on this area, including identification of where the shuttle stop is relative to the parking area and the routes to the falls. I'll explain further...

West to east, along Going-to-the-Sun Road, the first of these locations is the shuttle stop. It has a well-marked trailhead to these falls, and this is the most direct (i.e. shortest) route. The parking area is ~0.2 mile further east. A trailhead is here as well, but it adds ~0.3 mile of hiking (~0.6 mile if taken round trip). These trails intersect after ~0.3 mile along the route from the shuttle stop... The signage to the falls is clear, but still take note of which trail you took for your return trip later on.

Hiking from Sun Road to St. Mary Falls takes you through a landscape impacted by the **Reynolds Creek Fire of 2015**. Of the trails in this area, this route is my favorite, in order to observe this forest's progress towards re-growth.

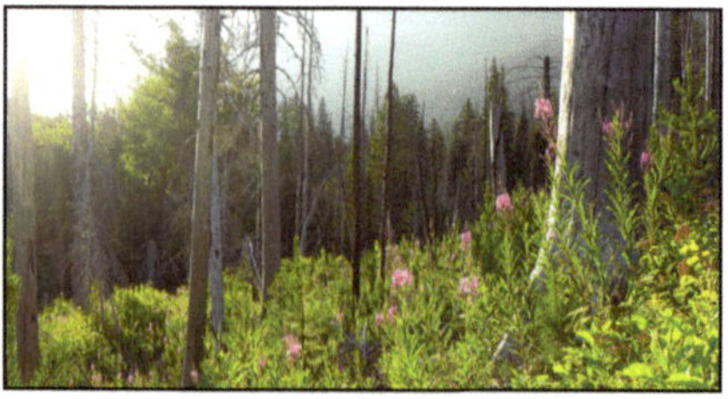

35mm f/4 1/160s ISO100

On the approach to St. Mary Falls you'll spot its adjacent footbridge. A path is present off the main trail for a clear view.

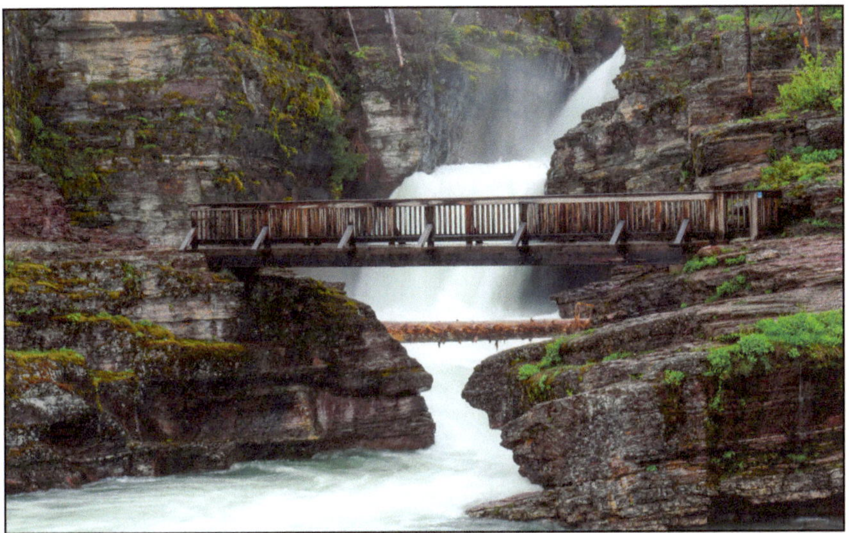

Rainy Day Approach to St. Mary Falls   100mm f/16 0.4s ISO100

St. Mary Falls can provide an extreme show with intense water flow, especially in the late spring and early summer. Even after it calms, the water throughput is remarkable. Once at the falls, try compositions from the bridge and from along top the broad rock platform on the opposite end of the bridge from which you arrived.

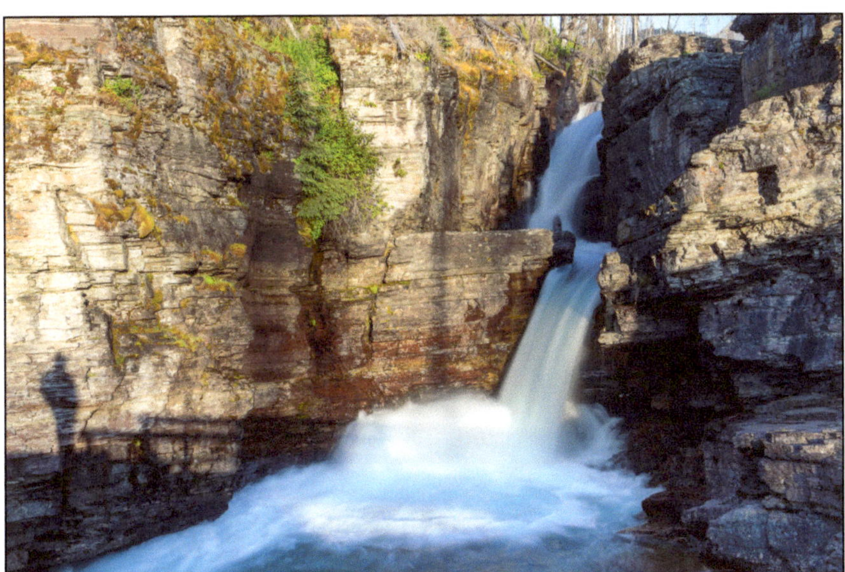

Silhouette Self-Portrait at St. Mary Falls   50mm f/11 0.5s ISO100

Continuing onward towards Virginia Falls, almost immediately come upon a sizable waterfall to your left... This is where some discipline is required. I recommend to stay the course and enjoy hiking past the numerous water features along the way. If compelled to photograph one or some, stop along your return trek. The route slowly ascends...

The first intersection in the vicinity of the falls points right to "Virginia Falls View Point" and lists 0.2 mile remaining. The distance is incorrect, but this is the route to take. Glance down and see a bridge over Virginia Creek. *Check this out on your way back.* (The area near this bridge does provide one of the three vantages of the falls.)

Once very close to the falls find a series of log bridges. I recommend continuing to the right and to begin with an up-close view of the falls. This location allows for a typical vertical perspective of the tall waterfall. Depending on the amount of mist, the primary challenge may be keeping yourself and your gear adequately dry.

My favorite location, however, is the middle option, accessed by the log bridge that was to the left (mentioned just above). Here you can walk along a wide, stone platform and capture the lower, shorter falls as well. From here, the bottom of the main falls is obscured a bit and so its height isn't as evident, but I like how the path of the water works its way across the frame.

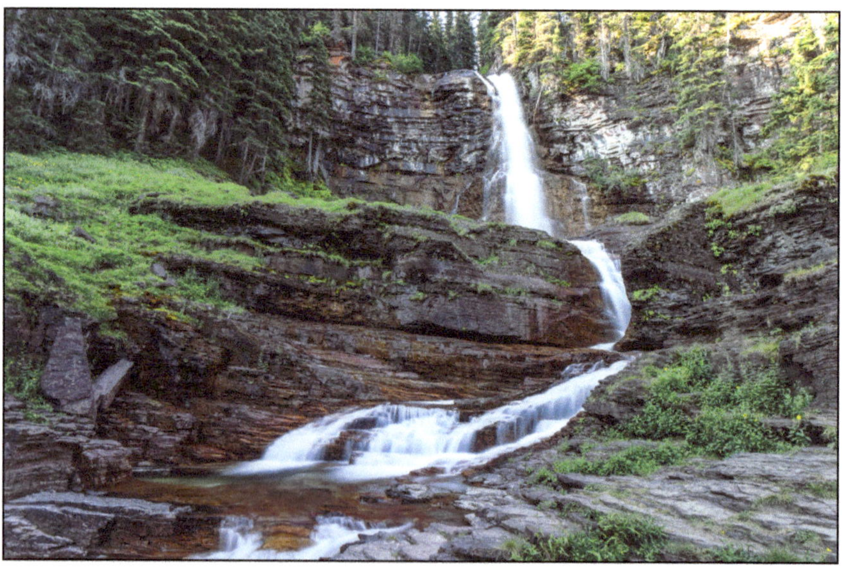

Virginia Falls   20mm f/11 1.3s ISO100

Once having exercised a number of compositions close to the falls, hike back to the intersection, cross the bridge, and find a distant composition available from there as well. If needed, a toilet is close by.

86

Time	Best Good									Reward			

Budget	45-60 min	Type	Out & Back	Effort	
RT Distance	~0.7 mi	Δ Elev.	~250 ft	Zoom	Wide, Norm

Here we have another coupled site, with two distinct points of interest... Baring Falls is easily the more interesting of the two, but Sunrift Gorge's close proximity to the road makes for an easy candidate to add variety to your Glacier portfolio, so it's a viable add-on.

Vehicle parking and a shuttle stop are near Sunrift Gorge and the trail to Baring Falls. Sunrift Gorge is on the north side of Sun Road, and the route to Baring Falls is on the south side. What's neat about this location is that access is provided alongside Baring Creek, *underneath* the arched Baring Creek vehicle bridge (constructed in 1931). Baring Creek makes its way through the gorge, then under the bridge, further downhill to Baring Falls, and finally to St. Mary Lake.

Of note, the gorge is accessed ~70 feet above Sun Road, and the falls are ~180 feet below Sun Road, for our ~250 feet in the table above.

I recommend a walk up the stairs first, for a visit to see Sunrift Gorge. While not really a remarkable site for photography, the feature captures the incredible power of water over the course of time. What I enjoy most about this location is the *challenge* it provides me each time I visit. Sunrift Gorge really seems to test my creativity and technical

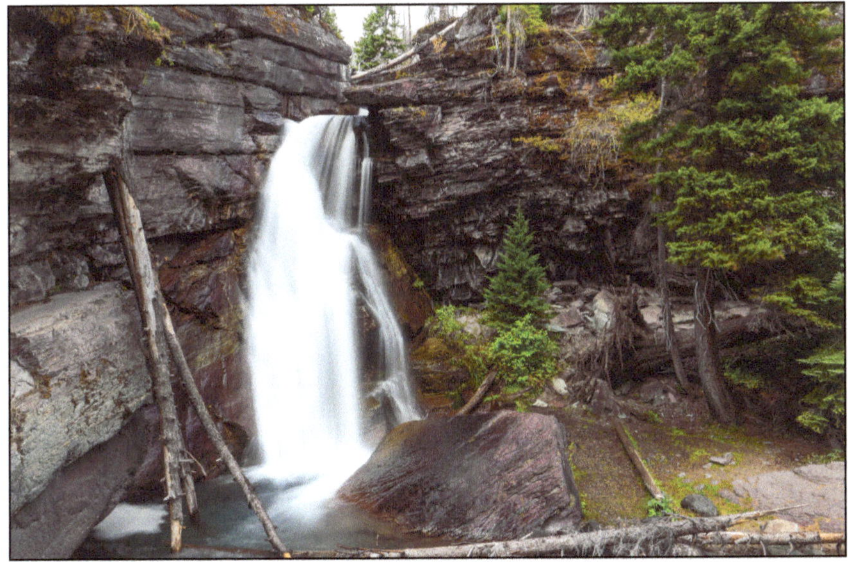

Baring Falls   24mm f/16 1s ISO100

know-how, to get the most out of it. This, I appreciate. Here we have a framing concept I like, highlighting the abundance of "long" (or tall) elements at play.

One alternative is to frame in a landscape orientation with a wider focal length, to capture the creek as it makes its hard turn towards Sun Road. With this, it's common to capture abundant forest debris that has forced its way through the gorge during spring snowmelt.

Descend the stairs and stay right, near the creek. A small cascade here is also fun to photograph. Continue to follow the creek and walk under the bridge. A trail sign points in the direction of Baring Falls, 0.3 mile away.

The area around the falls provides a variety of composition options. **Watch your step – some of the places can be slippery.**

The photo on the prior page was taken from near the beginning of a ledge along the left-side wall. A bright sky can challenge exposure here at times. The simple solution if the sky is not accommodating is to limit its presence in the framing. The scene performs well without the sky, so this can still produce satisfactory results.

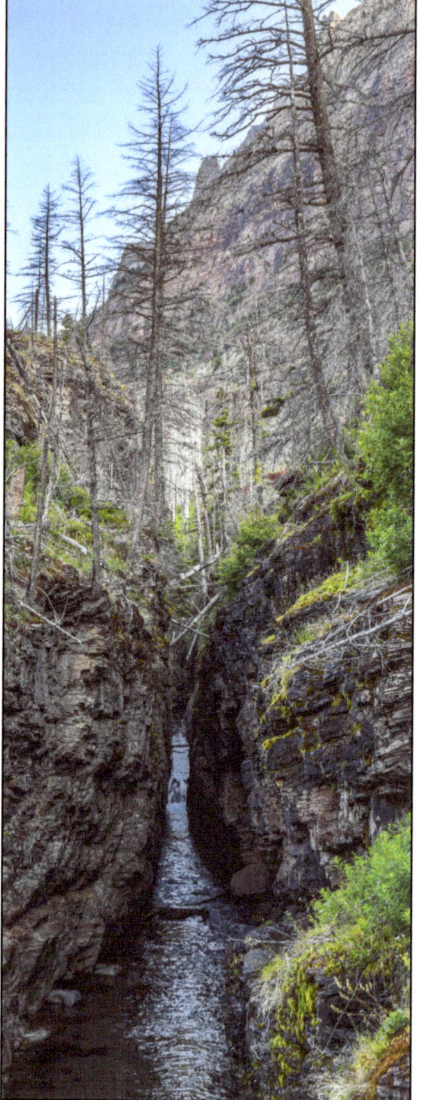

50mm f/8 1/50s ISO200

Once finished, retrace your steps back uphill to the bridge. Find a **colorful stone staircase** on the south side of Sun Road, leading back up towards the parking area. These steps are another good subject, particularly because of the varying colors in the stones used.

If visiting Baring Falls by way of the St. Mary Lake Boat Tour (21) an alternative trail to the falls from a nearby boat dock is utilized. It's the easiest way to hike to the falls, but of course it requires the tour.

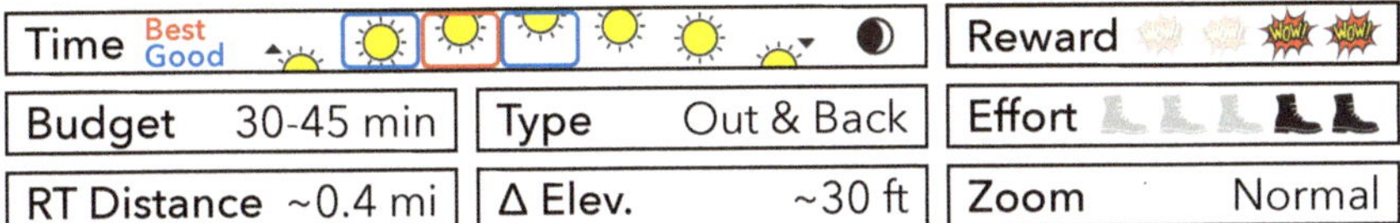

Time	Best Good	☀ ☀ ☀ ☀ ☀ ☀ ●	Reward	🌸 🌸 💥 💥
Budget	30-45 min	Type	Out & Back	Effort 👢👢👢 **👢👢**
RT Distance	~0.4 mi	Δ Elev.	~30 ft	Zoom	Normal

Near the southwest end of St. Mary Lake is Sun Point, once the location of the Sun Point Chalets (1911-1948). The view here may be the best one of St. Mary Lake, thanks to the just-right elevation above the water below.

A large parking lot serves this area and the Sun Point Nature Trail. I would forego the nature trail – the best use of time is to head directly to the point. Park near the vault toilets. The trailhead of interest, next to an information board, is a bit out of view to the left of the toilets.

Head downhill, and at the first intersection stay straight'ish, continuing further downhill. At a "Y" select your route up to the point. Both are of similar condition with somewhat loose dirt and rocks. Climb carefully.

Meander around the point, always mindful of the perimeter. **In some places the drop is sudden and dangerous.** Wind can be an issue as well here – secure hats and any loose clothing.

The area is riddled with snags (dead trees). They also make great subjects.

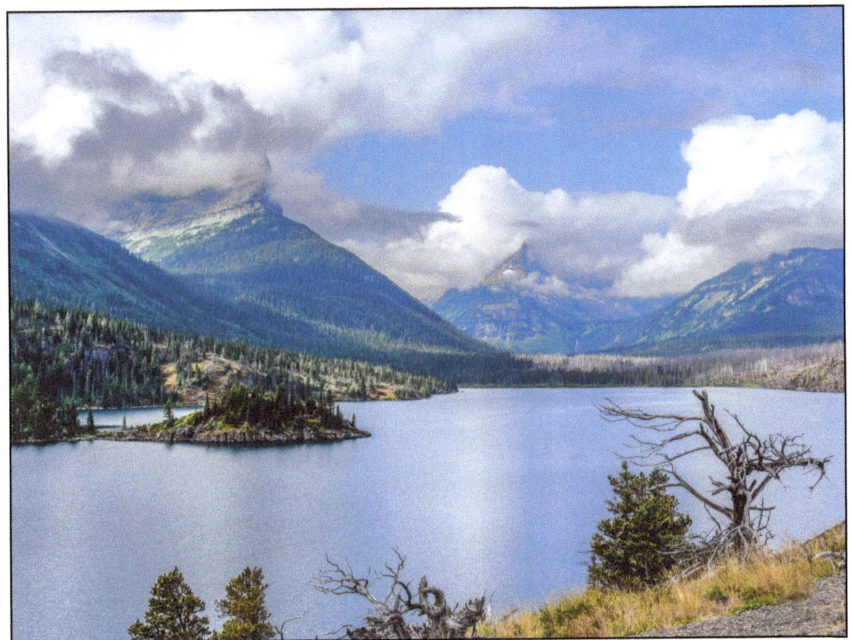

Sun Point – Looking West   50mm f/16 1/80s ISO100

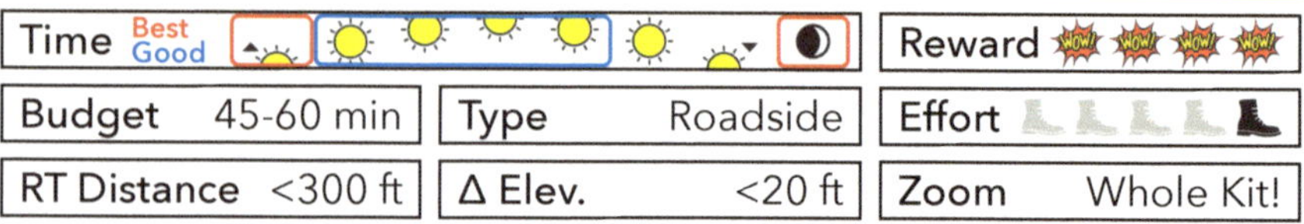

Time	Best Good	☀	Reward	💥 💥 💥 💥
Budget	45-60 min	Type	Roadside	Effort
RT Distance	<300 ft	Δ Elev.	<20 ft	Zoom	Whole Kit!

A composition of Wild Goose Island from its overlook is one of the quintessential photos within Glacier National Park. While deserving of its reputation, the location can present a real challenge for photography. The weather and sky redefine its personality throughout each day. If your experience is like mine, no two visits will be alike.

Please also reference the black and white photo on page 81 and the Milky Way photo on page 94. The black and white photo was taken mid-afternoon, and I believe it only turned out great due to the scattered clouds overhead with curious lighting. So anytime you're driving by, no matter the time of day, observe the conditions closely to see if a unique opportunity is present. The stormy weather on the day below provided rainbows, but only for about 5 minutes. I got lucky.

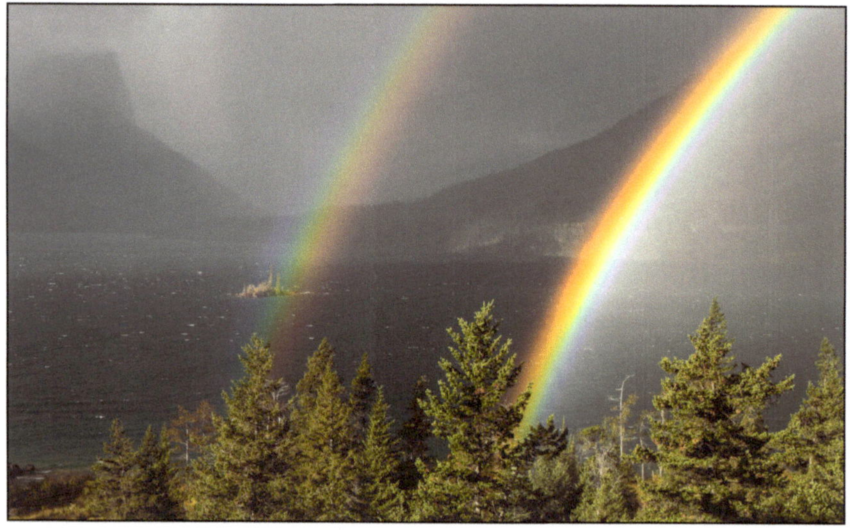

Rainbows at Wild Goose Island   50mm f/8 1/125s ISO200

The usual advice here is to arrive in time for sunrise (behind you). As it lights up the mountains, the soft colors will emerge ahead. The photo at right demonstrates these colors and an alternative focal length and framing option. The sky brightens incredibly fast here.

My go-to focal length at this location is 50mm, though I'm also sharing 20mm with the Milky Way and 150mm at right. With 50mm the broader scene (with the interesting mountains on the left) may be captured in a landscape orientation, or an interesting sky may be captured vertically (as on page 81).

The large viewing area where most visitors congregate is adequate, but an even better line of sight is down slightly to the left about 50 feet atop a large, flat boulder near the ground. Alternatively, if some mild climbing is acceptable, to the right of the main viewing area is an elevated rock formation, providing another perspective.

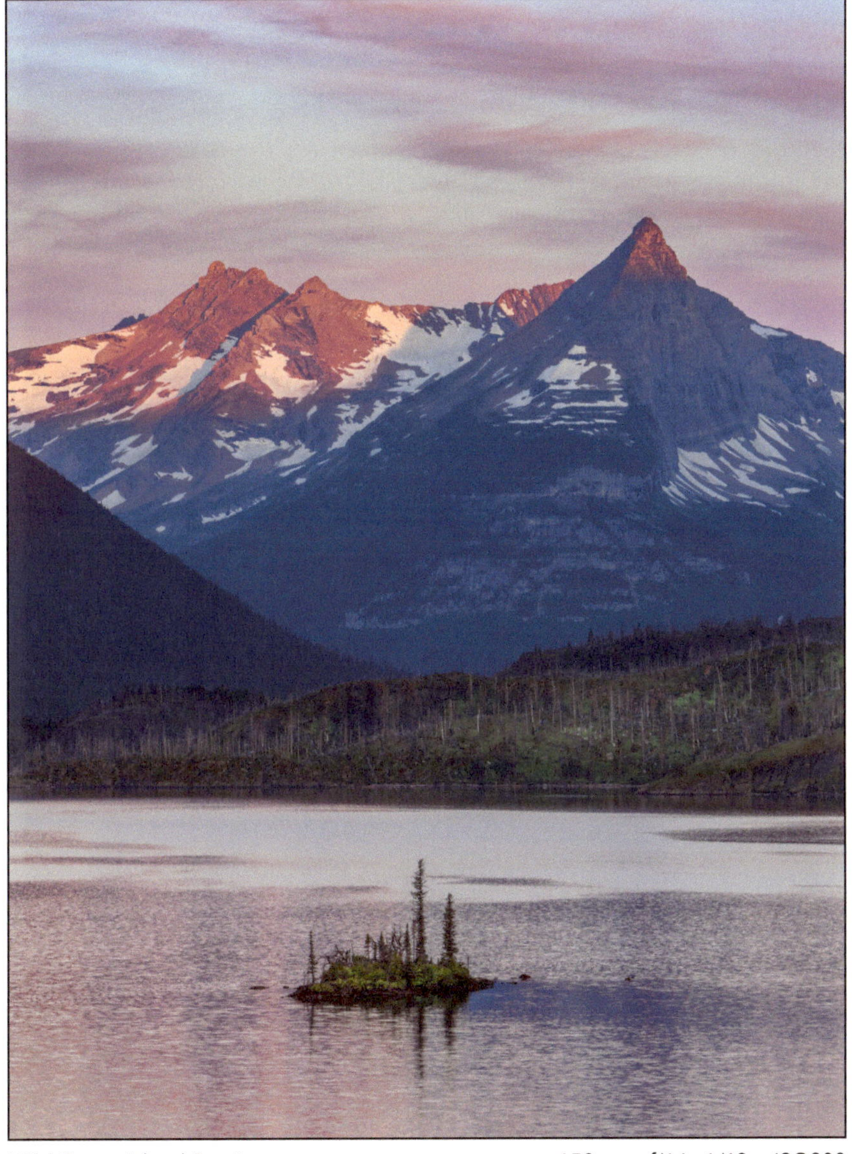

Wild Goose Island Sunrise   150mm f/16 1/13s ISO200

Time	Best Good	☀ ☀ ☀ ☀ ☀ ◗	Reward	🎆 🎆 🎆 🎆
Budget 30-45 min		**Type** Roadside	**Effort** 👢👢👢👢👢	
RT Distance <200 ft		**Δ Elev.** <10 ft	**Zoom** Wide Angle	

I think these are always fun – to look at, and to photograph – and I usually seek-out places in national parks where the effect translates well within a photo.

Here, we have a pretty unique topic, so I'll lay out an abundance of pointers specific to this activity.

My rule of thumb is that you're composing for 3 key features at minimum here – a car's tail light "trails," recognizable park features that capture "where you are," and an interesting sky. For this book, I have deviated somewhat from my usual routine under the stars to one closer to the "blue hour." It simply needs to be dark enough for the car lights to be evident in an otherwise darkened scene. A benefit to working during the blue hour is that cars pass by more frequently.

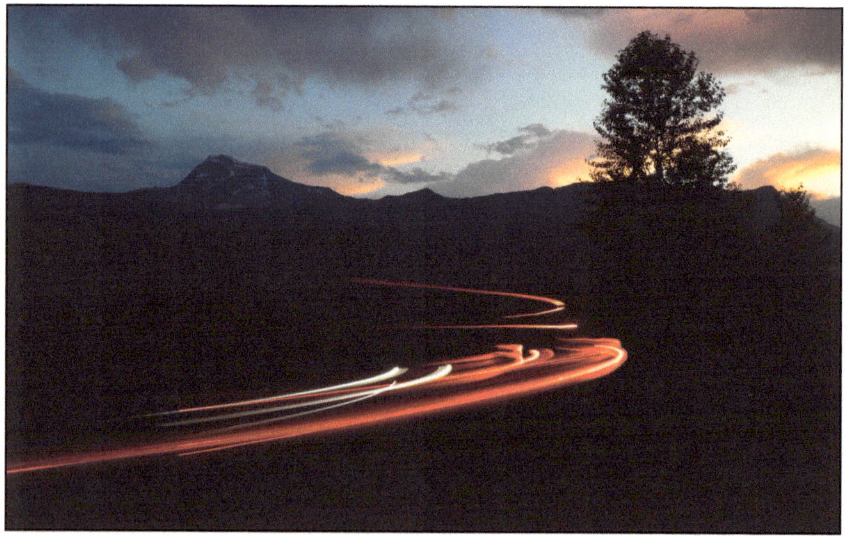

On and Off the Brakes at The Loop   28mm f/11 6s ISO50

Let's now tackle the technical how-to, from primary setup to final camera adjustments. (All photographers know the one truth about "rules" in photography are that they're meant to be broken, so please think of all the following as guidelines or starting points. Experimentation is encouraged!)

Assuming you are roadside (to your subject vehicle or vehicles), work in the direction that permits capturing the passing car's tail lights. The issue with headlights is that from this vantage the bright light will illuminate the inside of your lens and in essence totally wash out your exposure.

Some sort of rigid camera support is mandatory. I recommend a tripod. A headlamp or flashlight also helps immensely.

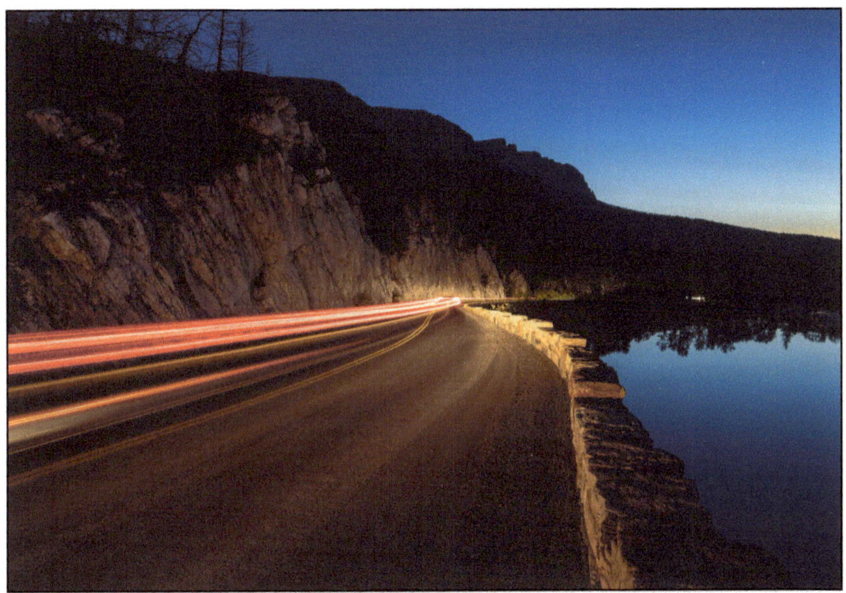

Tail Lights along the Golden Staircase   24mm f/4 20s ISO400

Lens selection... If you have the option, a fast wide angle is best. By "fast," I mean f/1.4-f/2.8. And by wide angle, 35mm or wider. You can use a slower lens, it just means there may be some compromises to ISO and shutter speed. Lenses with longer reach than 35mm will begin to struggle with depth of field and capturing the whole scene in focus.

Here, perhaps, is the hardest part... You're going to need to manually focus your lens to infinity and leave it there. Leaving autofocus turned on is the best way to a very frustrating outing. It just won't work. So, illuminate something in the distance, lock-in focus, and leave it there. (Hopefully your lens has a focus window, and if it does check the lens' setting occasionally, to ensure it hasn't moved.) Warning!: If you are using a zoom lens for this, you cannot zoom in or out after you have set focus. Focus is only set for a particular focal length. So if you're using a zoom, be careful of this as well.

Alright, we're getting close... Compose your shot, as best you can. (This can be difficult sometimes, depending on how dark it is.) After you take some shots, you can make some adjustments.

Set your camera body to Manual mode, and now we need a starting point... The following table lists some options under a *night* sky.

Aperture	f/1.4	f/1.8 or f/2	f/2.8	f/3.5 or f/4
ISO	100	200	400	800
Shutter Speed	15 sec	15 sec	15 sec	15 sec

You're ready to go. Now, using either a timer or a remote shutter release, listen for an approaching car, begin your exposure, and wait to see what happens! Take a look at your screen, and adjust accordingly.

Generally, you want to keep your ISO as low as possible, to minimize noise. Those of you with faster lenses (f/1.4 to f/2, for example) may find that you need to stop down to f/2.8 for depth of field (focus throughout your frame). Adjust the shutter speed to suit your needs.

That's basically it. Be careful, good luck, and have fun!

Oh wait, there's more good news! This same technique works well for photographing the Milky Way. The very short summer nights at Glacier National Park make capturing it a bit challenging. Wild Goose Island Overlook (19) is a great place for a composition. The below was taken in late June at about 3am. Another good location is near The Loop with Heaven's Peak beneath the starry sky.

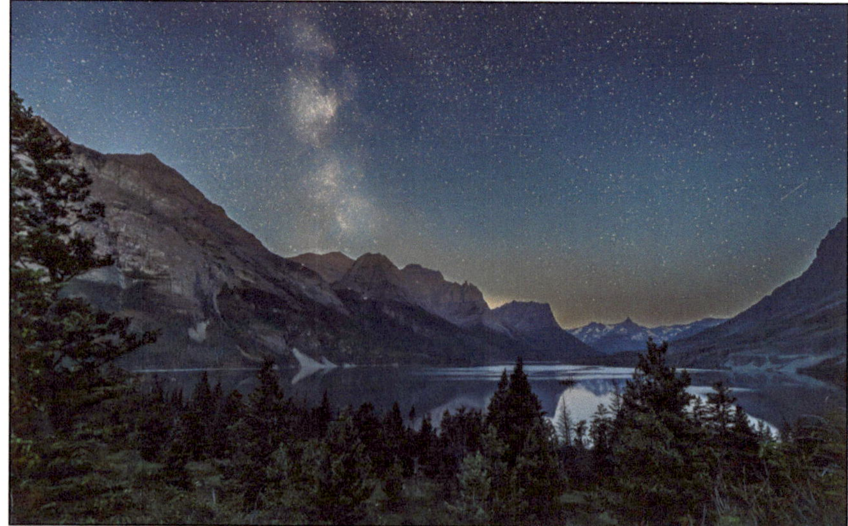

St. Mary Lake and the Milky Way   24mm f/2.8 30s ISO6400

Time	Best Good									Reward			
Budget	1.5 hr		Type		Out & Back					Effort			
RT Distance	~0.2 mi		Δ Elev.		~30 ft					Zoom		Wide, Tele	

Glacier Park Boat Company offers tours at Lake McDonald, St. Mary Lake, Many Glacier (25), and Two Medicine. They're all incredibly enjoyable – especially the captain's unique narrative along the way at each location, but I chose the two that I feel offer something "extra" for passengers. (We'll explore the Many Glacier Boat Tour on pages 104-105, so I'll leave the intrigue on that one for later.)

The area surrounding St. Mary Lake lacks a feature that this boat tour resolves... Most all of the vistas around the lake's perimeter are well above the water – very few access points exist along its shore. This tour closes that gap and provides passengers with water elevation views.

Glacier Park Boat Company operates the St. Mary Lake Boat Tour from the dock at Rising Sun. Parking is generous here and should not be an issue. The tour heads west along the lake (in the direction of the mountains and Logan Pass). At time of writing, all but the final tour of the day include a stop that accesses a short trail to Baring Falls. (See more about Baring Falls on pages 87-88.) Check the Glacier Park Boat Company website for current tour times and reservations. I recommend the 1.5 hour tour with the stop at Baring Falls.

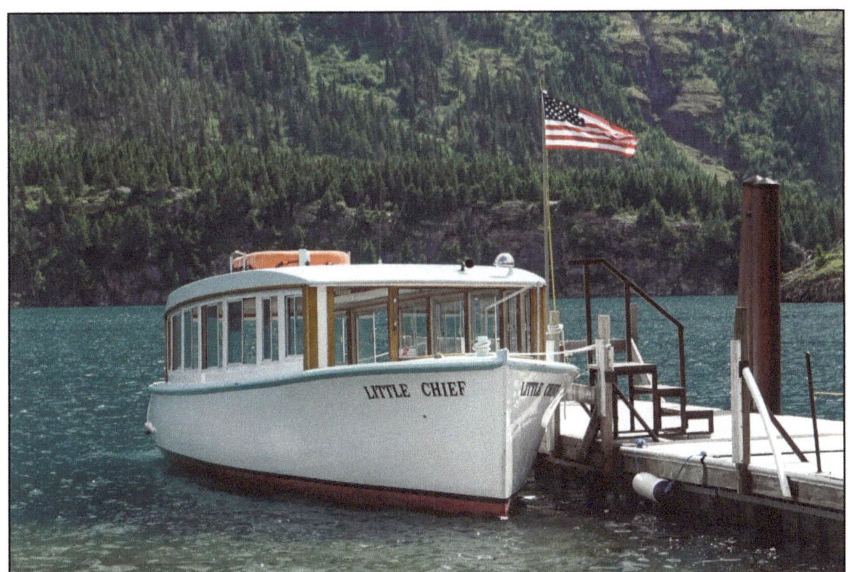

Little Chief   135mm f/8 1/125s ISO400

The route cruises counterclockwise around the west end of the lake. A window seat on the starboard (right) side allows for an improved view of the shore and its features (especially the **Golden Staircase**), while a window seat on the port (left) side allows for a great view of **Wild Goose Island**. Whichever side you sit on, when the weather permits and the captain allows an open air walk to the bow (front) provides the best views and photography. Visits there must be kept to a few minutes at a time to allow others the opportunity as well.

"Golden Staircase" describes *both* the Altyn Formation, a yellow-colored limestone *and* a stepped retaining wall along Going-to-the-Sun Road. The blocks along the wall's edge were blasted from this area and utilized in the wall. It's nice to drive by, but it's an even more impressive sight when seen from below. Altyn is some of the oldest and hardest rock within the park and what forms Wild Goose Island.

About the Baring Falls stop on the 1.5 hour tour... The hike from the dock to the falls is what's captured in the site table. The only "gotcha" if visiting Baring Falls via the boat tour is that you'll only have ~20 minutes for photography at the falls. This may be adequate for some, but others may feel rushed.

Following the stop at Baring Falls, the cruise continues its counter-clockwise route and ventures closer to the southwest shore of the lake. Cruise by a tiny island called "Rainbow Rock" by our tour captain. This island is very small and hard to spot from the shore.

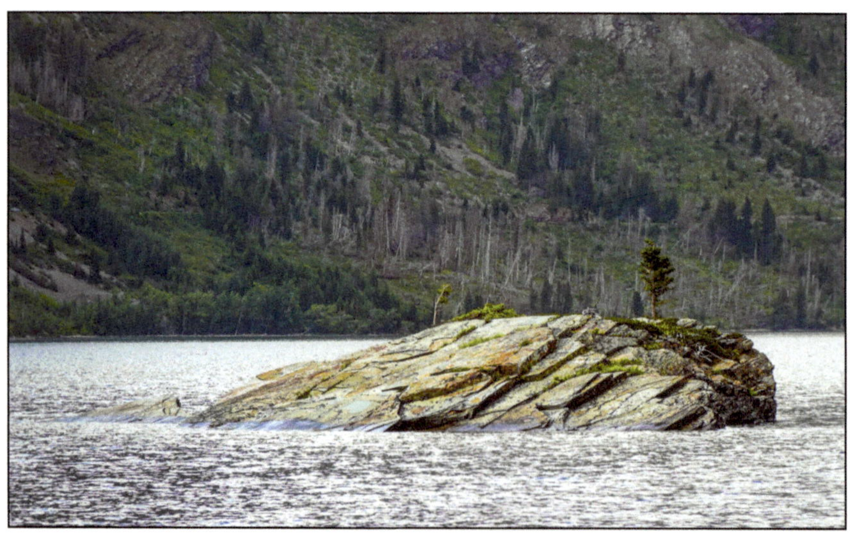

"Rainbow Rock"   200mm f/5.6 1/200s ISO200

Continue cruising and learning, and then return to the dock at Rising Sun. The tour does not venture further east beyond Rising Sun.

Time	Best Good	Reward
Budget	15-30 min	Type	Roadside	Effort
RT Distance	<500 ft	Δ Elev.	<10 ft	Zoom	Normal

Flashback to 1994! Locals affectionately refer to this bridge as the "Forrest Gump Bridge." On Forrest's *second* westbound cross-country run he crosses over the St. Mary River Bridge, constructed in 1935.

From upon the bridge, a wonderful view presents itself of Glacier's signature, shapely mountains to the west. Do not forego this shot. The St. Mary River fans out and makes for a good foreground.

Though, since I'm only sharing one photo, as you can see it is with the bridge as the subject and the mountains and expansive sky in supplementary roles. A trail leads to multiple paths down towards the river. I have tried them all. You might as well too! However, I found that the path halfway down this route seems to offer the best balance among the river, bridge, and mountains. The vegetation along the riverbank is challenging in places, and this "halfway" path minimizes its impact within the composition.

A brief explanation on the time of day... My recommendations on late morning and midday are in the spirit of capturing the entire scene adequately-lit. Prior to mid-morning there will likely be too much in the dark or in an early morning haze. The sun is combative in the afternoon.

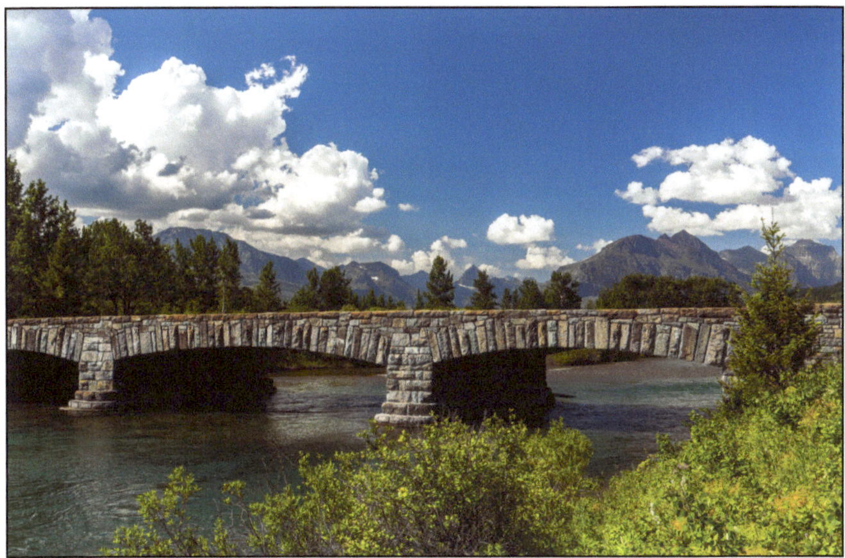

St. Mary River Bridge   35mm f/11 1/60s ISO100

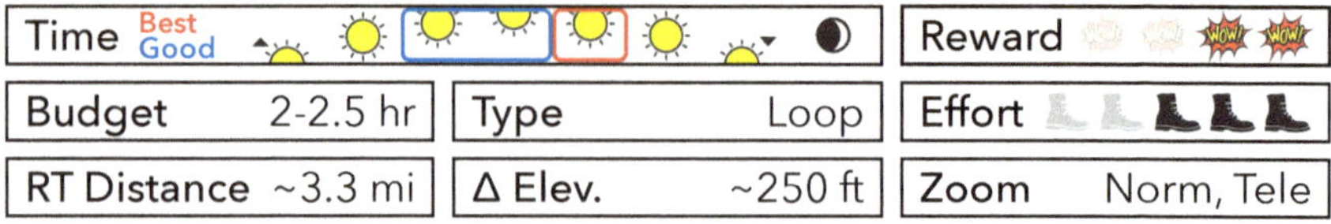

Time	Best Good							Reward				

Budget	2-2.5 hr	Type	Loop	Effort	
RT Distance ~3.3 mi		Δ Elev. ~250 ft		Zoom Norm, Tele	

Looking for a hiking option inside the park but outside the vehicle reservations system corridor? Beaver Pond Loop may be your ticket.

On Going-to-the-Sun Road between the Glacier National Park sign and the St. Mary Entrance is a turnoff marked to the "Historic 1913 Ranger Station." Follow the signs to a parking area that serves both the ranger station grounds and the Beaver Pond Loop trail.

One end of the parking area has a brown sign pointing towards the ranger station, and the other end has the Red Eagle Lake Trailhead. My recommendation is to hike the Beaver Pond Loop clockwise, so you will begin at the ranger station and exit at this other trailhead.

A short incline leads you to the ranger station and a barn. An information board provides a short history with illustrations and an entertaining story. As you can see below, fall here is stunning. The barn's appeal is the chinking between its logs, providing a two-tone interest.

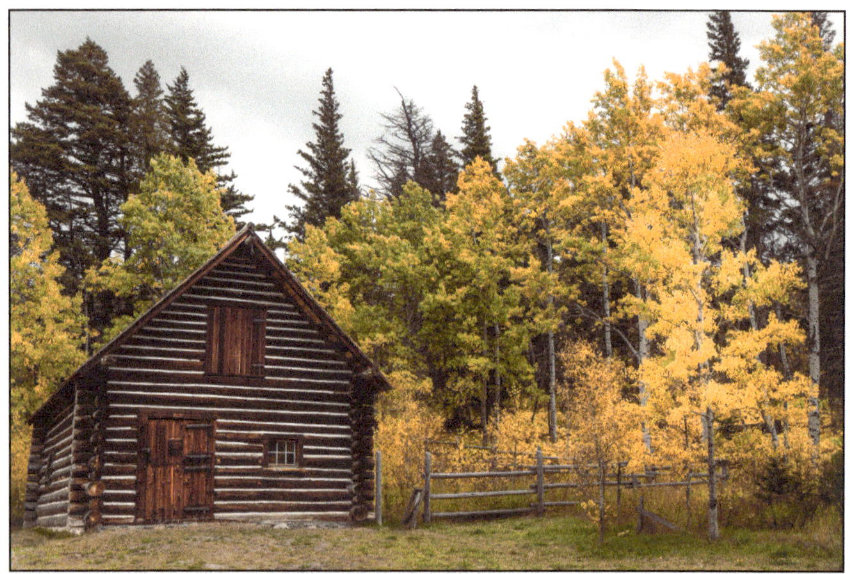

Lubec Barn   40mm f/8 1/125s ISO100

The trail begins at the forest's edge between the ranger station and barn. The climbs and descents are gradual along its length. The route to Beaver Pond varies through forest and small meadows. I believe this is the more interesting half of the loop.

Finally, after ~1.5 miles come upon the north end of the pond, seen downhill to your right. There are trails that lead down to the pond here, but the best vantage of the pond and the beaver habitat is at the far end. I recommend to continue on the main trail until you find near that far end a more well-trodden path downhill.

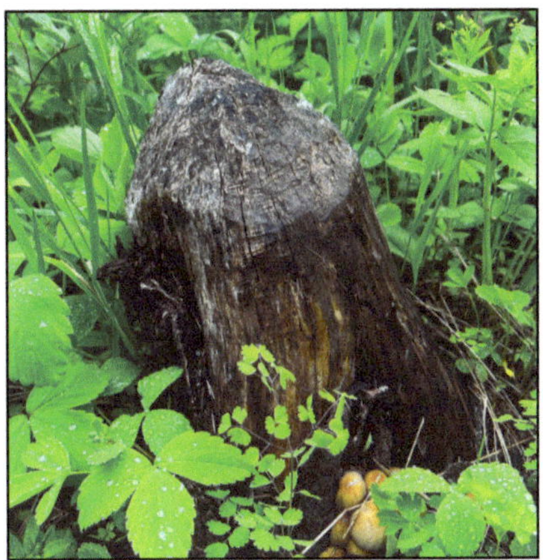

Take notice of the animal tracks in the soil. This is a likely watering hole – remain alert. Moose and bears frequent this area.

The downhill route to the pond may require some route-finding since multiple paths exist near the water's edge. **Step with care.** The area can transition from dry to muddy within a step or two. Please be respectful of the environment and stay out of the mud.

35mm f/5.6 1/60s ISO400

I have yet to see any beavers here, but their presence is evident.

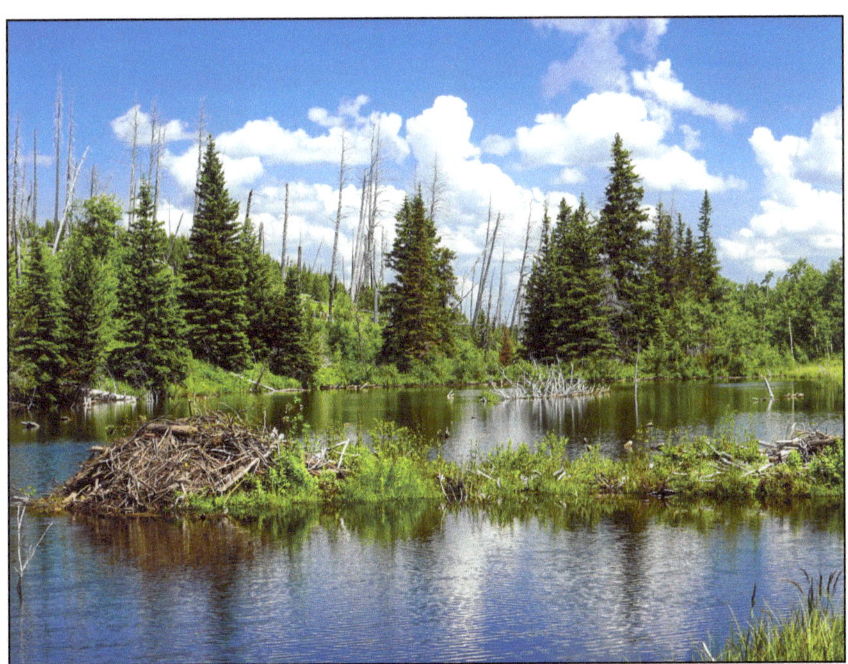

Beaver Pond

28mm f/8 1/80s ISO200

Back on the main trail, continue hiking under trees before emerging once again into another meadow. Finally, into the woods again and come upon an intersection along the Red Eagle Lake Trail. The posted mileage here seems off. Here, I have the hike at ~1.8 miles, with ~1.5 miles to go. Perhaps this is irrelevant, but I do find it curious. Anyway, turn right to continue the loop in this clockwise fashion.

The remaining hike remains mostly the same – the course slowly approaches the shore of St. Mary Lake, though such a distance away it's beyond a useful proximity for photography.

Wildflowers line the trail in places. This is the silver lining along this leg, providing opportunities to stop occasionally to study them and experiment with compositions.

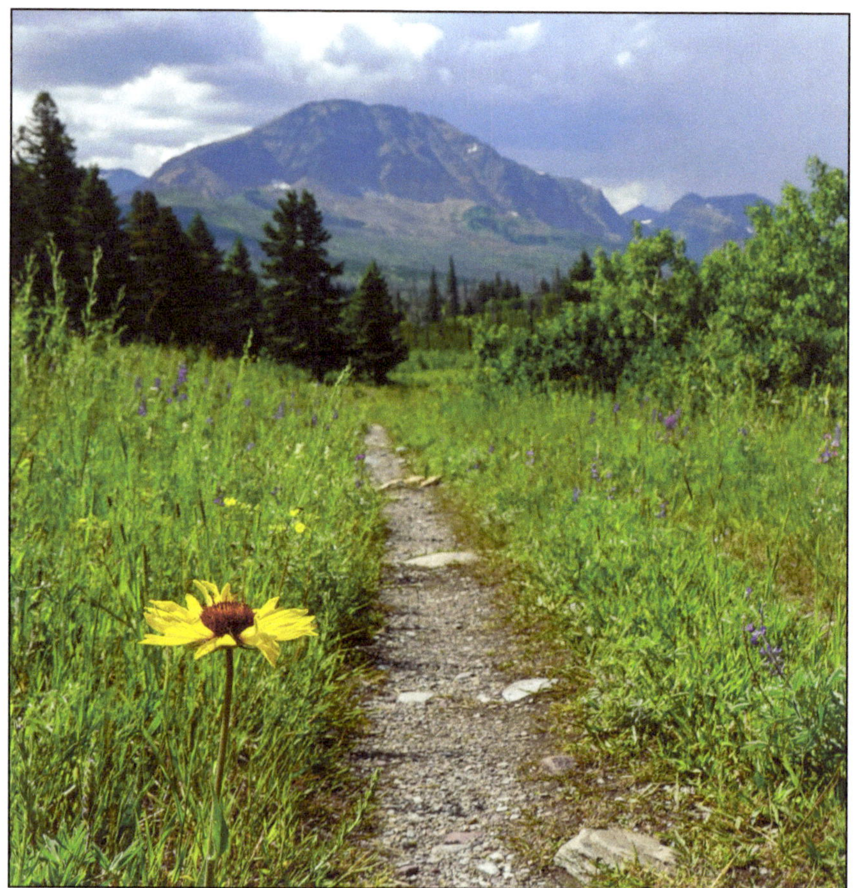

Wild Sunflower and Curly Bear Mountain   50mm f/8 1/200s ISO100

The final ¼ mile levels out and comes close to the southern end of the large meadow along the northeast side of St. Mary Lake.

Many Glacier

Many Glacier Entrance and Beyond

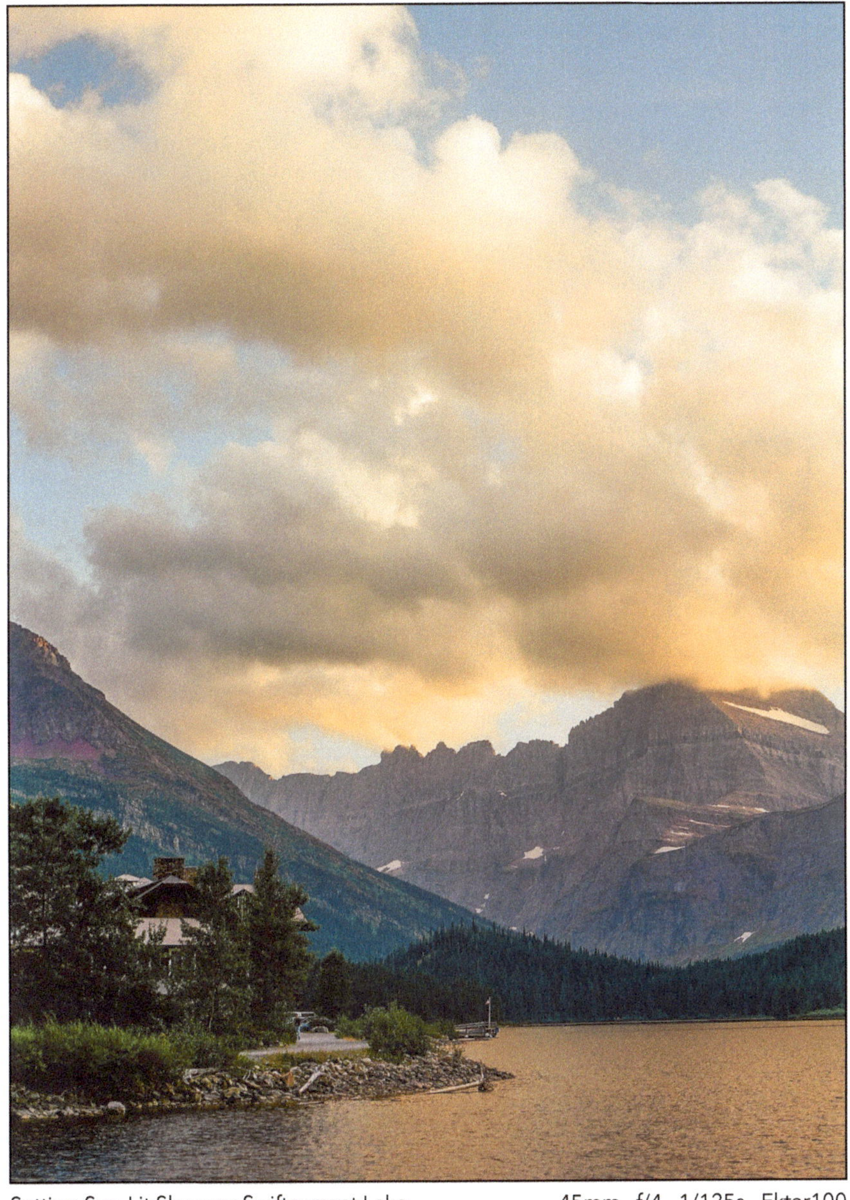

Setting Sun-Lit Sky over Swiftcurrent Lake   45mm f/4 1/125s Ektar100

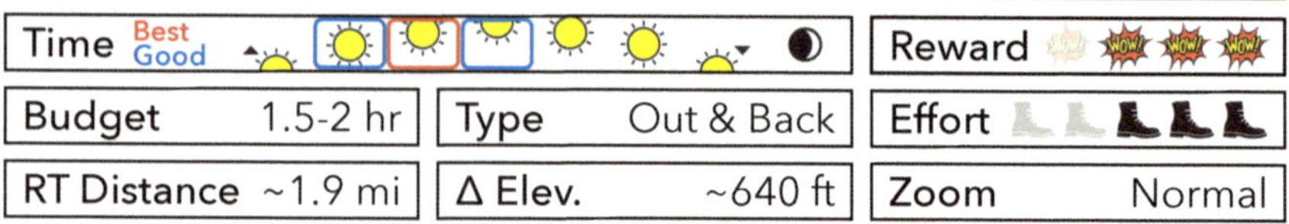

Time	Best Good									Reward				
Budget	1.5-2 hr	**Type**	Out & Back	**Effort**			
RT Distance	~1.9 mi	**Δ Elev.**	~640 ft	**Zoom**	Normal		

I don't normally grade the "grades" of hikes, but this one may take top honors among the lot in this book. It's relatively short, but it gains elevation quickly.

Apikuni Creek begins it swift descent on the far side of the adjacent Altyn Peak. The falls here are just tucked behind the eastern side of the mountain and out of sight from the road into Many Glacier.

A head-in parking area is on the north side of the road. Two trails are served here – Apikuni Falls on the west (left) end, and a trail on the opposite end heading to Poia Lake (6+ miles away).

The hike begins in a meadow, but quickly enters the forest. Find your pace and ascend… At about ¾ mile the hike levels out with the sound of the rushing water growing more evident. A peekaboo of the falls is to your left. The route meanders through scree to its finale near the falls.

There are multiple vantages to capture the falls. Some sure-footedness is required to safely explore the options. The one at right was taken near the end of the formal trail. Further downstream it is possible to capture Apikuni Creek as it continues to tumble downhill. With this option, less of the main waterfall is visible.

On this trip, I really liked how the falling water created a plumb of mist, thanks to its incredible volume of water. I opted for a faster shutter speed to better capture its vigor. ISO suffered somewhat, so that I was ensured to have the foreground rocks and the rim in focus with a small aperture. I believe Apikuni Falls is at its best in the late spring and early summer, when snowmelt is at its peak.

When finished, retrace your steps back… Your pace may be quite a bit faster than your way up, thanks to gravity now working with your stride.

Wildflowers do grace the meadow close to the parking lot. On out-and-back routes, I'm normally like a horse to water and seem to focus more on the destination than the opportunities around me. Here I made time on the way back for the flowers.

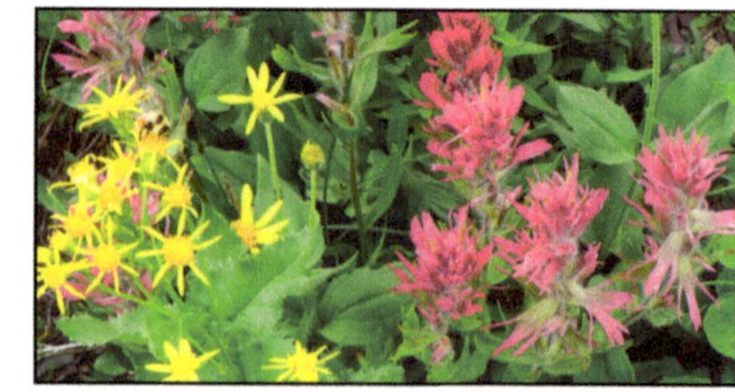

85mm f/8 1/160s ISO400

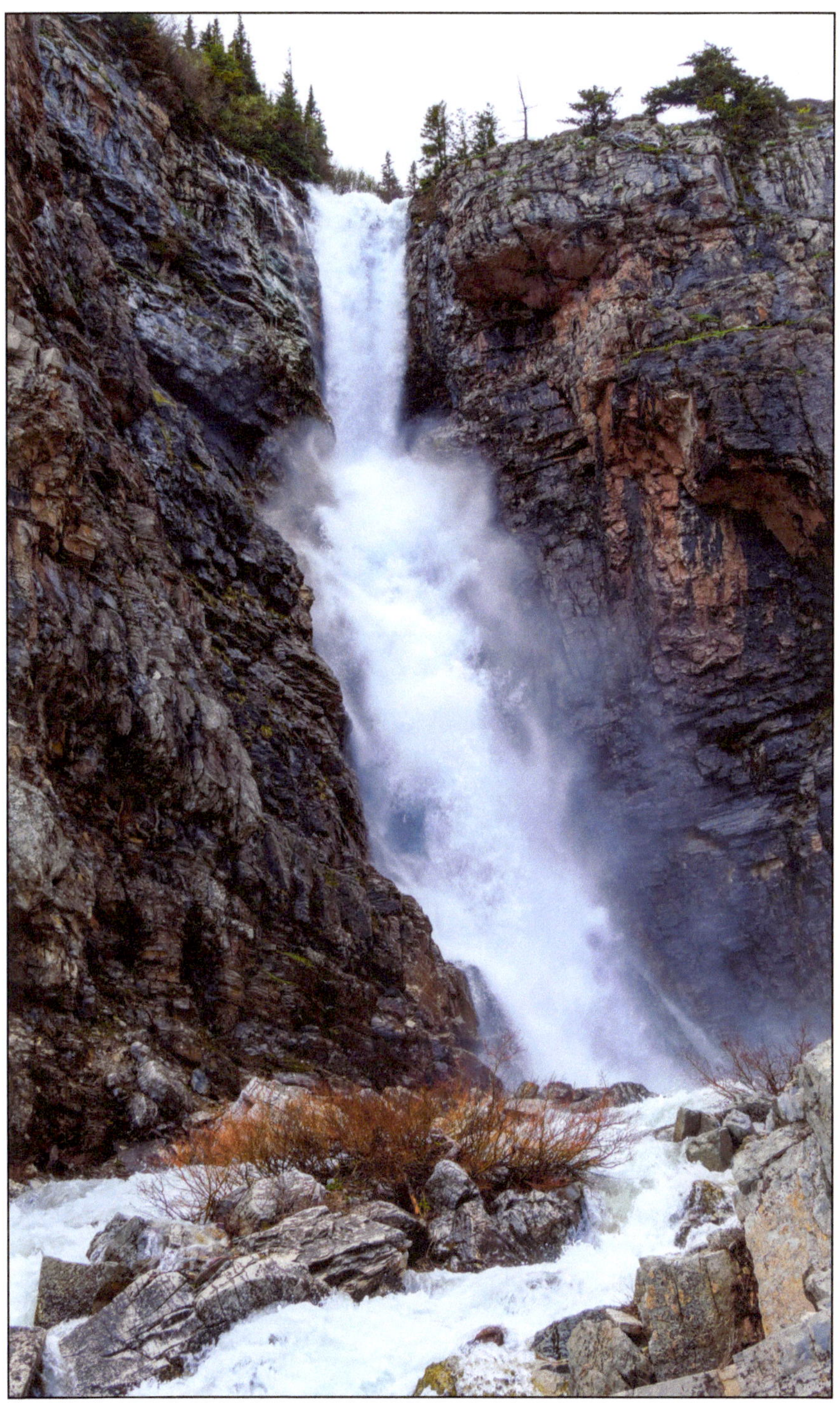

Intense Snowmelt over Apikuni Falls

40mm f/11 1/200s ISO400

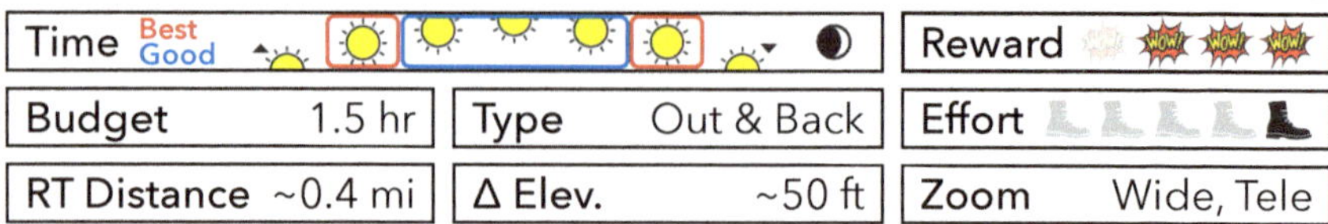

Time	Best Good	Reward
Budget	1.5 hr	Type	Out & Back	Effort
RT Distance	~0.4 mi	Δ Elev.	~50 ft	Zoom	Wide, Tele

The Many Glacier Boat Tour is **two tours in one**, including passage on Swiftcurrent Lake aboard the Chief Two Guns and then a short hike to Lake Josephine for another tour aboard the Morning Eagle. Two different lakes and two unique boats plus a short hike to stretch the legs... Outstanding!

Covered here is the round-trip, 1.5 hour tour that departs from the dock in front of the Many Glacier Hotel. Many Glacier Boat Company also provides one-way tours if interested in shortening your hike to either Grinnell Lake (27) or Grinnell Glacier (28). Check the Glacier Park Boat Company website for more information, current departure times, and reservations. A Frequently Asked Questions (FAQ) page is available as well, to help clarify their guidance on the one-way options.

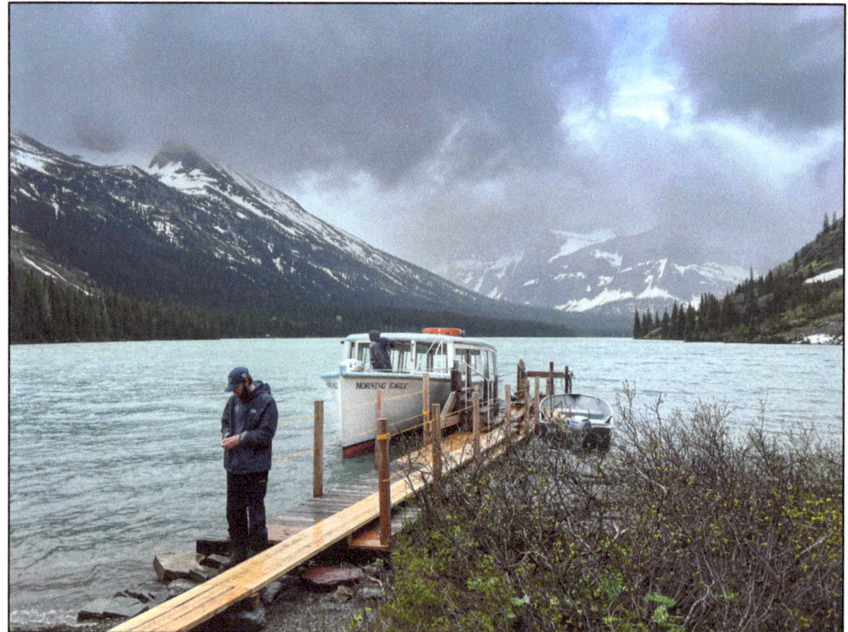

The Morning Eagle on Lake Josephine   35mm f/5.6 1/800s ISO100

Another two-fer — not only does the tour provide picturesque views along the water, but wildlife sightings here are not uncommon. This is where having a telephoto lens with you is desirable. As I see it, wide angle focal lengths will cover the "on lake" scenes, and the telephoto focal lengths are for distant subjects onshore, or for moose taking a swim in the water!

Each vessel will have its own captain, and their narration along the way is enjoyable and educational. When the weather permits and the captain allows an open air walk to the bow (front) provides the best views and photography. Visits there must be kept to a few minutes at a time to allow others the opportunity as well.

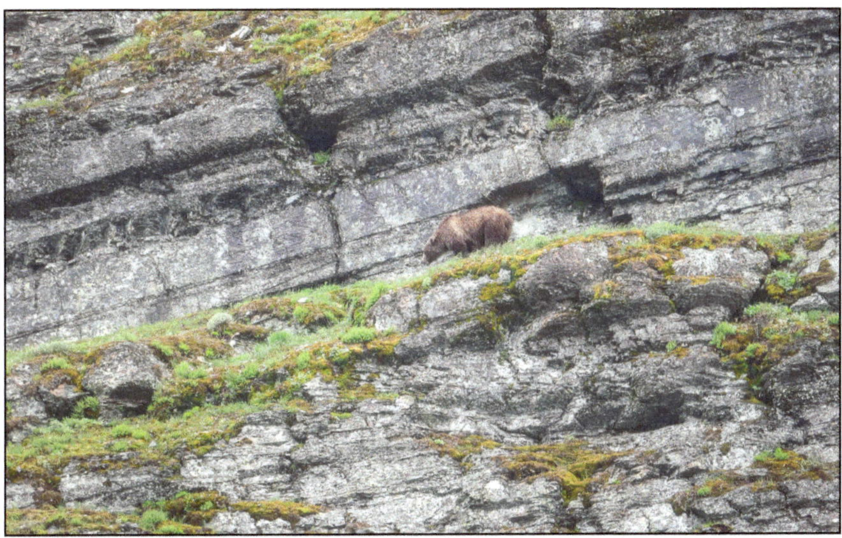

Grinnell Grizzly on the Prowl   400mm f/5.6 1/500s ISO400 (then 2:1 digital crop)

A short hike is required between Swiftcurrent Lake and Lake Josephine. The distance and elevation is covered in the table on the opposite page. The route is not difficult, but it is rocky. Leave your *boat shoes* behind and opt for footwear suitable for hiking.

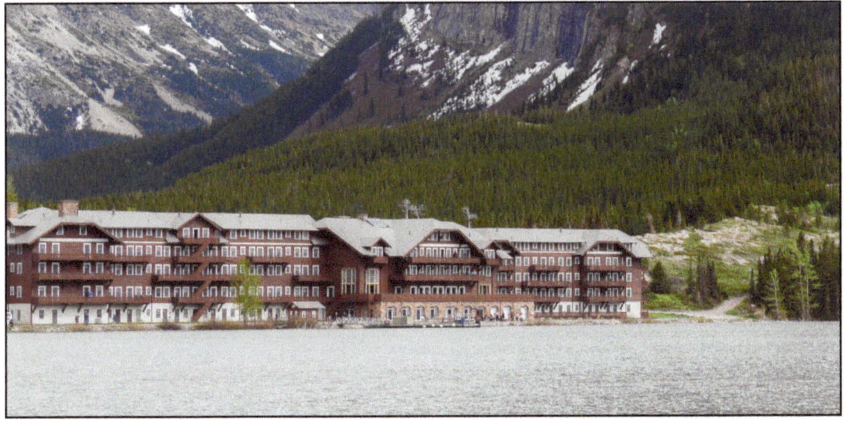

Many Glacier Hotel   80mm f/8 1/320s ISO200

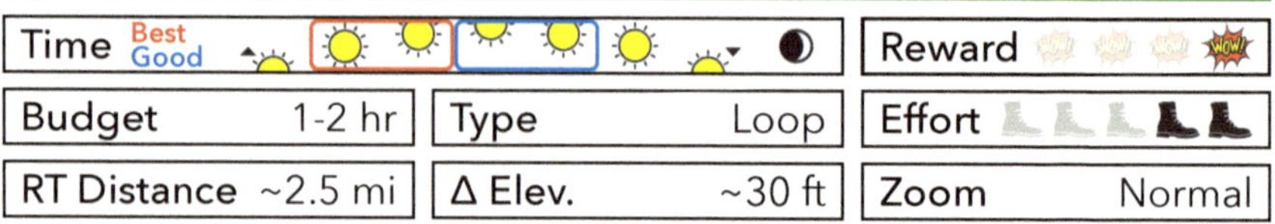

Time	Best/Good	Reward
Budget	1-2 hr	Type	Loop	Effort
RT Distance	~2.5 mi	Δ Elev.	~30 ft	Zoom	Normal

How about a casual hike around Swiftcurrent Lake? This is it. While views along this route are rarely sensational, the path around the lake is enjoyable (and one of the easier hikes in this whole area).

I recommend to begin and end at the Many Glacier Hotel, walking clockwise around the lake. The trail into the woods is easy to find to the left of the maintenance road in front of the hotel's south annex.

Signage at intersections along the way is clear... The only route curiosity is once you arrive at the semicircle parking area along Many Glacier Road, northwest of the lake. The trail picks back up near the road (but not on the road).

Views along the east segment of the trail seem to be best, as we have below near a boathouse with Grinnell Point in the frame. Once you cross the first bridge, clear visibility to the shore and beyond becomes difficult. The west side of the route is in the forest with interesting trees, including Aspen. The north section can provide good views of the lodge, especially in the afternoon when lighting is to your right.

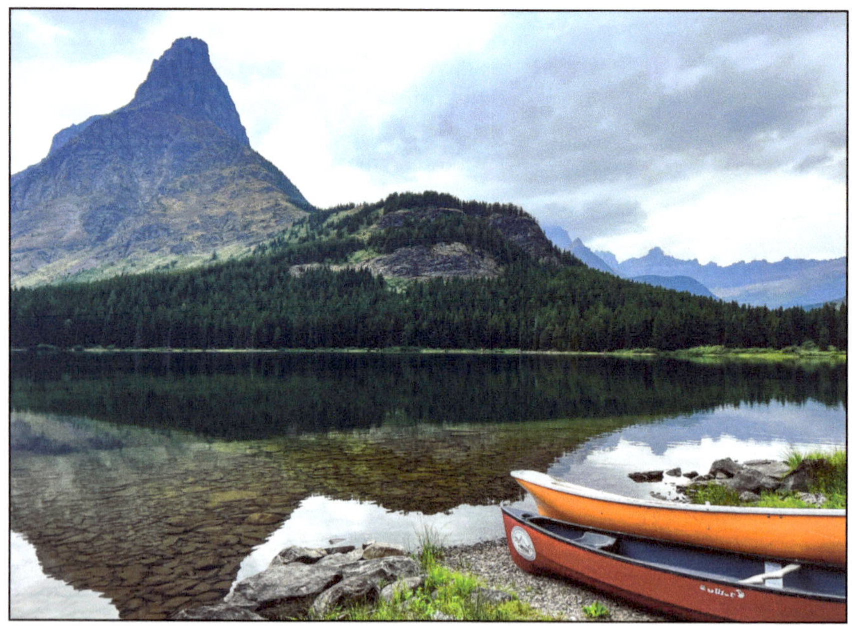

Canoes and Grinnell Point   24mm f/8 1/160s ISO200

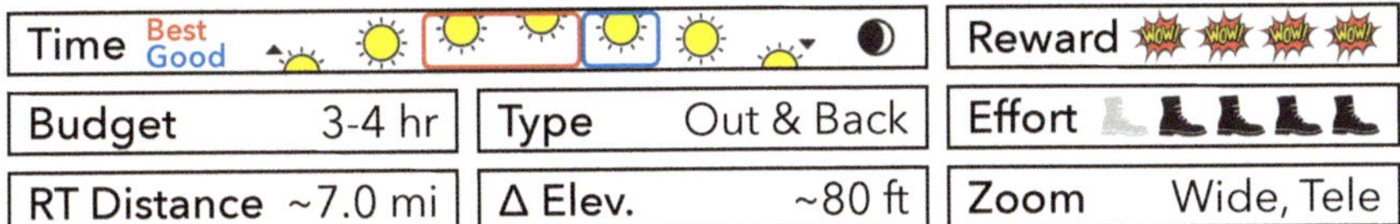

Time	Best Good								Reward	WOW! WOW! WOW! WOW!
Budget	3-4 hr	Type	Out & Back	Effort
RT Distance	~7.0 mi	Δ Elev.	~80 ft	Zoom	Wide, Tele

Grinnell Lake and Grinnell Glacier (28) are, without doubt, the two most popular day hike destinations in the Many Glacier area. They are deserving, and they are different. The route to Grinnell Lake is mostly flat, and so the only real effort here is covering its 7-mile round-trip distance. In contrast, the route to Grinnell Glacier climbs ~1,600 feet, and its total distance is longer. For families hiking with young children, Grinnell Lake appears suitable from the amount of kiddos I have seen at the lake. I have not seen many children en route to Grinnell Glacier.

While their namesake is the same, after George Bird Grinnell, a conservationist for the park in the late 1800's and early 1900's, **the routes to these two sites are separate from the head of Lake Josephine**.

On page 31 I listed the area trail maps, and I included a sample that is the map of Many Glacier. I highly recommend taking a full size copy of this map along with you.

A study of the trails around Swiftcurrent Lake and Lake Josephine reveals a variety of route options to the head of Lake Josephine. It is also possible to board and use the boats chartered by Glacier Park Boat Company to reduce the total hiking distance. (See page 104.)

For the recorded distance here though, we consider beginning at the semicircle parking area along Many Glacier Road, northwest of Swiftcurrent Lake. From here, the initial route is south along the Swiftcurrent Nature Trail to the connector trail with Lake Josephine. Hike the connector trail and then follow the trail along Lake Josephine on its northwest side. Next, cross one small bridge, one large bridge, and traverse a boardwalk towards the boat dock at the south end of the lake. Signage here points southwest for the trail to Grinnell Lake.

The most interesting features along this hike are near its end. The one exception I have regularly had some luck with is the aforementioned small bridge near the south end of Lake Josephine. Here I have seen **river otters** in this stream on multiple occasions.

The boat dock is at ~2.5 miles. A toilet is located here, if in need. Then along the dedicated trail towards Grinnell Lake at ~3.0 miles is another toilet. This is the closest toilet to the lake (at ~3.5 miles).

At ~3.1 miles reach a rather bouncy suspension bridge over Cataract Creek. The bridge is an attention-getter; you may not notice the subtle sign and trail to the left for **Hidden Falls**. I recommend continuing to Grinnell Lake... I'll address Hidden Falls after we explore the lake.

The trail ascends somewhat quickly and then descends for its final approach. Grinnell Creek appears to your right, and finally you arrive at a myriad of paths serving the east shore of Grinnell Lake.

Some exploration here is required to find a place to rest and also from where to take photos. I haven't found a spot that is "better than the rest" – it simply comes down to your preferences in the moment.

The one piece of advice that I can provide for photography of the lake is to be mindful of your shooting height off the ground. If too low, the vibrance of the water's color is lost. I recommend to shoot from at least head height or above to capture as much color as possible. Midday lighting also helps amplify the color.

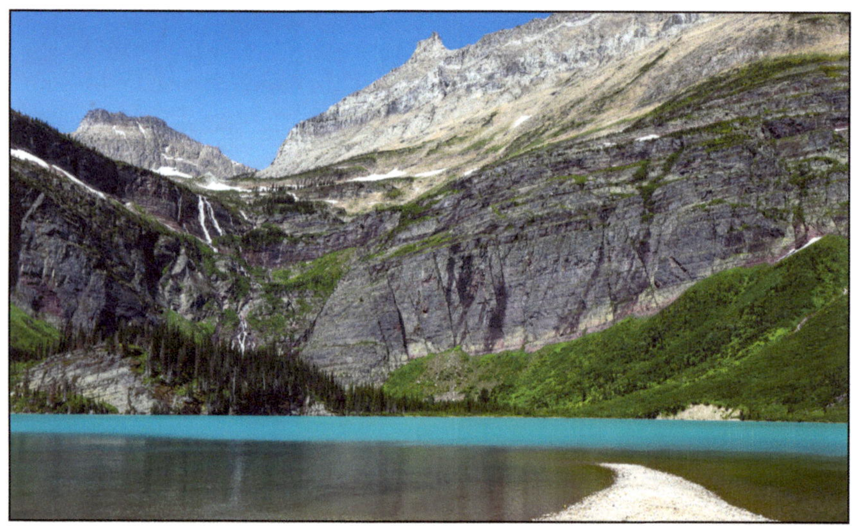

Grinnell Lake   35mm f/8 1/125s ISO100

Once rested and having exhausted photography options, head on back the same way you came. Cross Cataract Creek and now let's consider Hidden Falls... The good news here is that the signage is inflated on its distance of 0.2 mile. The hike is uphill, gaining ~80 feet but I believe the distance is less than 0.1 mile. The bad news, however, is that the view of the falls from the overlook is obstructed by trees and stone. I think a "pass," but go check it out if you're curious.

The rest of the trek, you already know. One alternative for consideration is the route along the southeast side of Lake Josephine. It's in the shade of the forest, and about ¾ the way up the lake is a wide clearing to the left with a nice view looking southwest along the length of Lake Josephine. The Salamander Glacier sits high above in the mountains.

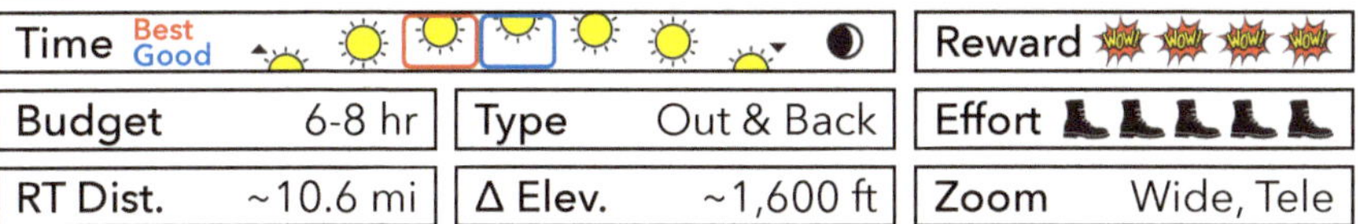

Time	Best Good		Reward
Budget	6-8 hr	Type	Out & Back	Effort
RT Dist.	~10.6 mi	Δ Elev.	~1,600 ft	Zoom	Wide, Tele

The route to Grinnell Glacier offers a lot for photographers.

In the spirit of saving space here, please read the first five paragraphs on page 107. Our route to Grinnell Glacier changes course halfway along the northwest side of Lake Josephine. A trail bears right as an alternative, more gradual ascent than the switchback option near the two bridges (also mentioned on page 107).

This trail ascends and continues without any intersections all the way to the end. Vistas of Grinnell Lake start to beg for your attention.

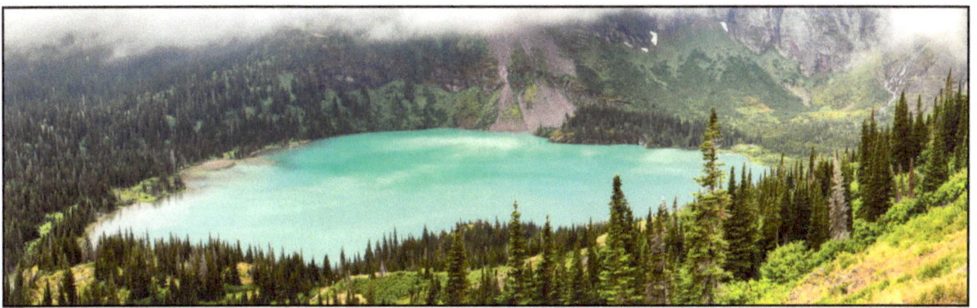

Grinnell Lake from the Route to Grinnell Glacier   35mm f/5.6 1/80s ISO200

At ~3.5 miles reach a series of waterfalls. This is a popular spot for a break – you may see many hikers here. The first waterfall is immediately in front of you. **Another waterfall is around the bend and at times can overwhelm the trail and hikers with water.** If this is the case, it's time to don something to keep you and your gear dry. A **poncho** can be of great help.

Views down to Grinnell Lake and the tall waterfall of Grinnell Creek from the glaciers above continue to improve.

At ~4.9 miles is a picnic area and toilet.

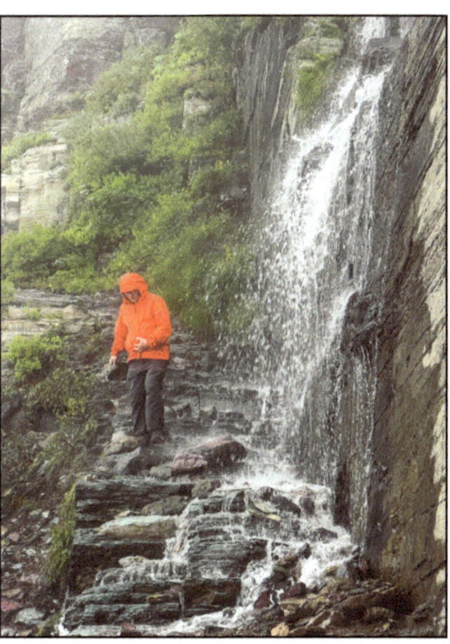

70mm f/8 1/100s ISO400

The final ~0.4 mile ascent is steep and really challenges tired legs. Wildflowers flank the trail in places... If in need of a breather, turn to some flower photography for a recharge of the legs and lungs. Finally reach the "top" of the trail – a broad area northeast of Upper Grinnell Lake. Straight ahead, perched above the lake is the Salamander Glacier. To your left (looking south) is the Grinnell Glacier. From here you can descend via one of many paths down towards the lake.

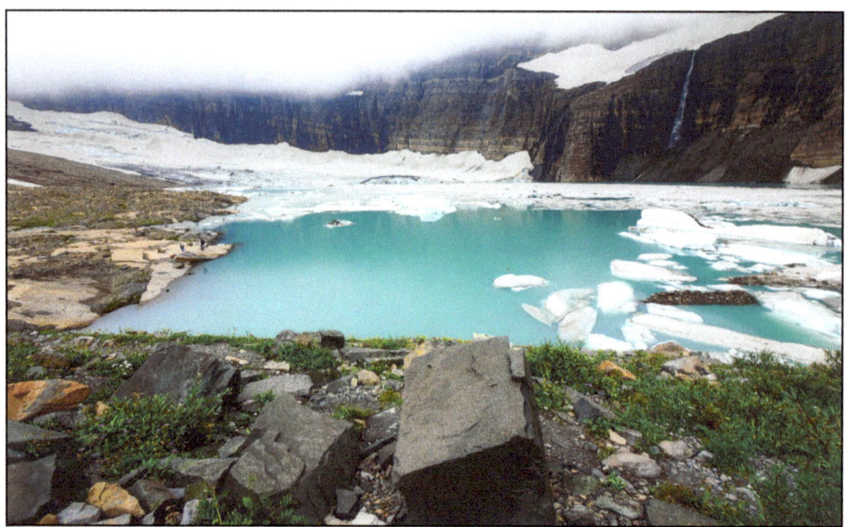

Upper Grinnell Lake and Grinnell Glacier   14mm f/5.6 1/200s ISO200

The reflections and texture of the floating ice are extraordinary.

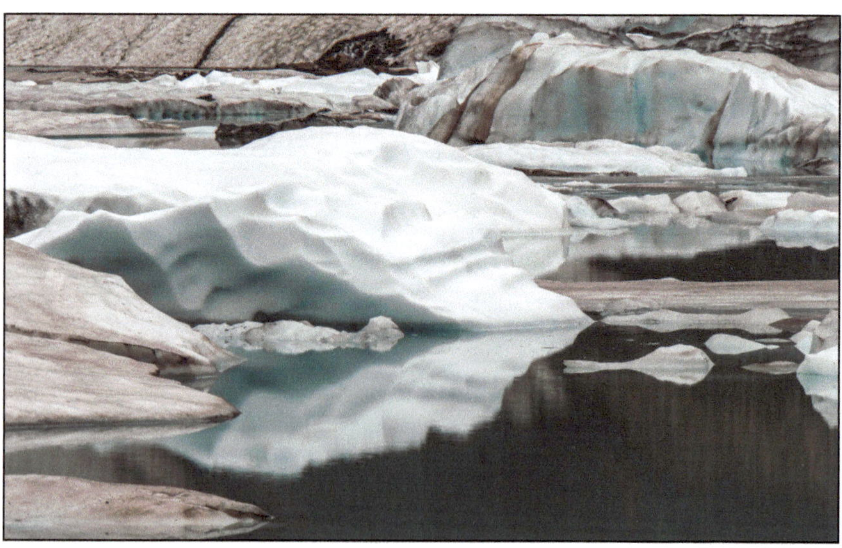

Floating Ice on Upper Grinnell Lake   250mm f/16 0.4s ISO100

Hopefully it is not too late to mention – **it can be cold here**. Packing layers for general warmth as well as protection from rain, wind, and even snow is advised. Add or remove layers, as the conditions warrant.

Have fun exploring the area, but do not get so lost in time that daylight becomes an issue for your hike back.

Also remain aware of what may be changing weather conditions while you're out this far. Though, sometimes a change in cloud conditions can provide for new or different vistas on your return journey...

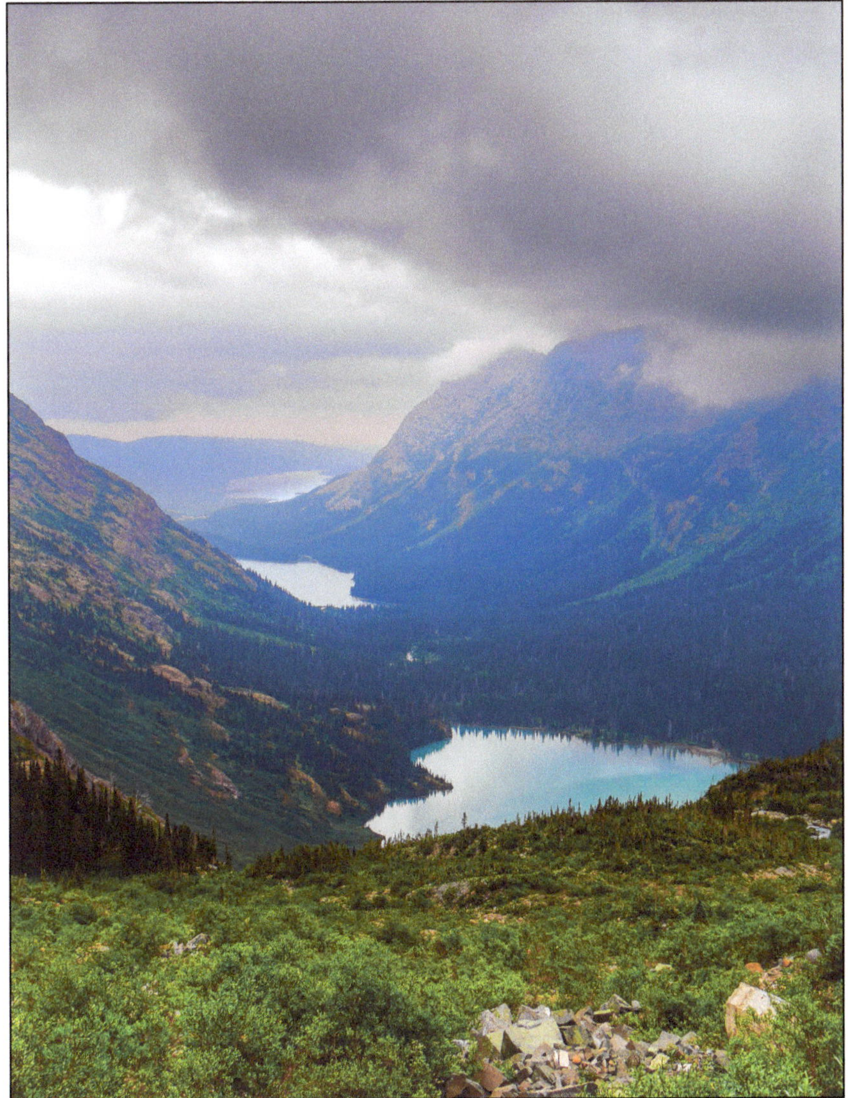

Josephine, Swiftcurrent, and Sherburne Lakes   35mm f/8 1/250s ISO100

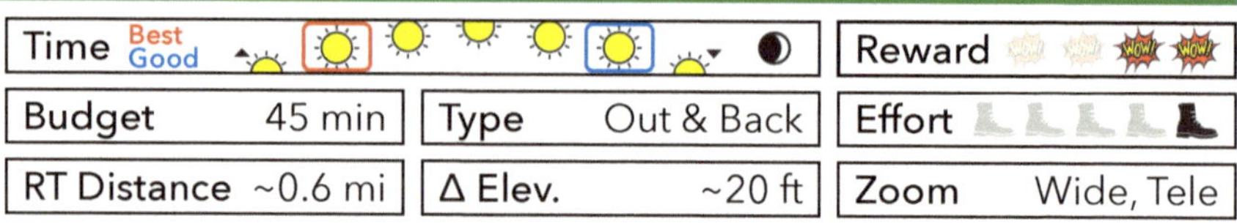

Time	Best / Good	Reward	WOW! WOW!
Budget	45 min	Type	Out & Back	Effort
RT Distance	~0.6 mi	Δ Elev.	~20 ft	Zoom	Wide, Tele

If you didn't see mention of Fishercap Lake on the main park map or the hike to it listed anywhere, you're not alone. This is perhaps the least advertised among easily-accessible sites in the Many Glacier area, if not the entire park.

The majority of this ¼ mile route is along the same trail that serves Redrock Falls (30) and beyond towards Swiftcurrent Pass. Begin at the far (west) end of the parking lot in front of the Swiftcurrent Motor Inn. Make one left turn towards Fishercap Lake at an evident intersection next to a cartoonish-shaped tree, or continue a little further to the formal trail, denoted by a weather-worn brown sign.

Moose and deer frequent the willows to the left and the distant shore. Coincidentally, their likelihood of presence in the early morning and late afternoon is also when the lighting is best for photography. Wider focal lengths are necessary for the lake, and of course telephoto lenses help with wildlife. If the water is still, as is typical in the morning, a polarizer likely won't be necessary... The reflections are usually sufficient without, and a polarizer can really interrupt the color of the blue sky in the corners of your frame if there are few to no clouds.

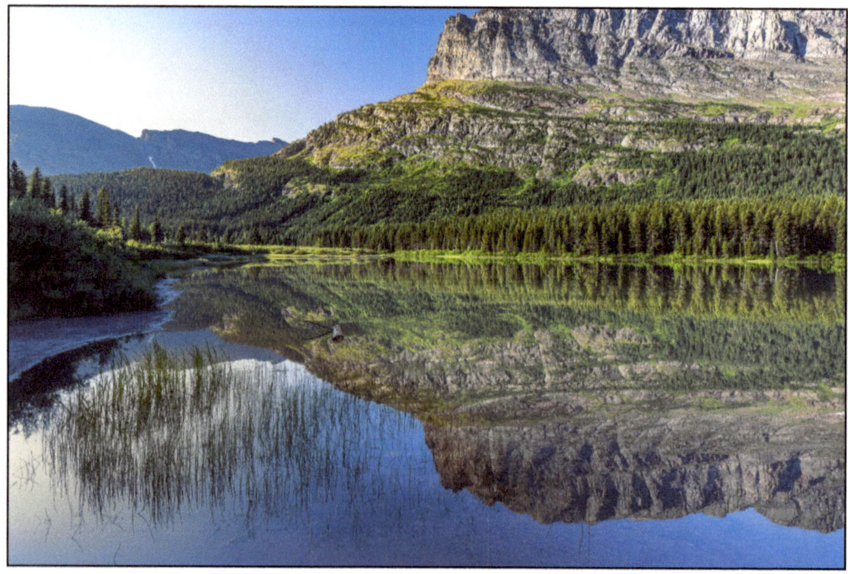

Grinnell Mountain Reflection   16mm f/8 1/40s ISO100

The mountain rising above the far side of the lake is Grinnell Mountain. **Grinnell Point** is on the left. The composition with the grass and willows on the left was what struck me first, but as I explored this short lakeshore additional opportunities became evident. A head-on shot of Grinnell Mountain is also marvelous. Looking west, the peak of **Swiftcurrent Mountain** is visible.

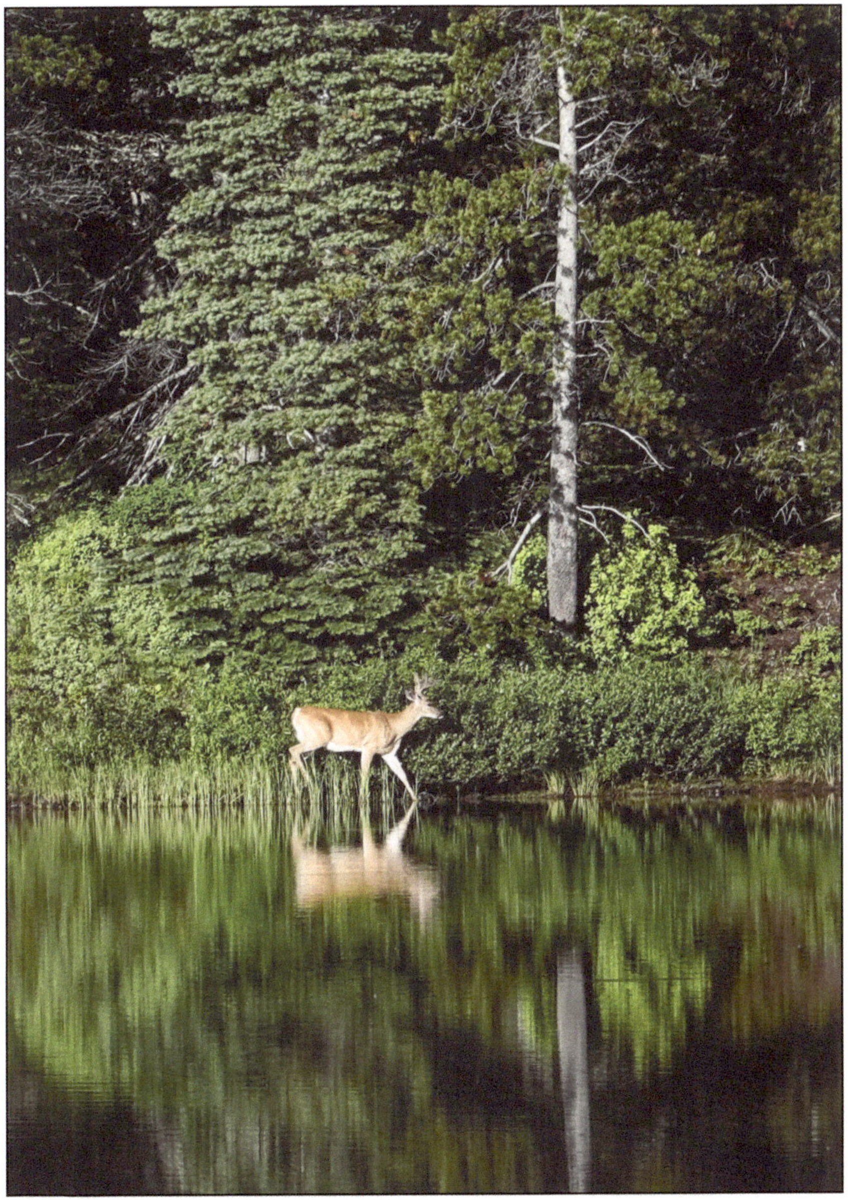

White-tailed Deer along Fishercap Lake   500mm f/8 1/400s ISO400

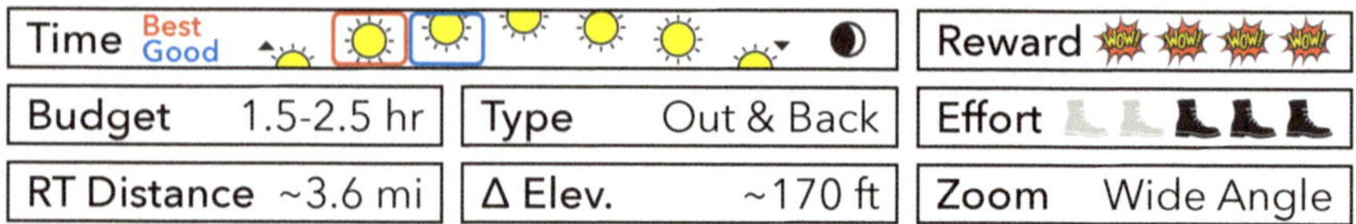

Time	Best Good	☀ ☀ ☀ ☀ ☀ ☀ ☀ ◑	Reward	WOW! WOW! WOW! WOW!
Budget	1.5-2.5 hr	**Type** Out & Back	**Effort**	👢 👢 **👢 👢 👢**
RT Distance ~3.6 mi		**Δ Elev.** ~170 ft	**Zoom**	Wide Angle

Beyond Fishercap Lake (29) and then beyond the next lake, Redrock Lake, is Redrock Falls. The color here is absolutely marvelous, especially when it's raining — as it was during this photo below.

I'll borrow from the Fishercap Lake trailhead orientation on page 112; the beginning of the route to Redrock Falls is the same. Ultimately, you will stay on this main trail for ~1.8 miles before coming to an obvious fork to the left, leading down to the nearby falls.

The route has mild ups and downs along the way, and a part of the hike is through a forest with some wildly curvaceous Aspen.

Photographing the falls is a straightforward exercise. An informal viewing area provides this head-on view. A wider field of view is best, hence the wide angle lens recommendation above. Depending on your taste, either use a ND filter (or stop down) for a silky water flow or shoot at ~1/100s to capture the charging water.

Be cautious: **Moose** sometimes peruse the willows in this area.

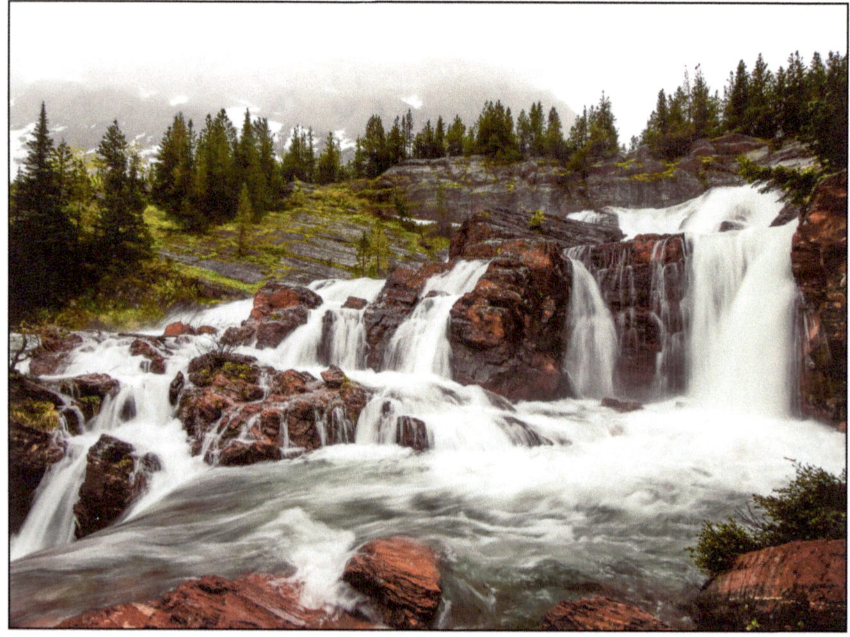

Redrock Falls   18mm   f/8   1/8s   ISO100

Two Medicine

Two Medicine Entrance and Beyond

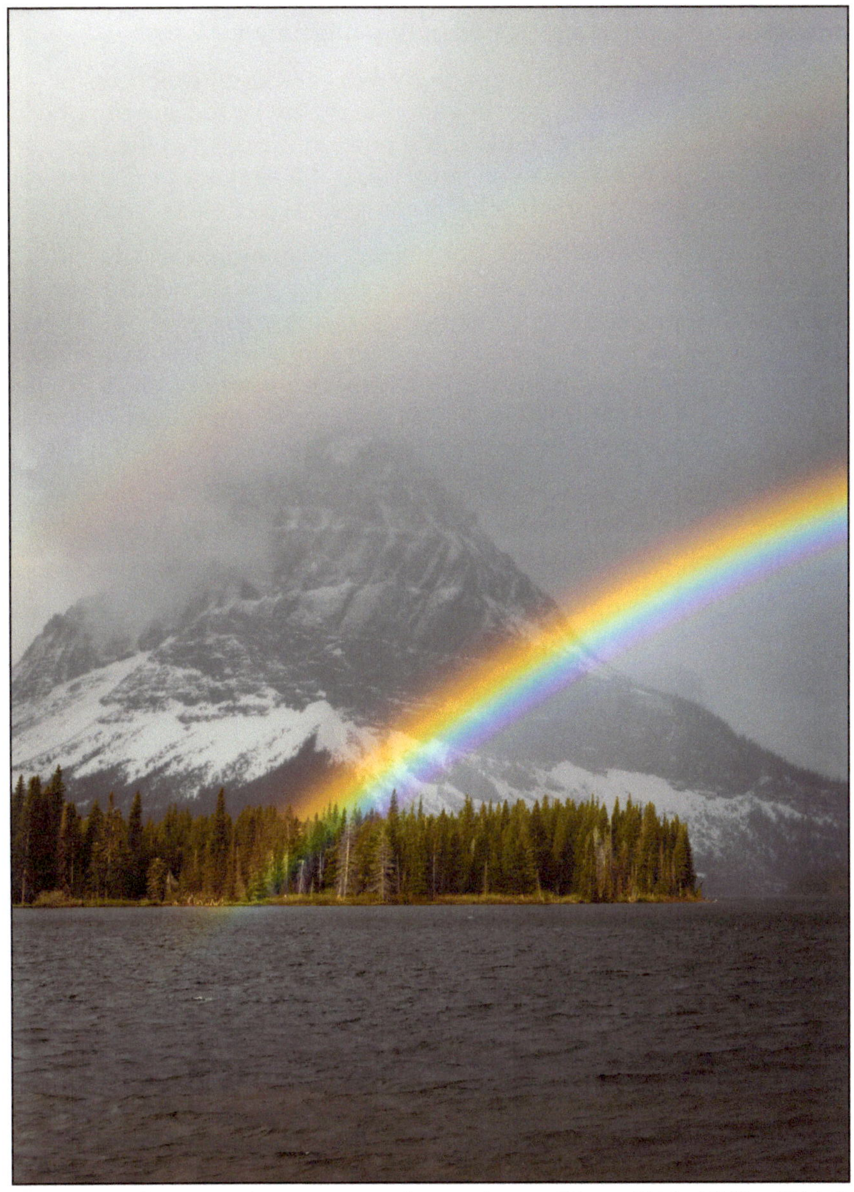

Morning Rainbows over Stormy Two Medicine Lake   70mm f/5.6 1/320s ISO100

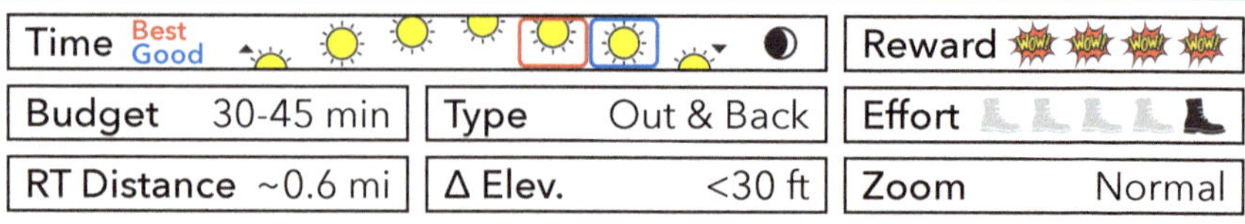

Time	Best Good		Reward
Budget	30-45 min	Type	Out & Back	Effort
RT Distance	~0.6 mi	Δ Elev.	<30 ft	Zoom	Normal

Running Eagle Falls is my all-time favorite waterfall, as it appears to originate from *within* a rock wall during midsummer flow.

The source of the falls includes Two Medicine Lake, which sits at an elevation about 200 ft higher. Beyond the top of the rocks in the photo at right is Two Medicine Creek, and it flows into a relief in the stone (a sinkhole) ahead of what we see here. This is the early stage of a natural bridge formation. In some publications it is referred to as "Trick Falls."

During spring snowmelt, the creek's flow is so abundant that the "trick" is masked – water rushes over the top, hiding this secondary flow of water behind it. Once the snowmelt slows, the volume of water from the top of the rock wall decreases and for some time a small waterfall comes over the top, joining the flow we see here through the relief in the stone. This typically occurs in the early summer. Finally, the characteristic flow at right arrives midsummer and lasts into the fall.

The parking area for Running Eagle Falls is the first well-marked stop when entering the Two Medicine area. Most visitors don't spend much time here, so parking spaces tend to turn over regularly.

The site hosts two routes, although it's not obvious from the parking lot. The primary trailhead is centered among the spaces and serves as the most direct route to the falls. Adjacent to this trailhead is an information board with a wonderful story of Running Eagle, an esteemed, woman Pikuni warrior. Beyond this information board, at the south end of the parking lot is the other entrance (or exit) to the **Running Eagle Falls Nature Trail**.

I suggest to begin at the primary trailhead, hike to the falls, and on your return divert to the nature trail. The routes are nearly parallel, so your hiking length is not really impacted, whether you choose to check out the nature trail or not. The nature trail has a series of signs, highlighting the flora in this area. We learn the furrowed bark of this **Black Cottonwood** helps it stave off fire.

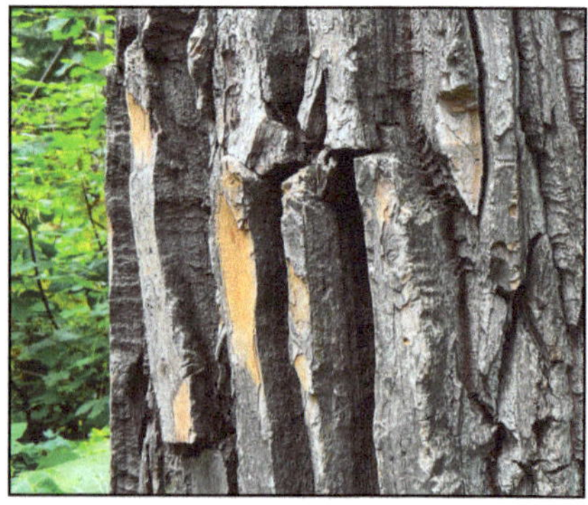

70mm   f/5.6   1/120s   ISO800

The route is easy to follow. Not far after the intersection with the nature trail spot a bench to the left. The view here is obstructed by trees... I imagine at one time it wasn't. Next is a short footbridge across Dry Fork Creek. Midsummer, this creek is often dry.

The formal route ends at a viewing platform. This is where the below photo was taken. At time of writing it is possible to explore beyond the platform (along the water's edge), though it doesn't improve the perspective much.

Sample different framing orientations along with various focal lengths and shutter speeds. A polarizer seems to help here as well.

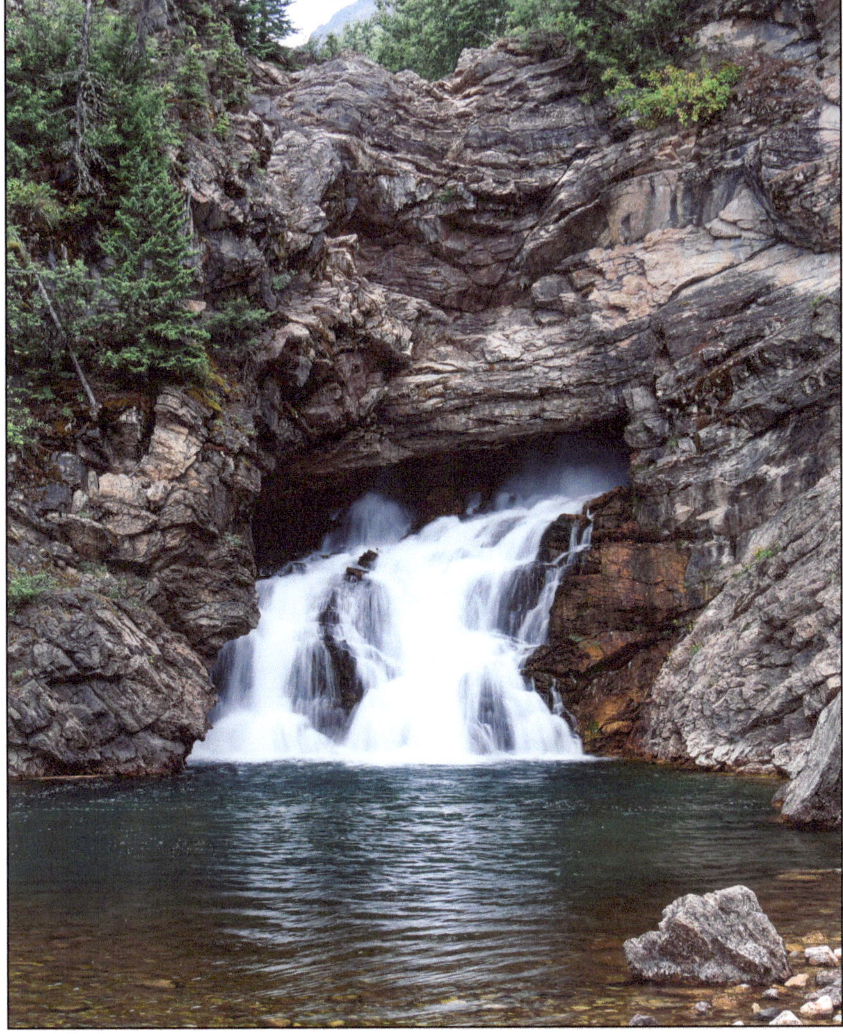

"Trick Falls"   50mm f/11 1s ISO100

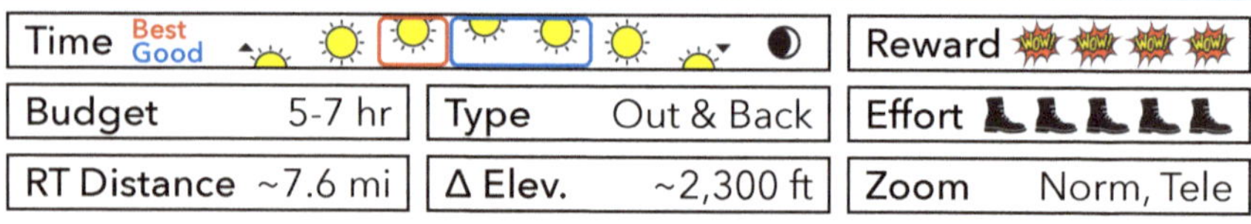

Time	Best / Good	...
Budget	5-7 hr	Type	Out & Back	Effort
RT Distance	~7.6 mi	Δ Elev.	~2,300 ft	Zoom	Norm, Tele

Scenic Point is a rock outcrop that sits high above Lower Two Medicine Lake. It's easily visible from Montana Highway 49, as seen on the right. It's what I consider a "vista" hike, providing 360° views from the point – east towards Browning and west towards the Two Medicine Valley.

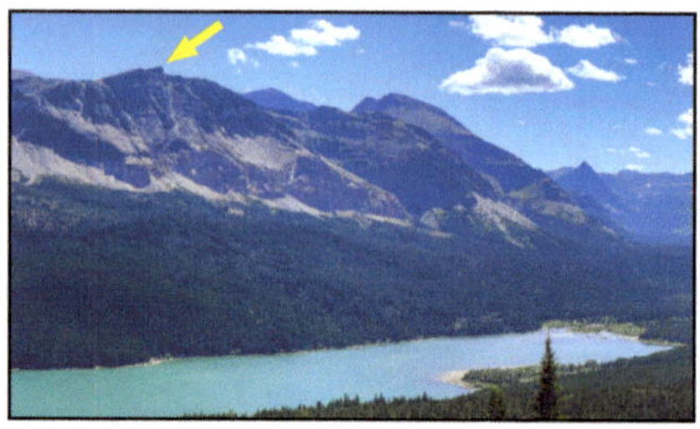

100mm   f/8   1/250s   ISO100

It is a rewarding hike and the vistas are enjoyable. However, if solely looking for the "best" vantage of the Two Medicine Valley (including an *unobstructed* view of Two Medicine Lake and some of Upper Two Medicine Lake to its west), a view from the ~2.0 mile point along the trail is all that's required. It's a fine place to turn around and why the site includes "Trail" in its name... Either choose to use the route in its entirety to the top or partially to this ~2 miles-in view.

The turn-in off Two Medicine Road to the Scenic Point Trailhead parking area is large, but the sign is small. If you are driving in and reach the Two Medicine Ranger Station, you've gone ¼ mile too far.

The hike begins in the forest and at ~0.6 mile a sign points to **Appistoki Falls** to the right. This trail to the right has loose rocks in places, making traction challenging. Further, it also skirts a cliff along Appistoki Creek. The falls are never visible without significant obstructions... **I recommend to skip this route and turn left at the sign.** You will arrive at the same wide, rocky point with the falls in earshot.

The route opens up here with a beautiful valley to the south. The hike remains exposed the remainder of the way. After 4 switchbacks, the route continues straight for ¼ mile, before reaching a switchback to the left and climbing towards the rocks. Along this long, straight section we are introduced to many snags (dead trees) in this area. They are wonderful subjects... Some more "interesting" ones lay ahead, so unless you see something particularly fascinating, I recommend to carry on. See page 121 for a sample of one using an infrared filter.

We might as well continue counting switchbacks here... Picking up where we left off (following the left switchback after the long traverse), the next switchback arrives after a walk over scree; it is to the right. In short order arrives 5 more switchbacks before the trail arcs to the north. A more mild switchback arrives at ~1.6 miles, to the right. Here the snags provide for a great foreground, now with a good amount of Two Medicine Lake visible.

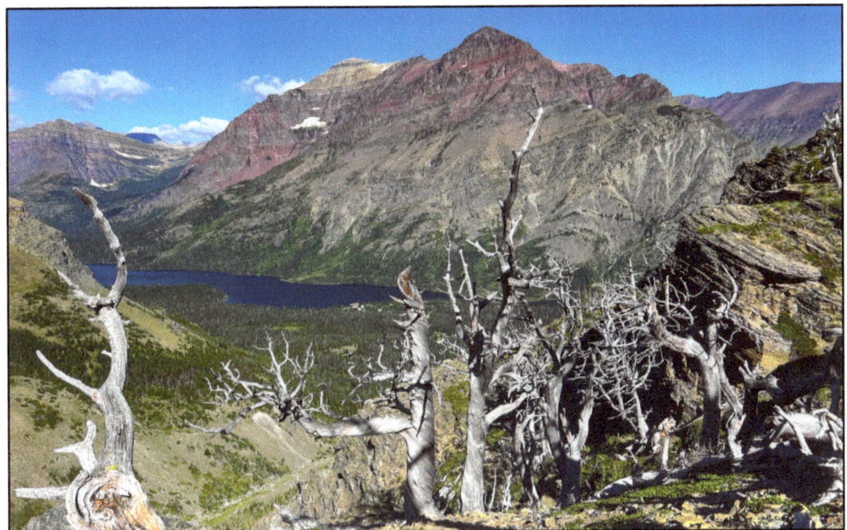

Snags and Two Medicine Lake - Mile 1.6   24mm f/16 1/60s ISO100

Now I'm not usually one to count switchbacks, and we are about done with the effort... Beyond this overlook, head uphill and the trail makes more of a left turn. Skirt some trees to your right, and finally at ~2.0 miles we have the switchback mentioned at the beginning. **A clear view of Two Medicine Lake is present**, with satisfactory elevation to also see some of Upper Two Medicine Lake.

If continuing on, head through trees to a switchback, for another tour through the same patch of trees (only up higher now). Find our last switchback I'll mention at ~3.0 miles. This one provides a view that is arguably the same as the prior, just 1 mile back. Visibility of Upper Two Medicine Lake is only slightly improved.

From here the hike feels straight but does curve as it makes its way up and over two ridges to the final, long approach towards Scenic Point. The landscape here is interesting, but I have not found that my photography adequately captures its curious allure. This stretch is more about the outdoor experience than take-home pictures. Perhaps a wildlife encounter would change things. Keep an eye out.

A sign at a trail intersection directs uphill to Scenic Point... A greater hiking effort is required for this final ~0.1 mile, and then you've arrived. The views are expansive on a clear day. One of the landmarks I enjoy seeing from here is Running Eagle Falls (31).

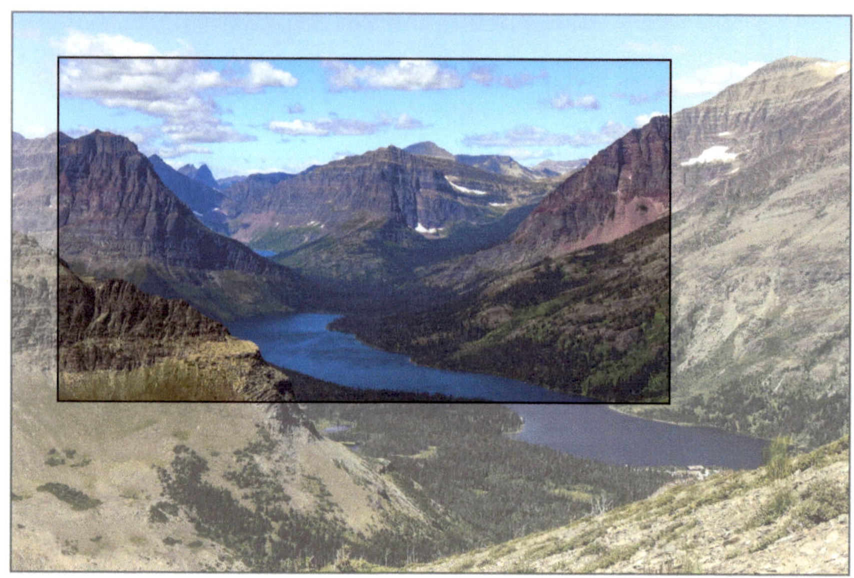

Two Medicine Valley from Scenic Point   50-70mm f/8 1/8s ISO100

Above we can see the impact the adjacent mountainsides have on our foreground... So we're left with a short telephoto requirement to eliminate them, but in doing so crop this end of the lake.

Find the **red rocks with ripples** – part of the Grinnell formation, from their once-underwater existence. Fascinating!

The return hike is as you might expect... Only perhaps easier because it's downhill most of the route. Keep an eye out for **hoary marmots** among the rocks and snags.

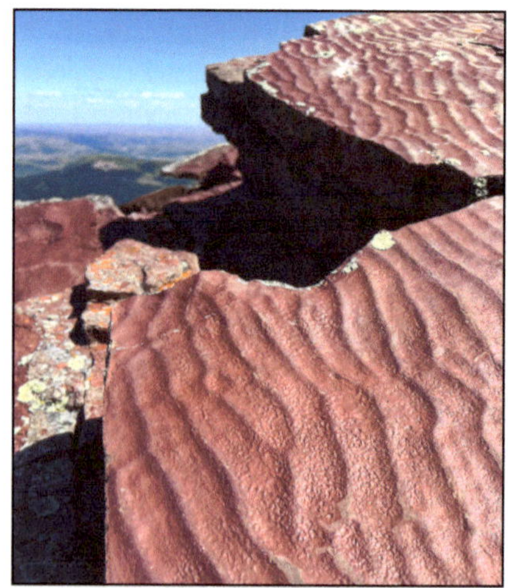

35mm f/4 1/800s ISO100

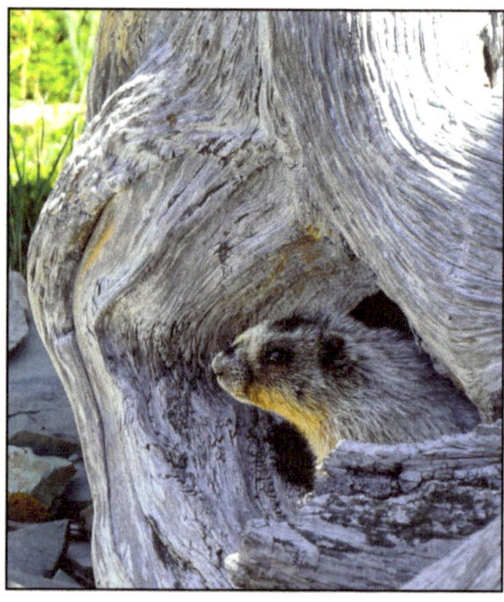

200mm f/5.6 1/200s ISO100

I have only just recently begun to explore infrared (IR) photography, with my first attempts in Glacier National Park. The ins and outs of this genre are enough to fill a book this size or larger, so I believe I'm left here only simply to promote it as an option to consider pursuing.

The tools that I use are a Hoya R72 filter along with my conventional digital camera. That is, to say, my cameras are not modified for IR service. I then process my RAW images with Adobe Lightroom.

Many online resources are available on this topic, and if this is of interest I recommend conducting some research as well as some experimentation near home before relying on this new process in the field.

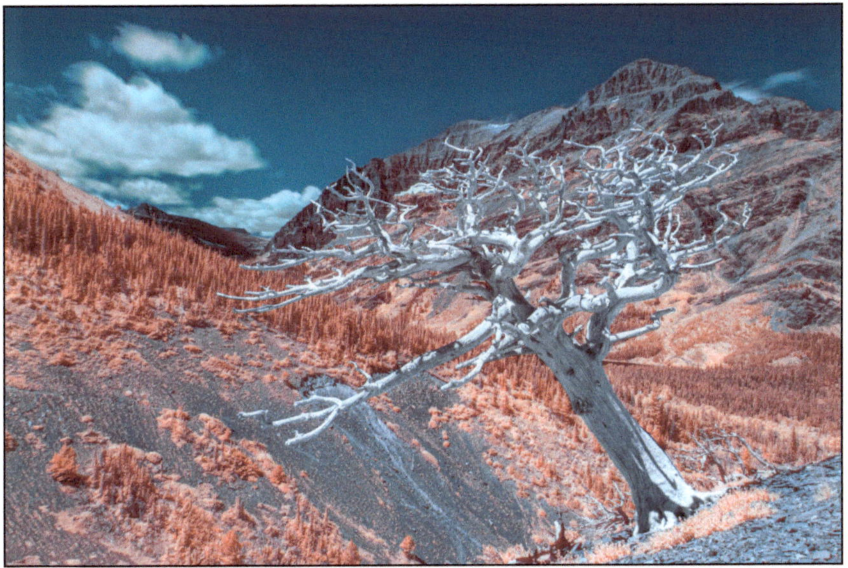

Along Two Medicine's Scenic Point Trail   24mm f/11 30s ISO100

A short list of things you will want to know, if considering this method...

* Exposure times will be long (10s and beyond).

* Your out-of-camera images will be monotone red.

* A fair amount of work is required in post-processing to arrive at a desirable, artistic representation with a photo. *This was especially true with my inaugural effort.*

I've found it to be a lot of fun, and I enjoy exploring the color possibilities once back home and in front of my computer. One major upside to IR photography – bright, midday light is generally desirable.

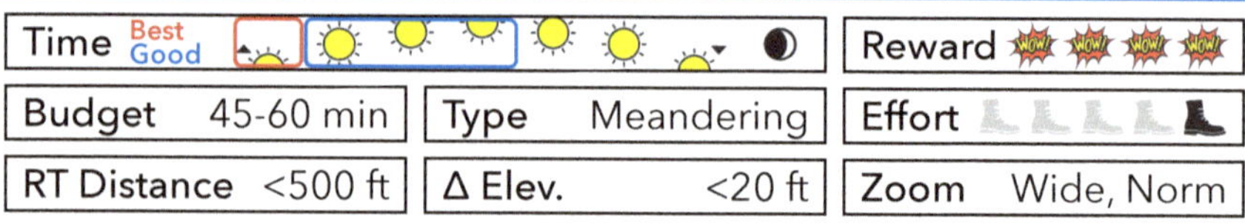

Time	Best Good		Reward	WOW! WOW! WOW! WOW!
Budget	45-60 min	Type	Meandering	Effort
RT Distance	<500 ft	Δ Elev.	<20 ft	Zoom	Wide, Norm

Windy. If I had one word to best prepare you for Two Medicine Lake, that would be the one. Now it's not windy here all of the time, but from my experience it is windy here *most* of the time. I say this, because I want you to arrive prepared. Sunrise here easily earns its 4-Wow rating, so it is certainly worth a visit.

Access is easy, with parking adjacent to the shoreline on the east end of the lake. Look to find a location to set up with the general store behind you. The view west lights up slowly as the sun makes its ascent.

If your visit happens to be on a calm day (rejoice!), then you could expect to use a low ISO and a longer shutter speed, typical for this type of composition. However, below I've elected to share my settings on a windy morning so that you can see the trade-offs I considered...

I remember first sampling a low ISO and longer shutter speed, only to be discouraged with the appearance of the lake water with its white-capped waves. I elected to embrace the wind and waves, seeking a shutter speed of 1/50-1/60 second. I also had started with the aperture set at f/11, for improved depth of field (sharpness), from the beach rocks to the distant mountains. But in order to achieve this faster shutter speed I was stuck increasing ISO and opening up the aperture to compensate. ISO 800 and f/5.6 was the compromise I employed.

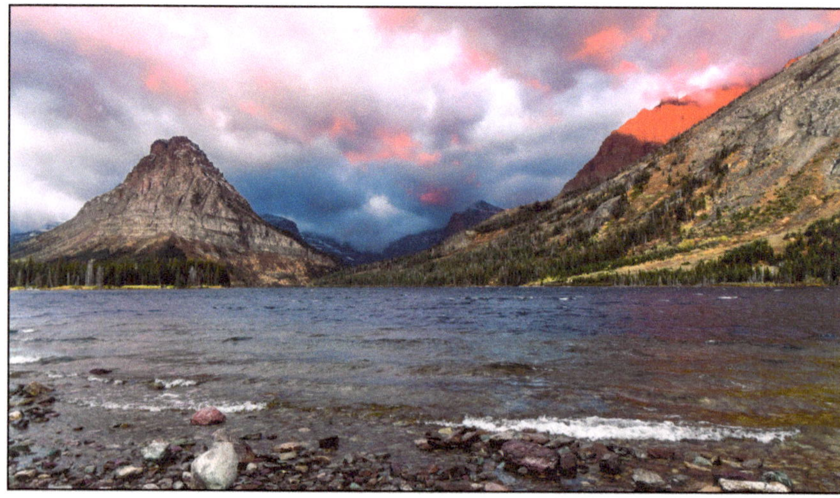

Sunrise at Two Medicine Lake

24mm f/5.6 1/50s ISO800

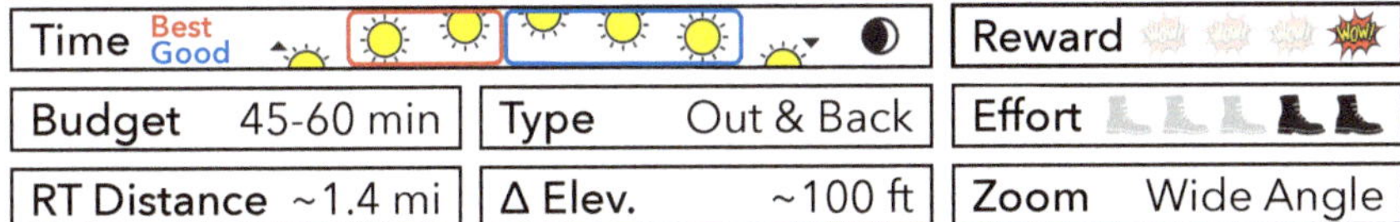

Time	Best / Good		Reward				
Budget 45-60 min	**Type** Out & Back	**Effort**
RT Distance ~1.4 mi	**Δ Elev.** ~100 ft	**Zoom** Wide Angle

The area around Two Medicine Lake has limited short hike options. If comparing to Many Glacier, the ~2.5 mile Swiftcurrent Nature Trail (26) fits the bill nicely, providing something shorter with a variety of views along the way. A series of trails can be utilized to circle Two Medicine Lake, but the round-trip ticket requires upwards of 7 miles. Yikes!

Our best option is the hike to Paradise Point, located along the southeast lakeshore, not far from the parking area and boat dock. This trailhead is the same as for Aster Falls & Aster Park (35), and the entrance is easily located at the forest's edge beyond the boat dock.

Most of the hike is in the forest, away from the lake. It begins a bit steep, but mellows quickly. At about 0.3 mile an intersection with signage points to the right for Paradise Point. Turn here and descend to near the lake level where a few route options to the "beach" are evident. The lake level may dictate which route will work best.

Rising Wolf Mountain consumes the north view across the lake. Good timing may provide for a photo of the Sinopah tour boat cruising by.

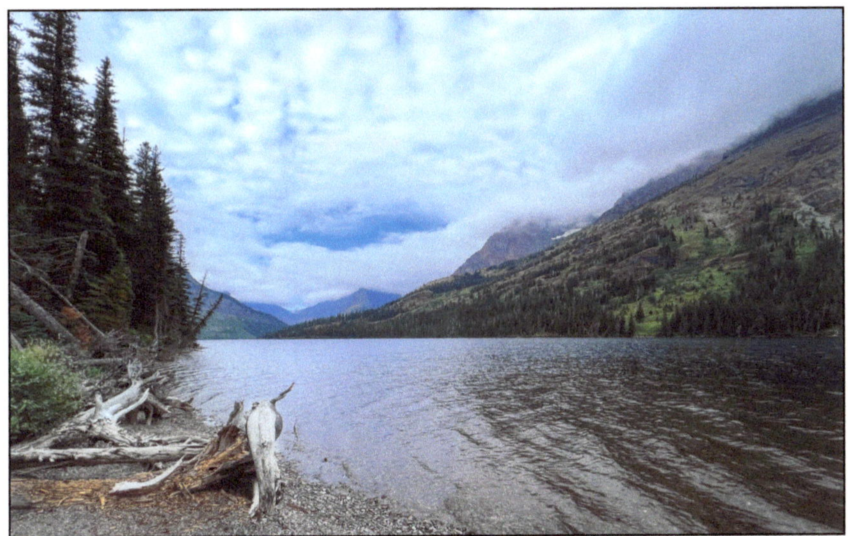

Westerly View of Two Medicine Lake at Paradise Point   16mm f/11 1/320s ISO100

See the next page for details about a set of ponds only ~0.2 mile past the aforementioned intersection, if interested in exploring more.

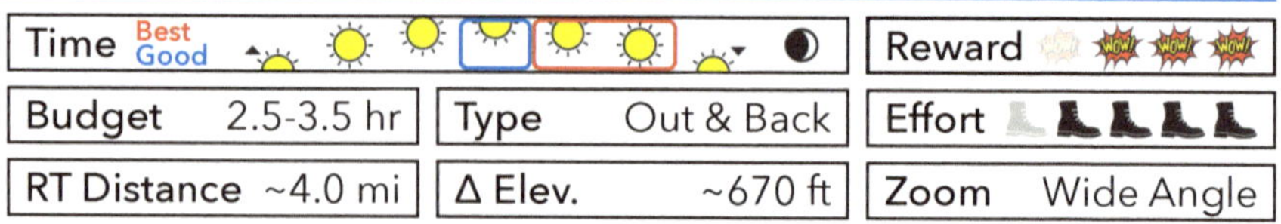

Time	Best Good	Reward
Budget	2.5-3.5 hr	Type	Out & Back	Effort
RT Distance	~4.0 mi	Δ Elev.	~670 ft	Zoom	Wide Angle

The hike to Aster Falls and Aster Park is arguably the only "½ day" hike in the Two Medicine area. The good news is that it's enjoyable and does provide multiple photography opportunities. Beyond this option, longer excursions are necessary, such as along the Scenic Point Trail (32) or to sites beyond the head of Two Medicine Lake. **Rockwell Falls** is an option you'll find on maps, but I'm compelled to state that if we're here for photography our time is better spent elsewhere.

Aster Falls is at ~1.3 miles into the 2-mile route. Some visitors hike only to the falls and turn back. This is a good option if in search for a milder outing. The trail between Aster Falls and Aster Park is **steep** over the last ~0.7 mile, gaining over 500 feet in elevation.

Please read the prior page on Paradise Point (34) regarding the location of the trailhead to Aster Falls and Aster Park. We'll pick up here at the intersection ~0.3 mile into the hike...

At ~0.5 mile the trail skirts a few, picturesque small bodies of water.

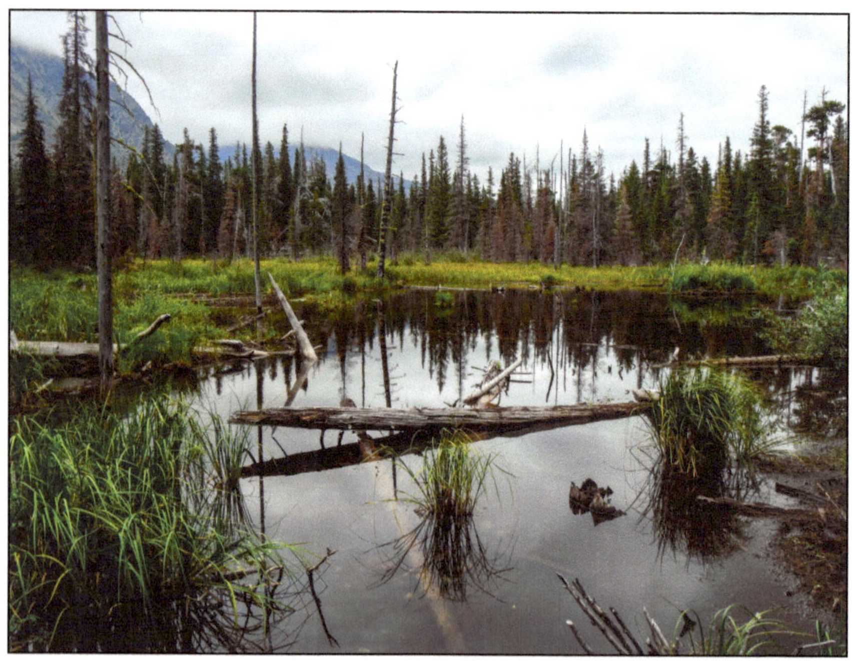

Tranquility in the Two Medicine Valley   24mm f/11 1/15s ISO100

Pass a clearing with more potentially interesting compositions, then over a bridge, and next at ~1.2 miles arrive at a well-defined intersection with Aster Falls and Aster Park to the left.

Some moderate climbing resumes... After ~0.1 mile find another intersection with a particularly interesting sign, pointing to the right for "Aster Park Viewpoint" with odd word spacing, as if something useful was eliminated... At any rate, what the sign doesn't state is that the trail to the left is to Aster Falls.

The area around the falls can at times be crowded. This trail to Aster Creek is short, so my recommendation (if you're planning to continue onto Aster Park) is to hike on down and see if the amount of people present is satisfactory for photography... If so, then stop here for a bit and take some photos. If it's crowded, then hike back on out and try again following your visit to Aster Park.

The area around the falls provides generous space for hikers to enjoy a break and a snack, but the view of the falls from the "end" of the trail is mediocre for photography. If the water level is high, then this may be as good as it gets. If though the water volume is low, then it is possible to carefully step out onto the large, flat boulder in front of the falls. Please – be wise if this is safe and be careful if choosing to do so. From this head-on vantage, the rest is straightforward.

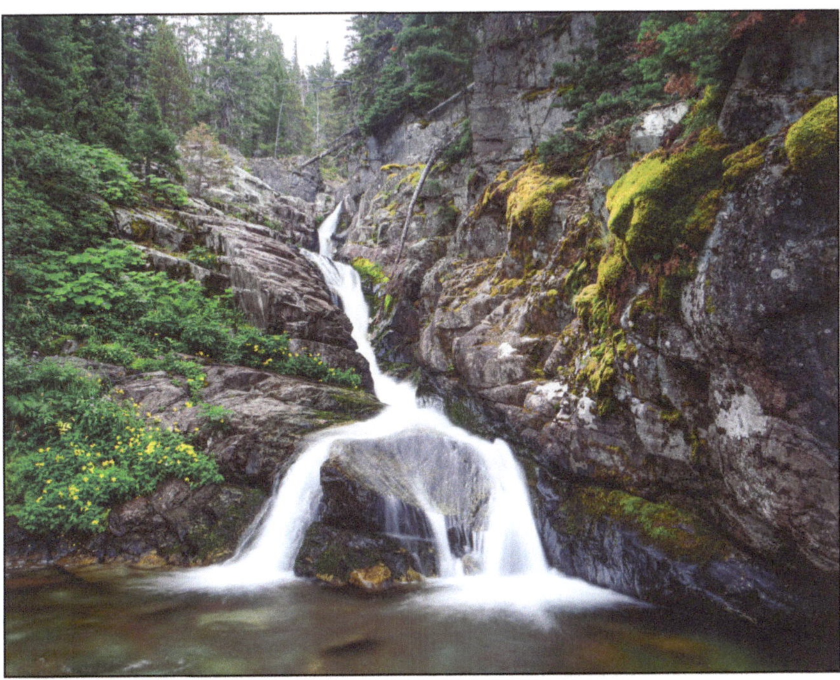

Aster Falls

28mm f/16 1s ISO100

Admittedly, my sky is blown-out in this photo of Aster Falls, but I kept it at a minimum in the frame. I'm delighted with the rest.

Back on the main trail towards Aster Park, the final stretch really pushes the legs. There's not a lot to capture, so as I like to say — find a comfortable pace and "motor on."

Near the end the trail makes its way into thinner trees and the grade becomes more reasonable. Make a bend to the right and find the rocky surface of the Aster Park Overlook (Viewpoint) ahead.

Some wandering around this small area will help. Many short trees fill the foreground, when looking down towards Two Medicine Lake. The trees are weather-beaten and add to the scene. I have tried to find a way to compose a shot with an unobstructed view below, but I haven't found a satisfactory one yet. Instead, I've learned to embrace the trees, as they add a welcome foreground element anyway.

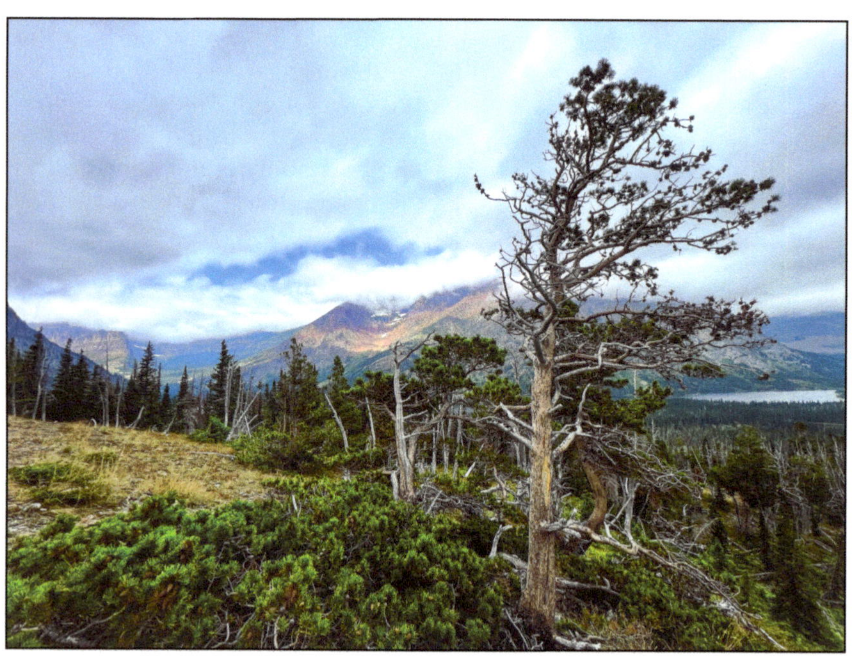

Aster Park Wind-Swept Tree   15mm f/8 1/400s ISO100

Other compositions are possible, with more of Two Medicine Lake in view. I liked the emphasis here of the moving clouds seemingly in the direction of the wind-swept tree. The texture in the subjects throughout this landscape is fantastic.

Be equipped with a layer for wind to stay comfortable up here. Once finished with the surrounding views, head on back the same way... Check Aster Falls once again, if desired.

On the Outskirts

Polebridge, Camas Creek Entrance, and Walton

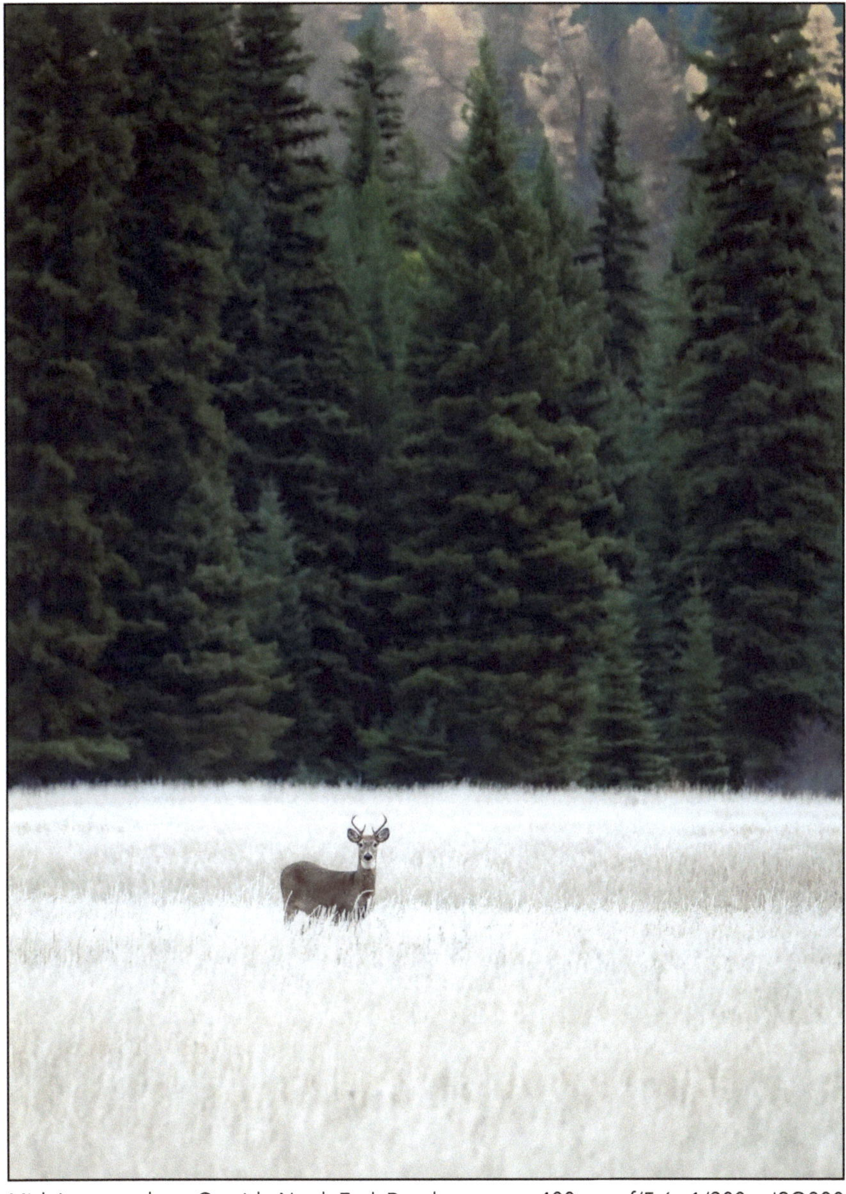

Mid-Autumn along Outside North Fork Road   400mm   f/5.6   1/200s   ISO800

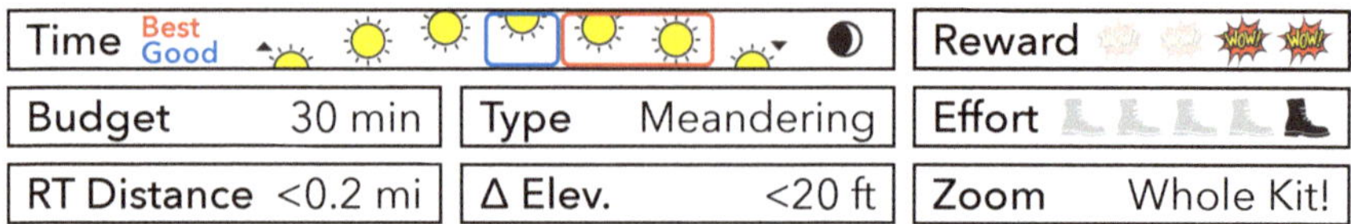

Time	Best Good		Reward
Budget	30 min	Type	Meandering	Effort
RT Distance	<0.2 mi	Δ Elev.	<20 ft	Zoom	Whole Kit!

You might be wondering, "Why would I drive an hour or more to a 2-Wow site that only takes a ½ hour to explore?" (And that's without yet knowing how rugged some of this driving can be!) Here's why...

A visit to the Polebridge Mercantile and nearby Polebridge Ranger Station with its primitive facilities and roads is *entirely about the journey*, where the focus on abundant photography takes the back seat temporarily. As these three pages demonstrate, it's of course a visually appealing place to visit, but for the amount of time and effort this just isn't as "efficient" as some other locations throughout the park if the primary purpose is pursuing a copious amount of photos.

Somehow I've made it all the way to page 128 without acknowledging the reputation of western Montana huckleberries and the many savory treats available in this region with huckleberries as the focal ingredient. **The Polebridge Mercantile & Bakery is reason enough for many to make this drive.** Their baked confections are delicious, and several options include local huckleberries.

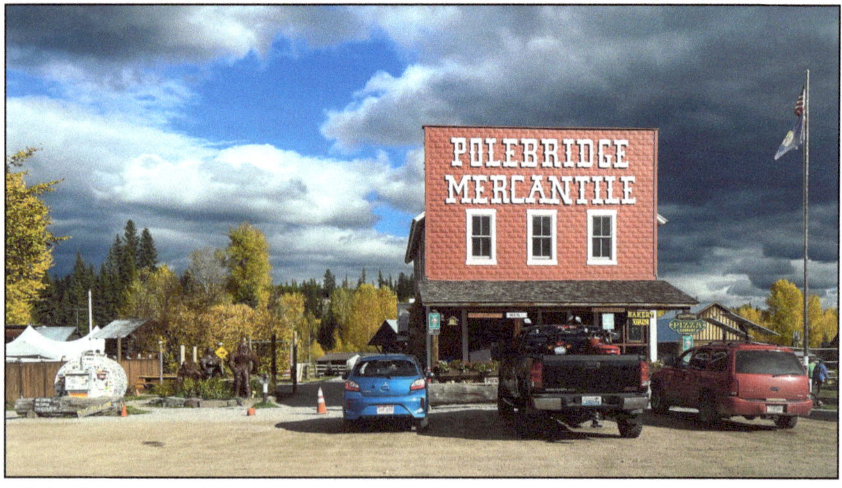

Polebridge Mercantile & Bakery   50mm f/8 1/250s ISO100

Alright, I'm now finished promoting this journey. Let's now take a look at the route...

Near the Camas Creek Entrance, Camas Road ties into the Outside North Fork Road. This road is gravel, and north from here its condition is normally pretty good. Begin north along this road, and after about 6 miles the road changes to asphalt for a drive through private properties with homes and ranches. Watch for wildlife near the road and in the adjacent meadows. Photography along this stretch should be limited to roadside, to honor property owners' privacy.

After ~13 miles arrive at an intersection with a short road to Polebridge to the right. Driving returns to gravel. The Polebridge Mercantile is straight ahead.

From the west end of Camas Road (where we started) to here is outside the Glacier National Park boundary. To access the park and the **Polebridge Ranger Station** turn left at the mercantile and head north. The drive typically begins to become very bumpy here. Cross the vehicle bridge and arrive at the ranger station complex.

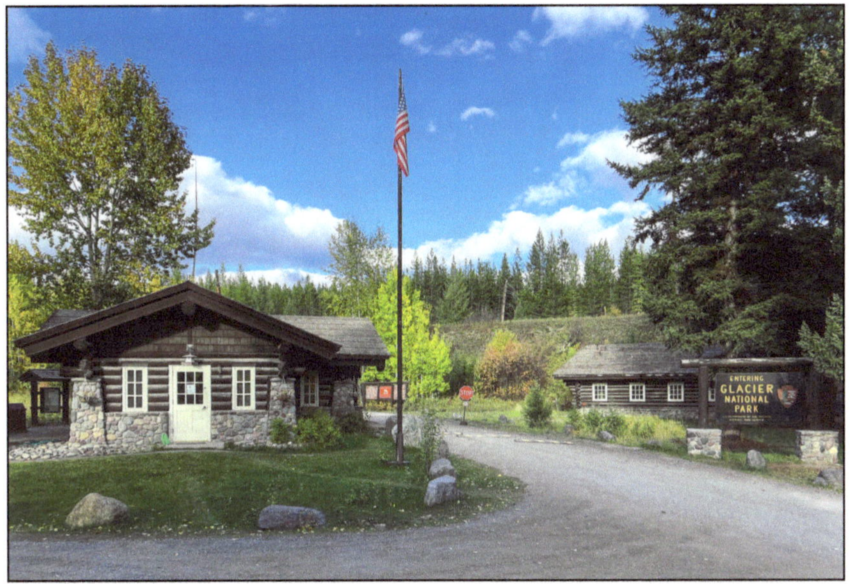

Polebridge Ranger Station   35mm f/8 1/100s ISO100

Find a lot of good information posted outside the ranger station, including recommendations for exploring this area and what to expect. The national park sign is interesting with its rustic design.

Continue straight along the road and after ~0.3 mile arrive at an intersection with the road to Bowman Lake to your right. The drive is ~5.5 miles and jarring, to say the least. **The National Park Service recommends a high clearance vehicle.** Expect a slow, ½-hour drive.

Bowman Lake offers camping, a boat launch, and a day use area with trailheads access. The day use area, adjacent to a comfort station, is where you want to park. (The area is a bit of a maze; do not be discouraged if a wrong turn is made and a turn around is necessary.)

A short walk leads to Bowman Lake. After that drive, a break is enjoyed on the lakeshore. Maybe a huckleberry pastry as well!

For photography, I believe two options are available – to use a wider focal length along with a polarizer to capture rocks below the surface of the water, or to use something longer to close-in on the mountains.

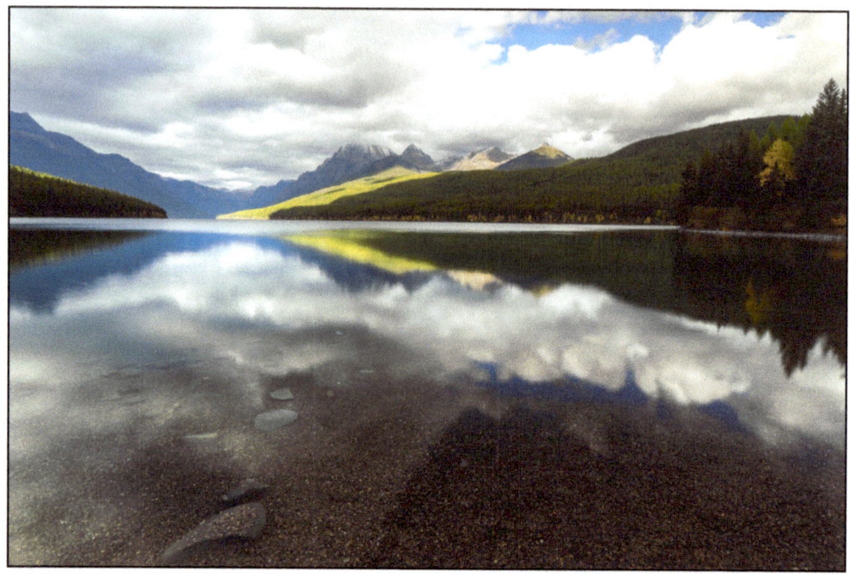

Bowman Lake

18mm f/16 2s ISO50

And that's the 30-minute photography effort. Really, as stated earlier, this trek is more about experiencing the more remote wilderness, so of course make some extra time and soak in the tranquility.

Fall color can be marvelous in this area. One afternoon after visiting Bowman Lake I stopped for a photo from the bridge over the North Fork Flathead River. The color, thanks to the lighting, was sensational.

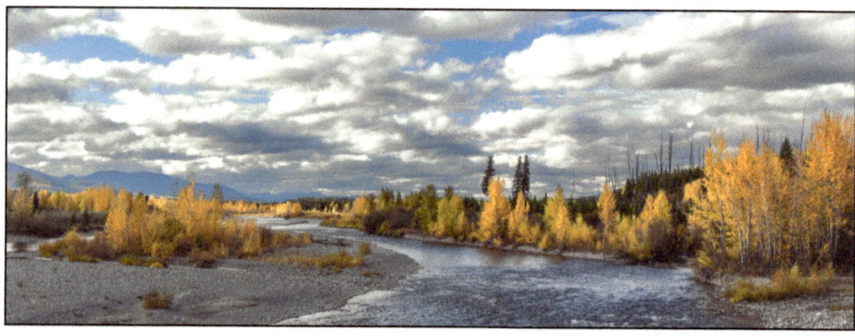

Autumn Gold near Polebridge

50mm f/8 1/80s ISO100

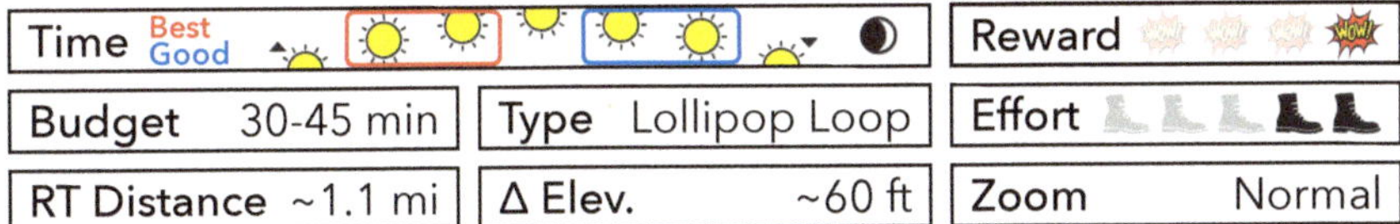

Time	Best Good		Reward	
Budget	30-45 min	Type	Lollipop Loop	Effort
RT Distance	~1.1 mi	Δ Elev.	~60 ft	Zoom	Normal

I believe that a lot of us – myself included – tend not to like the idea of forests precious to us being submitted to fire. The name of this trail was enough of a deterrent for me to postpone my exploration to *"maybe next time."* Finally, I obliged. And I'm glad that I did.

The site appears to have been recently renovated with an emphasis on awareness of the impact of fire and the evolution of the U.S. Forest Service's fire management strategy. A series of information boards are located in the small parking lot, providing insight on the history of fires, along with some other interesting facts. Admittedly, at times I'll hop onto a trail and conduct my due diligence afterwards. This one, however, warrants studying the information boards first. The tour through the woods is more insightful with this knowledge in mind.

The trail is a short lollipop loop, taking you through a section of significant regrowth in an area impacted by the **Moose Fire of 2001**. Abundant moisture and incredibly rich soil on this side of Glacier National Park allows for a fast-growing new growth. This young forest already masks much of the visible evidence from the fire, only a ¼ of a century later. Some large burnt tree trunks are encountered along the way, providing motivation for photography here – a study in contrast of vibrant life and scarred remnants from fire.

While more recent, the area impacted by the Reynolds Creek Fire of 2015 on the east side of the park is in a different ecosystem and seems to be growing back more slowly. Your portfolio of photos may benefit from visiting both of these areas. I highly recommend the hike to St. Mary Falls (16).

While the photography along the Forest and Fire Nature Trail may not be as sensational as some other sites throughout the park, the experience is relevant and rewarding.

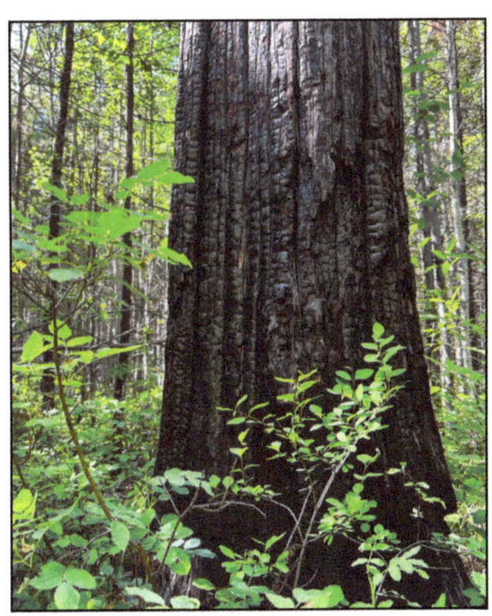

28mm f/5.6 1/30s ISO200

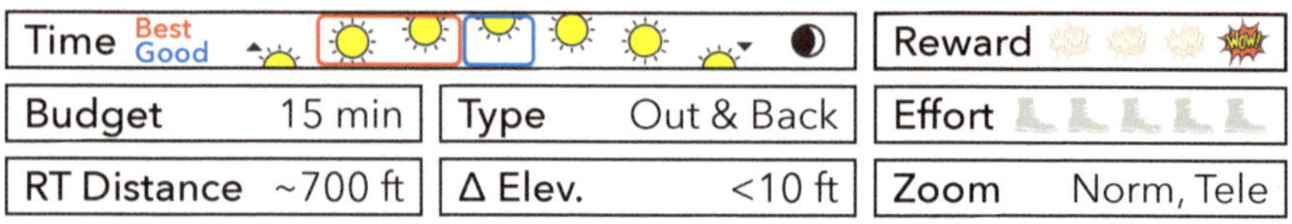

Time	Best Good		Reward			WOW!
Budget	15 min	Type	Out & Back	Effort		
RT Distance	~700 ft	Δ Elev.	<10 ft	Zoom	Norm, Tele	

Without hesitation, I recommend a stop at the Goat Lick Overlook along Highway 2, even if the likelihood of seeing any mountain goats is slim. I will admit – I have yet to see any here, and I've lost count how many times I've stopped for a 5-10 minute look. If nothing else, it makes for a nice break and provides an opportunity to visit with other curious passers-by at the two viewpoints here.

An information board explaining the goats' interest in the salt deposits along this gorge is adjacent to the parking lot. This is the first viewing point. **Search for goats along the green- and orange-colored gorge, visible below the trestle.** From my calculation, a focal length of 100mm will be more than adequate to see them along here, and 200mm+ would do better for a more detailed capture.

I've grown fond watching the frequent trains travel atop the trestle on the opposite side of the river. With accommodating clouds the colorful gorge and railway features make for an interesting composition if the wildlife pursuit doesn't pay off.

A second viewing area is to the right, at the end of a paved walkway.

Vault toilets are located at this stop as well.

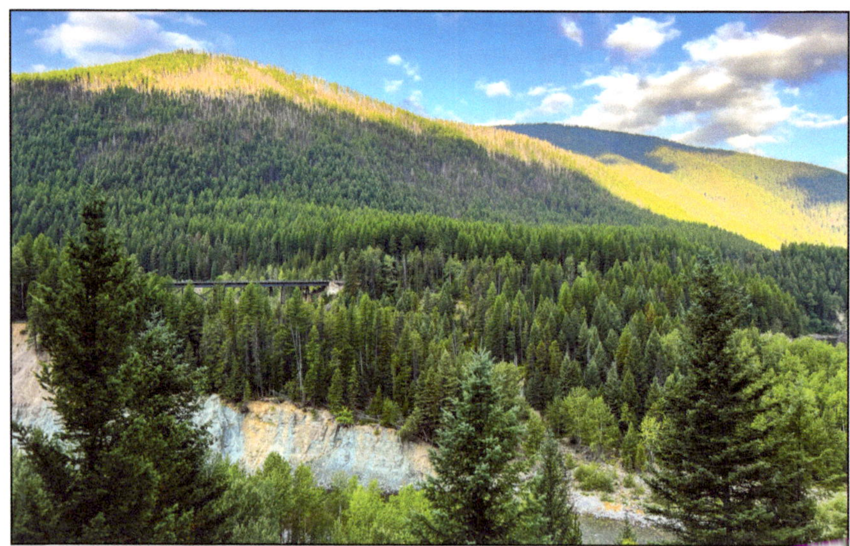

Trestle and Gorge at Goat Lick Overlook   28mm f/0 1/60s ISO100

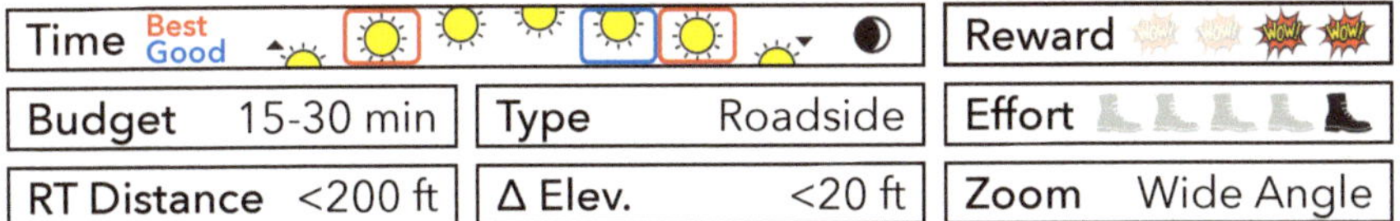

Time	Best Good	☀ ☀ ☀ ☀ ☀ ☀ ●		Reward	WOW! WOW! **WOW!** **WOW!**
Budget	15-30 min	Type	Roadside	Effort	🥾
RT Distance	<200 ft	Δ Elev.	<20 ft	Zoom	Wide Angle

Ironically, the final site in my previous book on Olympic National Park was for a location known as "Staircase." This was not planned, and I don't expect this to ever happen again. I mean really — what are the odds?

Much like Goat Lick Overlook (38), here we have another quick "point of interest" stop along the way between West Glacier and East Glacier Park.

This waterfall's intensity does vary seasonally. It is marvelous in the spring and early summer due to snowmelt, but by midsummer it slows to a mere trickle. Fortunately, it is visible from a broad pullout along Highway 2, so you'll be able to assess its state from your vehicle before loading up any photography gear. The pullout is between mile markers 188 and 189 on the south side of the road, approximately 5.5 miles east of the exit to the Goat Lick Overlook.

Trees are in abundance around the falls, so some clever framing helps to improve the composition. The image below was taken on a tripod, just off the informal space where most visitors stop and turn around. A strong breeze is typical here, but I threw caution to *that* wind and exercised a ND filter and long shutter speed, allowing for some blurred leaves.

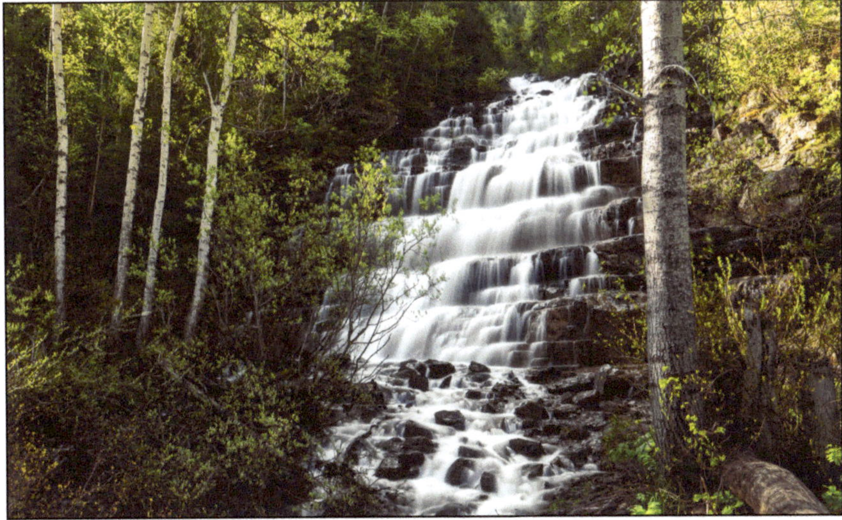

The Silver Staircase in June   24mm f/16 2s ISO50

No.	Page	Site	Time	
			Best	Good
1	46	Lake McDonald	SR & SS	AM+ thru PM+
2	50	McDonald Falls	-AM	AM+
3	52	Sacred Dancing Cascade	-AM & PM+	AM+
4	53	Trail of the Cedars +	-AM thru AM+	-PM thru PM+
5	56	Avalanche Lake	-PM thru PM+	MID
6	57	Other Lake McDonald Area Options…		
7	60	Red Rock Point	MID	AM+ & -PM
8	61	Bird Woman Falls Viewpoints	-AM	-PM
9	64	Granite Park	PM+	-AM thru -PM
10	68	Big Bend	SS	AM+ & PM+
11	70	Oberlin Bend	PM+	-PM
12	72	Highline Trail Outset	MID thru -PM	AM+
13	76	Logan Pass	PM+ thru SS	AM+ & -PM
14	78	Hidden Lake Overlook	AM+	MID
15	82	Siyeh Cascade	AM+	MID
16	84	St. Mary Falls & Virginia Falls	-AM thru AM+	MID
17	87	Sunrift Gorge & Baring Falls	-AM thru AM+	MID
18	89	Sun Point	AM+	-AM & MID
19	90	Wild Goose Island Overlook	SR & Nighttime	-AM thru -PM
20	92	Nighttime Car Light Trails	Nighttime	-
21	95	St. Mary Lake Boat Tour	-AM thru MID	-PM thru PM+
22	97	St. Mary River Bridge	AM+	MID
23	98	Beaver Pond Loop	-PM	AM+ thru MID
24	102	Apikuni Falls	AM+	-AM & MID
25	104	Many Glacier Boat Tour	-AM & PM+	AM+ thru -PM
26	106	Swiftcurrent Nature Trail	-AM thru AM+	MID thru -PM
27	107	Grinnell Lake	AM+ thru MID	-PM
28	109	Grinnell Glacier	AM+	MID
29	112	Fishercap Lake	-AM	PM+
30	114	Redrock Falls	-AM	AM+
31	116	Running Eagle Falls	-PM	PM+
32	118	Scenic Point Trail	AM+	MID thru -PM
33	122	Two Medicine Lake	SR	-AM thru MID
34	123	Paradise Point	-AM thru AM+	MID thru PM+
35	124	Aster Falls & Aster Park	-PM thru PM+	MID
36	128	Polebridge & Bowman Lake	-PM thru PM+	MID
37	131	Forest and Fire Nature Trail	-AM thru AM+	-PM thru PM+
38	132	Goat Lick Overlook	-AM thru AM+	MID
39	133	Silver Staircase Waterfall	-AM & PM+	-PM

Reward	Budget	Type	Effort	RT Distance	Δ Elevation	Zoom
4	45-60 min	Meandering	1	<0.3 mi	<30 ft	Whole Kit!
3	45-60 min	Out & Back	2	~400 ft	~50 ft	Wide, Norm
2	30 min	Out & Back	2	~800 ft	~30 ft	Normal
3	1-1.5 hr	Loop	2	~1.1 mi	~80 ft	Wide, Norm
4	2-3 hr	Out & Back	4	~4.0 mi	~500 ft	Wide, Norm
(Varies)						
2	15 min	Roadside	0	~250 ft	~20 ft	Wide Angle
1	15 min	Roadside	0	<200 ft	<10 ft	Norm, Tele
4	5-7 hr	Out & Back	5	~8.4 mi	~2,400 ft	Wide, Tele
4	30-45 min	Roadside	0	<200 ft	<10 ft	Normal
2	30 min	Roadside	1	<0.3 mi	<30 ft	Wide, Tele
3	1 hr	Out & Back	2	~1.3 mi	~120 ft	Whole Kit!
2	30-45 min	Meandering	0	<0.4 mi	~50 ft	Norm, Tele
4	1.5-2.5 hr	Out & Back	4	~2.8 mi	~460 ft	Whole Kit!
3	30 min	Out & Back	2	~0.3 mi	~30 ft	Normal
4	2-3 hr	Out & Back	3	~3.2 mi	~190 ft	Wide, Norm
3	45-60 min	Out & Back	2	~0.7 mi	~250 ft	Wide, Norm
2	30-45 min	Out & Back	2	~0.4 mi	~30 ft	Normal
4	45-60 min	Roadside	1	<300 ft	<20 ft	Whole Kit!
3	30-45 min	Roadside	0	<200 ft	<10 ft	Wide Angle
3	1.5 hr	Out & Back	1	~0.2 mi	~30 ft	Wide, Tele
2	15-30 min	Roadside	1	<500 ft	<10 ft	Normal
2	2-2.5 hr	Loop	3	~3.3 mi	~250 ft	Norm, Tele
3	1.5-2 hr	Out & Back	3	~1.9 mi	~640 ft	Normal
3	1.5 hr	Out & Back	1	~0.4 mi	~50 ft	Wide, Tele
1	1-2 hr	Loop	2	~2.5 mi	~30 ft	Normal
4	3-4 hr	Out & Back	4	~7.0 mi	~80 ft	Wide, Tele
4	6-8 hr	Out & Back	5	~10.6 mi	~1,600 ft	Wide, Tele
2	45 min	Out & Back	1	~0.6 mi	~20 ft	Wide, Tele
4	1.5-2.5 hr	Out & Back	3	~3.6 mi	~170 ft	Wide Angle
4	30-45 min	Out & Back	1	~0.6 mi	<30 ft	Normal
4	5-7 hr	Out & Back	5	~7.6 mi	~2,300 ft	Norm, Tele
4	45-60 min	Meandering	1	<500 ft	<20 ft	Wide, Norm
1	45-60 min	Out & Back	2	~1.4 mi	~100 ft	Wide Angle
3	2.5-3.5 hr	Out & Back	4	~4.0 mi	~670 ft	Wide Angle
2	30 min	Meandering	1	<0.2 mi	<20 ft	Whole Kit!
1	30-45 min	Lollipop Loop	2	~1.1 mi	~60 ft	Normal
1	15 min	Out & Back	0	~700 ft	<10 ft	Norm, Tele
2	15-30 min	Roadside	1	<200 ft	<20 ft	Wide Angle

About the Author

Anthony Jones, who friends and family call "AJ," lives in the Seattle, Washington area with his wife and their two daughters.

In April 2011 he visited Joshua Tree National Park, laying the foundation for what would become regular photography pilgrimages to many other U.S. National Parks.

AJ enjoys the planning and logistics aspect of a trip as much as the trip itself, and in so he realized a shortage of available books focused on the photographer's specific needs while visiting national parks. Thus, his idea to write a series of these types of books was born...

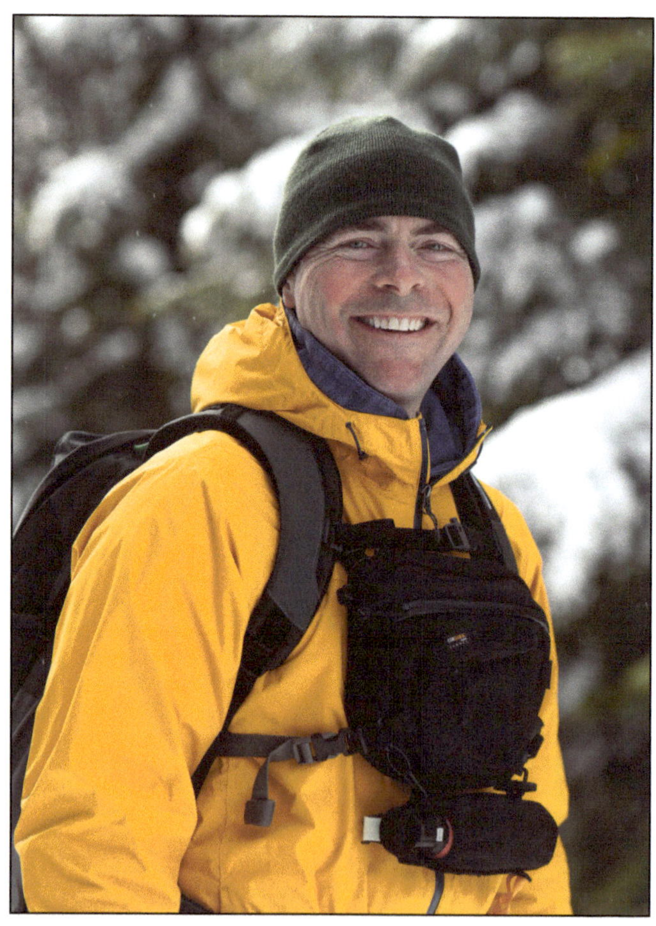

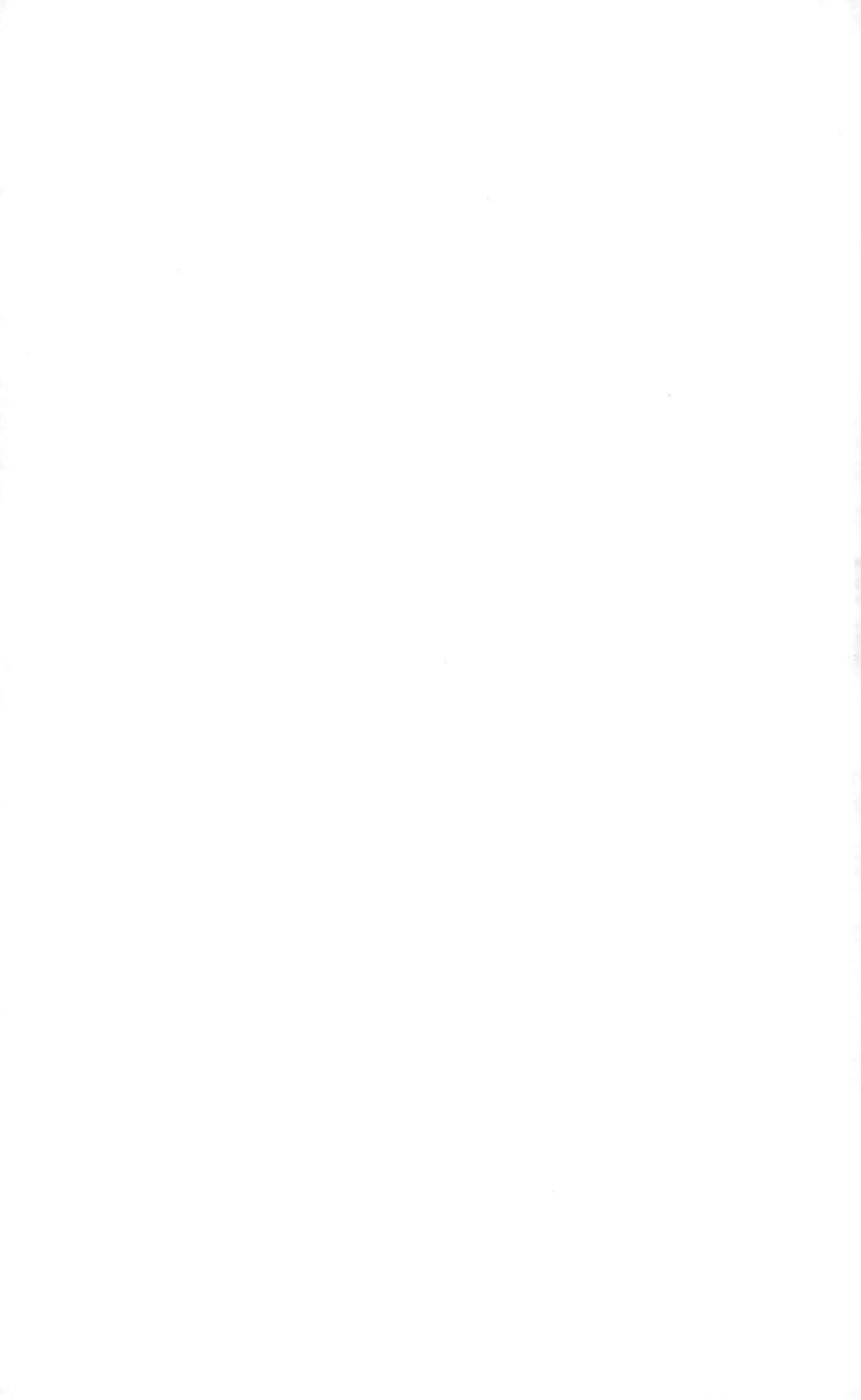

9 781732 168046

y life forever changed in 2019 when my son stepped off the roof of a seven-story hotel and plunged to his death. He was twenty-three, and his suicide was the final gut punch at the end of four years of ineffective hospitalizations, incarcerations, and homelessness. As he sunk deeper and deeper into a mental abyss, I also spiraled downward. I was a mom who always tried everything to keep my family well and safe. Yet I could not save my son.

I watched Calvin die three ways: to his bipolar illness, to a dysfunctional system, and to suicide. His severe mental illness (SMI) was treatable, but like many mothers I watched my son disappear within a system that wasn't built to save him. Calvin's death left me at the bottom of a deep and dark well. Alone. Books about grief didn't know my brand of pain, or what I might need to pull myself up to a place where happiness might be accessible again. This is my story about ambiguous loss and how I learned to live well alongside my grief.

If someone you love is lost in the abyss, this book is for you. You may feel like your person is gone, but you aren't really sure. They might get better and come back to you as someone you recognize, but they might not. That is the essence of an ambiguous loss, when someone is *gone but not gone*. You may not even know you are grieving because your loss is so unclear. Your hopes are mixed with dread. It's hard to take a deep breath when it feels more reasonable to hold it until something changes for the better.

Go ahead and let that breath out right now. All the way. It's okay. I've been there, and I was so glad when I started to breathe again. Now take a steady breath in, through your nose. Make your mouth into an "O" and slowly move the breath out, like blowing up a balloon. Easy does it. I hope you are breathing the whole time you're reading. I hope that by learning more about me, you will learn more about you. This book provides tools and a new way to look at your life and how you might begin to heal even if your crises are ongoing. If you feel like your life is on hold because of the ongoing trauma, give yourself permission right now to believe that you can start to feel better even if your life doesn't right itself.

This book supports your healing three ways, with self-directed coping guidelines, inspiration to share your story for advocacy impact, and tips for cultivating community. You may choose all three or focus on one or two. I offer self-help tips throughout the book, with "do now" suggestions. Make notes and spend time with those inquiries to get the most from this book. Feel free also to just read the book. You can come back to the exercises anytime.

Throughout your healing journey, please keep this big-picture question top of mind: *What is the thing you aren't doing because grief has gotten in your way?* My hope is that by the end of this book, you're going to know and start doing it.

> ### Do now:
>
> 1. *Choose a note-taking tool to use with this book. It might be a journal, a binder, a sketchbook, a word processing folder, or something else.*
>
> 2. *On page one, write this question: "What is the thing you aren't doing because grief has gotten in your way?"*
>
> 3. *Jot down any immediate answers, and leave room for more.*

How Do You Brace for Waves This Big?

If you're reading this book, you've probably been through something pretty rough. Maybe you're in the middle of it. Perhaps you see clearly that what's coming isn't likely to feel any easier for quite a long time. You may think your own self-care and coping will just have to wait for calmer days. Please keep reading, and stay open to the possibility of a mind shift.

I'm a surfer, so I like using the ocean as a metaphor. When you're a surfer, you watch the waves and try to anticipate what's going to line up with your level of skill, strength, and energy. To surf smart, you stay home when it's way too massive or when the tides create dangerous currents. But even when you're staying dry, you keep your eye on the conditions. When things settle enough for you to see your way into the water, you paddle out. You commit, even though what's about to happen is entirely ambiguous.

You know you need to go when not going feels wrong, like cheating yourself out of your own best reasons for being. When I first stood up on a board in Hawaii, just before I turned forty, I felt fear, anxiety, surprise, freedom, and pride all at once. I'm pretty sure our big blue planet paused for a moment while I perched on a peak of glory. That's called "stoke." I was so stoked. I also fell down. A lot.

As you find your flow on this journey of coping with ambiguous loss, prepare for a mix of emotions. It's normal to feel afraid or anxious. You may feel surprised by new concepts or perspectives. You may sense freedom as you let go of guilt or stop trying to control things that aren't yours to manage. You can expect to fall and get back up many times. Please be proud of yourself for trying new approaches! I hope you feel stoked, with a sense that turning back would be cheating yourself out of something important.

Grief may always come in waves of unpredictable size and power. You'll most likely carve through some with grace and tumble through others. Take a break when you need to steady your breath or reorient yourself. Then feel into what's happening, what you need to feel balanced. With practice, patience, and time, you'll find strength and direction while you teach yourself to heal.

> ***Do now:***
>
> *Write down and consider these questions:*
>
> *1. What am I eager to discover about myself?*
>
> *2. What am I afraid to discover about myself?*

As I think of myself twenty years ago, I'm glad I had no idea what was coming to knock me out of my life. I also see that I was discovering things about myself that would provide strength after everything changed. All in all, my forties was a fun ride. Bright memories flicker past like the montage at the start of a movie, setting up the plot by creating contrast. Life was so good!

Our family had a Eurovan camper, and we put a hundred thousand miles on it. We surfed the Pacific Ocean from Canada to Baja. We headed west whenever we could get away from our home and jobs in Vancouver, Washington. Calvin was a natural swimmer and learned to boogie board, skim board, and surf like he learned to scoot, crawl, and walk, a natural flow through his ages and stages.

Our glory days and his development devolved when SMI changed his brain, when he was nineteen and I was forty-nine. That math was always easy because he was born right before I turned thirty. He died when he was twenty-three and I was fifty-three. As I turn sixty at the start of 2026, I realize what a rough decade this has been, with ambiguous loss as a dominant theme. I've learned a lot to make it through. Grief will always have the power to hold me down, but now I know how to catch my breath and carry on.

Welcome back to 2015, the year my ambiguous loss story started on the Oregon coast.

The moment you first realize something is wrong with a child, seriously wrong, is burned into memory. My moment came with a phone call on a warm, sunny Valentine's Day. I was wearing red heart-shaped sunglasses and a pink-and-gray floral tank top with a long skinny skirt from the surf shop next to the pub where my husband, Matt, and I were enjoying a pint on the patio after a fun longboard session. My hair was still a little salty. I have a favorite picture from that afternoon, with me sitting on Matt's lap, laughing with other surfers. I call it the last moment of the "before times."

I had no idea about the horror that was ahead, but there was an inkling, a sense that all of our lives were going to change forever and not for the better. When my son called, he was talking really fast. He was extremely upset, but I couldn't quite figure out the details of what needed fixing. All I knew was that we needed to leave the beach right away to pick him up from college and take him home with us. I don't know if the weather changed, but a cloud came over me that wasn't going to lift for a very, very long time.

This book is my survivalist story and toolkit. I learned that I could recover alongside never-ending grief, and you can too. Our families are a club that no one joins by choice, but we are a community, and we can help one another heal. I hope you are helped by this book that honors my son, Calvin, who died much too soon.

Do now:

1. *Write this down: "I am not alone."*

2. *Make a few notes about the moment when you first knew your life was forever changed. Was there any clarity about what you were losing?*

What Ambiguous Losses Have Affected You?

If you are grieving because someone you care about has SMI, I'm talking directly to you throughout this book. You and I have been waiting a long time to be seen and understood. With all my heart, I want this book to support you.

Keep reading also if your ambiguous loss is unrelated to SMI. Maybe your loved one has dementia, or you've had a miscarriage. If someone you love was murdered or died from suicide, your losses include ambiguous elements that complicate grief. Even if you are grieving a more typical loss, perhaps because someone died in a car crash or from cancer, you can benefit from these guidelines that help you reorder your life around the loss. All flavors of grief unite those of us seeking a way onward.

My son's story exposes my grief wounds and shows how I learned to heal. You can too, and Part 3 is your coping guidebook. Skip ahead anytime you want to and read at your own pace. Take the time you need to really feel whatever is happening as you uncover emotions that could be locked up pretty tight. If you've been protecting yourself from those feelings, you will need to be extra kind and patient with yourself as you start to turn the key.

Some of this work is introspective, and some is best done in community. I urge you to talk with people you trust as you progress toward coping. You might even start a book club/support group using instructions I offer in the appendices.

If your loved one with a brain-based condition is doing pretty well, they might appreciate some concepts in this book. Their ambiguous losses are different from yours and uniquely complicated. I wish I could have taught my son the term ambiguous loss, to give him words to describe what hurt so deeply. I realize he got to be a child but lost his adulthood. He wanted to be a husband and father, with a home and a noble career. When he was very unwell, he had a fixed delusional belief that he was married to a young woman he barely knew but admired. His brain made up soothing stories, maybe to mask his deep sense of loss.

Because I've gotten so open about sharing my story, summarized in Part 2, I've come to learn that almost everyone has linkages to ambiguous loss and mental illness. It's usually a sorrowful story with only one or two degrees of separation from a person's immediate family. I hope this book helps all who are impacted by mental illness in unique and individualized ways.

If you're receiving therapy or counseling, ask the professional to consider ambiguous loss as part of what you work on. Some people who have studied with me have benefited from this approach. Your therapist may need additional guidance and can refer to books by Dr. Pauline Boss, professor emeritus of family social science and a family therapist who coined the term ambiguous loss and core concepts for coping.

One mom recalled learning about ambiguous loss years before she met me. "It was such a relief," she said. "What I was feeling had a name. I wasn't imagining it. So, armed with that description, I went to a therapist. I thought surely she would know about it and be able to give me tools to cope. But she had never heard of it. Her process, while it may have helped people with typical grief, was not helpful in my situation."

This book is informational, not clinical, but if you are a therapist or counselor, please consider ambiguous loss as an important aspect of what your clients might be going through. The tool of "both, and . . . " thinking, developed by Dr. Boss, is threaded throughout this book as an overarching concept for living with ambiguous loss. Healing comes when we can live with unresolvable losses *and* experience moments of peace or even joy. That's tough to feel in a society that tends to see grief as a pathology to fix before life resumes. If you take the approach that ambiguity isn't fixable and closure isn't coming, grief can be illuminated and honored while life moves onward.

There's more about Dr. Boss and my studies with her in this orientation. Part 1 also explains what I mean by severe mental illness (SMI), provides context for my professional work with families, and offers an overview of how the SMI treatment system got so messed up. This section might inspire you toward systems-change advocacy, which is an important part of healing for some people who have felt disempowered by injustice.

> ***Do now:***
>
> 1. *List people in your life that you have lost ambiguously and what led to the loss (SMI, dementia, suicide . . .).*
>
> 2. *List people who support you—those you might talk with about ambiguous loss at some point.*

You Up in the Night, Like Me?

Sleeplessness has chased me since my childhood. I was an anxious student anyway but also vulnerable to mean girls who saw how sensitive I was and used my tears to fuel their power trips. So I was no stranger to startling awake and preparing for battle when my little boy suffered night terrors and anxiety about cruel kids at school. Back then I knew how to settle him and take action to get the bullies off his back.

When his terror came at all times of night and day, and the taunts and jeers came from voices that weren't real to anyone but him, I was completely lost. My son's psychosis challenged everything I thought I knew about keeping him safe. That bully in his brain seemed to have all the power, and anyone with authority seemed as disempowered as a weary playground aide who watches and waits until someone has a broken nose.

During the worst years of Calvin's illness, I managed my nighttime panic attacks by reading and writing. During an early episode, I wrote about how people like Calvin are harmed by a treatment system that requires violence and therefore drives really unwell people straight toward jail. I called what I wrote "The Catch-22 in our medical/legal system that criminalizes mental illness."

I included this: "Can you imagine being desperately afraid because your son, twice your size, with eyes that are dark and wild, tells you to get away, because you are a witch, a devil, a vampire? Can you imagine calling the crisis hotline and doing your best to describe the terrifying, deep psychosis that is staring you down—and a bored-sounding woman tells you to lock your bedroom door, wear earplugs, and call the police if someone gets hurt? She says, 'There's nothing we can do. He's obviously quite symptomatic, but it's not illegal to be psychotic.' "

By then I knew about Treatment Advocacy Center (TAC), a national nonprofit focused on SMI. TAC was the only place that seemed to *get* me. Eliminating treatment barriers for people as sick as my son was their whole mission. I felt a bit more restful after I found my people.

I sent TAC what I wrote, and it was published as a *Personally Speaking* blog. Author Pete Earley, a Pulitzer-Prize finalist for *Crazy: A Father's Search Through America's Mental Health Madness*, republished my blog and it was read by thousands of people.

Publishing that piece about my predicament was validating. I now had eyewitnesses, and everyone knew ours wasn't the only family caught in this catch-22. As I found my voice, it helped me start to cope and to heal myself, even as my son continued to struggle and suffer.

My nighttime wonderings continued, fueling my daylight desire to speak in any venue with important ears. At public forums and legislative town halls, I explained injustices in the medical and legal systems that intersect with mental illness. I showed up at a library when Disability Rights Washington (DRW) reserved a room for "listening" to lived experiences related to criminalization of illness. I explained how my son was trapped by the criminal system because no one would hospitalize him before he got psychotic enough to get arrested.

I was shushed and told to stay "on topic." As it turns out, DRW and like-minded organizations fight against involuntary medical services, prioritizing autonomy at all costs. That evening, I used words that should not be uttered in a library—and not quietly.

My shrieking got shriller as my message clarified: "Someone has to do something about this!" A quiet realization forced me to settle down and take a good, long look in the mirror. Me. That someone who needed to do something meant me. Although I really only know this in hindsight, the catch-22 I wrote about on a night when I couldn't sleep launched my new life plan.

By writing about the systemic reasons for our plight, I also stopped blaming myself. I knew my son wasn't suffering because of bad mothering, and I knew good mothering wouldn't save him. I knew other parents like me, and my catch-22 essay spoke for all of us:

"We are struggling to rescue our children from medical and legal systems that don't make any sense. Our systems institute punishment when help is desperately needed. They deny access to services and then blame individuals who are severely impaired for not solving their own crises. They push people to a precarious edge and then kick. Mental illness has become a crime."

On April 1, 2023, working at TAC became my day job. No fooling. As resource and advocacy manager, I regularly speak with families in circumstances as dire as those I experienced while my son was living. Often a loved one has an SMI condition that renders them too sick to save themselves and yet not sick enough for any system to be obliged to save them. Meeting other families and troubleshooting is a perfect fit with my need for direction and purpose.

Shortly after I was hired, TAC named me its D. J. Jaffe Advocate, which honors the author of *Insane Consequences: How the Mental Health Industry Fails the Mentally Ill*. Jaffe, who died from cancer in 2020, has inspired many grassroots advocates like me, and I'm proud to contribute to his legacy.

I chose ambiguous loss as my D. J. Jaffe Advocate project and researched the topic in depth before building online resources for TAC's website and launching an online seminar program. One sleepless mom found my YouTube video in a moment of need. "I can't remember how I first learned about ambiguous loss," says Ellen F., "but at three am, in the middle of a grief meltdown, I hid my phone under the blankets so I would not wake up my husband and typed 'ambiguous loss.' I found Jerri's video, and she was talking about ambiguous loss in the context of mental illness. I thought, 'Wow! This woman gets it!' The next morning, I looked up TAC and called Jerri."

I remember taking Ellen's call while parked by a grocery store. She was so delighted to speak with someone who understood her. She paused our conversation to say to her husband, "She's real! She's on the phone with me!"

An excerpt from *The Velveteen Rabbit*, by Margery Williams, sparks in my mind: " *'Real isn't how you are made,' said the Skin Horse. 'It's a thing that happens to you.'* "

As people from families like mine started to see me, really see me, I felt real, no longer shushed and bullied by people who didn't want to hear the inconvenience of my truth. My son's illness and death crushed me, but my life mattered to people I hadn't even met. You are one of those people. The synergy of healing together has been a key feature of this ambiguous loss work. If you don't already know other SMI moms, dads, siblings, spouses, find us!

Ellen, who has two adult children with mental illness and is an active member of our seminar alumni community, says the ambiguous loss work has changed her life. "I don't know what I would have done had I not seen that video that night," she says.

Another participant listened through the hourlong weekly seminar sessions over two months, never raising her hand or unmuting herself during discussions. Near the end of the final meeting, she quietly shared, "Watching all of you try on your emotions makes me think maybe I can too."

Do now:

1. *If there are persistent thoughts or fears that interrupt your sleep, write them down.*

2. *Is what you've written just for you, or do you need to share it somewhere, now or later?*

Are You Ready to See Your Losses?

As you progress through this book, I encourage you to try on your emotions. Work at your pace, and give yourself grace as you prepare to consider who you might be now that painful things have happened that were not yours to control. If an ambiguous loss has made you sad, it's because you are a kind and feeling person who has been hurt—not because you are broken or lack the willpower to get over it and move on. Expecting that is cruel.

Through grieving with skill and intention, you can move onward, but no one gets over an ambiguous loss. I'm sorry, but this book isn't going to cure your grief. Because of ambiguity, there is no closure. If you can, take a moment to accept that right now. You cannot heal *from* an ambiguous loss; instead, you can heal *with* an ambiguous loss.

Think of it like purchasing a ticket for a journey toward healing. The losses will travel with you, but there will be a lot of other things to see along the way, and not everything will be hurtful into the future.

Do now:

Write down these statements and then say them out loud or inside your own head:

1. *There will never be closure because my losses are ambiguous.*

2. *Grief and loss are not everything that I am and do.*

3. *I can feel many things at once.*

Unrecognized loss leads to all sorts of issues, including emotions that may feel like a mismatch for the moment. If someone you care for is struggling with SMI, you may be asking, "Why do I feel like I'm grieving the loss of them while I'm spending every day and night trying to save them?" Or you might think, "People say I'm lucky they're still alive. Why do I feel entirely unlucky?" Or this: "It doesn't feel like they're living, even though they are technically alive."

If nothing is leading toward a solution to a loved one's ongoing and worsening SMI crisis, you may have feelings that your loved one's death would be a relief. I remember those thoughts clearly. Sometimes they came out like this: "When is this speeding train finally going to crash so I can get some damn rest?"

I've shared with other parents that my son's eventual death brought relief alongside grief. Some say they're grateful that I'm willing to say out loud what feels radical and uncondoned. I admit that those ambivalent feelings of grief and relief brought a lot of guilt at first. I kept them to myself until I had taken a deep dive into ambiguous loss work and learned how normal I was. I started by acknowledging that I'd lost things, big things. Are you ready to take a peek at your own losses? I'm right here. Give it a go.

> ### *Do now:*
>
> 1. *Write down at least three things that have broken your heart.*
>
> 2. *Look at your list, really look. What does it feel like to write down what's been lost? Sit with that for a few moments, and then consider these prompts:*
>
>   - *Does making this list feel like a release of pressure?*
>
>   - *Does it feel like you're breaking an unwritten rule?*
>
>   - *Do you feel guilty? (Hmm, what's that about?)*
>
>   - *What else do you need to write down, right now?*

Did you do it? Good job. This isn't easy.

Please take three long breaths, directing compassion inward for these things that have hurt you and are not your fault. If guilt is tugging at you, imagine giving it a little pat on the head, reminding it to quiet down and stop speaking out of turn.

There are no wrong answers to any of these questions. The point is to consider them, spend some time with them—and yourself! You will learn more about listing your losses in the chapter about how to make meaning, but here are a few more thoughts as you get going on your healing journey:

- Some losses are tangible. Some people impacted by SMI have lost their jobs, homes, finances, cars, and other major resources.
- Other losses are intangible: hopes, dreams, plans, goals, connections, understandings, traditions, sense of safety, etc.
- A complicated common loss is trust. When you always thought a person you love would be part of your safe inner circle, it hurts like crazy to see them on the outside of that circle because untreated or under-treated SMI has made them dangerous.

Keep your guard up against people who might say you are "worsening stigma" by talking about what's real and happening in your family because of SMI. If it's inconvenient for someone to know the truth, that's their issue, not yours. SMI-impacted families hear mixed messages: Wait until a loved one is so dangerous that the system must act, but please stop talking about SMI like it makes someone dangerous.

If you and your loved one with SMI stay invisible, the system is off the hook. Please tell your truth and help the world catch on that our families want what everyone wants: treatment before tragedy! We want help before trust is broken and there is risk of harm. That's how stigma stops, not by hiding in the shadows. First you have to deal with any sense of shame, though.

Taking out an order of protection to keep my son from coming home was a gut punch that still makes me nauseous to think about. I lost my ability to be that mom who always kept a hidden spare key and the lights on, with a warm meal and a freshly made bed ready and waiting. Oh, I felt so much shame about that! Talking to people in similar predicaments helps, knowing that there was danger—that my fears were based in facts. My son never physically hurt me, but I know so many moms who have been cut, beaten, shot, strangled. I'm not promoting stigma: I'm telling the truth! Untreated and undertreated psychosis makes someone unreliable and sometimes dangerous. Please keep yourself safe and find a way to cope with the emotions that come up because you must save yourself.

During the two years that Calvin couldn't come home, I often wandered through his bedroom, wishing him well enough to return one day. I burned a candle in there with the window open, to discharge painful memories. The cleansing felt helpful. It was something I could do when there wasn't much else.

In my young adult years, I was social, with multiple friend groups and a busy calendar. After my son got sick, I was lonely. I lost trust that other people would listen, understand, or even be kind. I felt bitter and unfriendly, and from my vantage point those expressions reflected both ways. The world didn't make sense anymore, and I lost trust that every little thing would actually ever be okay.

Now I know that without acknowledgment and active coping, losses like mine can lead to anxiety and depression, a confused sense of self, an overbearing need to control everything, and complicated relationship conflicts. Yep, I've felt all that. I didn't get stuck there though, and you don't have to either. This book offers new hope for a good life that can coexist with unresolvable losses. New hope is the sixth coping guideline, by the way. You'll get there!

I'll do my best to be a patient tour guide, but I'm just so stoked for you to learn what it took me a long time to figure out. Dang, I wish somebody had authored a book like this for me!

Your list of what you've lost is like the suitcase you're packing for your trip through this book. Welcome aboard!

Do now:

1. *Take three steady breaths, counting to four on the inbreath and four on the outbreath.*

2. *Look at your list of losses again. Is there anything you want to add?*

3. *On a fresh page, write yourself a short thank-you note for beginning this project.*

P.S. If you've bumped into resistance and don't want to journal or use these prompts, give yourself permission to just read the book, like auditing a course. It's okay. You can come back to these concepts anytime, when you are ready. If everything feels like a plane crash in your life right now, please put on your oxygen mask. Your self-care helps everyone in your orbit.

Who Came Up with the Term Ambiguous Loss?

As mentioned earlier, the concept of ambiguous loss was developed by Pauline Boss, PhD, whose theories informed this book. In her research and books, Dr. Boss describes two types of ambiguous loss: the kind where a person is psychologically absent but physically present and the kind where a person is physically absent but psychologically present. The first describes a loss caused by someone being emotionally distant or impaired by a brain-based condition. The second describes a loss when someone is missing, imprisoned, or physically inaccessible for other reasons. An ambiguous loss related to mental illness might be both types: For example, a person in psychosis could also be physically missing, homeless, or incarcerated.

A death can cause ambiguous loss if the person dies from enigmatic circumstances, such as homicide, terrorism, or suicide. Survivors can struggle if grief is frozen because the loss is intensely difficult to understand or accept. Keeping memories alive is a start toward coping.

According to Dr. Boss, an ambiguous loss is the most stressful type of loss because resolution is impossible and because it's related to a situation that goes far beyond human expectation. Let's spend a little more time with that last part and break it down. An ambiguous loss is related to a situation that goes far beyond human expectation.

- Ambiguous loss results from a highly stressful situation and is not a pathological condition. The situation is messed up, not you!
- This loss is beyond expectation, not something anyone could prepare to face. Not being ready for something no one predicted is not your fault, right?

> ***Do now:***
>
> 1. *Write down something in your experience that has caused grief because the situation itself goes far beyond human expectation.*
>
> 2. *Explain to yourself why this unexpected circumstance was not yours to control or prevent.*

Lessons learned from Dr. Boss are throughout this book. I was certified to train others about ambiguous loss in her online course from the University of Minnesota. I read her seminal book, *Loss, Trauma, and Resilience: Therapeutic Work with Ambiguous Loss*, which is valuable for clinicians as well as anyone experiencing ambiguous loss. I also read *The Myth of Closure: Ambiguous Loss in a Time of Pandemic and Change*, in which Dr. Boss describes what it means to lose trust in the world as a safe place. Ironically, I completed her online certification course while bedridden with COVID. I was too agitated by grief and loss to lie still and rest! Learning more about ambiguous loss helped me heal in every way.

That was four years after my son died, right after I started working at Treatment Advocacy Center in 2023. As a member of TAC's Helpline Team, I was doing my best to support people trying to navigate systems full of gaps and barriers. I felt inadequate when they shared their despair. One mom, whose adult child was going to the hospital for the fourth time in two months, said, "Every time this happens, it's like another death." These family members knew they were grieving, but they didn't know how.

Similar comments were common in online groups. I noticed this as a theme: "It's like he's dead, but I'm still trying to keep him alive. I feel guilty about thinking about my own grief while he's still suffering so much." It was while helping one of those confused souls find an article about ambiguous loss that I realized I wanted to know more about ambiguous loss—a lot more!

Digging around online led me to Dr. Boss, and I sent her an email to ask if any of her research specifically focused on SMI. The answer was no, although her books include mental illness as one common cause for ambiguous loss. Still, she seemed delighted that I reached out and encouraged me to take her course and then teach others to cope.

That's what led me to train people specifically impacted by SMI about ambiguous loss. Seminar participant stories are included in this book. A few wanted their names included. All gave permission for me to share their words and insights.

> ***Do now:***
>
> 1. *Try to explain ambiguous loss in your own words and/or write down this: Ambiguous loss describes an experience of loss when the cause lacks clarity or resolution.*
>
> 2. *Make a few notes about psychological and/or physical absence, as these terms relate to your ambiguous losses.*
>
> 3. *How would you tell a friend why these concepts are helpful to you?*

What Is Severe Mental Illness (SMI)?

I'm using SMI to refer to severe mental illness. I mean conditions along the schizophrenia, bipolar, and major depressive disorder spectrums. I'm talking about the most extreme versions of these conditions—those that come with psychosis and other symptoms that are chronic and disabling. SMI changes everything about how a family functions. Anyone can use this book as guidance for managing grief, but I focused on grief related to SMI because the experiences of families like mine are underrepresented in other books about loss and grief.

Many people with SMI don't know they're sick because of a symptom called anosognosia. This lack of self-awareness, also called insight, is the most common reason a person with SMI refuses or stops treatment. Just like you cannot convince a person experiencing psychosis that their delusions or hallucinations aren't real, you cannot convince a person with anosognosia that they have a mental illness. It's not that they refuse to admit they are ill: They know they are not ill. At least half of people with SMI experience anosognosia some or all of the time.

Skipping appointments and tossing medication, like my son did in the weeks before he died, seems rational when a person with anosognosia is unable to see the illness or recognize the benefits of treatment. My son was diagnosed with severe bipolar disorder with psychotic features, and for him anosognosia cycled alongside his extreme states of mania and psychosis. His inability to see that he was sick when he was most definitely sick made everything about helping him more difficult. Anosognosia also made my sense of loss more heartbreaking because I could see how vulnerable he was, but he couldn't.

Other writers and many researchers define SMI as "serious" instead of "severe" mental illness. Those definitions are generally broader and might include anxiety, eating, or personality disorders that can significantly impair a person but don't always come with psychosis and/or anosognosia.

People impacted by any mental illness may experience ambiguous loss and can benefit from intentional approaches to coping. This book is for all, with a special nod to the SMI-impacted families that often feel additionally marginalized by the mental health treatment system, including for their own care and recovery.

> ***Do now:***
>
> 1. *Write down any illness conditions that have contributed to the ambiguous losses in your life.*
>
> 2. *In your own words, explain how those illnesses weren't caused by anything you did or didn't do.*

What Makes an SMI Loss Ambiguous?

Grieving is typically something people do while a death certificate is on its way through the mail. With the exception of deaths that lack clarity (suicide, homicide, terrorism), ambiguous losses don't usually come with direct evidence of what's been lost. When it's hard to prove your loss, it's hard to see grief is a logical and necessary human response.

That struggle is real if you love someone with SMI who is "gone," as they once were but still around as a new version of themselves. They are *gone but not gone*, the type of ambiguous loss described by Dr. Boss as physical presence with psychological absence. How much better they might ever get depends on so much that is unknown, so grieving the loss of them can feel really strange. I promise it's appropriate. You've lost so many hopes and dreams, expectations, special connections. Yes, your losses are real: They just lack clarity because they are ambiguous.

Your person with SMI also might be missing, incarcerated, homelessly wandering, or required to keep their distance because of a no-contact order. You pine for them, knowing they are unreachable. That's the type of loss Dr. Boss describes as physical absence with psychological presence. It will probably be difficult for you to give up trying to control what happens next. You can do it. You may need to read and reread the chapter about adjusting mastery.

If someone you love has died for a SMI-related reason, including suicide, their death may lack logical sense, leading to another version of ambiguous loss. Peace about the death is elusive because of what might have been with a different mental health system or different endings to the various tough episodes or conversations. *What if?* It's so hard to stop wanting the past to play out differently. You can let go of old hopes and put agency toward what is still possible. I did it, and you can, too.

I've experienced all these flavors of ambiguous loss. My son was gone *before* he was gone for good. He also had ambiguous losses of his own. He didn't get to finish college. His relationships fell apart. He kept turning up without a place to live, without a job, dazed and confused about why those things were taken from him. I remember how frustrated he got while trying to memorize a script for a sales job that never panned out. His memory had always been a steel trap, and it didn't work the same anymore. He had lost his brilliant mind.

I wish I'd had a chance to talk with Calvin about his losses. As you get comfortable with the ambiguous loss concepts, please seize any opportunity to talk among yourselves as a family about what's helping and what's still confusing. If you can think empathetically about what loss must feel like to your loved one with SMI, you may be able to have a valuable conversation. If not, having a pretend conversation with them in your own mind might help you feel closer to a part of them that you still need to cherish.

When talking about loss and grief, it's easy to get caught up in comparisons. I refuse to gauge which types of loss cause the worst grief. A wise counselor once explained that "grief contests are a cruel exercise," and I've embraced that. Seeking out and supporting others who know deep grief is a valuable human endeavor. Comparing whose grief is more troublesome can damage the connection by putting everyone in separate rooms. Everyone's pain has unique features that can be discussed more openly if all are welcomed but judgment is barred at the door. How a hurt person heals depends on so many things! When we see one another and hold each other up, we heal together.

Our SMI community benefits from understanding ambiguous loss. Most of us grew up with cultural norms that offer common ways to help one another after a typical loss from disease, age, or an accident. You drop by with soup, lasagna, a box of tissues, a pie . . . and talk about the person who passed with nostalgia or even a sense of peace that they are no longer in pain. Certain religious faiths offer something more specific, such as the Jewish tradition of sitting shiva, a protocol for mourners that lasts seven days.

No such guidance exists for ambiguous losses, and very few people outside our SMI community have any skill to help you talk about your complicated version of grief. Many turn away—perhaps because they feel inept and scared. If you are reading this book as a friend or community member, please consider delivering a literal or proverbial lasagna to someone who is grieving because of an SMI situation. You may be the first to say that you understand they are in grief.

A lack of empathy worsens isolation, which is typical for families impacted by SMI. If you're the one starved for empathy, be specific when explaining what you are hungry for: an ear that can listen, a shoulder to cry on, even a casserole when cooking feels out of reach. Explain that you are a person in grief who needs grief support, just like you would if someone died. Ask if they can be that friend for you, even though your loss is unclear and ongoing.

On the fourth of July in 2023, seven years after my dad died from cancer, and four years after my son died from suicide, I journaled about my own typical losses versus my ambiguous ones. It was right before I took the online course by Dr. Boss, so I was contemplative and a bit anxious about what I might find out about my own grief. I was at the beach, in our RV, while less-than-ideal weather and waves were also wracking my nerves because I wanted to surf but also didn't want to.

Here's what I wrote that morning, while gazing at a picture of Matt and me with my mom and dad (Judy and Jerome Niebaum), Calvin, and his friend, Christian Audova: "Sitting in the trailer this morning after a surf check (windy, a bit bigger than I prefer), I'm looking at this picture from a fun family trip along the coast when the kids were teenagers. I realize I'm remembering that I had a dream about my dad last night. I think I was arriving in death, and he was greeting me with some regret, 'I'm sorry to see you here . . . '

"I burst into tears, realizing that I'm experiencing a deep grief for the loss of my dad. I miss him so much and wish he was still here. I realize also that these feelings are ones I haven't leaned into very often. When he died, there was so much trauma. Calvin was in a psychiatric hospital. His illness cycled dangerously from that point onward, and then his death three years later took over most of the grief space in my head and heart. I lost my dad, and nothing ever felt quite right in our family again.

"Maybe this is bubbling up because I'm reading a book about ambiguous loss. Losing my elderly dad to cancer wasn't ambiguous, but my grief process was layered with the anxiety and profound fear I was experiencing at that same time because of Calvin's out-of-control illness and my confusion about my role in trying to save him.

"It was obvious that I could not save my dad. Bearing witness was the best and only way to be while he said a final goodbye. I could not gracefully bear witness to my son's messy episodes that tipped him toward death over and over before his actual death. I felt forced to act—but what action would make any difference? That confusing ambivalence was terrifying. How could it have been anything but?

"As I prepare to do Dr. Pauline Boss' training on ambiguous loss, stuff will continue to come up for me. I think that's going to be difficult and helpful. Today, I must decide whether to surf or observe the waves. There's a good metaphor."

That was when ambiguous loss became part of my ongoing internal dialogue. Over time, I got brave enough to talk about this concept with others. I notice when some of my seminar participants are in that timid space of watching versus doing. Some prefer to "audit" the training before they tuck into the self-reflective work. At the conclusion of one seminar, a participant was in tears as she said she wasn't sure yet if she was ready to try the exercises but that her grief was "newly different." She was curious about her subtle shift but admitted her fear of going any deeper. I've heard similar trepidations from other seminar participants, and you may experience something similar.

I hope this book emboldens you to keep going with the self-work of coping. Choose a pace that challenges but doesn't overwhelm you. You might start with a new approach to questions that inevitably come from others. For example, if someone asks how you are when nothing is okay, consider a new way to talk about the question itself, one that recognizes the tough place you are in without disclosing details of your immediate story that are too painful for the moment.

You might start with this: "Thank you so much for asking how I am. I really appreciate you for noticing my difficult situation. Have you ever heard of ambiguous loss? It's something I'm learning about.

One thing to know is that I won't ever get closure on grief because my losses are ambiguous. It's a challenge for me to even acknowledge that's what I'm going through, and that's about all I can say for now."

Here's an alternative answer if you don't have the energy to explain what ambiguous loss means: "I'm happy to talk with you about it sometime when we both have the energy, but I just don't right now. In short, I'm in grief because of losses that are beyond human expectation that are related to my loved one with a complicated mental illness. I appreciate your being my friend."

If they are a true friend that you know might be supportive, you might share an article, video, or this book about ambiguous loss. You can explain how helpful it would be for them to understand some of the things that you're also learning. Always explain that it's okay to not have words to express something. It's nice to just know that someone wants to show up as a friend.

Do you need to pause right now? Be honest. Unless you've learned about ambiguous loss on your own, this might be all new information. If this is lighting up something in you, take a moment to pause and breathe. You are not alone. Families throughout the SMI-impacted community are similarly overwhelmed by ambiguous losses and unmanaged grief. One reader of an early draft of this book said, "I can relate to the terror and horror, and I am just so sorry that someone else fully gets this nightmare."

Welcome to the club that none of us joined by choice. I'm sorry that you're here, but because we cannot quit the club, we may as well continue learning to support ourselves and one another. Thank you for being curious and willing to learn something new. Remind yourself that ambiguous loss is not your fault. This grief is hard because it's hard, not because there's anything wrong with you.

Do now:

1. *Write down the name of someone you want to talk to about ambiguous loss, now or in the future.*

2. *Out loud or in writing, practice explaining that you're in a rough place right now but learning about ambiguous loss and how you might cope.*

Can Advocacy Help You Heal?

If your family is impacted by SMI, then you know the treatment system is built of gaps and barriers that make it more a sieve than a container for people in desperate need of care. If you feel disempowered by unfair and discriminatory systems, like I did, advocacy toward change may be part of what you need. I hope the brief historical context I offer in this chapter helps you see how we got here and what might turn things around. The "do now" options at the end include a few advocacy projects to consider.

It took a while for me to realize that our family hadn't missed the train to good care and happy outcomes. No, nobody laid down those tracks or even planned a clear route. Here's a question no one ever answers: *Who is responsible to make sure the sickest of those with SMI are okay?*

When my grandsons were toddlers, my daughter taught us a game. If there was a stinky diaper, she who smelt it first would touch her nose: "Not my problem," the gesture meant. The last to notice did the cleanup work.

In a not-funny way, state, federal, and private medical systems have all touched their noses to tap out on caring for those who are the sickest with SMI, especially the unsavory among them who cry and complain that they aren't sick and don't want anyone's stinking help anyway. That person is left with their own nose exposed. "Fine," these systems say, "Your life: You figure it out!" The result is destroyed families, homelessness, early death, and frequently incarceration—because jails and prisons are the service system of last resort.

This rigged game is the outcome of various decisions and indecisions by people with mixed motivations and limited scope. I see our mental health system like a jumble of puzzle pieces. A few shiny services pop out, among them certified community behavioral health centers (CCBHCs), coordinated specialty care (CSC) for early episode psychosis, and assisted outpatient treatment (AOT) for court-ordered community care. I wish like everything that my son had gotten those way-too-rare services. But those centers of excellence don't notch into a cohesive bigger picture.

The puzzle we need to put together is called a continuum of care. The trouble is that nobody knows what the corner pieces might look like, what framing could scaffold the costs, or who could take charge to design, build, or run it. There's no container for noting the number of pieces needed to make a complete picture.

Meanwhile, we moms dig around behind the couch hoping to find a random piece when someone we love is in terrible trouble. Oh, and we're doing that with our hands cuffed behind our backs. One damned thing that got glued into this slapdash puzzle is that privacy protections are sacrosanct.

HIPAA, the Health Insurance Portability and Accountability Act, contributed to my lost motherhood. Although it wasn't written to block families from caring for their loved ones, misunderstandings have led to strict nondisclosure policies that have worsened patient care and torn families apart—including mine.

My blood runs hot remembering the icy day Calvin was driven 127 miles from jail in Clark County, Washington, to Western State Hospital in Steilacoom, to have his "competency restored" as part of a criminal trial. Every major road was closed for safety reasons, but my very sick boy was sliding north in the back of a squad car. My jail contact was kind enough to say that, yes, he'd been given shoes.

All morning I watched ice enshrine every outdoor surface. My heart raced as time slowed. In early afternoon I was certain he must either be at the hospital, dead, or stranded, so I called. I explained as quickly as I could: "I'm not asking for protected information or records. I want to confirm my son's safety. The ice. The roads?" Before hanging up, a monotone receptionist read a familiar HIPAA script: "We can neither confirm nor deny the presence of a patient in our facility."

I wept, wept, and wept more on that snowy December day, certain that this cold-blooded world was going to kill Calvin by Christmas if winter roads hadn't already done the deed. Eventually my son himself called, confirming he was clothed and warm, being fed. I had lost him, but he was back, sort of. Nothing was clear, and no tangible reassurance was coming any time soon.

Staff at Western State never provided a release of information for him to sign, although Calvin said he wanted one. He always signed one, even when he was really confused about whether I was who I said I was. Western State never shared a thing about my son's well-being or treatment; it just wouldn't take my calls. He called a few times, sounding fine but not fine.

Having no information about Calvin's condition or treatment was a huge problem when, after fifteen days, they abruptly drove him back to jail. It was two days before Christmas. We posted bond, knowing his tenuous stability would not last back in jail and wanting him with our family for the holidays.

Calvin met us at a nearby bail bonds office. His hair was bushy, and his fingernails were awful, but he greeted us with a broad smile. We saw our son in him: He was there! Our celebration was so short-lived.

I quickly learned that he had no prescription and no idea what pills he'd been swallowing at Western State, which still wouldn't answer the phone. Our money meant the jail was done with him, and an outpatient provider wasn't available for a week and a half. No one was any help.

I located some of his older prescriptions and became his doctor, pharmacist, therapist, case manager, parole officer. Trying to also be his mom stretched me beyond thin. I was really out of my scope. He took the pills for a few days to appease me, but he didn't believe he was sick, and his old friend mania was calling from just around a bend in his breaking mind.

Thus the "system" protected my psychotic son's privacy rights while denying him any coherent care and leaving decisions up to me, a family member kept in the dark by design. I was keening into the echo chamber of my own grief for the death of my son as I'd known him, struggling to keep what was left of him alive. After cuffing my hands, the system stepped away, a finger on every nose.

My son's psychosis was on full display by the time we made it to an outpatient appointment. There, a prescriber proud of her "person-centered care" catered to the whims of a psychotic person and delivered Calvin the perfect reason to stop taking his medicine: *He didn't want it.* He explained how upset he was about the devil's plot to poison and dismember him. The pills were clearly part of that evil plan, which his mother knew about and played into.

With dark and darting eyes, Calvin startled a nurse who attempted to take his blood pressure and nearly got evicted. They were happy to wave him onward, with permission granted to titrate down or even off his medication—up to him! The provider threatened to call security because I was angry.

That was that. Calvin spiraled. He quickly became a person no one could live with safely or sanely. All our lives were at risk, and no one who might care was willing or able to care. That prescriber never saw Calvin again. It's common for a person as ill as he to be let go as "too difficult to serve," including by some hospitals that file trespass charges after pushing out a patient.

Such abandonments are sometimes characterized as protections for a person's "autonomy." Like many moms, I was accused many times of trying to "control" my son—or "take away his choice." Oh, my dears, psychosis took his power to choose so long ago. If only someone had listened to his mom. My role was taken from me, and nobody was responsible to step up and be sure my son with SMI was going to be okay.

Ambiguous answers to the question about who's responsible may explode with importance into the near future as federal funding cuts threaten already skimpy resources and public insurance. Those few shiny puzzle pieces are getting sucked up by a powerful vacuum cleaner. We need more and better services, but instead the gaps get bigger, making it harder to imagine a continuum of care that we could ever Mod Podge and display for all to admire.

An important book about historical reasons for this mess is by E. Fuller Torrey, MD, founder of TAC who wrote *American Psychosis: How the Federal Government Destroyed the Mental Illness Treatment System.* Dr. Torrey describes the process of deinstitutionalization that coincided with the Community Mental Health Act of 1963, the final legislation signed by President John F. Kennedy before his assassination. Kennedy was inspired to envision a better treatment system by his sister, Rosemary, who was lobotomized in 1941, when she was twenty-three.

Same age as my son when he died: Ouch! Watching him die before he ever grew up was an unbelievable loss and smacks me with a back-bending fatigue every time I think about it that way. I suspect Kennedy's family experienced a similar grief.

Despite some good intentions, decisions of the 1960s were short-sighted. In *American Psychosis*, Dr. Torrey chronicles what he describes as a "lobotomy" to an already unwell system. By taking over community mental health (the body) and severing it from state hospitals (the head), the federal government essentially made an incongruent Franken-monster of public mental health.

The private medical system seems to have watched with a macabre curiosity but no interest in scripting itself a heroic role in this horror film. Tending people with SMI is hard, with loads of liability and little payoff. Many psychiatrists keep their couches clean by serving private-pay clients with mild or moderate mental health disturbances. Those patients generally arrive on time, with please and thank you on their lips and money in their pockets. Advocates call this cherry-picking.

I'm bitter about it because Calvin never got a dedicated doctor, but I do see both sides. Doctors have the right to build the lives they want with the credentials they earned. Yet it means that people with the most advanced degrees in psychiatry usually don't treat people with the most advanced psychiatric illnesses. In truth, doctors need to be incentivized and supported by public programs if they're being asked to step into this emergency situation.

Kennedy wanted to put the federal government in charge of the sickest folks, by funding mental health centers across the United States. His ideas made some sense, as disreputable asylums had become dumping grounds for poor people and others there for the wrong reasons. Ken Kesey's 1962 novel *One Flew Over the Cuckoo's Nest* evoked public furor. The sane main character was "imprisoned" at Oregon State Hospital and mistreated by an evil nurse. The solution to his problem wasn't mental health care but escape from the evil place.

My son read Kesey's book in high school, and it was still on his bookshelf when he came home from college after his first psychotic break. A memory that gives me creepy chills was when he hid that worn paperback all over the house for me to find and put back into his room. I realize now that he believed he was being mistreated like Randle McMurphy in the book. My son actually had SMI, but he didn't always know that. He needed better health care, not to escape from treatment! I eventually buried that disturbing book in our outside trash can.

Kesey's book became a movie starring Jack Nicholson in 1975, inspiring the general public to cheer loudly as most state hospitals were mothballed or radically downsized. Meanwhile, Kennedy's vision for community mental health melted like a mirage in the rear-view mirror, leaving no plan for severely sick people pushed from hospitals to homelessness.

Another catalyst for terrible outcomes was a federal law that imposed discrimination disguised as social justice: When Medicaid was established as part of the Social Security Act in 1965, it excluded inpatient reimbursement for adults receiving care in any facility with more than sixteen psychiatric beds, which was the random number assigned to define an "institution for mental disease (IMD)." Repealing the IMD exclusion is a federal advocacy project underway.

Another issue is that most remaining state hospital beds are reserved for competency restoration, kicking to the curb patients who need a bed *before* psychotic behavior leads to arrest. Those who finally get hospital beds as criminal defendants get less care because now the goal is "fitness for trial," not recovery.

Criminal and civil commitment systems need a reboot, documented in 2024 by a TAC report, "Prevention Over Punishment: Finding the Right Balance of Civil and Forensic State Psychiatric Hospital Beds." I'm quoted in TAC's qualitative supplement to the report, specifically for explaining how my son's one and only placement at Western State was ridiculous to even him. I asked if he was getting good care and he laughed: "Mom, I get pills in a cup and court classes." My heart sank with many of my last remaining old hopes that day.

Making states make their beds better is one of many tasks angry moms are taking on. We've had reasons to rage for a long minute. While offering pretty awful treatment options from the 1940s through the 1970s, psychiatry chose to also overtly blame mothers for the brain-based illnesses of their children. In *Shrinks: The Untold Story of Psychiatry*, Jeffrey A. Lieberman, MD, identifies psychiatrists as "the black sheep of medicine" while describing a full menu of misguided and outright abusive past practices, including those related to an unscientific "schizophrenogenic mother" theory. Dr. Lieberman offers his field redemption through focus on evidence-based practices. That shouldn't be pie in the sky, but the crust isn't rolled out yet for baking that idea into a starved system.

The residue from being shamed and blamed hasn't fully cleared around modern moms who are still accused of being aloof refrigerators or overbearing helicopters. Whether you're a mom, dad, sister, brother, husband, wife, or some other family member or friend, this systemic discrimination is part of why your own healing is critically important. You cannot defend your loved one or envision a better system if you don't defend your right to be respected and supported, including with your own self-care.

Phew, this chapter took the wind out of me. How are you? Please take a few steady breaths. Like me, you're just one person. One person can only do what one person can do.

There's a lot to fix, and some of this stuff is so bad a B-rate filmmaker probably wouldn't touch it. I hope these points help you digest what you've just read so you can consider what you need to prioritize for yourself.

Do now:

1. *Commit to focusing on mental health for yourself. Reading this book and integrating coping into your regular life is enough. The rest of this list is entirely optional.*

2. *Consider sharing parts of your story that highlight systemic errors with neighbors, local or state lawmakers, medical professionals, or just about anyone who will listen! (I admit I'm a terrible party guest because what's important to me doesn't make good small talk.)*

3. *Consider writing a social media post or a letter to the editor.*

4. *Pick one or two topics that you want to learn more about. Here are a few options: gaps in the continuum of care, bed shortages, HIPAA, SMI criminalization, IMD exclusion, anosognosia. Visit Treatment Advocacy Center's website for resources: tac.org.*

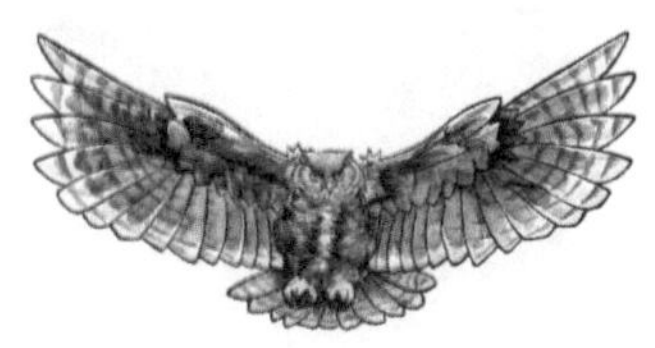

Part 2

My Ambiguous Loss Journey

While my son soared through mania, piloted by psychosis, I couldn't begin to describe how lost I felt. SMI had set fire to our family's carefully mapped plans and dreams, and I was stumbling around in the dark hills of lonely dismay. As I look back and see myself in that disorienting place, I feel self-compassion. Oh, I longed to be a confident young mommy again, walking alongside my little boy with a hand ready to help if he might teeter.

As he crash-landed into adulthood, Calvin was as unreachable as if he'd parachuted onto a remote island skirted by rocky cliffs. No compass could locate him within his disoriented mind, and I had no idea how to navigate the tumultuous seas that separated him from me. A tear-soaked nineteenth-century widow's walk comes to mind: Each heavy step was exhausting, but I wasn't getting anywhere, and no lantern illuminated a clearer direction.

One night in Seattle, I was trying to connect with Calvin. We rode the Monorail from Seattle Center downtown for sushi in a restaurant with a conveyor belt that shuttles food among the tables while you nibble on whatever you pick up. Afterward, we were planning to see a movie. We didn't make it that long.

The air felt electric. He was there but also not. His eyes darted. He muttered under his breath and kept tilting his head to the side, listening to something I couldn't hear. I knew almost nothing about hallucinations, and I knew even less about what to do while he had them.

We picked up bits of food and took a couple bites. I made small talk to pull him back toward me and the reality of us in the restaurant. I asked how things were going, said I was worried, that I wanted him safe. At once, he stood next to our booth and stared past anything in visible view. His eyes went black, unblinking. His body was frozen; his mind retreated into a realm unknown to me.

I looked around, appealing to the restaurant staff, other patrons, anyone in view. All looked away. My twenty-two-year-old son was clearly having a medical emergency, but no one cared to even notice us. I kept my voice calm, "Hey Calvin, it's okay. How about you just sit down, and we can finish eating. This sushi is good. I'm sorry if I said something that upset you. It's okay. I'm so happy to be here with you." No response. None. He stood there for maybe five minutes, frozen.

As abruptly as he had stood, he bolted out the door. It's the only time in my life I've left a restaurant without paying. No time. I chased him, block after block, tried to explain that I was sorry and just wanted us to have an evening. At some point I stopped trying to scurry alongside him or talk to him and just followed. Breathless, I called my friend, Linda Wiley, who lived in Seattle. As mom to a son with schizophrenia, Linda knew my plight. That night she was in the city with a friend. Between their two phones they called 911 and tracked my movement.

I chased Calvin for well over an hour until, lost and exhausted, I saw a police cruiser with red-and-blue top lights spinning but no siren. The cruiser pulled up next to Calvin on an overpass; two offi-cers got out and approached him. In an instant, he snapped into the world and smiled, held out his hand: "Hello, officers. How can I help you this evening?"

They chatted amiably for a minute or two, a length of time that my son could pretend to be fine. They waved him on. As I watched him walk away, my mind struggled to veer from a searing memory, the morning he called after jumping off a highway bridge into a raging winter river. A surfer's survival instinct to swim had saved him, despite a voice taunting him to stop working so hard and sink into an easier escape from further pain. "I didn't want to live anymore, mom," he told me on the phone that day, almost two years earlier.

Through my tears, watching my son disappear onto the other side of that Seattle highway overpass, I said inside my own head what he could not hear: "Oh, my dear boy. I could not catch you then and I cannot catch you now. Nobody will help us tread these troubling waters. Please keep swimming."

The officers were kind enough, apologized that they couldn't do anything: "He's not hurting anybody. Hope you can get some rest." Linda located me and drove me to my hotel. Her good-night hug was a lifeline. We were mothers grieving the loss of our living sons, and there wasn't any clarity about what that really meant. Grieving a "death" when there's no proof of death is complicated.

That night, I grappled with the incongruity of feeling like my son was gone for good while knowing he might not be. In keeping with the nightmarish life I'd gotten used to, it wasn't until morning that I knew he'd lived to see the day. As always, my relief was stained by my growing grief. All of that described the confusion of ambiguous loss, but I didn't know that term yet.

It would be years before I found techniques to ground myself when flooded by fear. I mostly kept my head above water by grabbing any bit of encouragement or support that drifted past, like sushi on that conveyor belt. One place that shored me up was our unique community at Shanti Yoga Center in Vancouver, Washington. We didn't just move our bodies there; we stretched our minds.

My teacher, Sundari SitaRam, shared a Mary Oliver poem that plagued me, "The Journey," about orienting through dark times by shining light on yourself. The first time I heard it; the poem totally pissed me off. The implication was that I needed to put myself first. That was an abhorrent suggestion. Just no! I would do anything for Calvin. My role as his mom was to protect him.

I was so deep and so lost in the world, so unsure of where my next steps needed to land. Oh, that poem challenged me! Could I become determined to save the only life I could save? Was that going to be mine, then? What could my life be worth if my treasured son didn't make it out alive? Escaping the world myself definitely tempted me. If I jumped ship, then I wouldn't have to watch his suffering. I didn't want to end my life though.

Mary Oliver's poem offered a different viewpoint. For one thing, if I didn't survive, I couldn't do anything at all to help my son into the future. Also harmed would be my daughter, my husband, my newly widowed mom, my brother and his family. None of us knew how to save Calvin, but we all knew we needed each other. I began to see that all the people I cared about deserved a world with me in it, doing things that I alone could do. For me and for them, I needed to stop chasing Calvin and ease down some other road, but heading where?

Also bugging me was a nudge to become an activist. So much of my son's circumstances made little sense. His psychosis was in charge, and medical-legal systems seemed fine with that, watching him struggle and deteriorate in plain sight. As his mom, I saw this hands-off approach ending badly. Very badly. His odd luck would absolutely run out.

To get his life back, Calvin needed help, not abandonment. He needed access to a hospital bed when he was severely unwell, so he could stabilize and get set up to recover across time. He needed the right medications, in the right dosages, managed by a well-qualified provider. He needed counseling to help him see how treatment would improve his quality of life. He needed that before he got hurt or hurt someone else, not after. Why was none of that available? Why did people keep telling me my son needed to get dangerous in order to get help? Why was I the only person who wanted to make sure he didn't get dangerous?

As the inaction of an illogical system deepened my sense of loss—and stole my ability to sleep—it began to dawn on me that there were messed-up things in the world that I was seeing in a unique way. My voice mattered, and I wouldn't be heard if I was entirely out of breath from tailing my son's every wrong turn. Not only did I need to survive, but I also needed to save the only life I really had power to save—my own.

Early tentative steps helped me rethink who I was and where I might go to develop a new sense of purpose. Ending my war with reality helped me pause to light a lantern on my losses and illuminate my profound grief. I had to weep before walking onward. As a new version of my life began to emerge, I chose to be awake and aware while traveling at my own pace. Despite not getting what I originally wanted, I had the drive to seek a meaningful life that was still possible. My journey with ambiguous loss thus began.

Whether you are miles into your own ambiguous loss journey or about to take the few first steps, I hope my story helps you orient yourself and collect tools for coping with more ease than how I stumbled upon them. Some parts of my story could be triggering: As you now know, my son's journey with SMI led to his death from suicide. If you want to skip to the coping guidelines in Part 3, go ahead!

> ### *Do now:*
>
> 1. *Now that you know another part of my story, consider a part of your own story that highlights a moment when something was lost.*
>
> 2. *Write a few bullet points, sentences, or paragraphs—whatever feels doable.*
>
> 3. *Did you know at the time that something was being lost? How does that moment look different to you now?*

As I retell my story, I notice times when I had no clue about how to cope and other times when I was figuring things out. Even when everything felt impossible, I was seeking self-empowerment. You may notice that for yourself too. If you've opted out of journaling (*A friend once said she'd rather eat frogs than write, so I know that's a thing.*), consider talking to a friend, your dog, or the walls—anything that helps you articulate what you're processing.

I anticipate that many of you will see something of your own story here. After being featured in the news, I typically hear from various people that I just told "their story." They seem surprised— and glad to know they're not alone—so it feels important for me to keep sharing what has happened to me. If your story is really different, that's no problem. You can identify with the feelings of grief and loss because those are what unite us.

One mom of an adult son with schizophrenia was napping in front of her television one day when she awoke to my face on her screen, telling a bit of Calvin's story while imploring the state of Oregon to improve its treatment laws. She said it felt like I was speaking directly to her because what I was talking about was what she was living. She found me online and we've been friends and fellow advocates since. Sometimes you have to open up to yourself to open up to others. That's where healing happens the fastest.

Okay, you've been prepped. Read on for more of my ambiguous loss story.

> ***Do now:***
>
> 1. *Was the story about my son's first suicide attempt a trigger for you?*
>
> 2. *What can you do to ground yourself? Breathe, drink soothing tea, look at clouds, go touch a tree, pet your cat. . . . Please choose something so you can take a break and recharge.*

The Night I First Lost Calvin

The night I first lost Calvin began with confusion and ended in terror, as it dawned on me that I was being plunged toward a despair that most parents could not imagine surviving. Trying to talk to him was like trying to get ahold of something slippery and hot. His sentences were intensely emotional and full of weighty words. I knew there had to be sense within those sentences because he was so dang smart. I clung to the words as they tumbled out of him, trying to connect them one to another so I might understand. He was very upset, and my mother's heart ached for him.

There was something about a girl who had lied and got him in trouble with his debate team—the reason he had gone to Willamette University in Salem, Oregon, in the fall of 2014, with a merit scholarship. The debate team had turned mean—blocking him from their meetings and events. At the start of his second semester, a fraternity had recruited him with open arms and then dropped him, ordering him to stay away.

That night, about a month into the second term of his freshman year, his relentless discourse included complicated descriptions of his emerging spirituality, his insights about public elections and Constitutional law, and his noble ideas for helping homeless people. His college professors were teaching him about the impacts of racism and politics on suburban landscapes. He'd bought a new game he wanted us to play called Suburbia. Characters from his all-time favorite game, Magic the Gathering, threaded through his tangled storytelling.

Earlier in the day, some of this came out by phone, when my post-surfing reverie was interrupted by his call. His topics were too intricate to pick apart long-distance, and I could tell something was very off. Matt and I abandoned our weekend away to pick up our nineteen-year-old son from his dormitory. He never went back. After we got home that day, the conversation resumed around our dining table in Vancouver, Washington, where Calvin was born and grew up.

Our house is special to us because it took all we had to meet the terms for a thirty-year mortgage in our thirties. Calvin was six when we moved in, ready for first grade. His room on the second floor has a peekaboo view of his elementary school. Walking him to and from his classroom was an early joy of living in our forever home, which backs up to a greenspace filled with firs and massive maples. We've always loved our hardwood floors and having a triple car garage, big enough for bikes, skies, surfing and camping gear, and two cars.

That night, I tried to cling to normalcy. The lighting was the same. My favorite mug with surfboards on it was the same. I kept touching the tile-and-oak table where we played so many games and shared so many meals. Spaghetti and tacos were everyone's favorites.

Still, nothing was normal that night. Calvin was there but not quite there while I kept trying to figure out what I needed to help him fix. I'd witnessed his brilliance with words since he started speaking in full sentences around age two. As a young child, he always asked the most fascinating questions, "Mom, what's under our house, holding it together and making all the things work: the lights, water and all that?"

He won first place in his first-ever speech and debate contest as a high school freshman. The trophies and medallions piled up quickly after that. His capacity to meter out facts and references to form a persuasive argument earned him a state championship in extemporaneous speech during his senior year. The achievement was additionally notable because he overcame verbal tics and other significant symptoms of Tourette's Syndrome while becoming so eloquent.

I beamed with pride watching Calvin at national forensic tournaments, where he performed well among the best in the nation. He put ideas and facts together to frame an argument that could persuade almost anyone on just about any topic.

But that night, the more I heard, the more his concepts and conclusions tumbled apart. As I listened and listened, long past midnight, my writer's mind could not force the jumble of words into any thoughtful structure. Well into a fourth or fifth cup of tea, rubbing my eyes and looking deeply into the shiny dark pupils of my brilliant son, I at once realized what was truly happening:

This was mental illness. It felt as though everything about my safe and stable home trembled with me. What could I possibly know about how to fix this?

There was a distinct moment twenty years earlier when I realized I was pregnant. My eyes went blurry and there was a reverberation in my head like a taut rubber band being plucked. The ground tipped. Back then I realized that a new life grew in me. My dream of being a mom was coming true! I had faith that the world was a fair and rational place where I would love and care for a treasured child. We would raise him to think critically. I knew he would be smart and do important things.

His entire childhood reinforced my predictions. His success and our lovely home, with the fridge always stocked and the beds always made, demonstrated that my motherhood had been a job well done. Oh, my self-satisfaction was so naïve!

Like when I first felt my pregnancy, my experience on the night I first lost my baby boy to mental illness was physical. The world tipped. My vision blurred. I felt instantly like I would throw up from dizziness, which again felt like the reverb of a plucked rubber band. But this time I was not feeling the start of a life. In that instant of emotional freefall, I recognized that this would be the beginning of the end of everything I had dreamed of for my son and our family. The life we had known, and all of my expectations for my son's life into the future, were in the early stages of a death.

I've always been pretty cool and calm in emergency situations. I tend to be the problem-solver, the one who thinks to call 911 or get a warm blanket and elevate the feet of someone in shock. I got my infant son to the hospital when he had a croup and couldn't breathe right. Same when he slammed his finger in the car door and needed stitches. I stayed calm in the ambulance on the way down the mountain after he broke his femur snowboarding.

That night I had no idea how to triage my own shock or the realization that my son's brain had lost its tether to reality. I knew almost nothing about mental illness, only that someone with it might not make much sense, like my son. His paternal grandfather had a severe form of bipolar disorder, but the family had been silent on any details. I knew mental illness required medical attention, but I had no idea where to go or whom to call.

It was somewhere around three a.m. Matt had retreated to our camper van in the garage, out of earshot from the incessant conversation inside the house. I was exhausted too, but the later it got the more animated my son became.

In my moment of realization that this might be mania, psychosis, or both, I stopped trying to connect the loose threads of our conversation in order to seek solutions to any of the presented problems. I remember getting very quiet and trying to think through how to possibly end this never-ending nonsensical dialogue. I offered that sleep would help us clear our heads and that we could talk again in the morning. I asked if there was anything I could do to help him feel more restful.

He seemed confused by the offer and disappointed that our animated debate was ending. After a cup of chamomile tea and a few more attempts to get me chatting again, he acquiesced and went into his childhood bedroom. I closed my own bedroom door and felt nausea rise to replace the false calm I'd been carrying throughout that long night.

What could I possibly know to help me care for this new version of my son? He clearly had no idea that his agitated mind had been struck by an illness and that all his troubles at school probably resulted from his disordered perceptions. His brain was lying to him, but he believed that people he loved were now sworn enemies and that he was being called to crusade against spiritual evil-doers. Words like paranoia, mania, and grandiose delusions weren't part of my vocabulary yet. I only knew that my son was not my son anymore—and that I would do anything in my power to get him back.

Do now:

1. *Write down this question and then an answer: Was Calvin's psychotic break Jerri's fault?*

2. *Write down this question and then offer an answer: Have I blamed myself for something that is not my fault?*

Death by Degrees

Calvin was diagnosed with bipolar disorder. On the morning after he came home, he charged through the house screaming of demons and barred me from ever again entering the downstairs guest bathroom, where he excised an entity but couldn't be sure it wouldn't return if I was careless enough to open the door. Amazingly, a family friend who was also a functional medicine doctor agreed to see Calvin right away and he agreed to go. He liked and trusted her because he knew her daughter from the high school debate team.

The doctor provided the initial diagnosis of bipolar disorder and lithium, which calmed his mania enough to get us a few nights of sleep while we hunkered down at home and figured out what we might do next.

My son's brand of bipolar turned out to be Type 1, the kind that's associated with psychosis and more mania than depression. Right away his rapidly cycling moods ran with hallucinations, delusions, and paranoia. It's probable that if he had lived long enough he might have been diagnosed with schizoaffective disorder, which is a type of schizophrenia spectrum disorder that includes extreme moods alongside positive symptoms, like psychosis, and negative symptoms, such as social withdrawal.

Calvin's manic/psychotic episodes soon led to car crashes and run-ins with law enforcement for doing things like selling hot-dogs off a TV tray in the city and preaching from a wildlife protected butte. He ran up enormous bills on credit cards he never should have been able to get, once purchasing an entire case of books on how to get rich quick! His depressive episodes brought anger and self-harm, although I didn't know for sure until after he died that he'd been cutting and burning himself.

I'll never know if he drank and used drugs to calm his symptoms or whether drinking and drugs triggered the onset of illness, but I do know that his illness made him feel isolated and afraid and that substances helped him feel like he wanted to feel—until they didn't.

He told me one time that hanging out with a group of people using marijuana was a place where he felt like he was popular and well liked. That broke my heart because being smart had always been his thing. Most of his friends who used alongside him got through that phase of life okay and eventually grew up and found healthier ways to feel good. His brain wasn't so adaptable, and he was pissed about that.

More than once he called while stoned, completely confused about where he was or how to get home. Cannabis made him believe he had died, left his body, fallen into a very dark place. I was a yoga teacher then and used grounding techniques to help him feel his feet on the floor, his legs above his feet, his breath in his belly, and so on . . . often while driving to the place where my GPS told me he had dropped a pin to help me locate him.

Here is a poem I wrote after one of those nights:

A Mother's Dilemma

> Your whole life, my job has been to keep you safe.
> So when you called that night, terrified, I came.
> "Help," you cried. "Find me. I don't know where I am.
> I made a mistake. Fix it. Please. Have I died?"
>
> You asked for my help, and I was flooded.
> Fear. Anger. Betrayal. Confusion.
> Was this really happening?
> My whole being charged to the task.
>
> What tools? A phone, with maps.
> And you, clinging to my voice.
> Wanting me to talk you down, to bring you home.
> "Will I, can I be okay? Make me be okay!"
>
> I've been looking for you ever since.
> Watching. Waiting. Holding tight.
> Keeping track. Eyes ever open. Exhausted.
> But fear has a vigilance that surpasses logic.

Mothers being tortured by terrorists
Hold their babies until they die
From exhaustion, their arms just don't
work anymore.

You are not a baby. I don't know
What you are ready to fix on your own.
I don't know when to set you down,
And see if you know how to walk away from danger.

Do now:

1. *Take a moment to reflect on this poem. Can you see how writing it was helpful to me in a moment of grief?*

2. *Does writing help you process? If yes, what do you want to write down right now? If not, what can you do instead to express what this poem brought up for you?*

Some people are susceptible to permanent, chronic psychotic illnesses from cannabis use. I suspect my son was one of them. Each time I saved him during one of those episodes that was worsened by the drugs, he promised he would stop. The allure of feeling better—and belonging—made those promises very difficult for him to keep.

One weekend, early in his diagnosis of bipolar disorder with psychotic features, he used something stronger than cannabis while Matt and I were at the beach. We got a call from a neighbor before dawn that our front door was open and there was blood—a lot of blood. No one appeared to be home. We called a friend who presumably had been hanging out with Calvin that weekend and learned that he'd been taken to the hospital by ambulance in the night. We drove two hours to pick him up from a locked room in an emergency department. He had cut his chin just below his lip and had quite a few stitches. He thought he'd done it on the glass in my curio cabinet but wasn't entirely sure.

No one at the hospital asked us for any information about our son's diagnosis or care plan. No mention was made of a psychological assessment or need for further treatment. In fact, the entire pick-up was pretty much accomplished without anyone saying anything at all. At the time we didn't know this was poor care. We just knew we were scared, and our son was frightened, exhausted, and ashamed.

It was still early in the morning when we got home. The neighbor had closed the unlocked door, which we opened to what can only be described as a horror movie scene. There was blood everywhere, on every piece of furniture, every section of floor, in every room of our two-story home. Glass from my cabinet covered the family room floor, along with broken stemware from our wedding and crystal tchotchkes I had inherited from my grandmother. It took the entire day, using an enzyme cleaner intended for cat urine, to clean up the blood. We were emotionally numb and physically spent for weeks.

I commonly pass that cabinet in my family room and recall that rough time, but what I see behind the replaced glass is only partially clouded by pain. There are pieces that survived that night, like a Tiffany bowl from my great-uncle LaRue Watts, whose New York City career included designing Christmas trees for famous people. Other wedding gifts in there are crystal goblets that Matt and I toast-tested and chose because we liked the sound of the chime they made. A top shelf holds a porcelain angel that belonged to my grandmother Doris Johnson and used to sit on a dressing table in the guestroom I loved when I was a girl. Next to that is a Bunnykins dishes set from my childhood and a mini tea set I bought in San Francisco's Chinatown when my daughter Michelle was little. Generations of memories live in there, and those touchstones help me tap into what's deep and meaningful inside of me. I'm more than my pain, and so is that time capsule cabinet.

When my son came home from the hospital that morning, my emotions were so overwhelming that I don't remember giving them much attention at all. Anger and fear were obvious, but I'm pretty sure I got mad for a bit and then just shut it all down. I certainly didn't think to notice grief. I see it now. This was profound grief, like the kind of grief mothers have when their children go off to war and get blown to bits. My son's life had blown to bits, but a few pieces kept wandering back in the form of my son that I was trying like everything to save from the ongoing explosions. I became hypervigilant, afraid of every phone sound that might announce the next disaster.

One thing was clear: The person Calvin had been before his first psychotic break was gone and our lives would never be normal again. I was acutely aware of that. My son was there but not there. I was witnessing what felt like a death by degrees, as each crisis sped my family further and further away from who we had been. A child-sized mug in my cabinet says, "God who holds the children dear watch over little me." I wanted to believe that all might still be okay, but my faith in the future was slipping away.

A metaphor I've thought about often over the years is a penny funnel—those plastic make-a-wish whirlwinds at kid-friendly museums. You watched your coin roll its way around and around the sides of a yellow cone until it finally disappeared through a hole in the bottom. You were supposed to make a wish while you watched. That's what it felt like watching my son spiral downward. There was no stopping him once he got going, and no one willing to put a hand in and pluck him out. The myth was that once he disappeared through the hole at the bottom, someone would pick him up and shine him up for some good purpose. Of course I could wish for that, but I was really confused that my wishing was about the only strategy we had.

During the first two years of his illness, my son played peek-a-boo with his sanity and with his father and me. He would pop into focus sometimes, with his true quirky grin and a smart comment, and then disappear again into his psychosis, without leaving the room. Now I know I can call that a "confusion of absence and presence." His psychological comings and goings were also mixed up with his tendency to literally disappear, sometimes for days without calling home. I reported him to police several times as a missing endangered person. I compare my sense of confusion and loss then to that of a mom whose child might be kidnapped by pirates or recruited by a violent gang.

The incongruity I experience now is the kind where my son is physically absent but present in my heart and memory. I'm left forever wondering what could have been and why his life ended so badly. When I look at that child-sized mug, I want to have faith that a guardian angel in another realm is looking after my little guy. My memories of him as a child playing soccer or as a teenager surfing alongside me are treasures more valuable than anything in my curio cabinet. What I'm doing is called "letting go while remembering," a comforting concept I learned from Dr. Boss. This concept applies regardless of whether your loved one is physically alive. The point is to allow yourself to enjoy your memories without attachment to things being other than they are now.

I wrote this poem on the first Thanksgiving after Calvin died, after walking over the shadowy imprint left by a perfectly shaped maple leaf on the sidewalk.

Life Leaves

> There is life, and there is the imprint life leaves.
> The beauty of the imprint is up to those who see.
>
> What shape shook the world a little or a lot,
> and left it changed?
>
> What shadow lingers, to remind others,
> that something important visited here?
>
> All have the power to pause, give thanks,
> And wander on in wonder.
>
> What is temporary is made permanent
> By the remembering.

Do now:

1. *Write down a memory that brings a smile, sense of peace, or feeling of importance.*

2. *Explain in a few words why treasuring this memory feels valuable to you.*

How Waves Flow with Emotion

While Calvin grew up, I was a stay-home mom who taught yoga and dance—ages thirty to fifty. Right in the middle of that I learned to surf, mostly in Oregon where water temperatures are typically in the low fifties. Yes, I wear a hefty wetsuit, booties, and gloves. Being a cold-water girl is a kooky thing for a Kansas-born woman, for sure. I'm sixty and still surfing, which makes me even more of an anomaly. Maybe you are scratching your head, wondering, "Wait, you *surf?*" I want to share a bit more about my surfer self because it's part of how I am still healing, and it connects me to treasured memories of my son.

Yes, I really do surf. On a nine-foot longboard. I even have four trophies from the Cape Kiwanda Longboard Classic, held in an Oregon town called Pacific City. I got first in my division when I was fifty-nine. There's nothing like the smell of salt in my nose with the cool coastal air steaming off the five millimeters of neoprene that covers my pumping heart. I squint toward the distant sea, wondering what's coming. A rising line on the horizon means a new set of waves to gauge before choosing when to lean back, pivot my board in the direction that the wave is headed, and lie belly down with my back arched and my feet tight together. The trick is to time the swim just right to slide into the pocket of the wave, that specific place where whitewater curls onto the glassy face. Carving into that sweet spot is where the juice lives. Sometimes I pop right into it and time stands still while the ocean and I cruise together toward the beach. Sometimes I'm late, or slow, or just off balance. Oftentimes I swallow water instead of riding it.

The unpredictability of surfing the ocean has shown me the thrill of doing something with no idea how it's going to go. Calvin understood that too. He was really good at turning down the line and walking the nose on his red-and-white board. He had a wave tattoo on his bicep with the phrase "surf your waves" that was adapted from a Jon Kabat-Zinn quote, "You can't stop the waves, but you can learn to surf." He got the tattoo after he got sick.

Being willing to go with the flow is a way to practice being uncomfortable doing things with an uncertain design to them, also like doing improvisational theater, dancing, or cooking without a recipe. By intentionally playing with ambiguity over time, you get increasingly more comfortable with what is unknown. It's a way to become more tolerant to ambiguity.

In February 2017, two years into Calvin's illness, he, Matt and I paddled into an unusually big but clean Oregon Coast swell. The waves were double-overhead and pumping. They peeled from the south heading north, making them "lefts" for us surfers. Matt and Calvin rode "goofy," which meant they put their right foot toward the nose of the board. Those waves were "frontside" for them.

I'm "regular," with my left foot forward, which meant that day I was surfing "backside," which is harder. I couldn't have been more anxious. Calvin was surfing for the first time in a long while. He was doing okay but not entirely stable on his medications. Still, he and Matt were amped and surfing together like they hadn't in years. They were strong and in their happy place.

I was beaming to be out with my boys, but the swell was outside my comfort zone and not moving in my favorite direction. I screwed up every ounce of my courage, paddled into a wave, popped up and rode. To this day, that was the biggest ride of my life. It was so heavy that it felt like water flowing over a freight train. The guys teased me later that I "got the windows all the way down," which is a way to say that my arms were spinning at my sides to help keep my balance.

Still, I rode that wave, and I was proud. We three had such a blast cheering each other on. I'm so grateful that I was courageous enough to show up for every bit of that day. I faced my full-on fear and uncertainty and emerged with strength and confidence. It's a darned good metaphor for riding waves of loss and grief.

Some peaks aren't rideable though. Not everybody makes it down the line, and sometimes the ocean's energy is too strong for a soul. *Trigger warning: This next paragraph is grisly, so skip to the next one if you don't want to know.*

A weird combination of wind and wave energy one time tossed my board into the air behind me while I was underwater after ending a chunky ride by falling off the back of my board. When I bobbed to the surface, my board came down on my face, fin first. The center skag fin is like a big knife, and it sliced through my forehead like a hatchet in a coconut, all the way to my skull.

It took seventeen stitches and a couple of weeks to heal. My son was there that day, too, and I'll always treasure how kind and concerned he was. It was one of our last beach trips together. The ocean absorbs my tears from time to time as I wish like everything that my son was still surfing by my side. That loss is one I visit sometimes when I finger the thin scar just below my hairline.

> *Do now:*
>
> 1. *Take a moment to think about a person connected to an ambiguous loss in your life. Can you recall a time when you were in flow with that person?*
>
> 2. *Write down something about that moment. Can you experience this like pulling open a drawer and finding a treasure you forgot you had?*
>
> 3. *If sketching brings you any sense of pleasure (even if you're a kindergarten level artist like me), make a quick sketch to go with your memory.*

Gone but Not Gone While the System Fails

During Calvin's first two years of illness, I was his committed care-giver. I found him a psychiatric nurse practitioner and also signed him up for homeopathic and yoga therapies. I hired one licensed therapist who was also a meditation coach and another who ran his holistic practice from a tiny home in his backyard. Several of those professionals established trust and rapport with Calvin.

My son and I went to the gym and took long walks. I sat up with him many nights when he needed help to quiet his mind. Together we read *An Unquiet Mind*, Kay Redfield Jamison's memoir about her journey with bipolar disorder. The book was both inspiring and frustrating because the level of psychiatric care she needed and got was out of the question for Calvin. His reticent nurse practitioner was not about to rescue him like Jamison's doctor rescued her during crises.

If I got a do-over on that part of my life, I would fight like a tiger to get him into a coordinated specialty care (CSC) early episode psychosis program. It's not my fault he didn't get that, though; it didn't exist yet in Washington State.

Upon Calvin's request, I helped him enroll in local colleges a couple of times, but none lasted more than a few weeks. I helped him get part-time work, which always ended badly when his symptoms showed up on the job. I believed that our stable family filled with love and my intrepid attempts to find resources would be enough to help him through this rough patch in his life, but everything I tried lacked a key ingredient: his motivation to stick with a treatment plan when he couldn't always see that he was sick.

Let me be crystal clear: Voluntary treatment is always preferred, but anyone as sick as my son will suffer and die prematurely without changes in the system that enable access to "unwanted" treatment until a person is well enough to want the treatment that will obviously save them. Treatment works, and people who deny that mental illness exists or that involuntary treatment saves lives are deluded by their own idealism about what autonomy actually means.

I learned through layers of loss that this game is rigged. Like any eager, organized suburban soccer mom would, I sought every possible resource and kept looking for more. I called all the dozens of psychiatrists in our insurance company's network and was blindsided at being rejected by each one. I had assumed psychiatrists would eagerly open their appointment books if I explained how serious this was. Silly me.

I eventually learned that people with SMI usually get "prescribers," not doctors. A prescriber is someone with less training who is legally allowed under state-specific licensure laws to prescribe psychiatric medication, like a nurse practitioner, physician assistant, or in some locations, a psychologist. I'm not suggesting that these professionals aren't well trained, compassionate, and qualified, but it seems odd to me that psychiatry is the only medical specialty in which the most educated rarely help the most unwell within their area of practice. Can you imagine if people got only nursing assistance after a heart attack, instead of ongoing checkups with a cardiologist?

Calvin's nurse practitioner knew what she was up against with my son. She warned that stopping his medication would be unwise. She told him his life wouldn't work out very well. She emphasized her impending retirement and willingness to continue as his prescriber only if he would cooperate. In hindsight, I realize how exhausted she was from working for many decades with patients who lacked insight and thus didn't follow her treatment guidance. The game was rigged for her too, with laws that blocked her from intervening if her patients were too sick to know they were sick. I wish she'd been able to motivate Calvin to want what she offered, but it's typical that she couldn't.

I explained in Part 1 that very few psychiatrists choose to work with the SMI population. I know a few extraordinary exceptions, including Dr. Robert S. Laitman, co-author of *Meaningful Recovery from Schizophrenia and Serious Mental Illness with Clozapine: Hope & Help*. Dr. Laitman is also dad to a man in recovery with SMI, and I wish I'd met him before Calvin died, not after. Another notable exception is Dr. Xavier Amador, whose book, *I Am Not Sick, I Don't Need Help!* provides excellent guidance about how to help someone accept treatment when they cannot see that they are even ill.

I read Dr. Amador's book about a half a year before Calvin died. I think it improved our final communications, and for that I'm glad. During that first year, though, the callings of mania were much more enticing to Calvin than what the medical system offered. He hated antipsychotic medicines that dulled his intellect and made him feel heavy and slow. Of course it wasn't long before he ditched the meds and canceled all appointments.

As he grew increasingly symptomatic, he sought speed and momentum. He wrecked the Mustang he'd inherited from his grandfather and used the insurance settlement money to lease a Ford hybrid. He found a job with a messenger service. Staying home was excruciating, so a job that paid him to drive all over Washington and Oregon at all hours of the day and night was a good fit for a while. I'm pretty sure he lost that job for preaching nonsense at a retirement home while delivering medication to an elderly person, but the terms of his firing were never totally clear.

His drive to go, Go, GO remained strong after his job ended. That method for managing mania was pretty unsafe, but we had no control. He was an adult with a car and a driver's license. One night he drove off with his car stuffed to the roof with random things he took from our house: cat food (but thankfully not our cat), pictures from our walls, decorative pillows, Halloween decorations. Before he left home he took every picture down from every wall in our home, "to close the portals," he later tried to explain. He didn't fill the tank because he believed the car would run off his energy, so he of course ran out of gas. Law enforcement found him asleep in his car barely off the highway and took him to a hospital. His leased car was impounded, and we didn't help get it back.

Another time he put on his business suit and packed a briefcase with stuffed animals and plastic beads so he could move to Seattle and seek others whose sole purpose was to make bracelets with meaningful patterns and wear them all the way up their arms to parties and concerts. I remember making him pancakes that morning, a favorite since childhood. Matt and I played along but drove to the hospital instead of the train station, convincing him that he needed to be medically cleared for travel.

Despite our stealth efforts, the emergency department turned Calvin away without an evaluation, explaining for the umpteenth time that being psychotic wasn't illegal and did not indicate a need for hospital-level care. He couldn't afford the train trip without our money, so he came back home—untreated, very psychotic, and extremely angry.

Each time we tried to help our son access medical care, he got more threatening. We all felt betrayed, by each other, by the failing system, and by literally anyone anywhere who just wasn't helping us through something so impossible to navigate.

At some point during that time, we became not only afraid for our son but afraid of our son. In psychosis, he was menacing. He picked up furniture and other heavy things he threatened to throw, got in our faces with a cruel grimace. He screamed into the trees behind our house and was furious if we asked him to quiet down to respect the neighbors. He made creepy altars with knives, sticks, bits of random food, and sometimes his own blood. He got upset if they were disassembled. At one point he told us to move out of his house. Talking him out of that delusion was, of course, impossible.

I've decided not to tell the entire narrative of my son's illness. I cannot keep living in those weeds and maintain my own growth. The drawers in his old bedroom are stuffed with his rambling writings that I don't need to read. Details from those drawers are not going in this book. You don't have to retell your whole story either to access healing from ambiguous loss coping work.

What I most want to share here is that systemic failure contributed to my ambiguous loss and grief. I first lost my son to a terrible illness, but before I lost him to suicide I lost him to the system. If you're in it, you know this: Our so-called system is a meshy mess of not-enough-beds, outpatient programs without proper staffing, filthy beds under bridges, civil courts that deny beds, and criminal courts that put people into jail beds instead.

I described how the system failed my son in a feature article called "My Son's Story" that I wrote for *Kansas Alumni* magazine, a publication for graduates of my alma mater, the University of Kansas. I earned a journalism degree there in 1988 before working for seven years as a full-time *Kansas Alumni* writer. Telling my story was an empowering act of advocacy, and I'm glad I captured the essence of our struggle. Being a writer is part of who I am, and I feel a stronger sense of self when I write. Other people rediscover themselves through art, photography, or music. There's more on that in the chapter about reconstructing identity.

Keep remembering your core question: *What is the thing you aren't doing because grief has gotten in your way?* I encourage you to jot down any answers that occur to you along your way through this book.

I was discouraged and unempowered after the first two years of my son's SMI, after everything I did to ensure he would survive and thrive. It will forever boggle me that despite our family's deep bonds, eagerness to problem-solve, and college degrees, our smart but super sick son didn't stand a chance. My old version of myself as a mom didn't stand a chance either. I had to become a whole new me to keep getting up in the morning and putting a foot in front of the other. Pretending to still be my old self would have immobilized me.

Please, don't let me discourage you if you are still in the fight! Some people with SMI make it into lasting recovery, maybe due to happenstance or simply better luck at finding the right resources for the right help in the critical moments of need. Many of Dr. Laitman's patients are doing well. My friend Eric Smith is a model for schizophrenia recovery and was featured in the February 27, 2023 issue of *People* magazine. I like to tell Eric that he reminds me of my son, but with a rewritten future because he got assisted outpatient treatment (AOT), a service I think would have benefited Calvin.

Something I tell other families over and again is this: If you do what you can, with what you know when you know it, then you will be okay, no matter what the outcome. How you rethink your own identity is how you survive, regardless of what happens to your loved one.

Always know that the choice you make in a ridiculously hard moment is the only logical option among probably lots of bad options. You are only one person, and you can only do what one person might. Take care of your own need to feel integrity in your choices and you can be okay. Although you want to with all your heart, saving your loved one is ultimately not up to you alone. I think figuring that out on my own probably saved me.

> ***Do now:***
>
> 1. *Write this down: I am doing what I can, with what I know when I know it. That's all any person might do.*
>
> 2. *List a few kind or helpful things you've done to help the person you've lost ambiguously, recently or in the past.*
>
> 3. *Write this: "Thank you, self. That was the right thing to do in that moment."*

Bearing Witness to a Living Death

Calvin's condition severely devolved after year two, and my attempts to use logic and love to get him the right level of care during crises were most often met by refusal from him and indifference from the system. Services were built to prioritize stringent treatment laws and personal autonomy over saving his life. When he was at his sickest, symptoms rendered him unable to see his illness or believe that treatment would improve his quality of life. At the same time, court-ordered treatment wasn't available until he was very near death's door.

When he jumped from a highway bridge into a raging winter river to try to quiet the voices and end his pain, he met the criteria. When he burned things indoors, refused to drink water, and arranged bloody knives to scare away evil spirits, he did not. During his worst illness episodes, the system's stoic bias toward personal autonomy—even when his psychosis called all the shots—meant he got incarceration instead of treatment.

As Calvin's psychotic episodes became more frequent and closer together, I learned at some point that he probably had the worst kind of bipolar disorder, with "mixed states" and "rapid cycling." Trauma compounded upon trauma. He said to me in one moment of medicated clarity, "Mom, they didn't guarantee my civil rights. They made sure I would lose all my rights by going to jail." It was an ongoing struggle to admit that he and I had very little control over how his SMI would play out.

I was bearing witness to a living death. Everything about it was confusing and isolating. As he slipped more frequently out of reality, he often ditched his phone and wallet so he couldn't be "tracked." Helping him find or replace those items became an arduous regular project. He was sometimes afraid to eat or drink, paranoid about being poisoned. An ongoing delusion was that he had married a girl he barely knew. Sometimes there were "children."

These are common behaviors and thought distortions, but those of us living these lives don't always know that other people are having these bizarre and terrifying experiences. I mostly remember that my life's scariest moments made my friends' eyes go big but rarely impressed anyone with the power to assess Calvin for a hospitalization.

I was often told that "being psychotic is not illegal" or that "he'll be better off if he commits a crime and goes to jail." Of course, that contributed directly to my helplessness, confusion, sense of loss, and worsening grief.

At one point I reached out to a group of his former debate friends to try to explain to them that I needed to know if he'd ever been violent or threatening. I tried to help them see that those were the criteria I needed to prove to save his life—that without the risk of suicide or homicide he'd never get the level of care he needed. They didn't believe me or didn't understand. None responded.

I started advocating for mental health systems to change while Calvin was alive but struggling. He attended one event I hosted for about a hundred people in the Seattle area, and he wasn't doing very well that night. Still, he spoke with clarity and honesty when he said he was glad his mom and others had helped when he was too sick to see how to help himself. That was an important moment for all of us: Too few self-advocates who have been as sick as Calvin are able to explain that even though they didn't like being involuntarily hospitalized they know they needed hospital-level care.

Calvin's symptoms nearly always slid below the required threshold of danger. The basic criteria were the same everywhere, including when he crossed state lines between Washington, Oregon, and California: He had to be overtly dangerous, not just really, really sick and completely confused about why his life was falling apart.

While everyone watched and waited for a true and proper danger, he went through all the things someone might experience under these circumstances: eviction, homelessness, incarceration, suicide attempts, betrayal, victimization. A podcast called *Lost Patients*, a collaboration between the Seattle Times and National Public Radio affiliate KUOW describes this wasteful and unhelpful cycling as "the churn."

The loss of friends was an ambiguous loss that my son and I shared because of his SMI. The difference was that I knew his SMI was the problem, and he didn't. While stuck in the churn, he just thought the whole world had turned against him. And that broke my mama's heart. I hated that so much for him, but I couldn't fix it.

Do now:

1. *Write down a few ways that the mental health system has failed your family.*

2. *Write this: Those errors are bigger than me and not my fault.*

3. *Consider looking up "Lost Patients," wherever you access podcasts.*

A Suitcase by the Door

Trying to pull my son out of the churn, I lost all ability to maintain my veneer of normalcy. The more extreme the struggles became, the more I isolated myself. I lost work, social connections, and my sense of self. My marriage persevered, and for that I'm grateful. We were able to see ourselves united by grief instead of divided by it. We clung to one another. Matt's journey, though, has been much more internal than mine and I'm respecting his privacy by not sharing much in this book about his involvement and perspective.

With Calvin at home and struggling, we both lost the ability to rest with peace and comfort in our home. At night, we locked the bedroom door and made sure to have a suitcase of essentials perpetually packed for a speedy exit. I escaped to the homes of friends a few times when Calvin's delusions made him especially aggressive toward me, while Matt was able to keep a safer emotional distance. Calvin probably sensed how intensely I wanted him to get better, and it made him mad because he was certain that he wasn't ill. His misunderstanding made me the problem.

I lost my ability to fall asleep and wake up refreshed. I lost my ability to focus on basic tasks. I recall half-packing a grocery cart and bolting from the store before I finished shopping. This happened more than once. I was afraid of seeing someone I knew or being asked by a grocer, "How are you today?" It was easier to avoid human contact than attempt to answer without being crude or cruel.

One time I saw someone I used to work out with during my Masters Swimming years, and I just dumped on her. She listened, but I could tell by the time I let her off the hook that I'd been entirely inappropriate. I don't think I ever saw her again, and I still feel guilty about how much I appealed to her to understand something she couldn't possibly understand.

I lost my ability to make small talk, and friendships were strained. I didn't have much to give, and all of my unmet emotional needs likely made listening to me entirely exhausting. Some people probably experienced a subconscious fear that my obvious and extreme pain might somehow transfer to them if they listened. A few friends were amazing, and I'm forever grateful to those who were willing to let me vent or spend a night when I needed respite.

Poorly equipped to help my son make more organized plans and unable to convince him that we were not the enemy, our family struggled to make sense of anything and often argued. Sometimes the police got involved, and eventually there was an arrest.

Calvin spent weeks incarcerated in solitary confinement while he retreated deeply into his psychosis. He was catatonic at some point, but it was difficult to get updates about his mental health when he was locked out of sight. After he got out, we kept trying to set him up with places to live, providers, and part-time jobs, but everything fell apart pretty quickly when he stopped taking his anti-psychotic medication. The losses piled up.

After a hearing at the county courthouse during Calvin's first incarceration, I wrote this poem. Calvin attended by video because he was too unwell to transport.

A Cup of Tea on a Bitter Night

> The pain that is indescribable:
> It is the pain that most needs to be described.
> I need to touch it, to feel its barbs and know its roughness,
> Perhaps to know where it has not stabbed me yet.
>
> What is left when the worst has happened?
> When the nightmare you shook off—not true, not possible,
> Enters a court room with tables, chairs, fluorescent lights,
> And normal-looking people bear witness to your horror?
>
> You do not awaken, because sleep never happened.
> And your eyes and ears are not deceiving you.
> Life, that trickster, made you think you had a right,
> To a shiny life bubbling along in happiness.

Your murky new reality brings you face-to-face with
A black-eyed man with blue hair, panicking, begging,
Because this penalty means no paycheck to pay with.
The unimpressed judge gavels him into a catch-22.

This desperate man with shocking hair and piercing eyes.
Might sit down to lunch with your son, stare at him.
Will they commiserate, exchange names? Who knows?
When sad souls cram together in a small, dark space.

Punished for illness, when promises and pockets are empty.
Keeping him out was impossible, and dangerous.
Self-preservation has a price, and this is happening.
Him on screen in a safety vest with a swollen eye. Hurt how?

Your child. The one person you carried into the world.
You wanted him with all your longing, defended him
Against mean kids, weary teachers, terrors in the night.
He was amazing, and you were proud. And then he broke.

At first, confusion. Where was the enemy to annihilate?
In his head: him but not him. He loved you but spat hate.
You lost a bit of him at a time, like now, on this screen,
Talking like a crazed robot before a judge just doing a job.

Back home, an empty bed holds a tossed teddy bear.
The night comes; clouds cover the moon; your heart panics.
How to describe a day such as this, a pain such as this?
The only calming option is to search for words.

I need words to explain the nature of my predicament,
Words to help me locate myself in the forest of my dismay.
Like breadcrumbs, words mark a trail toward a safer place.
Home. Chamomile tea. Warmth in a cup with a cool handle.

Do now:

1. *Do words help you explain the nature of your own predicament?*

2. *Write down anything that comes to you.*

3. *Make tea if that suits you, and use every sip to remind yourself that you are not alone.*

When I Gave Hope a Second Chance

Although he had been aware of his original bipolar diagnosis, Calvin lost insight that he had a mental illness after multiple severe and prolonged psychotic breaks. At some point I learned to call his lack of insight anosognosia. Very few people, including providers, know this, but it's visible on brain scans, and in 2024 anosognosia became a billable diagnosis under code R41.85, applicable for patients fifteen and older.

The frontal and parietal lobes, it turns out, have bits and pieces that are supposed to light up when a person is thinking in ways that are self-reflective. In people with anosognosia, those areas are pretty darn dark. In addition to being unaware that they have a mental illness, a person with anosognosia might not notice that they are cold or developing wounds on bare feet that have been walking for hours through polluted city streets, for example. My son's ability to recognize his condition got dimmer with each episode, and he experienced all of that.

Frustratingly, providers don't always have training to identify anosognosia and adjust their treatment methods accordingly. During one hospitalization I tried to ask his nurse practitioner about her treatment protocols to accommodate for anosognosia. There was a long pause, and she asked me to repeat the word more slowly. When I started to explain what the word meant for my son and his needs, she hung up on me.

Learning about these symptoms didn't help me slow my son's progression toward a cliff's edge, but it did help me cultivate compassion, shifting me away from being directly furious at him. I learned to see that anosognosia set all of us up for ambiguous loss.

Calvin could not self-reflect or understand his rightful role in relationships anymore. I know he was bothered by what he couldn't understand, and that's the brutality of untreated SMI. He couldn't know what he couldn't see and was left alone to lash out until everything about his life was utterly chaotic. He also lost gray matter in his brain, which happens with prolonged episodes of untreated psychosis.

Our losses were also financial. Calvin broke a lease at one rental to seek a new life in California, where he lived on a communal farm at our expense until he got involuntarily committed there. When he was discharged, he cashed out the whole life insurance policy I took out for him on the day he was born to buy a train ticket from San Francisco to Seattle. I'm not entirely sure where the rest of the money went but at some point he was handing out twenties to homeless people. He was a bit proud to tell me that. How I felt was a mix. We didn't have those bills to spare; still, his soul was generous, and I saw that.

He lived in a few places in and around Seattle, with us paying most of the bills. He had dozens of encounters with law enforcement and got hospitalized once when the stuff that scared a landlord rendered him dangerous enough to meet criteria for involuntary treatment. It turns out that waiting and watching for a threat of death in the moment is intensely traumatic. That poor woman and her young children lived across the street from her rental where Calvin roomed for a few weeks. She courageously testified at his commitment hearing, and I expect she'll be forever impacted. That hospitalization happened, but not for long enough. Ultimately, it was just a quick stopover on his way back to jail.

Each crisis represented another ambiguous loss while I watched my son disappear in plain sight. For the most part, I stopped hoping because hope was unhelpful. It felt like lying to myself. I was exhausted by disappointment. Somewhere around that time I wrote in my journal about embracing hopelessness:

"When used as a replacement for necessary action, hope is a dark place where there aren't any reasonable options left, and no one wants to help. Hope is what is left when I have to submit to an outcome that is unlikely to end well. Hope is an exhausting exercise in rainbow chasing when I know darn well there is no way out of the storm. Hope wastes energy when there's work to do."

My purposeful decision to forego hope was challenged when Calvin's final incarceration resulted in him getting set up with Social

Security and a subbasement studio apartment in a dingy but stately old Capitol Hill building. He loved it and was proud to say he was living independently in Seattle—his first choice for a city. We helped him outfit his kitchen and regularly brought groceries or reimbursed friends in the city who delivered them. He enjoyed a walking group with his Program of Assertive Community Treatment (PACT) team. I had a job that took me to Seattle fairly regularly. Calvin and I met for meals and toured landmarks whenever we could get together.

By then I was an invested mental health advocate. I knew then-governor Jay Inslee and was actively working with lawmakers to pass new legislation to slightly improve treatment access laws. There were reasons to imagine a brighter possible future for my beloved son—and others like him.

Calvin was reconnecting with extended family, and we had Christmas 2018 together at my brother's house near Chicago. We played games, watched movies, laughed, hugged, cried. My heart skipped a beat each time I let myself believe that he might not only survive but that he might find a way back to happiness and a meaningful life.

The last time Calvin, Matt, and I were together was in the train depot in downtown Vancouver, Washington, just after that Christmas trip to Chicago. Calvin's train back to Seattle was delayed, and I'm so glad for that. Seated on a worn wooden bench, we played cards, a version of rummy we've always played with Clark house rules. We were a little weary but happy to be together. We had a full-on normal family moment. What I wouldn't give to have normal back.

In January 2019, I was featured on *PBS NewsHour*, within a segment called "Brief but Spectacular." In keeping with the segment's theme, I clapped my two hands together before concluding, "Mental illness should never be a crime." Producer Steve Goldbloom meticulously edited that segment into a treasured time capsule of that point in my family's story.

For a brief but spectacular moment, I dared to hope that my son would be one of the lucky ones. Loss was still the defining feature of our lives, but we had reasons to reenvision a life into the future that might be okay. I was still terrified of the sound of a ringing phone, or a siren, or my own nighttime what-iffing: My fingers were crossed against my fear. For good reasons.

> ***Do now:***
>
> 1. *Think about what hope means to you: Is it a helpful tool, a concept that feels like a trap, or something else entirely? Did this chapter change how you think about hope? If you want to, make a few notes.*
>
> 2. *Write down something you have hoped for that isn't possible anymore. What is possible instead?*

Gone but Still Present in my Heart Work

Trigger warning: This chapter includes a description of suicide.

My son took his own life in 2019, when he was twenty-three, after he'd been sick for four years. Calvin's death galvanized my ongoing work in advocacy as I struggled to cope with this new version of grief fueled by intense anger. The way I see it, the system withheld treatment while we all watched Calvin deteriorate and die—with his "civil rights" intact but his humanity destroyed.

My feelings of loss pierced through new layers. Even with a death certificate, there wasn't clarity or closure. His death wouldn't have happened if the right treatment had been provided at the right level at the right time. The mismatch of my logic and the illogical system added to my furious grief.

Keeping Calvin's memory alive through my work at TAC has aided my recovery. Despite his physical absence, I sense his presence in my commitment to change as I move through each day of working with personal and systems change advocates. Acceptance of his absence but also his ongoing presence has provided valuable healing.

When he died, Calvin was still living in Seattle but had gone on a trip to St. Louis with a group connected to the Seattle Clubhouse, which is part of the Clubhouse International system that accredits day services for people in SMI recovery. At the Seattle location, Calvin made new friends, helped organize gaming events, and edited a newsletter. My journalist self was darn proud of that!

My mom, Judy Niebaum, and her new husband, Dave Marden, live in Lawrence, Kansas, where I grew up. They drove up to see Calvin while he was in Missouri, not too far to drive. I'm so grateful that my mom was the last family member to see Calvin alive because she never gave him any reason to fear that her unconditional love would be impacted by his behaviors. She knew he wasn't doing very well, but she just loved him up during their brief visit, which was right before she and Dave married. She bought a new pair of shoes for her upcoming wedding that she proudly showed Calvin. He liked them and praised her good taste. They shared a pizza. He was in psychosis, but there were those moments of normal gramma-grandson love. They had that.

After being in St. Louis for about a week, Calvin somehow hacked his way onto the roof of his seven-story hotel and jumped off. My mom and Dave had already driven back to Kansas. No one saw him, so the details will forever be unknown to me. I've no desire to visit that city or the hotel.

For years I've had recurring nightmares about trying to catch him. The dreams aren't literal. Sometimes I'm catching him as a baby, a young child, or a being that isn't even human. The details are always a little blurry when I awaken, but I always know that I've just tried to insert myself into that moment of his death. *Did you feel it, Calvin? Were you afraid? Were you pleased with yourself? Was it amazing until you landed, and then did it hurt before you passed on?* That last question stops my heart.

My longtime friend and chiropractor, Paula Smith, knew Calvin well. I believe her when she explains that she sometimes sees or understands things others cannot. Her intuition is a helpful gift. She says his spirit left before he landed. I choose that version of how Calvin's human life story ended. He wanted to fly away.

We later found Calvin's antipsychotic medication on the floor of his apartment back in Seattle. I know from people with him on the trip that he was in psychosis. I don't blame them for what happened. They loved Calvin and he loved them. He reassured all that he was okay, and they were following the rules by letting him be. Psychosis ought to be treated as an emergency, but it's not.

I'll never know what blend of choice versus psychotic delusion was the impetus for his final act. I think he felt like he lost a piece of himself when he took the medication because it dulled his intellect and made him too languid to exercise. He was upset by the weight he gained while taking antipsychotics. I don't think any of his providers tried hard enough to improve his medication management. I had dared to hope that treatment would bring him back and save our family from this final, irreversible loss, but no.

Calvin's leap from the hotel was undoubtedly impulsive, but I also believe he made a choice. On his dresser back in Seattle was his drafted poem, "I hope I die on a Monday," which he said would be the title of a book he planned to publish one day. He took his own life on a Monday. His pain was so severe that he likely saw suicide as a rational Plan B. I believe he was wrong in thinking his pain was unresolvable. With time, patience, and trust in his family and others he could have recovered and lived well.

Still, Calvin knew his life was not working out as planned. That was an ambiguous loss for him, and he didn't stick around long enough to learn to find new hope. He would have felt joy into the future. He absolutely could have surfed again, laughed again, and experienced shared love. I wish I had an opportunity to talk with him about ambiguous loss and how to live well in its presence.

The elusiveness of closure surrounding my son's death has led me to a place of acceptance that life's ambiguities are unresolvable. Grief from loss is not something to overcome, like a strep throat infection, and there is no magic portal that will pull you out of it. I've learned to use the coping approaches in this book to walk alongside grief in mostly amiable fashion.

Keep this in mind: Grief isn't linear, and it doesn't care how much you've worked on setting it aside or tucking it away. It shows up whenever it wants, wherever it wants. Knowing how to see it, greet it, and seek meaning and direction from it is the key to onward momentum.

When I began this book, I realized I'd been shushing my own grief through the sixth anniversary of my son's death. Sitting down to write helped as words and tears poured out. I let myself remember all I could about the day he died.

That day, I was juggling many tasks. Midafternoon, I went to Starbucks to meet a woman who might help me turn my grassroots advocacy organization into a nonprofit. I ordered a chai latte, a treat I didn't indulge in very often. We were just saying hello. I don't remember her name. A friend was there too, another mom with her own terrible story. She was my lifeline that day, later driving me home, handing me my chai to drink on the way.

My son had been sick for so long; of course I had PTSD about a phone ringing. When my cell chimed, my heart raced. The phone number was from St. Louis. Was he in a hospital or a jail? Would the voice be his?

"I have to take this," I told the woman I would never see or speak to again, as I raced outside for privacy. The voice on the phone didn't make any sense. He was a doctor in a hospital. Was my son there? No, that wasn't why he was calling. He kept asking me questions.

Did I have a son named Calvin?

Yes, of course: "Is he there, in your hospital?"

No, ma'am, well, yes, ma'am, but no he's not okay.

He was sorry. There was nothing to be done.

The coroner's office would need to call to verify his identity.

They could do it by phone.

No reason to suspect a homicide. Please take care of yourself.

A police officer knocked on my front door later that day. I greeted him, said I already knew. He held his hat over his chest. Mothers of children at war came to mind—what it must be like to see the official car in front of the house and to want the person taking off his hat to turn toward someone else's house. Matt was home by then. I had to tell him. I made sure he was sitting down. His heart cracked in line with mine. I got a migraine that night and took a pill.

Do now:

1. *Please take a break. Hug your dog, cat, a healthy family member, a pillow, stuffed animal, and/or yourself.*

2. *Think of anyone in your life right now who needs support. Envision them wrapped by a golden light. Imagine that your heart and their heart are connected by an invisible string. Take a few breaths, envisioning that string and how the protective light around them can brighten because of your connection.*

Happiness Might Not Be the Point After All

While clearing our son's Seattle apartment after he died, I felt wide awake to every detail of his apartment: the smell of his favorite wool coat, the unmade bed with a comforter I had recently given him, stuffies and books that had been his since he was small, pots and pans from our wedding that we'd passed down to him, notebooks filled with writing that revealed the depths of his illness and his despair.

A KUOW reporter, Deborah Wang, asked to interview me and Matt while we worked. I welcomed the opportunity to reflect on the experience. Something I said became part of her headline: "We get it wrong when we say the point is to be happy."

I was having a moment of clarity that being curious was more interesting than chasing happiness. I also said this: "I think the point is to explore all of life's complexity, and Calvin's very complicated life gave me layers of complexity that I couldn't possibly have had without him."

I hadn't studied ambiguous loss then, but I realize now that I was already beginning to seek meaning from my losses. On my first Christmas without Calvin, I wrote this poem, which referenced an actual postcard that came in our mail from Ford, about the car he leased when he was jetting around in mania:

Uncompleted Recall

The postcard arrived just before Christmas.
Your name so familiar, the addressee.
A smudge from the postal machine blurred the text,
But instructions for *What You Should Do* were still legible.
Expedite Repairs. Call the 800 number. Immediately.

I breathe in, and I breathe out. Sort the rest of the mail, but I set
this aside.

It was a terrible day, when you were so ill,
And you believed the devil pierced your tire.
Your call that day was a turning point for us,
A clear sign you were you but not you.
The car became a symbol for your decline.

I breathe in, but the out gets stuck.
I feel compelled to trace your name with my finger on this card.

You will not be calling. Repairs are past making.
They do not know that you died, long after
The car they are so worried about was impounded.
There was no safety recall for your brain,
When you believed your mind would fuel the car.

A breath out is barely possible, followed by a shallow in.
The message is funny, not funny.

I cannot remember whether you ever drove again.
Memories linger from your sixteenth birthday,
The gift of Grandpa's Mustang, fast and fun.
The world was an open road then.
Welcoming you to take the wheel, your steady eye.

Breath comes and goes, but I do not notice.
Staring at the postcard, with its weird metaphors.

Our service center authorized to perform repairs
Or any updates necessary. Do not delay.
Years too late to repair what?
What might have saved your life?
Why was the repair plan for your mind so unclear?

A loud breath leaves. A sigh: A cry. Ford Motor Company.
One of your delusions. They wanted your soul.

No service center was authorized
To conduct an assessment or order new parts.
What broke was an enigma, no fault no blame.
But, ouch, the shame. Yours and mine,
We were ill-equipped to turn back time.

Under my breath, that song—
About mamas who once sang to their kids, now stressed-out
adults.

Reality slipped; the songs became screams.
You crashed your way through a few painful years.
But the road closed. Warning signs everywhere.
No directions. No map. No roadside respites.
Your life was completely unfinished. Undone.
A breath interrupted. *Uncompleted Recall Notification.*

There was no silver lining to Calvin's death, but I was looking for a way to connect with loss and realized grief was teaching me things about myself and the human condition. I learned later about coping with ambiguous loss by identifying the losses and asking what those losses mean. I'm glad I figured out some of that on my own, but it's even better when you start with helpful vocabulary. That's where we'll begin with our coping guidelines, in the next section.

Do now:

1. *As you prepare to read Part 3, write down a few of your personal goals related to coping.*

2. *Write this: My life is important. I will be patient and kind with myself as I consider new ways to heal alongside ambiguous loss.*

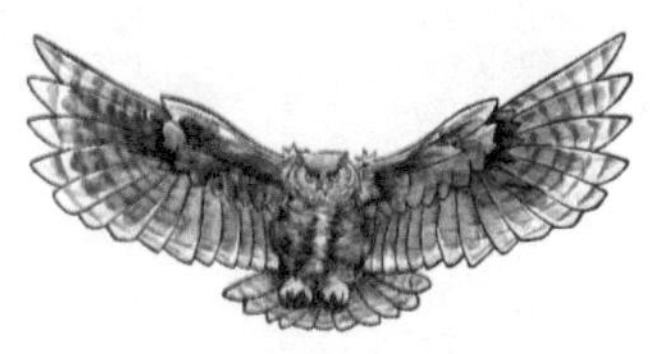

Part 3

Coping Guidelines

Think of your grief like a persistent child that becomes increasingly petulant when disregarded. My youngest grandson—he's eight—often hollers from across the house: "Gramma, come here!" If I don't, he calls again. He eventually comes to find me. "I'm hungry!" He's skinny and scrappy, without an ounce of fat to hold him until his next meal. When he notices he's hungry, snack time is *now*, or a meltdown might be around the corner.

That little voice of your ignored grief? She may not cry loudly at first, but there will be fallout if you don't find her, turn on the lights, and ask if she needs a little something. I call my little voice "Grief Girl"—a she. As a mom I guess it helps to anthropomorphize my grief because I've always been pretty good at taking care of others, just not always myself. If she's a hurt someone who needs my help, well, that's a situation I can rally for! Please use any pronoun or name if it helps you understand this entangled relationship between ambiguous loss and your grief.

Picture Grief Girl mostly hidden inside a shadowy figure that grows and shrinks, disappears or looms large. You might know grief's in there, but you're struggling to see it because of this thing obscuring your view. That amorphous anomaly is your ambiguous loss. Because it's so hard to pin down or identify, grief can seem misplaced. It's easy to turn your back, tell Grief Girl she has no right to bother you with her troubles.

Here's something really important to know: Grief Girl isn't the one shapeshifting. She's solid, seated, and waiting for much-needed nourishment, while her shadowy partner *loss* creates chaos and confusion. Your loss is ambiguous, not your grief!

Your grief is deep within you, there because of your personal experience with loss, but the loss got in there because of something that happened to you. The ambiguity is in the situation that led to the loss. You were going about your business, doing life, when this stormy thing roared through and rearranged all the rules. Loss left a residue in you because you care—because you are a human being—not because you failed to duck and cover.

Once inside, an ambiguous loss hovers around the grief it made. The edges will always be fuzzy, but once you get your bearings you can navigate into the cloudiness. Call your loss by its name, and things might settle long enough for you to find your way to Grief Girl, delivering a tray of soup and crackers before she gets so hangry that you can't think straight. Eventually, you taking care of you becomes the most logical and natural thing you can do. If you're already starved from lack of self-care, please be extra tender as you feed yourself love and kindness one bite at a time.

What does it feel like when grief goes unnoticed and unfed? You may feel stuck, frozen, physically ill, or really, really mad. You could be consistently sad, jumpy, insecure, or uncharacteristically unfriendly. You might not want to talk to other people at all, unless you must open your mouth to talk to your boss or maybe to order a sandwich. During the worst years of my son's illness, I was a grumpy grocery store guest. I would catch myself glaring at other shoppers while growling under my breath, "Get out of my way." I knew I was behaving badly, but I was really pissed off at the whole dumb world.

When someone called to ask how I was doing, I might randomly rant about politics, relishing any opportunity to unload on a topic easier to talk about than my family falling apart. At some point, I realized the problem wasn't innocent bystanders; it was me. But it wasn't easy for me to figure out that I was irritable because I was grieving. My losses were tough to pin down, and other people kept pleading for my reassurance: "At least he's still alive, right?!" Yes he was. Then I should be happy, right, not angry and depressed?

Until I got tools to work with these confusing inner struggles, I just felt off—really, really off—like being lost inside my own skin. I feel that a lot less now, but progress has been in fits and spurts. Sometimes I forget that coping isn't ever over. When I slack on my self-care, Grief Girl has to get ugly loud to remind me that I can do better by her—better by me.

Six years after Calvin died, his death anniversary was in the middle of the week. In past years, Matt and I hiked or surfed, scattered some of Calvin's ashes in a meaningful place. We buried one small biodegradable urn by a tree in Oregon's Deschutes Forest, on the property of our dear friends Kim and Andrew Audova. They loved Calvin like an extra son and keep many of his books and toys for children visiting their bed-and-breakfast. When we visit Red Cone Lodge, we stay in the suite by "Calvin's Corner," giving me a place to love up Grief Girl.

On another anniversary Matt and I carried a small urn of Calvin's ashes to the top of Angel's Rest, a rocky outcrop on the Oregon side of the Columbia River Gorge. Three bluebirds sang to us as we tossed Calvin's ashes to the wind; those were the only songbirds we saw that day. I always felt like the veil between this realm and the great unknown was thinner that day—like everything meant something. Maybe it's because I was more sensitive and paying attention. For five years Calvin's death anniversary was special like that.

Heading into year six, I decided to keep up with my regular routine. There was a lot going on and I was fine. Big mistake! By week's end I was weepy and saw very few reasons to pull my head out from under the covers. I had a sinus cold, so there were multiple explanations for my messy misery. Still, I knew this inertia went deeper. I dragged myself around the house for a few days, did only what was absolutely required.

At some point, realization slapped me upside the head from the inside out. It was her, my little Grief Girl: "What the heck you doing? Calvin, your son, the one you honor with all this work. Yeah, he died, and you just let March 18 come and go like any other day. I am not cool with that. Stop. Do something different. Now!"

It was illuminating and embarrassing to admit that I didn't take time to honor my grief. I was teaching this stuff! It helped to tell my ambiguous loss seminar participants what I'd done. They got me. We had a chuckle. It was so good. Once I paused long enough to pay attention to what was happening inside of me, it became clear that I needed to pivot.

I canceled a work trip, knowing I would spend the week tending my head, while my eyes and nose sprung leaks for all the reasons. Despite being sick with grief and a head cold, though, I wasn't restful. Around five one morning, I shuffled into my office and opened my laptop, not sure what tasks to address since I'd cleared my calendar of the trip I didn't take.

Without totally knowing why, I opened a blank file in Word. Maybe I'd write a few things down. Or, a little voice deep inside me said, maybe it was time to write *my book*. "Wait," I thought. "What did I just hear myself say?"

"It's time to write your book," that little voice said, a little louder and firmer. In my jammies, feet stuffed into fuzzy socks, with hair sticking out in every direction, a box of tissues at arm's length, I started to type. My nose ran, my eyes ran, and lines of text ran down page after page. I found a flow for three days, and on Friday evening my eyes widened to see that I'd assembled more than ten thousand words. That Mary Oliver poem, *The Journey*, whispered to me: " . . . there was a new voice, which you slowly recognized as your own, that kept you company . . . "

As I strode deeper and deeper into my story, I felt a renewed determination to save myself by really, truly reckoning with my ambiguous loss and the grief it caused. Sure, I'd been coping, using strategies, even teaching them! But there were so many layers, and I needed to go deeper. I knew I was on the right track, honoring my grief, because I started to feel better.

Writing is self-care for me. It's hard, sure, even excruciating sometimes. But after I've given words to an experience or really described a feeling I'm having, I know myself better. It is through knowing myself, and greeting myself with as much patience and kindness as I can muster, that I keep getting better at healing myself. As I heal, I've got more to give. I feel more connected to all that's happening in the world and how I might best help.

An all-time favorite quote is by Anne Frank: "How wonderful it is that nobody need wait a single moment before starting to improve the world." What she wrote in her journal was a statement, not a question. Everything about Anne's awful circumstance was ambiguous. Still, she turned her helpless and unjust predicament into an opportunity for reflection, taking notice that the actions of every single person matter. She also seems to have sought words to soothe herself. We are lucky she did, because her writing has impacted many generations.

We can be more like Anne. She had thought long and hard about what she was going through, and writing down her reflections was an act of defiance against systems that tried to make her forever invisible. Her losses were ongoing, and her life ended horribly. Still, she illuminated an experience that needed to be seen; the light she left lingers importantly.

SMI doesn't have a seat in society's front parlor either; it's in a back room, behind a trap door, hunkered down and waiting for rescue. To open doors and expose the harm, we need our voices to be strong and clear. Not everyone needs to be an activist, but if we're all honest and open about what we're going through, we will be a force for change. Sincerity starts with how you treat yourself.

When I taught yoga, I learned about Indra's net, from Vedic tradition, which blankets all and is strung with multifaceted jewels. Each jewel is reflected in all others, such that any dull jewel diminishes the entire net. The metaphor accentuates how self-care is never selfish. Here's a more Western analogy that you've likely heard: You obviously cannot help someone with their oxygen mask on the plane if you're suffocating because you left your own mask dangling.

Go ahead and take a deep breath right now. Notice that you're breathing—what it feels like to really breathe. Drink it in and notice that you are taking care of your body. While you do that a couple more times, take a moment to give yourself grace if you don't breathe deeply very often. You've been hurt. It's scary. I know. I've been afraid to breathe deeply too, thinking it might show me something I've been too afraid to look at. It's okay. You're okay. Breathe.

I wrote this book because not writing this book was hurting me. That's why your big-picture challenge as you journey toward healing is to ask yourself: *What is the thing you aren't doing because grief has gotten in your way?*

As you work your way through the coping guidelines, you might find barriers behind barriers. Each guideline includes at least one common barrier to overcome to move deeper into your coping. When you meet up with resistance, ask yourself questions about what might be blocking you. Encourage yourself to rest. Take your time, but keep going.

I'm sorry, but my book doesn't offer a five-minute fix. Coping with ambiguous loss takes time, patience, and consistency—like tough physical therapy instead of a quick pain pill. I told yoga students this: "Yoga works because you do yoga, not because you believe in yoga." The same is true here. The more you practice coping, the more you benefit. And like with exercise, pushing too hard might make you want to quit. Use the Goldilocks principle and try to seek that sweet spot of just right.

Stay with it. I promise it's worth it. Your life matters. If you're not really living life right now because of ambiguous loss, it's time to get quiet, kind, and patient enough to really listen to the voice that's been trying to tell you about what hurts and how you can help yourself heal.

Do now:

1. *Practice square box breathing: Envision inhaling up the left side of a square as you count to four, then hold your breath across the top of the square for four. Envision sliding down the right side of the square for four and hold the breath out across the bottom of the square for four. Repeat three times.*

2. *Write these questions, and consider any answers:*

   a. *What are you not doing because of feeling stuck?*

   b. *How can coping help you unlock your potential?*

Self-Care All Day, Every Day

The six coping guidelines developed by Dr. Boss and adapted for this book are all about self-care, but it's going to take some time for them to be part of what you do all the time. This chapter is the warm-up. You may need to rethink what self-care even means. It's not just a day at the spa or a getaway vacation, although those special treats are nice. True self-care is available in every single moment. How you talk about yourself inside your own head can be self-nurturing or cruel, for example. Take charge and change the channel when your inner dialogue is critical. If inner voices are beyond your self-control, please seek help from a professional.

You do self-care any time you pause to notice your breath or your feet on the ground. Make a cup of your favorite tea and really, really notice the taste and feel of that first sip. Call it "a sip of peace," and relish everything about it: the taste, temperature, the feeling of the cup in your hand. . . . Here are a few other ways to integrate self-care into even the busiest schedule: Prepare food that makes you feel good, stay hydrated, make your bed, step outside, use your favorite hand lotion, cut yourself some slack. Please make your own everyday list, and commit to it.

This is your number one job because how you meet your own needs for well-being, rest, self-love, kindness, and emotional safety impacts everybody in your orbit. If you don't heal, your family, your community, and the world suffer the ambiguous loss of you.

If your physical and/or emotional safety are compromised because of living in close proximity to someone with untreated or under-treated SMI, please clarify your physical and emotional boundaries. I've spoken with many moms and dads who are willing to lie down on a proverbial railroad track to try to save the person they love, often because of treatment criteria that require direct evidence of harm. Please remember that a person who may be unwell now would not hurt you when they are healthy. When in recovery, they would be horrified to know if you were hurt because of them. Everyone is harmed if you are harmed. Set clear boundaries and maintain them.

When self-care becomes your habit, your instincts will guide you about what that means for your specific circumstances.

As you begin this self-directed journey toward healing with ambiguous losses, you might find that the process feels very private, or you might feel like you want to talk it out with people you trust. Follow your instincts and consider that choice as an act of self-care.

Our brains are hard-wired to pay closer attention to negative experiences than positive ones. I'm no neuroscientist, but I know that something bad and scary sticks to memory with a firmer grasp than something pleasant. It's a survival thing. To override this hard-wired habit, called the negativity bias, you have to pay attention when you feel comfy or pleased. Incorporate that knowledge into your self-care plan. For example, if there's a sunrise or sunset, stand there in awe. Really notice every color, the smell of the air, any breeze, the temperature. Whenever an opportunity presents, pause to really see a bird out the window, or an interesting cloud. Pause at a doorway threshold or while turning on a light to take a breath, feel the ground, and really show up. You are settling yourself in the moment, and you are making memories to revisit whenever you need a peaceful sensory infusion for your nervous system.

Do now:

1. *Take a moment right now to notice your breath in your body. If you can, try to feel your breath moving from your feet to your head and back down again. Surrender your weight to the ground, a chair, a pillow—anything you are touching. If it doesn't feel too weird, put your hand on your heart and take a few breaths while you feel your own heart beating. See if you can steady your heartbeat by beaming a sense of kindness there.*

2. *Use this moment to acknowledge that what you are going through is hard and sad. Give yourself the grace you would give someone else in your situation. Recognize grace as an act of self-care.*

3. *Make a list of simple daily things you can do to care for yourself.*

If self-care and self-directed healing are not enough for you, please consider if you need professional help. Call 988 to access the national Suicide & Crisis Lifeline or find a local alternative number for crisis support.

Make Meaning

My baby boy's brightness illuminated my life the moment he slid out of me and into the world, flooding me with purposeful plans for our future together. The places we would go! I always kissed him good night, then stood over his crib to watch him fall asleep while I whispered, "You are so important." To me, that meant he would grow up strong and confident. He would become a force for goodness, someone equipped to fix wrongs that needed righting. I was certain his life would amaze me, and we named him accordingly, after the philosophy-inspired character from the comic *Calvin and Hobbes*. Of course my baby had a stuffed tiger.

Bill Watterson ended his ten-year-old strip on December 31, 1995, a month after my Calvin was born. On their final Sunday morning together, comic strip Calvin and his tiger friend Hobbes went sledding. It was a "day full of possibilities." Back then we got an actual newspaper delivered, and we laughed and laughed at the perfectness of the comic as we launched our new parenting journey with this sparkly baby boy. The wide-mouthed cartoon Calvin said, "Let's go exploring!"

There was so much meaning in everything we did then. Being Calvin's mom meant I had a little buddy to cart around at the grocery store, one whose rosy cheeks and dancing eyes often caught the attention of another friendly shopper who would stop and smile, tickle his tummy, admire his stoutness. I was so proud to have made that little person! When he was two, I sewed him a Winnie-the-Pooh suit on my grandmother's 1936 Singer. My life felt rich in the past, present, and future. I hummed and sang Pooh truisms; "It's so much friendlier with two!"

My preschooler would strut with importance through our neighborhood parks, making friends as he learned to pump all by himself on a swing, ride a scooter, pedal his bright blue bike with training wheels. I presumed all those milestone achievements meant I was a good mom, doing all the things to raise a little person who would be ready to take on the world one day. I documented his growing up in elaborate scrapbooks. That was a thing we moms did then.

His lovey was a floppy clown, with legs that pulled down to make the music box inside play, "You Are My Sunshine." How happy he made me, even when skies were gray.

That verse has an ending though: "Please don't take my sunshine away."

What is meaningful often reveals itself most profoundly when there is contrast. It took me years to make use of my sorrow, but eventually it became clear that Calvin's enduring importance was up to me. I saw no choice but to make meaning from his painful, psychosis-surged years and my journey onward from a very dark place. His beautiful childhood creates a contrast that is impossible to unsee, providing perspective for those who might misunderstand mental illness as always being caused by a mother's mistakes.

Just no! The gift of Calvin's too-short life means I can stand up with other mothers like me and speak truth to power. Our children's illnesses do not mean we were bad mothers. This is not our fault! Across the United States there are Angry Moms and Mad Moms (yes, those are real groups) uniting to share our stories. The system is broken and breaking our families, but we didn't start out broken.

Mental health advocacy has been my way to make meaning and find purpose from my losses. As you feel ready to look back at what has broken your own heart, I encourage you to consider with nonjudgmental openness how your own losses might reveal something meaningful for you. Please don't misunderstand this as a quest to find a silver lining. Not all things happen for a reason, and I despise that phrase. My son's life and unnecessary death were not a "gift." Hard no.

Still, what happened is done and I cannot change the past. Finding meaning in my rearranged life is really my only way to locate a purposeful path to stride onward. The gift is my own ability to look around with awareness at what I've been through and where it has landed me. The gift of this darkness is to feel into the magnitude of what it means to be a hurt person—and to know (really know!) that I'm not the only one feeling the weight of the world.

I've stopped worrying when I feel stuck. Being held down by grief doesn't mean I'm helpless or broken; it means I'm normal. I do what I need to do to care for myself, contemplate my circumstances, and find what I need to move onward again with meaning and direction. I've rounded up enough tools to know that my only other choice is to lose myself forever in grief. I want more for my own life and for my memory of Calvin's. I want to map my way, not leave things up to chance. In one comic, Watterson's Calvin wondered whether a person's destiny is predetermined "by the stars." Practical Hobbes thinks more like me. "No," he answered, "I think we can do whatever we want with our lives."

Do now:

1. *Write this down: Make meaning.*

2. *Under that, write these prompts, leaving room to jot down answers that occur to you now and more to come:*

   - *What have I lost?*

   - *What do these losses mean to me?*

   - *Are there "both, and . . . " experiences?*

When I do this exercise myself, my list of losses gets long quickly. What those losses mean takes longer and can feel pretty fluid. Here's what I've got right now, in the predawn of an early spring morning when once again grief drew me away from sleep and into my writing: Losing Calvin means I got to be a mom to a son through childhood but not adulthood. I taught him things for the purpose of "when you grow up," and sitting with that takes me all over the place emotionally.

Did it matter that I didn't buy soda, to protect his "you-only-get-one-of-those" liver from high fructose corn syrup? What difference did it make that I taught him to separate light clothes from the dark ones? All the colors blurred to gray anyway. All those scrapbooks were supposed to be his—to show his kids, passing on all those memories. I'm keeper of the stories now, repurposing them to shine light on mental illness from a mom's eye view.

It might surprise you to know that my losses do not mean I'm strong, and I don't like being told that I am. I feel weakened by loss, with less stamina for new traumas. I didn't choose to be a supermom charging across the universe to try to save my son from his evil illness and the sinister system. I did what I could to keep him alive, and now I'm doing what I can to keep myself that way. I have found some strength, sure, but I'm no Wonder Woman. I'm just me.

You're just you, and you might be stronger than you think, but it's also fine to acknowledge when you feel weak, tired, unmotivated, discouraged, and all the other things that are real and that show you're a human person in a situation beyond human expectation.

This is a really important point. If you are grieving, it's because you are a person experiencing something intensely sad. Recognize your sadness and lean softly into what sadness feels like for you. Steeling yourself against it can freeze your grief, and you won't be able to continue onward until it thaws. Here's more about what this coping approach isn't:

- This is not a call to "get over it and move on." That's a cruel, stoic approach that can make you bitter.
- It's not instruction to hyper-focus on the anxiety and trauma: Chances are you're already good at that!

Because undoing the past is not an option, pause to consider how becoming wizened by loss is logical. By naming what you lost and what it means, you expand your vantage point.

Do now:

1. *Look at something in the room you're in. Hyper-focus on it. Don't let yourself see anything but that. Notice how narrow your vision gets. Then come back to the book.*

2. *You back? Okay, great. Thanks for doing this with me.*

3. *Now pull your eyes back and look all around. What is the farthest thing you can see? How many things can you actually see at once? What does it feel like to lean back a little bit, visually and physically?*

You can also think about this as being like putting marbles in a jar. When the jar is full, more marbles don't fit, right? You solve the problem by getting a bigger jar!

Expanding your vantage point is sort of magic. Your jar just got bigger, and now you have capacity for a fresh sense of purpose. You've got a place to put some moments of peace. Carve out some space for even happiness, so it doesn't get squished out if it happens to show up for you.

Here are a few empowering statements to enhance this project of making meaning while expanding your perspective:

- I am sad because sad things have happened to me and my loved ones.
- I feel grief, and I am more than my grief.
- I have the right to purpose, hope, and joy, despite grief that is ongoing.
- I have room for all of my experiences.

Do now:

If any of the sentences above feel especially important to you, write them down or highlight them to revisit later.

In each of my ambiguous loss coping seminars, participants have explored the coping guidelines in unique ways. Some write in a journal, paint, write song lyrics, take photographs, or talk through the prompts with people they trust. One participant sketched herself in a downcast kneeling position with a broken heart on her shirt. Surrounding her are scattered pieces of paper, with words related to her loved one's condition: "psychosis, diagnosis, unstable, suffering...." Next to each page is a word that describes a loss: "time, health, peace of mind, faith, sleep, joy, friendship, money...." When she shared her art with the group in our online meeting, there were tears and heads nodding in solidarity.

Another participant wrote a song dedicated to her young adult daughter. Her lyrics reflect life dreams lost to SMI and new meanings still being discovered:

"There are things I wanted you to have
Things I wanted to share with you
Your first job, driving a car
See you grow and thrive

"I may seem strong, but I often feel weak
Each day I'm just trying to hold on

"Your wedding day. Your children at play
So many things forever lost . . .

"But I will love you
For every day that you are still here
Visiting you with your brain so hurt
Not the life I wanted for you."

This parent explained that writing the song was cathartic. "The lyrics bubbled out in a way that spoken language can't," she said.

At the start of each seminar, I ask participants if they feel open and curious or resistant. The answers are always a mix, and I remind people to regularly check in with how they are doing because the answers can change. You can do the same!

Sometimes you will probably feel open and curious. Other times you may bump into resistance. When that happens, give yourself permission to pause and consider what it's like to sense resistance within yourself:

- Is there fear or anxiety?
- What is that like?

Let your intuition guide you as you patiently explore what you feel. Whatever you bump into is okay: You can feel what you feel without doing anything about it. There is no need for judgment when you are on a tour of your feelings and emotions. Take a look around and listen for any inner wisdom that might speak to you. Just because you think something doesn't mean it's true, and just because you feel something doesn't mean you have to do anything about it.

As you contemplate what you've lost and what those losses might mean, keep watching out for "both, and . . . " emotions. I am both furious that my son died and grateful that his too-short life gave me an important new life purpose. His death came with both grief and relief because our lives had become such a struggle. These statements and contemplations are all part of my ambiguous loss healing journey.

As you approach this self-work, you may feel both excited and reluctant. It's possible that you will feel grief in a new way, and it's possible that listing your losses will bring some measure of relief. None of that may be true for you, so pay attention to your unique experience. One day's list might be really different from another day's list. See your list as something that will never be finished and that you can return to whenever you want.

> **Do now:**
>
> *Now that you've made an initial list of losses and thought about their maybe meaning, pause to consider these questions:*
>
> 1. *How did thinking about these questions make you feel?*
>
> 2. *Are your emotions a mix?*

Some seminar participants said making the list made them feel sad. That makes sense! It's not bad to feel sad; it's honest. One person said the list "raised old wounds." Others felt this: "angry, unburdened, anxious, unsettled, emotional, inadequate, sorrowful, regretful, afraid to have hope."

Try to stop yourself before you jump to judge your emotions as good or bad. Instead, get curious. For example, are any of your mixed feelings opposites to one another—like cold and warm? Think of standing in the snow, with chilled cheeks, while your fingers are toasty warm in woolen mittens. You can feel both things, right? You obviously don't need to decide if the cold cheeks or the warm fingers are good or bad. In fact, all feelings and emotions that contradict one another can coexist without getting marked by gold stars or red slash marks. As you journey along your coping pathway, try to get comfortable with all kinds of incongruities and let them be what they are.

Mixed emotions are further addressed in the section about normalizing ambivalence, and there's a thought experiment at the back of the book to help you take that guideline to the next level. For now, just know that it's normal to have mixed feelings about what has happened to cause ambiguous loss in your life. Start to adopt a "both, and . . . " approach whenever you can.

If you experience frustration or mental blocks when you try to make your lists, you might want to consider barriers that commonly get in the way. Remember that you're on a quest to figure out if there's something you're not doing because grief got in the way.

Do now:

1. *Think about what you've done so far with this first coping guideline, which asks you to think about your losses and make meaning from them.*

2. *Note any resistance, without judgment but with curiosity:*

   - *Is something stopping you from getting started?*

   - *Is there something specific that might be making you afraid to name what's been lost?*

Barriers to Making Meaning

There are a few specific reasons that people might struggle to make meaning of their losses. Below are some of them.

Revenge and hate: Focusing on spite can make you rigid, halting progress toward resiliency, which means being adaptable. Imagine if a tree stood stoically in a stiff wind until finally cracking and breaking in two. Wanting revenge or focusing on hate is like that for you—making your whole being brittle and vulnerable to collapse. To be clear, resiliency isn't the same as stoicism.

The tree that bends and sways with the wind can survive, and so can you if you soften your self-defenses. Keep in mind that revenge and hate most likely blow right past the people you're mad at anyway, swinging around to hurt you instead. Because of that typical blow-back, getting kinder and softer is super important to self-care.

Start small, with random acts of kindness: Offer help when an opportunity occurs naturally, like if a friend asks you to walk their dog, or a stranger needs you to hold the door because their hands are full. Enjoy what it feels like to be kind and helpful and how those choices impact how you see yourself. I'm not encouraging you to slip into a habit of always putting other people ahead of yourself. To counter feelings of revenge and hate, these small acts of kindness need to feel doable and energizing.

When you're ready, graduate toward bigger challenges, like how to rethink family traditions that aren't working anymore. For example, if your family's regular Sunday brunch is strained by arguments related to a loved one's unpredictable psychotic behaviors, the event could simply end with everyone feeling angry and hateful. Is something different still possible? Could family members meet up for a regular walk in a public park? Would they be willing to gather on Zoom? Who might want to schedule a regular one-to-one phone call?

One year our typical holiday get-together wasn't possible when Calvin was pretty unstable. Matt and I adapted by booking a hotel room not too far from Calvin's apartment and bringing him over to spend Christmas morning in the hotel lobby. I filled the stocking his grandmother painstakingly appliqued when Calvin was a baby and placed it among our little collection of gifts and traditional treats on the hotel lobby coffee table. We watched a classic movie and laughed together. Our day was meaningful, and I treasure those memories. I'm so glad I didn't spend that holiday stewing in my own fury.

> ***Do now:***
>
> 1. *Make a note if revenge and hate have created brittle resistance instead of resilience. What does that mean for you?*
>
> 2. *Make a note of any family traditions or rituals that have been impacted by your ambiguous loss circumstances and any ideas you have to adapt them for the current reality.*

Isolation: Despite being a lifelong extrovert, I pulled inward as loss and grief related to my son's SMI made some human interactions painful and confusing. My Bunco friends expressed caring and concern, but it was hard to roll the dice while merrily rolling along with their stories of children making their way into the world with success and happiness.

Still, I knew it wasn't healthy for me to isolate myself. A wise counselor advised me to add new friends, especially parents who were going through something similar. Not long after getting that good advice, I was asked to speak at an annual fundraiser for my local affiliate of the National Alliance on Mental Illness (NAMI). I talked about how my son's illness was criminalized, how help required harm instead of preventing it. I got a standing ovation and that felt validating.

Afterward, a long line of people waited to shake my hand or give me a hug. Somewhere in that line was Heidi O'Connor, whose son with schizophrenia was a little younger than Calvin and struggling too. He'd been discharged from a hospital without proper clothes, in the middle of winter, hundreds of miles from home, with no phone. The hospital "honored his civil rights" by not telling his family he was being discharged. He was a missing person for about a week before he turned up, nearly starved and fully terrified.

Heidi and I became friends, and through Heidi I met Jacki Elsom, the woman who was with me the day I got the call about Calvin's death. Heidi and Jacki were both part of the core group I formed and called Mothers of the Mentally Ill (MOMI) to advocate for systems change in the Pacific Northwest. Those two amazing women rallied to organize my son's memorial service, including by recruiting help from my Bunco friends and others. I cannot imagine that point in my life without those friends. No one should be alone in times like those.

I have found friendship and solidarity in groups of mental health advocates, but your connections don't need to have anything to do with mental illness.

Do now:

1. *Ask and answer honestly: Are you spending too much time alone?*

2. *What is possible for you to seek community, anything with a shared endeavor: an online group, gardening club, group bicycle rides or hikes, yoga or cooking classes? Where can you unite with others who share an interest?*

3. *Even if you don't feel ready to venture out right now, write down what feels possible into the future.*

Keeping secrets: Stigma and discrimination related to mental illness can get in the way of coping with ambiguous loss if you or your family are hiding in the shadows, embarrassed or ashamed of the SMI situation. Educating yourself about the illness can help you fully understand and accept that this is not your fault. A support group can provide a safe place to practice speaking openly about what's happening.

Families struggle to find resilience if they don't reconstruct themselves around the truth of the situation. Like revenge and hate, keeping secrets makes people and families rigid, frozen in a place of fear and denial. One mom noted how helpful it was to connect with another parent whose adult son with schizophrenia has also been cruel. "Oftentimes, the delusions become so threatening, and the accusations are so disturbing," she said. "It can add another level of shame that we don't often talk about."

Stephanie M. wrote about the silent treatment her son was about to get on his twenty-fourth birthday. "The last time we celebrated his birthday was three years ago, when he turned twenty-one," she wrote. "The thought of him not celebrating his birthday with his loved ones is heartbreaking." Since his schizophrenia diagnosis shortly after turning twenty-one, his milestone moments became lost jobs, a fire he started on a family member's property, a poorly planned move to another state, and a long episode of homelessness.

"He became someone I didn't know," she said. "Angry, full of rage. He tried to attack me. I feel I no longer have a son, and I feel like a failure as a mom. I can't stand the fact that I don't know what's going on with him. He was the apple of my eye. It's a lonely feeling because I never thought his life, my life, would turn out like this. Nobody wants to talk about him. So not a lot of my close friends or family will talk to me either. Because this is who I am now, not the former self I used to be."

For what it's worth, my own son celebrated his twenty-first birthday in jail. Ouch. I can barely type that, let alone say it. I know how important it is to speak openly about what's happening and what's happened, but I haven't told many people that unpleasant truth. I'm taking a deep breath right now. Thanks for listening.

Seminar participants sometimes reveal that our discussions are the first time they've talked openly about the situation with their loved ones with SMI. In one group email thread, Marla Knauss wrote, "I now have a circle of friends that share my same experiences. This truth really feels good and comforts me!"

Please seek people who get you. I promise others are out there looking for the same. If you connect well with someone, figure out if you might have coffee or a regular phone call or a Zoom meetup. I put myself out there and found sisters in solidarity. You can too.

Start to notice if you are stuck in a rut of revenge and hate, if you are isolating yourself, or if you're keeping everything bottled up inside, like an untouchable secret. Find ways to expand outward, through random acts of kindness, finding new friends, and talking openly about what's happening.

> ### *Do now:*
>
> 1. *If you haven't already started your list of ambiguous losses, take a moment to begin now, with whatever small step feels doable.*
>
> 2. *Write yourself a note of congratulations, perhaps to include this sentence: My journey toward coping with ambiguous loss has begun!*

Adjust Mastery

If you're on a quest to save a loved one with a severe brain-based condition, you've probably acquired skills you never expected to need. In the midst of your grief, you may feel like you're visiting the outer reaches of your own patience and emotional self-control while living in a foreign land and trying to learn the lingo.

Maybe you're searching for "magic words" to get a crisis intervention team to come for your loved one who is lost in psychosis and has no idea. Perhaps you've stayed up all night learning the names of complicated medications and how to ameliorate their side effects, but your loved one won't go to the doctor anyway. Maybe you've learned how to take calls from jail, put money into a commissary fund, or post bail. Maybe you can map out homeless shelters like a champ. Perhaps you've done an amazing job of retrofitting a bedroom, backyard shed, tent, garage, or basement into a makeshift psychiatric hospital.

I remember one week, while my son was in jail, that I spent all day, every day, combing through paperwork and notes I'd spread across our massive dining room table. There were names of people and programs, acronyms to define a thing I might ask for, people to call to get another phone number for another person, place, or thing. All my plotting and mapping kept routing me back toward confusion. I couldn't fix this.

If you know, you know. At the center of all this messy helplessness is a broken relationship. You might use every possible communication tool to reach the person behind the illness, knowing they are in there, but never get through. You still love them, but they might say they don't know you anymore. They might even be angry with you or blame you for something related to their own confusion. They may be threatening to hurt you. It's so hard to keep hoping that you might ever see a real glimpse of them again. Sometimes that hope is the very thing you need to stop trying to control.

If you've been there, I know. I see you. None of this is your fault. I could not be master of all things, and neither can you. Please be so kind to yourself!

I didn't plan on this job as an SMI subject matter expert, and if you're a family member you probably didn't either. Neither of us broke the mental health care system, and our families cannot fix it on our own. I see you. I am you. I wanted to believe that if I uncovered every stone I would find a magic wand to call forth the right provider, the right treatment plan, the future our family deserved. Calvin's future wasn't mine to design, and to save myself I had to step back into my own present reality. I had to adjust mastery.

Before I figured that out though, this was me: I was chasing a train speeding toward an inevitable crash, running faster the more tired I became, wearing myself out while getting nowhere. That train was not catchable, but I just kept running.

You too? Take a breath. I eventually stopped chasing that train, and so can you. Pause. Did guilt come knocking? Don't answer that door. Read this:

- This does not mean giving up!
- This does not mean you should stop trying to help your loved one.
- This does not mean lying down in dismay, hoping something will magically transport you back into a time when you felt safe, and life made sense.
- This absolutely does not mean giving up on unconditional love.

Here's what adjusting mastery enables you to do:

- Give yourself a break by adjusting what you expect from yourself.
- Pursue what is logical to try.
- Pursue other activities where you feel confident and competent.
- Expect and accept imperfect relationships.
- Stop endorsing your own guilt for things that aren't your fault.

I was pretty unreasonable about what I expected from myself when I was chasing that train. I believed that loving stronger, caring harder, and trying with every ounce of energy was my job. When things slipped out of my control, I blamed myself. I let guilt drive me harder. That attitude didn't work and needed to change, not only so I could survive but so I could continue to show up for my son and others counting on me.

> ***Do now:***
>
> 1. *Write this down: adjust mastery.*
>
> 2. *Under that write these prompts, leaving room to jot down answers that occur to you now and in the future:*
>
>   - *When do I struggle for control?*
>
>   - *What can I do instead to foster feelings of strength/resilience?*
>
>   - *What helps me let go of idealized relationships?*

A helpful framework is a beginner's mind. Needing to be an expert in all things shuts down new learning and exploration, including when your relationships are shape-shifting. Do not expect your relationships to look like those in the movies, especially when there's an ambiguous loss that has changed all the family dynamics.

Adjusting mastery can be difficult in a society that idolizes self-determination and achievement. Signs and posters are rich with platitudes: "You got this!" "Play to win!" "Make it happen!" Believing those are true and reasonable makes it hard to admit this: "I have no idea what to do here!" Or this: "I've tried everything I can think of and it's not helping."

There is also rampant messaging that can instill guilt and shame. Here's my least favorite: "You are only as happy as your most unhappy child." If that were true, I would have shriveled into oblivion long ago. I would have stopped myself from laughing with my daughter and giggly grandsons. I would have felt too guilty to enjoy the surf without my son. I would not have been able to enjoy my favorite tea or the sight of a bird building a nest without reminding myself that

I was supposed to be sad. I would have been too consumed by grief to write this book.

My son would not have wanted that for me! My son's illness wasn't my fault, nor was his happiness mine to supply.

Simple-minded pillows and placards set you up to struggle, but learning to adjust mastery enables your self-growth and opportunities for a rich life despite the complex grief caused by ambiguous loss. You can find happiness that is yours and yours alone, and you can experience moments of happiness that live alongside grief. Keep taking a "both, and . . ." approach.

Keep remembering that this situation is not your fault. It's Not Your Fault! It's also not yours to single-handedly fix. Start to adjust mastery by stepping back, getting real, and giving yourself grace! Review the section in this book about self-care if you need to remember how to prioritize yourself. Always remind yourself that self-care is not selfish. Your being healthy and whole helps everyone.

Do now:

Highlight or write down these empowering statements:

- *My loved one's illness is not my fault.*
- *These circumstances are not my fault.*
- *I can only do what one person might try with the information and resources available in any given moment.*
- *I would not expect more from anyone I love, and I cannot expect more from myself.*

During my seminars, the moms seem to struggle the most with giving up control. One wrote, "Whenever I think about my son and wonder where he is, how is he living, his loneliness, etc., I want to invite him home and fix it. But I can't. I know now that I can't control the outcomes of his SMI."

In that same email thread, I shared a moment from my own experience, when my son was homeless in Seattle and asked to come home. He was unwell, disengaged from treatment, and cycling through psychotic episodes that matched what had made him unsafe at home in the past. That night when he called I had to be a mom like I never expected to be a mom.

"It was one of the most profoundly sad moments of my parenting life," I wrote. "My son called from the streets, describing the place he was going to sleep, wrapped in the tent we'd bought before he was born, poles lost. He was cold and only about three and a half hours away, but going to get him would not have helped him or preserved our own health and safety, so I just had to say good night. I told him that I loved him to the moon and back. I encouraged him to keep calling. I don't regret that decision because I've worked on coping. Without this appraoch, I would have a hard time ever accepting that at one point that indeed was my reality as a mom."

One mother admitted this coping guideline was super hard but also said it helped. "Although I haven't stopped trying to help my daughter," she said, "I am more able to let go of outcomes that my efforts cannot control."

While giving up control in areas beyond your scope, look for other things you can do that help you feel strong and resilient. These examples might fit but more likely are metaphors:

- If your daughter in psychosis won't talk to you right now, will she sit down and watch a show together? If not, let someone else fill that seat on the couch.
- If your brother with schizophrenia is in jail, will your sister bake sourdough with you?
- If your wife's psychosis makes her believe you're an imposter, can you find a moment of solace mowing the lawn?

Do now:

Write down these prompts and fill in the rest of the sentence in a way that suits your situation:

1. *Right now, because my person is . . . , I cannot . . .*
2. *Instead, I can . . .*

This is not about distracting yourself. It's about taking care of your human need for a break and some nourishment. After you choose your thing and do it, it's important to celebrate: "I did that. I did it well. I'm pleased with me."

Is guilt trying to get in again? Say hi, but don't open the door. There's no need for guilt about doing something that enriches your life. Your loved one with SMI doesn't suffer more because you do things that are good for you and others. Do anything that refreshes you, empowers you, strengthens your sense of self-worth, and creates a reason to get up in the morning. Call it your "adjust mastery workout." Know that it has value because it helps you be who you need to be for yourself and others.

You may need to revisit the prompts related to adjusting mastery over and again to uncover your own pathway forward with this coping guideline. Here are comments that came up as one of my seminar groups contemplated these three prompts:

1. When asked to describe times they struggle for control, they made a word cloud with these topics: "when chaos breaks out, when I get bad news, when my loved one is doing very poorly, when nothing changes, when life doesn't go as planned, when I'm trying to fit in."

2. In answer to the second prompt, about what brings a feeling of strength or resilience, some answered: "helping or listening to others, going to the gym, walking, prayer, yoga, advocacy."

3. In answer to the third question, about letting go of idealized relationship, one person said they felt "grief and acceptance." Others said they felt "hope, stuck, angry, sad, disappointed." One participant was "trying to be realistic" while another took it "one step at a time."

As with all the coping guidelines, keep asking and contemplating the questions. Notice if your feelings about the questions change over time. Know that you are doing important self-care when you give yourself a break from trying to control something that's not yours to control. Keep looking for activities that foster your feelings of strength and resilience, and remind yourself that idealized relationships are a thing from fiction. If you're really stuck, consider if you might be too disempowered to get going on this part of your healing journey. Remember to keep asking yourself what you are not doing because of this unmanaged grief. That's what makes all this work worth it.

Barrier to Adjusting Mastery

Learning to adjust mastery can foster resilience, which is adaptability and recovery from hardship. However, disempowerment related to injustice or victimization can block this coping approach. It might make everything worse to think this: "It is what it is." Some things aren't livable and should not be taken lying down. No, not all things just are what they are.

When your personal safety is at stake, make a change to stay safe. When a policy or law is causing harm, look for any ways you might influence a systemic change. For example, if your loved one with SMI keeps getting kicked to the curb by hospitals that say they aren't sick enough, take a look at the laws or how they're being interpreted and ask yourself whom to call. Call on providers to discharge in ways that meet professional standards as safe and appropriate. Telling your story to impact change can feel like a giant leap forward for your own healing.

I felt so small and inconsequential when I kept hearing that the "best thing" might be if Calvin got arrested. Well that happened, and it was absolutely not a good thing, not a good thing at all. Explaining that to horrified lawmakers and others with power to influence change mattered. I exposed a dirty secret in the system, that providers were teaching families to hack the system by encouraging crime and harm. The system still isn't working, but there are people who understand the problems better because of me, and that has helped me heal.

A man in one seminar described his struggle to feel any control or empowerment. His wife was getting sicker and sicker in their home while crisis responders perpetually said she wasn't ill enough to meet criteria for hospitalization. She used a hammer to destroy the control panels on their home's security system, to tear apart the circuit boards and wiring. She also removed all the smoke detectors and dismantled most of the light switches and electrical outlets. A fixed delusional belief had convinced her that the CIA connected the home's electrical system directly to her nervous system and was using the alarm system to control her and shock her.

At one point, this unwell and untreated woman called the White House to issue a complaint. Her husband could not convince treatment providers to intervene until his own life was directly threatened, leaving him with almost no options for staying safe in his own home. "I certainly have no control during her almost-daily psychotic episodes," he wrote.

His wife ultimately left the United States to live with family in another country, where she's doing poorly. He is left with the enormity of his loss and seeks ongoing empowerment through advocacy. "I'm also thinking about educational opportunities," he says. "During my journey I ran into pockets of people who understood the dynamics, but there were way too many who didn't. For instance, my wife's primary care provider was totally clueless about how to deal with a patient with psychosis, explaining that she seemed 'fine' and giving permission for her to stop taking medication. It was most definitely not the proper response. Ugh."

If your despair over poor care, discrimination, victimization, criminalization, and other SMI injustices consumes you, find a place to share your story. The final chapter in Part 1 of this book provides more context for how the SMI treatment system got so bad. You may want to contact an elected official, write a letter to the editor, or contact a public health official to ask for a change in law or policy.

Adjusting mastery may be one of the hardest coping guidelines to follow. Keep looking for things you might do to feel a sense of confidence and strength. Catch yourself and ratchet down your expectations if you are unrealistic about how a forever-changed relationship might be going. If disempowerment is getting in your way, here are a few additional tips to overcome that barrier, which might manifest as feelings of helplessness, related to injustice:

- Seek actions that leave you feeling empowered.
- Seek solidarity and help from others on a similar path.
- Approach advocacy in small bites that feel within your scope of influence.
- Rest when you are overwhelmed.

- Treatment Advocacy Center offers support and training for grassroots advocates; email advocacy@tac.org with questions.

Do now:

1. *Is there anything in the list above that speaks to you?*

2. *Write it down and mark it with a star to remind yourself to follow up.*

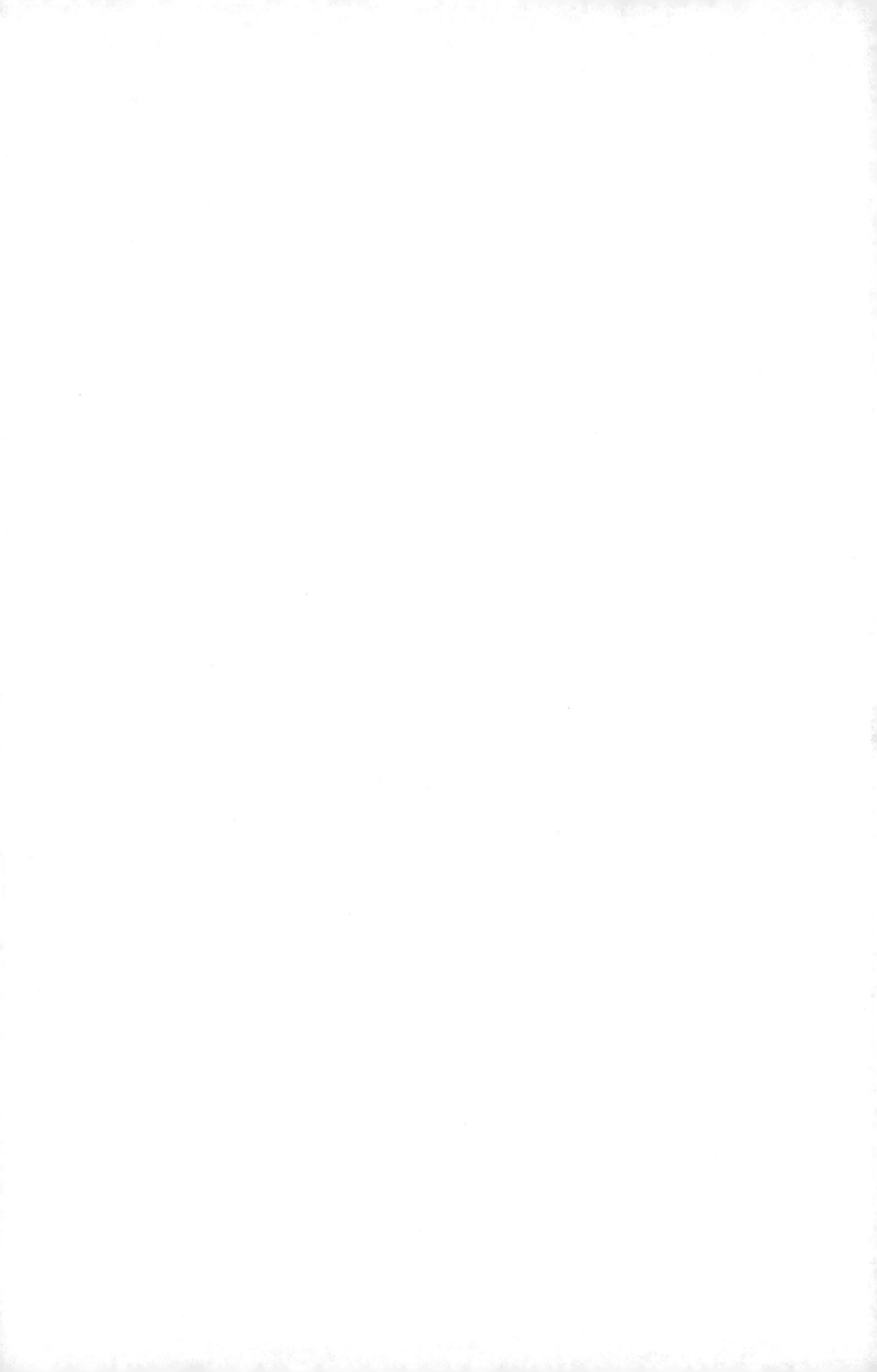

Reconstruct Identity

When mental illness roars into a family, it shakes the foundations of home, health, and happiness. People lose track of how to talk to each other, hold each other up, and share quality time. Of course, family can mean by origin or by choice. Within the group, each person's role shape-shifts, so everyone might go through an identity crisis. It's no one's fault. The ambiguous losses are to blame. If you're confused about who you are and what you're supposed to be doing, it's because you're having a normal response to a very abnormal situation.

In yoga years ago I learned a century-old poem by Juan Ramon Jimenez, "I Am Not I," long before I had a clue what it might mean. Now I realize how potent that poem was to my process. It took stepping back to observe myself—to see how I wasn't being authentic—to see that I needed to integrate my everyday self with the self that I knew had a higher purpose. Here's a funny sentence, but it's true: The self that observed myself helped me rebuild my sense of self.

By sense of self, I mean who you are, your roles and purpose, and how you relate to others within your family and beyond. All of that gets shuffled around when a loved one gets really, really sick. Like when a house is shaken apart by an earthquake, you're going to need tools for this reconstruction project.

Do now:

1. *Write this down: reconstruct identity.*

2. *Under that write these prompts, leaving room to jot down answers that occur to you now and more to come:*

   - *Who am I now that I have experienced these losses?*

   - *Where do I belong and find purpose?*

   - *Can I let go of wanting or needing an absolute identity?*

Keep in mind that your answers, like your personal identity, won't ever be entirely clear. Starting over can feel strange, disorienting, or overwhelming. As always, take your time and be super kind and patient with yourself as you get into the work of it. Remember that the goal is not to get over your losses and move on, but to walk alongside your losses with some sense of who you are and where you want to go next.

Marilyn King, a seminar participant, shared that her son's schizophrenia forever changed her family, her sense of self, and her expectations. "The relentless search for answers, the self-blame, and the shame—these have all been agonizing parts of the journey, and my identity has shifted dramatically," she wrote. "I am no longer just the mother of a successful young man: I am a caregiver, a role that demands constant adaptation and resilience. My son, too, grieves the loss of his former self, the young man he once was before the illness took hold.

"Despite the immense grief, I find moments of profound joy in the simplest things: a shared laugh, a walk in nature, a quiet moment of connection. These small, precious moments illuminate the darkness and remind me of the enduring love that binds us. The grief, however, remains a constant companion, a sharp, intermittent pain that is an undeniable part of my new reality. I've learned to acknowledge its presence, to integrate it into my life, to understand that it is just okay to feel this way."

Without active coping, you might feel lost or stuck, uncertain about what to do or how to do it, unable to make decisions, pay attention, or concentrate. These can also happen with depression, but with ambiguous loss the mental blocks are caused by something outside of you. That's why you have to get outside yourself to cope. You're going to need some friends for this approach to work its magic on your life.

Keep in mind that you don't have to share every detail of your story to talk about your coping work. Knowing that can make it easier to talk to people who don't understand mental illness very well but do understand you as their friend. Find a time and place to talk about how you're figuring out who you are again, now that everything has happened.

Remember, what happened is not your fault. Please say this to yourself again and again, emphasizing each word: *This is NOT my fault. This is not MY fault. This is not my FAULT.* Your normal human responses are something to notice and handle with care as you take a look at how you've been hurt and where you might go from here to rethink who you used to be, who you are now, and how you fit with other people and the world.

I had no idea what to call it when it was happening to me, but my sense of self was severely shaken when my son came home from college in psychosis. I became a blank shell of who I'd been before. There was me in the before times and there was me in the after times. Like most people, I wasn't just coping with my son's illness: It was a whole life do-over. I hope by giving you a tour of my identity crisis and how I kept remaking myself that you can see a useful process to consider yourself.

My before times: I was a yoga teacher who shared wisdom about personal care habits and seeking inner serenity at various studios and health clubs in Vancouver, where I tended our yard and flower gardens and greeted neighbors with a smile and easy small-talk in our tidy suburban neighborhood. I was that mom who made home-made meals, often with ingredients thoughtfully sourced from local farms. My home-canned tomatillo salsa was a late summertime treasure, and a few jars made it to Christmas for gifting to our most important people.

I have been a dancer since childhood and performed with the Lawrence School of Ballet and Prairie Wind Dancers in Kansas, where I lived as a teen and young adult, 1980–1995. After Calvin was born, I kept that part of me moving as Teacher Jerri to earnest young dancers at a Portland studio called The Center for Movement Arts. I was so proud of my beginning ballet students when they took their bows each spring in the annual recital. A favorite piece I choreographed was set to ragtime music, with the one boy in class carrying a prop I built to look like an old-time camera. The girls were so darling as they swirled around, vamping for their photographer with bright red hair bows catching the stage lights. In early elementary school, Calvin was in those recitals too, and we shared delightful mother-son moments.

I was a proud mom who accomplished a lot to get to the point where our beautiful daughter, Michelle, was done with college and Calvin, ten years younger, was just beginning. I had been lucky to get Michelle as part of the deal when I fell in love with her dad, Matt Clark, when she was six. As her brother started college, Michelle was in love, getting married, and buying a house.

I was the wife of a successful information technology professional. I was athletic, outgoing, and enthusiastic toward new challenges—like learning to surf in my forties! I was a master packer when we geared up to travel up and down the West Coast or snow ski on Mount Hood. Right before Calvin got sick, the hard work of mothering was in my rearview mirror. I was fluffing my feathers in an empty nest and awaiting grandbabies to buy little tiny wetsuits and skies for.

My after times: After my son's psychotic break, neither yoga nor my home provided serenity to overcome this surreal place of panic that I lived in. While chasing my son through psychotic episodes, I became an unreliable and often exhausted employee. I tapered way back on my classes and stopped teaching entirely after spending two months helping my mom and dad, during my dad's two months of hospice before he died from cancer, on my fiftieth birthday.

Right before my dad died, Calvin had a psychotic episode that included suicidal thinking scary enough that he took himself to the hospital—his first and only voluntary admission. He had a unique and special connection to his Grampa Jerome. After sitting with my dad while he passed—and quietly with my mom for an hour or so after—I checked my phone. Calvin had left a message from his hospital: "I know Grampa died because he came through me." Staff had disregarded him when he fell to his knees on the floor of the milieu and announced his grampa's death. They assumed it was another hallucination and were stunned into silence when I said otherwise.

Michelle struggled to understand what was happening with her little brother and went silent while serious conflicts in her own marriage consumed her. It would be years before we could reconnect and support her needs again, after her husband (father of our two grandsons) died from substance use disorder two months after Calvin died.

Every pressure point in our small but previously close family threatened to blow us apart. Matt struggled to keep up with the demands of his IT job, and I stopped earning money. The upheaval was way outside my scope of control. I had no idea who I was or what I was supposed to be doing. I just knew I needed to do things differently and that I would never again be the smiling mom in the apron, canning salsa and day-dreaming a dance I might choreograph for the spring recital.

So, yeah . . . my before times became ash and rubble. Showing up for the ongoing fire of the after times took focus and courage. Sometimes I tried hiding under the blankets, but that didn't work for me. I knew I had to stroll into the world as a new version of myself to make progress, so I made a point every day of making my bed, pulling on shoes, and stepping outside. While I walked I thought about my predicament and my ongoing goals. I became determined to figure out who I was now, and where my skills and the needs of the world might meet up.

Do now:

If this question intrigues you, write it down and consider possible answers: Where do your skills and the needs of the world meet up?

My after, after times: Coming up with my own answers sets up this addendum category. Overseeing the injustices that happened to my son and our family, I felt called to do something noble. I was new to the term "advocate," but it felt like a fit. I was going to a weekly support group at my local NAMI. The affiliate's executive director asked me to join a speaking team, called "See Me," that trained first responders (firefighters, ambulance drivers, etc.), about mental illness and how to be compassionate.

I joined the team. It was my job to explain what it was like to be a mom watching a son disappear behind his psychosis. I implored them to think of everyone they encountered as someone's child—to try to see the person like their mom would, as a kind and bright person, trapped beneath symptoms: They're confused, not criminals! I made a lot of people cry, including one paramedic in training who knew my son in high school. He was sorry to hear what happened after graduation.

Since I wasn't teaching yoga and dance anymore, we needed money. Through my NAMI connections, I found a job at a Washington State nonprofit called PAVE, which supports families and young people impacted by any disability. Much of my work intersected with behavioral health, and I started inserting myself into statewide meetings where I could share hard-won wisdom about SMI. As I found my voice and helped other people, I found a renewed sense of purpose. Plus, I got really good at using acronyms!

I read books about mental health system dysfunction, including *Insane Consequences*, by the late D. J. Jaffe. That book led me to begin my grassroots group called MOMI—Mothers of the Mentally Ill. A Facebook page and simple website provided enough visibility for families to unite and impact some changes in Washington and Oregon. Although much work remains in the Pacific Northwest and elsewhere, what I did mattered.

Calvin was proud of my work, and he helped with a few projects. I was becoming a new version of his mom. I was a caregiver, but also someone who could shine light on what wasn't working system-wide. Positive improvements in Calvin's life during his final few months helped me see where to point the flashlight. I was talking to lots of stakeholders by then, and this was my message: "See, when someone gets better help and a place to live they can start to climb back up again. My son is living proof that whole-life support, with better medical care, helps people get better!"

On the Monday he died, hours before I left for a late afternoon coffee with the woman volunteering to help make MOMI a nonprofit (I never did that), an email from Calvin came through. He said he couldn't help with the presentation we were planning together about a savings account called ABLE—Achieving a Better Life Experience. ABLE is for people with Social Security disability benefits to save money for future qualifying needs. Calvin helped me write an article about ABLE for PAVE's website, and we were working on a slideshow for a conference.

I had no idea that the note contained a suicide message. There would be no savings. No future. No logistical life needs to meet eligibility criteria for access to those funds. The last words he communicated to me wished me luck. He signed it, "Love, Calvin."

My new version of being a mom fell off the hotel roof with Calvin that afternoon, about 3:30 p.m. my time and 5:30 p.m. where he was. End of day. End of me as the mom of a son with a life full of meaningful struggle, with a future that could show the way for living well with SMI. The empty shell I'd been filling up with new plans and purpose was purged and flooded instead with new feelings of dark fury. I did everything I could, and my efforts failed. I was an advocate for everyone in the system, sure, but mostly him. He died anyway.

After times again, again: I had to reconstruct my identity as an advocate all over again. Dedicating my work to Calvin helps. Knowing that he loved me and was proud of me does help. My identity as a mom has evolved while watching my daughter learn to parent two non-stop-motion boys. I'm Gramma Jerri now, an honor that keeps me on my toes despite retiring those pointe shoes long ago. The boys sleep in Calvin's old bed, read his books, play his games. Most of the time, that makes me glad.

Sometimes it is incredibly sad, and I have to step away. The boys are too young to know details about how Uncle Calvin and their dad died, but they understand why various family members cry, sometimes randomly. We talk about how sad it is that those important people died so young. I've had a talk with each of them about why they could be especially vulnerable to drugs like marijuana. I want them to understand how important it is for them to take good care of their bodies and their minds, so they can live long and important lives. Helping them grow up is a role with heft.

Knowing I'm important to those boys has helped me reenvision myself. So has providing support and resources to family members through my job at TAC. I know that I matter, that I impact people. One time I talked very openly with a mom whose daughter was threatening suicide. I told her things I wish someone had told me long ago, especially that your unwell child cannot be expected to reassure you that they are okay: "Make sure she knows that it's okay with you if she's not okay. Let her know that you're available to listen to anything she needs to say, even if she knows it might upset you."

I advised that mom to find new ways to meet her own needs so she could let her daughter off the hook. I said, basically, "Stop talking and start listening." A few months later, that mom wrote to thank me for saving her daughter's life. She said her daughter told her that changes in their relationship helped her stay alive.

So yes, I matter to people. But to get there, I had to put myself out there. It wasn't without struggle and effort that I opened myself to other people's pain. I've worked on how to be empathetic but then let other people's problems move on through, so they don't get stuck in me. Sometimes I have to back off—especially when random people dump on me because I'm a pretty good listener. Boundaries: I've worked on those.

In hindsight I see that my version of myself as a mom, gramma, employee, advocate, and friend is never going to settle down in a single location. My identity will forever be somewhat ambiguous as I walk alongside my lifelong loyal traveling companion—loss. Sometimes I have to pause and sit with my experience before I make a choice about what to do or say.

Do now:

1. *Make pages or columns labeled "before times" and "after times." If you want to, add pages for "after, after times," like I did.*

2. *Make a few notes now if you feel inspired and ready, or leave plenty of room to work on this project another day.*

I hope that by telling you all of that about me you might start having a conversation with yourself. How you see yourself, listen to yourself, talk to yourself, and guide yourself has a huge impact on your inner well-being. Keep considering how to make self-care a regular routine. Your needs cannot go unmet day after day, year after year.

Many seminar participants have struggled with the homework related to reconstructing identity. Responding to the first prompt (*Who am I now?*), many identified emotions that were consuming them, rather than roles or other features of identity. They said they were "scared, uncomfortable, misunderstood." They described lost faith. Many quit friends because it was too hard to connect about big stuff and small talk wasn't worth the energy.

During our seminar discussions, many resisted describing themselves as anything beyond a worried and anxious observer to a crisis unfolding in real time. Yet by the end of an eight-week seminar, some participants relished discovering new aspects of themselves: artist, photographer, musician, hiker, new friend, activist.

In one email thread, a number of participants shared about their baby steps toward a personal identity beyond caregiver. One wrote, "I wonder about my identity. I've been overly caring for others, at my own peril, for decades and decades. Who am I if I let go of overly caring for others? My new hope is that I can get really good at caring for myself (I've started on this journey)."

When she reviewed that note, months after finishing the seminar, she shared her progress: "It's taken a long time for me to figure out that I identified mostly as a person who finds her worth in caring for other people. Now I realize that I can use my caretaker skills to care for myself. Better late than never! It's fun and gratifying."

When asked about where they belong, participants reflected with honesty that their sense of belonging was sorely challenged. Some said they found a sense of belonging "with others who understand their grief," "when leaning into their religious faith," or "in nature." One participant admitted, "I have no idea."

When asked about where or when they feel a sense of purpose, participants expressed that helping others, exercising, and doing personal or systems change advocacy provided purpose. One participant responded that they were "waiting to figure this out."

Please keep asking the questions and actively seeking answers. Reconstructing identity requires patience, curiosity, and sometimes discomfort as you put yourself out there to figure out where you feel part of a flow, moving with others toward something purposeful. Remember that your goal is to get unstuck, so you can do that thing that you might not be doing because grief got in the way.

You may want to make a list of your own feelings and consider how they relate to your identity struggle, if you're having one. Here are some feelings listed by seminar participants: "stressed, numb, sad, angry, foggy, shut down, indecisive, unmotivated." If you are overly discouraged and cannot seem to get going on this coping guideline, take some time to wonder about what's getting in the way. Is it one of these barriers mentioned below?

Barriers to Reconstructing Identity

Stigma: Trying to "pass" or mask who you are and what's truly happening can block resilience and adaptability. In the SMI community, the barrier of stigma is tall and wide. Although self-stigma is misunderstood as the primary reason a person with SMI might refuse treatment (anosognosia or lack of insight is the primary reason for that), stigma is a common reason people with SMI and family members don't discuss their circumstances. It's hard to reframe who you are and what you're up to if you don't admit openly (or even to yourself!) that you have changed, your family has changed, and everything you get up for every single day has changed.

I find it frustrating that antistigma campaigns related to mental health have in many ways worsened the stigma for families impacted by SMI. An unintended consequence has been to normalize mental health to such an extent that people think they're supposed to talk about it like there's nothing wrong with anyone. Through that cultural lens, you might feel like you're not supposed to describe a grim or terrifying psychotic episode because it could "perpetuate stigma," even when the details are absolutely true and harming your whole family!

Getting real with people you trust is a starting point. Try to find someone willing to listen and learn with you—maybe in a support group or just with a friend you love and trust. Ask first, with a trigger warning, to make sure they understand that you need to get this off your chest. You can explain that this is part of your ambiguous loss work, that you're feeling pretty lost and confused about who you are because you never thought you'd live as a character in your own horror movie. You might mention that stigma related to SMI makes this difficult for you, and that you trust them to understand that.

> *Do now:*
>
> 1. *Write down the name of someone you want to talk to about your situation and how it's impacted your sense of self.*
>
> 2. *Outline a basic conversation starter and estimate when/where you might make that meet-up happen.*

Isolation/disconnection: Talking with others is important because other people help you know where you belong. Putting yourself into any social situation where you share ideas, goals, or simply friendship can be extremely helpful while you rebuild your sense of self.

In her book, *Loss, Trauma, and Resilience: Therapeutic Work with Ambiguous Loss*, Dr. Boss mentions the peril of identifying only with the illness condition that has disrupted the family. "When a family has a member with chronic mental or physical illness," she wrote, "healthy members must find identities beyond the illness so that they do not become the alcoholic family or the schizophrenic family."

My friend Linda Wiley got a job as a guest experience host at Seattle Mariners baseball games. While her son with schizophrenia struggled to stabilize and stay out of jail, she said, "Having this job has dramatically changed my life of nonstop worry, distress, and sadness."

A single parent, she added, "My job at the Mariners is to greet fans, answer questions, talk with them about baseball (which I love), and offer any assistance I can to make their visit enjoyable. The guests are happy (even when we lose) because they are there to enjoy themselves. When I'm at my job I truly forget about the problems and worries regarding my son, although he and I sometimes discuss the baseball game in detail afterwards.

"I care deeply about my son and the heartbreak of his illness, but I can coexist with those concerns and losses while I am also living my life and spending time in my happy place. I love having co-workers who know me as a co-worker and a fan; none of them know I have a disabled son."

> *Do now:*
>
> 1. *List any activities unrelated to your ambiguous loss experience that help you shore up your sense of self.*
>
> 2. *Make a commitment to keep those activities on your calendar.*

Clinging to an absolute identity: In my seminars, I share a photograph of the yellow-roofed house that I played with as a child born in the 1960s. My chubby toddler fingers would hop those wooden cylindrical family members all about on their plastic yellow stairs, brown lounge chairs, and blue-foam-topped white beds. I would talk for the mom, dad, brother, sister, and dog—playing out roles that fit perfectly with my nuclear family.

I presumed my own turn at motherhood would look like my own happy childhood but with me in the master bedroom and maybe a different mix of kids and pets. I knew I would be a loving and helpful mother. I became that, to the best of my real-world ability.

I had no idea my good intentions would never be enough, and it took a long time to accept that my son's illness had nothing to do with my parenting. Internalizing those true points was necessary for my own healing.

> *Do now:*
>
> 1. *Say these phrases out loud or in your head:*
>   - *My good intentions may never be enough.*
>   - *This illness is not my fault and didn't happen because I failed to be a good [parent, spouse, child, friend, etc.].*
>
> 2. *Make a list of things you've done to be helpful, even if the results weren't what you wanted. Remind yourself that you didn't control the outcome.*

Letting go of an old version of yourself may feel really hard. Hard is okay, not impossible. One seminar participant is a mom to three smart sons. They lived happily for decades in a stable suburban community until one son developed a psychotic illness. He got dangerous enough to get detained by a SWAT team in front of their home. Shortly after that, this mom found herself living in a new home, at an undisclosed location for safety reasons, with no sons living there and neighbors she didn't know.

"We all had to leave our old house without a typical good-bye," she says. "It was so full of emotion. It was awful. I had been a mom, and now I'm a middle-aged woman with everyone gone: my sons, my friends. I'd been in that neighborhood for twenty-six years, and it was comfortable. We were thrown out on our heads, and every piece of comfort was taken. I fought finding a new identity because all I wanted was to hang onto what I had."

That mom is now a mental health advocate who makes herself available to support other families trying to navigate complex systems. She's found purpose in the work and recognizes that adapting to a new sense of self and purpose was painful but necessary.

You can adapt too. If you haven't already, go ahead and write down who you were in the before times and who you are now, in the after times. Remember, you created placeholders in your journal. You might add a third list: "who I'm capable of becoming."

For this project, try to avoid a list of only emotions. Write down roles you fill or might fulfill. Include places where you belong—or places you might insert yourself that could be a fit. Describe your importance, skills, and perspectives that you uniquely share.

You might seek professional counseling to support this part of your coping journey. If so, ask for specific help to rebuild your sense of self. Be sure to mention that you've been impacted by ambiguous loss and that you understand your identity crisis is related to relationships that have been disrupted because of SMI. Try to find a professional with training and skills to address these topics.

Please commit to rethinking who you are, where you belong, and where you find purpose, because your life matters. You matter. When you feel right in your own skin, you'll know you're headed in the right direction.

Revise Attachment

Wendell Berry's poem, "The Peace of Wild Things," calmed me many times while I chased the train that was my son's life with mania and psychosis. "When despair for the world grows in me," the verses begin, followed by a reference to fearful awakenings. That has so often been a fit for my state of mind! While walking through the woods behind my house, listening for birds and frogs, touching bark, and sometimes plopping down among the leaf litter, I often was grateful to Berry for giving written permission to "rest in the grace of the world."

I knew in those moments that I would endure if I could remember to breathe in the scent of the earth and look to the sky. I did that long before I understood ambiguous loss and how I might cope. I'm so glad I did that.

I must admit, however, that those moments of woodsy reverie were perhaps fewer than the times I wailed for hours into nothingness, disconnected from every sensation except the monstrous pain that flooded me. Sometimes my throat was scratched for days, my eyes so sore I couldn't wear my contact lenses. I didn't know how I would ever survive and sometimes didn't want to.

I hated most of the advice coming at me. It worsened my agony when people told me I needed to "let go." I clung to what I wanted back. Desperately. I would not give up on my son, but pleading with the universe to make him better while he kept getting worse was killing me. It took a long time to figure out what it might mean to release the pressure on myself without ending the battle for my son's life.

This coping guideline is about attachment, clinging. If you're feeling anxious, worried I might urge you to "let go," relax. That's not where I'm about to take you. But before I explain more about what it means to *revise* attachment, I want to share a few more things about why this topic can be triggering.

In my Helpline role at TAC, a mom shared that a provider told her to stop trying to help her adult daughter with SMI because "she doesn't want anything to do with you anyway." That mom knew her daughter loved her beyond measure but was pushing family away because of delusions—untreated symptoms. The solution to their relationship struggles was treatment for her daughter, not total detachment! That mom needed to tend her own grief wounds and pace herself, but she wasn't giving up on her daughter. Encouraging her to "let go" was gross and unprofessional. That mom stayed in the fight.

When I was in it, one of the people who recommended I "let go" was the psychiatric nurse practitioner who gave Calvin permission to end his anti-psychotic medication because he believed it was poison. That prescriber refused to discuss the care plan with me, despite my well-researched attempts to get her to consider a trial of clozapine. I knew it had potential to reduce my son's suicidal ideations and explosive anger, as well as his persistent psychosis. She dismissed me entirely, firm in her position that I was the problem and needed to "let go."

Let go of what? Loving my son? Wanting him to have a happy life? Expecting the medical system to use evidence-based and available treatments to care for him? Keeping him alive and out of jail? No! No, thank you!

Still, even as I was a momma Hydra facing off in all directions to contain the fire that was burning through his life, I understood that this inferno was way too big for me to tamp out on my own. I did need to take a step back, tend my wounds, and rethink how best to direct my energy. That never meant I would "let go" of loving my son and doing what was possible to preserve his life. It meant I couldn't burn down my own house, with myself inside. That wouldn't save either of us.

Now we're getting closer to what this coping guideline is about. The first word is "revise," which means to reexamine or make alterations to something. When you adjust, you don't cut ties and let something loose. Instead, you give yourself a break from clinging to the point of exhaustion and save some energy for what's within more reasonable reach. I gave up on that prescriber, but I never gave up on my son.

Several key ambiguous loss concepts come up with this coping guideline, including the one that inspired the title of this book. Take a look at the prompts below and make some notes to orient yourself, and then keep reading to see what the boldface phrases mean.

> ***Do now:***
>
> 1. *Write this down: revise attachment. Underline the word <u>revise</u>.*
> 2. *Under that write these prompts, leaving room to jot down answers that occur to you after you've learned what these phrases mean:*
>   - *Can I accept that someone may be **gone but not gone**?*
>   - *What helps me accept that **what is real may not be ideal**?*
>   - *How do I **let go while remembering**?*

Gone but not gone: Accepting that someone might exist or cease to exist in more than one realm supports coping with losses filled with ambiguity. Here are examples of what that might look like:

- A person is physically present but also absent because of emotional disconnect or mental or cognitive impairments. A person may be so changed by SMI that it can feel like grieving their death at the same time you're trying to save their life.
- A person is physically absent because they are missing (lost, kidnapped, incarcerated, homeless) or they've died for reasons that lack clarity (suicide, homicide, miscarriage, act of terrorism). Their presence lives on in the hearts and minds of people who care for them and, in some cases, might be looking for them.

If the person you love is gone but may not be, try to see the paradox. If you let both sides of the truth exist, you stop using energy resisting the ambiguity and can instead work toward something you might realistically influence or change.

Dissonance and *incongruity* are other words to use when you're thinking and talking about this part of coping. A person with SMI is still the person they were before they got sick but also really different. Your memories and your reality might not match, and that dissonance can make you uncomfortable. What your loved one with

SMI does every day might not fit your hopes and dreams for them, and that's incongruity.

Reconciling paradox, dissonance, and incongruity starts with accepting that none of this may ever get resolved. What's been lost is ambiguous. See the messiness and take a next step anyway to find your way toward resilience. Find new ways to love despite your confusion, and you can foster new versions of your relationships. Stay engaged in all aspects of your life, not just those connected to caregiving, and your life will have meaning, even though grief isn't going anywhere.

Those important next steps are really hard to take if you're stuck trying to resolve the unresolvable paradox of someone who is both gone and not gone. Accepting the truth gives you some breathing room. You can start by using that phrase—*gone but not gone*—to describe your circumstances.

Stephanie M. recognized how hard this can be. "I continue to seek answers about my son's illness," she said, "asking police to do safety checks on him in his last known whereabouts . . . I still think I'm in a nightmare, that this can't be happening to my son. But it is real. I continue to struggle with how to be happy knowing my son is battling demons in his head every day. He is both there and not there."

> ### Do now:
>
> 1. *If this is true for you, write this down: My loved one is gone but not gone.*
>
> 2. *Think for a moment about how it feels to acknowledge that paradox.*
>
> 3. *Also write these words: dissonance and incongruity. Make a few notes if those words help you describe something about your circumstances.*

What is real may not be ideal: This phrase is a good one to repeat like a mantra while you figure out how to come to peace with the ambiguity of a loss. To be clear, you may never have peace with the loss itself—because it's ambiguous!

You can, however, find peace with the ambiguity, by accepting that closure isn't waiting around the next corner. Here's a place where letting go has usefulness. What was once ideal may no longer be possible, so can you let go of that? When you do, you make space and save some energy to explore what's really still possible.

This can feel like a bit of a brain tangle. That's okay. If you're managing an ambiguous loss, you may feel tied up in all sorts of knots. Loosening them takes time and agility in the way you think about your predicament. If you've ever done isometric physical therapy exercises—where you tighten up an irritated muscle in order to loosen it—you might use that analogy as you consider this next activity.

> ### Do now:
>
> 1. *Notice a place in your body where there is a tightness associated with your sense of loss.*
>
> 2. *For just a brief moment, tighten up your muscles to feel like you are pushing on that place.*
>
> 3. *Then just stop trying. Feel the release of pressure in your body. Take a few long, even breaths. Notice what that is like. Can you accept that the loss is still here? Can you see it without giving it all your energy? Is it possible for the loss to be there but take up less space?*

This isn't a one-and-done kind of project. Try it now and then, across time, always with curiosity and kindness. You'll never win a battle to kick the loss out of your life, but you can stop wasting energy trying to fight the ambiguity.

Here's another thing: Without proof of death, detachment isn't possible. Read that again: detachment isn't possible. That mom I mentioned, who was told to stop caring about her daughter in psychosis? That was an impossible ask! She knew her daughter wasn't dead. That mom could never detach from loving her daughter. She could only accept that her daughter may be gone but may not be . . . and then pace herself in choosing what might still be possible while loving her daughter from afar.

Another seminar participant shared that she and her husband had a birthday party for their estranged son. Because of his untreated psychotic symptoms, he was not safe to be with his family, and they had an order of protection—a heart-breaking choice. On his birthday, they ate a special dinner and dessert and talked about their son's birth and childhood, honoring him while missing him. The evening was imperfect, yet it soothed their souls.

Many seminar participants struggle to accept the lifelong standoff between real and ideal. In an informal survey, half of one seminar group said they were uncomfortable with the dissonance but starting to shift. A few said the topic made them very anxious, that they couldn't accept the reality they were living.

In response to this concept, given as homework, seminar participant Rania Dima wrote her thoughts while witnessing a sunrise in the mountains. "This campground is my haven," she wrote, "my place to be shielded among the trees while I sort through my emotions.

"My son is gone but not gone, hidden behind the monstrous mountain of his illness. Behind me, laughter spills out from the camper. My girls have woken, giggling from their bunks. Their brother should be here, groggily laughing alongside them. I can't accept that he is lost to his illness any more than I can accept that a piece of me is gone. But I have no choice. . . .

"The reality of his illness poured black paint into my ideal world. As the dark and light colors swirl and merge into gray, my brightness dims. I become darker, more haunted, a shadow of myself. And so, I sit on the mountainside desperately waiting for the sun to rise high enough for me to catch a glimpse of its rays between the tree trunks.

"Around me, with or without their canopy, the trees stand mighty and tall. Their leaves fall one by one to the ground as they let go. My dreams and my tears fall with them. As they crumble into the earth and turn to dust, I have to remember that they also nourish the soil that brings forth life. Holding on will not stop the change of seasons. Holding on will not heal my son's mind. No one is guaranteed a perfect life. I close my eyes, I breathe. Perhaps the only control I have is choice, to let the wind scatter my memories or to stand here, grounded with the trees and allow myself to feel."

> ***Do now:***
>
> 1. *If you have internet access, look up Wendell Berry's Poem, "The Peace of Wild Things."*
>
> 2. *Are there times when you allow yourself to rest in the grace of the world?*

Let go while remembering: Long after my son got sick, I still clung to an old version of him. That played out one morning when he was sleeping off a prolonged episode of mania. He was about to sleep through a college class he'd enrolled in. I wanted that future so much for him—the degree, the job opportunities, the intellectual stimulation that fueled him through high school. I woke him up! Nothing went well that day. I eventually understood that I could remember and appreciate the brilliance of my son without trying to force him back into being who he was before his brain changed with illness.

The concept of letting go while remembering also relates to my journey in advocacy for my son. When systemic barriers and gaps got in the way, I was forced to let go of expecting help from a professional or program that didn't exist or wasn't set up to serve him. At the same time, I kept telling everyone what my bright, kind, loving son was capable of if he got the right help. I made them keep remembering that he was a person, with a loving family and a life, who deserved good care—even if they weren't providing what he needed.

Since his death, I've treasured memories of who he was, and I've kept his importance alive through my work. That process of remembering is richer because I've let him go. He died, and I cannot bring him back. I could have gotten stuck in a loop, denying the forward motion of my life. My grief could have frozen me in time. I wanted more for me and for his memory. I've learned to let go while remembering.

Do now:

1. *Write this question: What memories do I treasure?*

2. *And this one: Is it possible to honor those memories without demanding that life return to the way it was before?*

3. *If you don't have any answers now, that's okay. Leave some space.*

4. *Take a look at the next section, and make a note if clinging, rigidity, or being a brick wall feels familiar. You don't have to fix anything, but you can thank yourself for getting curious.*

Barriers to Revising Attachment

The barriers to revising attachment are pretty literal. Keep them in mind if you're struggling with the prompts for this coping guideline. All three have to do with attitudes that make you feel stuck or frozen. The concepts don't sound complex, but that doesn't mean they're easy to overcome!

- **Clinging**: Wanting things to go back to the way they once were.
- **Rigidity**: Inability to see that absence and presence can coexist.
- **Being a brick wall**: Inability to accept the disconnect between what is real and what is ideal.

I've always seen parallels between my thinking and my home. For me, wanting things back the way they once were meant I kept Calvin's room just like it was for a long, long time. Same with sections of the backyard, where for many years his childhood play structure stood witness to his haunting absence.

Then, about two years after he died, it was time to change it up. We pulled apart the monkey bars, where he got strong. We used to hang our mama, papa, and baby-bear sized wetsuits there for washing and drying. We took down the climbing wall, with the little bell he first proudly rang when he was about seven. The swinging bridge that connected the deck to his play tower came apart and was gifted to a friend whose kids would use the wood for a makeshift treehouse. The old deck, rotted after twenty years, was hauled away and replaced with a clean new composite deck with black aluminum railings.

Once the new deck was done, I hired a young woman with a gift for color and texture to arrange flowerpots in all the fresh spaces. Matt worked to shore up the flagstone steps and walkways I originally built—with seven-year-old Calvin occasionally helping—in the way back when.

Around the same time, I cleaned out Calvin's room and journaled about all of it: "A weekend at home, doing some projects. Our new deck is fully finished, decorated with beautiful potted flowers. I remember so well the very hot summer day when I built the first stone steps. Chunking away the sod, terracing the dirt, choosing the stones that would puzzle together to make a waterfall of stairs leading to the deck attached to a swinging bridge and play structure. . . .

"Matt and I were commenting this weekend that the last time we did this set of tasks we were in our mid-thirties! We feel different, not different. The passage of time is remarkable to witness and somewhat breathtaking when I pause to reflect on the magnitude of it."

In my journal I mentioned a *Seattle Times* feature article that included stories about Calvin's time spent in homelessness. Published July 25, 2021, the article was part of the newspaper's Project Homeless series, titled: "Becoming homeless in Seattle helped him find psychiatric help. His mom says it shouldn't have taken that long." The article featured a picture of me looking sad, sitting on Calvin's bed, with his debate trophies and surfing décor on display.

That picture—a time capsule, really—showed me holding the gray tweed cap Calvin wore all over Seattle, with his collection of pins and buttons on it, including the NAMI suicide prevention button I gave him. The hat came home from Seattle after we cleaned out his apartment, and it lived on his childhood dresser for two years, next to the Wizard of Oz figurines he meticulously placed the last time he was ever in that room. I tried really hard to help the reporter understand that when he was homeless it was because of his unmanaged illness, not because his family didn't love him and want him to click his heels together, wake up from his frightful delusions, and come back to us.

In my journal, on that weekend of deep cleaning, I wrote how the *Seattle Times* article helped me stop clinging to some of Calvin's possessions. "I decided today to pack away the debate trophies and to put his hat on a shelf in the closet," I wrote. I was pleased to make the room more suitable for our grandsons. "The room isn't a museum. It's a bedroom. I'm letting go a little bit at a time."

The stuff in his room was a complicated paradox, with decades worth of birthday cards mixed with letters he got and wrote from jail. He had scribbled angry and bizarre messages across many of the envelopes. On one, a flow chart described how he was picked up for a DUI, hospitalized, sent home, arrested, and incarcerated for the same DUI because he couldn't be in court and a hospital at the same time. Even in the throes of psychosis, he knew that didn't make sense.

After reading only a few of those letters, I put some into a drawer and others in the trash. I wrote this: "I like the room a little more alive, in the present. Gone are the books that marked the last years Calvin lived here—mostly about getting rich quick and God. It's not that business and religion aren't valuable topics, but they were symbols of his mania. His delusions about being a rich prophet with a business enterprise were such a profound part of his illness. His touch with reality was lost when he started talking about getting rich, sermons he would preach. My momma's heart aches for the dreams he believed were real but weren't really him."

How you sort through your own internal and external stuff is personal, but I encourage you to weed through the physical stuff you might be clinging to if you feel stuck in this project of revising attachment. Start small with one drawer or shelf, a couple of sentences in a journal, whatever helps you feel like you are loosening your grasp on something you don't need anymore, to lighten your load.

One seminar participant described how she overcame a sense of clinging by leaning into her grief before choosing what to release. Her story might trigger you if you are still in a place of fostering old hope, so please read this knowing that this mom arrived here after years of selfless efforts to help her son with a severe psychotic condition and no insight about how to lift himself back toward health. Her helplessness against his extremely complicated illness and an ineffective treatment system required her to chip away at her brick walls.

"I believe that I'm starting to accept that my son's old self is gone," she wrote. "A different man with schizophrenia has taken his place. I don't have the previous creative, loving, joyful, friendly, emotional, exciting, and engaging son that he was, anymore. What helps me accept this is that he's not a part of our life anymore. He's physically, emotionally, and mentally not with us. The longer that he's away, the more I come to realize that this is what it is.

"It's certainly not the ideal that I dreamed about when our children were young. I am letting go of that dream. We were never promised a life without pain. Another thing that helps me accept our reality is knowing that I am growing because of this. Growing in ways I may not have wanted to, but still growing, nonetheless. My hope is that I am more supportive of others with heartbreaks now. I also want to be able to say, at the end of my life, that I did the best I could with what I knew at the time."

Do now:

1. *Name anything you may be clinging to that doesn't serve you anymore. It might be physical, mental or both, like my son's hat that perched on his childhood dresser for more than two years.*

2. *Write how you are clearing that, perhaps with an affirmative statement like this, "I no longer need . . . so I'm choosing to . . ."*

3. *If what you want to clear is internalized, consider writing it on a rock that you toss into a body of water or elsewhere in nature.*

Normalize Ambivalence

Ambivalence is the state of having mixed feelings or contradictory ideas about something or someone. When I introduce this topic in my seminars, I include a slide with a cactus sporting a fluffy yellow flower. Soft and prickly exist on one plant. It's easy to appreciate the flower, but what about those prickly bits? Sure, they're okay to look at, but do you want to feel them? The metaphor is helpful as you practice noticing how quick you might be to judge and reject a "negative" sensation or emotion. We all do that, but is it the best option?

Like mad, sad, worried, sick, tired, cold, and cranky, prickly falls under the "bad" category of human feelings: Down the chute they all go, like the recalcitrant Veruca Salt in Willie Wonka's chocolate factory. Good riddance!

But here's the thing: Expelling emotions you don't appreciate can leave you living a pretty superficial and even dishonest life. Not everything is a sweet paradise, and expecting that is a setup for struggle. By accepting the truth of what you feel, you can ease toward grace.

That's the essence of this coping guideline. Normalizing ambivalence is about being honest with whatever occurs to you emotionally, even if what you feel isn't pleasant or feels contradictory. If your life is impacted by ambiguous loss, you probably already know what mixed emotions can do to you. A family member once shared with me that she struggled to look at photographs of her son when he was young, before his SMI changed him. "Part of me is happy to be reminded of those years," she said, "but I'm sad because I miss that."

By normalizing ambivalence, you give yourself grace to feel whatever you feel, with all the messiness and contradictions just as they are. You can be happy and sad at once, and sad doesn't have to move out to make way for happiness. There's room for both when you expand what you're willing to acknowledge.

> ***Do now:***
>
> 1. *Write this down: normalize ambivalence.*
>
> 2. *Under that write these prompts, jotting down answers that occur to you now and leaving room for more after you learn more about this approach:*
>
>   - *What mixed emotions do I feel?*
>
>   - *Can I give myself grace to feel what is real?*
>
>   - *Can I sit with strong emotions to avoid explosive, unintended actions?*

After considering these prompts as part of her seminar homework, one participant noted that she was seeing for the first time a jumble of emotions that tumbled around at once, mostly without her acknowledgment. "No wonder I felt that I was such a mess," she said. "I'm starting to allow myself to feel them."

She experienced an inner conflict when relief crashed into guilt and anger. Her sense of relief, she explained, was because her family member with SMI moved out. "It was so awful to live with him and see him deteriorate," she said. Even though the shift in living arrangements was needed for her safety, she felt guilt. Also anger. "The anger is tough because I don't know where to point it," she said. Knowing that her ambivalence was normal helped her relax and simply validate her mixed feelings. "It helps to journal about these strong emotions," she said. "I tend to hold them all in and then explode when it gets to be too much. The explosion doesn't help anyone. It makes my relationships even more tense."

During the seminar, she became brighter and more talkative, eventually laughing and smiling with the group. In the group email thread after the final session, she wrote, "I have learned so much during this class. I don't want to be stuck anymore. I want to remember and also move on."

Guilt comes up a lot during the seminars—as it did for me when I was struggling to support my son and after his death, when guilt contrasted with relief. Here's what I know:

- Feeling guilty doesn't give you control over something beyond your control.
- Your guilt doesn't make someone else well or safe—now or into the future.
- Experiencing guilt doesn't always mean you are *guilty*, or that you've done something wrong.

All of this is why it's so important to sit with your emotions, notice their nuances and let them slide around in your consciousness before reacting unnecessarily or rashly. If you give yourself grace to feel what is real, you can see that we humans have complicated emotional experiences. They're extra complicated when they are mixed up with ambiguous losses. Still, the best way into your emotions is through them.

> **Do now:**
>
> 1. *What are you afraid to feel? Write it down. Be honest.*
>
> 2. *What might happen if you go ahead and feel that?*
>
> 3. *You don't need to feel that scary thing right now, but write this down: I'm open to the possibility that feeling what I feel will be possible in time.*

Ignoring emotions: Repressed emotions are a stormy barrier to normalized ambivalence. Consider the metaphor of a developing storm, with a cumulonimbus cloud gearing up for a twister. Somewhere over the rainbow, water droplets cycle and recycle through the sky while low pressure and high pressure battle it out. The vapor forms a cloud that grows darker and taller until it finally reaches the troposphere, where the winds get going. If you've lived in the Midwest, you recognize that green tint to the sky, after those drops have become hailstones that refract the light just before all hell breaks loose and tornadoes start to form on the shelf clouds low in the sky.

Think of your unseen emotions like those water droplets. If they don't rain down, they get wicked and can fly out with uncontained evil when you least expect it. Yeah, I grew up in Kansas: The Wizard of Oz and tornadoes are kind of a thing with me. I know you do not want to screech like the Wicked Witch of the West, so let's talk about how you might discharge before there's a twister.

The most important thing to do is notice what you're feeling when you're feeling it. That doesn't mean you have to react or do something. In fact, it's best that you don't. Just pay attention. I'm about to share an example that might feel real for you. Maybe it won't. You'll see the point either way. Trigger warning: I'm about to talk about suicide. Disclaimer: This is not suicide prevention counseling. The character I want you to notice is the one who would be you. This scenario will play out a couple of ways. Here goes:

Your son who is severely depressed says he doesn't want to live anymore. You panic, get angry, terrified, defensive, worried. . . . A thought flashes by that his death might bring relief—no more suffering—and your emotional explosion is topped off by a huge helping of guilt. You immediately turn off the tap on all those feelings: *Nope. This. Is. Not. Happening.* Right away, you say something like this, pretty fast: "Oh, honey, that's a permanent solution to a temporary problem. It's okay. You'll be okay. I'm here for you. I love you." Let's say he stops talking at that point, and you hug it out. You don't think about it again, and if it starts to bubble up you immediately distract yourself.

A few days later, you're exhausted after a busy day with work and chores. Your son has been sleeping all day, every day, and frankly he smells bad. His room is a mess, and his hair needs a trim. He's angry at you for asking him to get up and clean up. "Why can't you just leave me alone, Mom?" he screams at you. "I hate living here! I hate you! You're ruining my life!"

Now your blood is boiling, and you spit back with everything you've got: "If you're going to kill yourself, why don't you just do it!?"

Ouch! You did *NOT* mean to say that. You would never say that. But maybe you just did? Where in the heck did that even come from? The troposphere of built-up emotions.

Let's try that another way.

Your son whose depressed says he doesn't want to live anymore. You pause, breathe, look at him, sit down. You notice that your heart is racing. You feel angry and scared all at once. You don't know what to say or how to say it, so you say nothing, just notice the feelings in your body. You notice that your mind is spinning scenarios, imagining this house without him in it. It's quiet and clean. There's relief. Yikes! You realize you're going to need to take another look at that later. You say none of that. "Tell me more," you say, and then have a short back-and-forth conversation. He's not doing very well, and you're worried, but there's not much you can do. He's not going to meet the state criteria as overtly suicidal so you're going to have to live with this ambiguity for a while. (Of course you do all the things to make sure your son cannot access things he might use to harm himself, but that's not the point of this role-play.)

Later that evening, you close your bedroom door and lie down on the floor with your legs up over a chair. You think about how complicated this situation is. You notice that you're really afraid for your son's life. You might notice that you're also contemplating what it might be like if he died. *Awful! The worst possible outcome!* And, behind all of that is a niggling notion that there might also be a bit of relief. He's suffering, you're suffering, the whole family is suffering, and there's no relief in sight. Let's imagine your internal dialogue goes something like this:

"I can see how it would be somewhat of a relief if my son who is suffering didn't have to suffer anymore. I would be in charge of how my house looks and smells again. That doesn't mean I wish he would die. I just wish he could get relief from his suffering. I'm suffering too. In fact, I'm overwhelmed by my own suffering right now. I'm out of ideas and energy. I need to let things play out for a while without spinning my wheels so much, so I can get some rest and rethink my strategy. I'm feeling grief about the ambiguous loss of my son, and it's normal that I might think about how a change in our circumstances could bring relief. I need to give myself grace for having human feelings, and I know I won't say anything hurtful to my son. I love him so much. There's stuff here that neither of us can control. That's just true."

In the first scenario, the unplanned outburst occurs because of repressed feelings. None of the immediate emotions got noticed, and there was no digestion of them later. Even if you don't think you'd ever say anything so awful, be honest with yourself that you've got some really big emotions about this ambiguous loss situation. If you don't take care of yourself—including your emotions—you may not be able to fully control what you say in a heated moment.

Naming emotions is your first step toward taming them, a strategy I learned from Dan Siegel, a neurobiologist who recommends you "name it to tame it." Taking time to think about your feelings turns on the problem-solving part of the brain and eventually helps to settle the brain's more reactive and impulsive parts. In one seminar, participants built an extraordinary word cloud of mixed emotions they've noticed in themselves. You may notice that relief showed up quite a few times: "joy and pain, relief and devastation, relief and guilt, defeat and determination, shame and pride, sorrow and happiness, relief and frustration, quiet rage and quiet compassion."

When you notice you're feeling more than one thing at a time, give names to those feelings and notice their different features. Instead of pushing away feelings you might typically label as wrong or bad, you might laugh at your own desire to send them down the chute like that incorrigible girl in *Willie Wonka*. Lighten your mood a bit by having a chuckle at that and let yourself off the hook. Consider how your emotions are normal internal reactions to something you are going through. Think about what those feelings have to share with you, like in the case scenario.

A thought experiment to explore opposite emotions can be useful. The roots of this simple practice grew from a course I took from Richard C. Miller, a clinical psychologist and yogic scholar who has blended counseling practices with ancient meditation techniques to support people impacted by trauma. There's a longer version in the back of this book that you might share with a friend.

Do now:

1. *Scan your body, feet to head, noticing your felt experience in each section of the body and what your body parts (especially feet) are touching. Notice your breath while you look around inside yourself.*

2. *Notice if you feel an emotion calling out for attention. Give it a name. Notice where you feel that emotion within your body. If there isn't an obvious felt location, then choose one. Spend some time there, just noticing, not judging.*

3. *Consider if your emotion has an opposite and name it. Notice where you experience that opposing emotion in your body or assign a location. Spend some time there, just noticing, not judging.*

4. *Begin to toggle between the two emotions, using their physical locations in your body to support your experience of feeling into them. Notice what happens as you go back and forth between the two, without requiring your experience to be anything in particular.*

5. *When you feel finished, return to the experience of being in your body, in the space that you occupy, paying particular attention to your feet and what they are touching.*

6. *Finish with five conscious breaths, just bringing awareness to the experience of breathing with intention. Make a few notes about your experience, if you want to.*

After completing this exercise in an online seminar session, one participant said she didn't usually allow herself to breathe deeply because it felt too scary. She did that evening, she said, because she felt safe in the group. She shared that she felt calmer after giving herself permission to do the practice.

In an informal poll during that session, very few participants said they regularly sit with their feelings. About half said they were slightly comfortable with their feelings, but almost as many said they often distract themselves when they start to get uncomfortable with what they feel. A few admitted that they regularly push away their feelings because feeling numb is more tolerable.

You might feel those things too, so I'm sharing this to help you know that you're not alone! If you have a trusted friend, you might ask them to take turns with the thought experiment in the back of this book, written so you can read it to one another. If you both want to, you can talk about what it felt like afterward.

Learning to feel what you feel requires a certain surrender of control, asking you to revisit what you've already discovered about adjusting mastery. Keep remembering that it's okay to feel confused, angry, frustrated, guilty, and all the other things. You are feeling those things because you are a normal person going through something abnormal. It's not your job to guard the gates and keep out any emotion that shows up unannounced. By giving all of your emotions permission to exist, you can sort through them to see what's real and what needs some attention. Feel what you feel and respond, instead of repressing feelings and later reacting like a twister tearing the house apart.

Here's a bit of really good news: Once you make room to feel lots of things at once, you'll have more internal space for joy, enduring love, and happiness. None of the tougher emotions have to move out to make room for those dear ones that you'd love to see more often.

I cannot share this enough: Your loved one is not going to get better because you feel guilty about being happy. Your loved one wants you to be happy! And this: Grief and even guilt don't need to disappear in order for happiness to appear. When you feel more than one thing at once, no single emotion dominates you.

I experience ambivalence a lot when my grandsons visit. They play with toys that belonged to Calvin. We read his books. They sleep in his bed. I feel immense joy at being a grandma, and I'm aware that beneath the surface of my current experience is a deep grief that my son's childhood didn't lead to a happy adulthood. It breaks my heart again and again that he doesn't get to wrestle around and give horsey rides to his playful nephews. He would have loved that.

I'm so glad I've learned that my grief and my joy can coexist. I don't feel guilty for enjoying bright moments. I also don't blame myself when a grief shadow darkens an overwise bright moment.

I've gotten much better at holding onto many emotions at once. You can too.

> ***Do now:***
>
> 1. *Write this down: My loved one is not going to get better because I feel guilty about being happy.*
>
> 2. *Make any notes about your experience of mixed emotions while reading this chapter, including during the thought experiment.*
>
> 3. *Write down the name of a friend you might share this thought experiment with, and take a look at the version printed in this book's appendices.*

Find New Hope

Hope and I have struggled to get along over the years. When I launched a website for my grassroots organization, MOMI, I wrote a blog with this title, "Let's Stop Hoping and Get to Work." I explained how banishing hope freed me: "Tethered by hope, I felt like I was holding my breath. Hope felt like waiting in a stage of extreme anxiety. Weighted down by hope, I was completely stuck. When I cut the string, I drifted toward a ground I could push against."

For an essay published on a former mental health website, *Brave Expressions*, I wrote more about my disdain for hopefulness: "Hope is stuck in the future. Agency is right now. I decided to focus on what I could do instead of waiting with hope for things to sort themselves. I also had to give up hope that doing the right thing would get me what I wanted. Seeking right action was worth it either way."

I realize now that what I called right action aligns well with new hope, giving me a good reason to befriend hope again—but with clear boundaries. The concept of new hope connects all the coping guidelines, like a Möbius strip, because it gets to the meaning of your losses, your control issues, how you see yourself, what you might be clinging to, and whether you're honestly accepting your emotions.

Do now:

1. *Write this down: find new hope.*

2. *Under that write these prompts, leaving room to jot down answers that occur to you now or after you've read more of this chapter:*

   - *Am I ready to let go of old hope?*

   - *How might I play with ambiguity to increase my tolerance for it?*

   - *What is still possible, despite not getting the outcome I originally wanted?*

Let's take a pretend trip to the garden to plant these concepts firmly. Think of old hope like a rocky yard stripped of topsoil with a clay base. Your shovel won't go in, and water just puddles and slides off. Trying to make that garden grow is exhausting and yields little. To start over elsewhere, you need new soil and fresh seedlings. Think of your new hopes like fresh flowers and veggies that you grew from scratch. While you tend these new hopes, you fertilize your tolerance for ambiguity, which is really hard to see through the sweat and tears if you're still chunking away in that old rocky yard.

I hope (aha, said it!) that you have a bit of fun with this analogy and this coping guideline. Check out the word *play* in the second prompt. In the course I took with her, Dr. Boss said she loves to "go for a walk to get lost," especially in Estes Park, Colorado. I love that for her! She called it "playing with ambiguity." It's something you do knowing that you don't know how it's going to go, showing yourself that you can handle the not knowing.

My favorite ambiguous activity is surfing, never knowing how the wave might play out or if I'll even catch a ride before taking a salty swim. You might cook without a recipe, play games that require improvisation, or build a garden path of meandering mismatched stones.

If you try one of those things, you might hope that your walk to nowhere in particular will take you past lovely wildflowers or even a waterfall. If you surf like me, you can want a long, pumping ride. You can dream up the best charades clue, spontaneous pantry cookies, and new landscaping. But when you start, you can also choose to let all that go and say, "I'm just going to see what happens; whatever it is will be okay!"

Here's another way to bend your mind around what this might mean: When you know you don't know how something's going to go, but forge ahead anyway, you're gently inoculating yourself to your own discomfort with what is unknown. Be sure to choose something you enjoy, so there's playfulness in your experiment.

Fun and humor—even the macabre variety—can help when you're struggling to let go of old hopes. In my seminar, the slide deck on this topic includes a picture of Humpty Dumpty, the egg from the

English children's rhyme who fell off the wall and splintered into too many bits for all the king's horses and men to manage. That image nearly always brings some smiles—and who doesn't need to smile at something silly?

My dad, who died on my fiftieth birthday, used humor until the end. After he was given a fatal diagnosis in the hospital, he cheerfully greeted staff who came by, sometimes gifting them little treasures or a silly riddle to muddle. "I think we made him feel better," he quipped after his oncologist visited.

My dad wanted to sort through some of his things but could barely walk, so he turned the project into a treasure hunt. He'd give meticulous clues about which room, which drawer, and what to move aside to find the thing. When I brought some medallion or special trinket to his lounge chair, his grin was genuine when he said, "This is fun." Having fun was still possible, despite our obvious wish that his cancer would disappear, and we could keep on keeping on as a family.

Sweeping away old hopes is seriously helpful. I have a well-worn copy of *When Things Fall Apart: Heart Advice for Difficult Times*, by Pema Chodron, a Buddhist nun. Well known for approaching happiness through hopelessness, Chodron helped me see how relating directly with the dark moments of my life created the contrast I needed to see the light when it peeked out.

New hope blends well with a "both, and . . . " approach. Even when you're not getting what you want, you can have experiences that are rich and interesting. When you're hanging out with your emotions, try using sophisticated adjectives. If all you identify is "good" or "bad," you're not really exploring your emotions; you're just kind of judging yourself. Instead of feeling "bad" about your loved one's illness, for example, you might notice that you feel *agony, defeat, confusion, earnestness, exhaustion* or something else and all of the above. Using your thought experiment from the chapter on normalizing ambivalence, you can consider opposites to those words, such as *endurance, survival, intelligence, inspiration, rest* and consider what is possible for you to cultivate into the future.

> ***Do now:***
>
> 1. *List emotions related to how ambiguous loss circumstances have crushed your old hopes. Choose descriptive words, using a thesaurus if helpful.*
>
> 2. *Consider opposites/antonyms to those words. Are there choices you can make to cultivate those expressions, to feel more empowered?*
>
> 3. *Think about how empowerment and new hope relate to one another.*

Like while cleaning out my son's apartment after his suicide, I've put effort into exploring a range of emotional experiences—not just the happy ones—and it has created momentum for me. But before you get annoyed with me for sounding smug, I want to be perfectly clear that this has been a hell of a journey. My sorrow has been huge and dark. There were times when my own suicide seemed like a pretty decent exit plan. In the context of anything real and meaningful, I will never say, "It's all good." It most certainly is not all good! I have to pause and calm down when someone says that, or this: "Everything happens for a reason." No, just no! Dying way too young from a treatable illness was not my son's life purpose. He should have gotten good treatment and lived his full life. Yeah, I'm still really pissed off that he suffered and died.

What I'm saying is that flowers are still beautiful, and vegetables are still amazing. Things that grow from seeds still stun me with amazement, and I'm flabbergasted at my own human capacity to still seek joy and pleasure, despite everything I've been through. What I'm saying is that I didn't rediscover hope by sitting back and waiting for it to show up for me. I got there with intention. You can too. But if you're stuck in the rocks and weeds on this coping guideline, here are more ways to think about the barrier of old hope. Your new hope might relate to that thing that you know you're supposed to be doing, but haven't started yet.

The barrier to new hope is clinging to what is no longer possible. Old hope:

- Causes you to deny an ambiguous loss, perhaps believing "I'll fix this, and things will go back to the way they were."

- Leads to an expectation of closure, perhaps thinking, "This is just a blip in my life, and everything will work out fine, just like I always wanted, once I get through this brief interruption."
- Focuses on the past, perhaps causing you to say, "How I was before is what I'll keep striving for!"

Those positions block new hope from forming, but it makes sense that you might have them. Our Western culture values fortitude and often equates hope with strength and courage, making it logical to deny that anything could be unresolvable. Believing that all problems have a solution pushes suffering into the far future, as something avoidable with proper planning. When the future arrives and brings with it the pain of an unfixed issue, the only option is to look back with regret and self-blame that you must have missed a step.

That old hope mindset is a trap. New hope offers escape. When you see ahead of time that this ambiguous problem won't resolve, you let yourself off the hook. There is no magic rock to overturn, with a solution written on its underside. You decide up front that you will do what is possible with what you know as you know it. All along, you can protect your own boundaries and well-being and watch with curiosity to see what evolves. Your heart will still feel broken, but you won't blame yourself for your pain, and grief won't be your only available experience.

One seminar participant laughed while admitting during our final session that she signed up assuming her grief would get fixed. "Because of the course, I have finally been able to give up the hope that my children will ever return to me on the path they started on, or even return to me at all," she said. "I don't have a fully formulated new hope, but I am certain my old hope is gone."

Reviewing that quote months later, she said a recent annual holiday family gathering gave her a chance to practice her new perspective. Instead of begging her daughter to show up, as she has done in the past, she issued an invitation jend then let it drop. "Last year I was very upset when she didn't show up," she said. "This year not at all. Instead, I focused on my gratitude that our son and a dozen friends did show up. I thoroughly enjoyed the event."

Another seminar participant wrote this: "You can't understand it until you've lived it, but letting go of hope was the first time my brain started to be able to heal from the trauma of watching my loved one deteriorate mentally. . . . Until I was pushed to my limit I had no idea what was possible. Letting go of hope wasn't possible; revising it was. Finding joy wasn't possible (and still isn't); breathing through 'what is' without needing it to be joyful is where I land on peace."

While I was writing this book, I attended a conference sponsored by the University of Washington, called "Psychosis Care." Among presenters was Meghan J. M. Caughey, M.F.A., a clinical assistant professor at Oregon Health and Science University. A professional artist and writer informed by her experiences living with schizophrenia, Caughey led an art exercise during the online conference. I'm a total nonartist, so I was surprised by how much I enjoyed trying to draw a lotus blossom that represented me, noting and scribbling around the murkiness it emerged from and the potential it grew toward.

I bought Caughey's memoir, *Mud Flower*, right away because I wanted to know more about her experiences of loss and grief. I found that many of her perspectives matched mine. For example, she explained how her recovery didn't rely on clarity or closure.

"One can go into the fire—and just be there—in the middle of the flames—and survive," she wrote. "We don't always know if there will be another side beyond the flames. This spot, in the middle of it all, is where true courage is practiced. We stay in the flames and allow everything extraneous in ourselves to be burned away. We just stay."

As you look back on the journey you've just taken through these six coping guidelines, I hope you feel empowered to stay right where you are, with curiosity and patience about what might happen next. If you've kept your distance from the suggested exercises in this book, that's okay. You can come back to them any time you feel ready. If you're still reading, then you know you are yearning for something. Keep looking. Please stay interested in what's possible.

If you've explored the self-directed exercises, you've begun to name what's been lost and what it means to you. You've looked at your desire to control outcomes and how you might adjust mastery to let yourself off the hook. You've perhaps begun to see how your identity can adapt to these new life circumstances, and how you might revise attachments when clinging means you cannot move onward. I hope you've become patient enough to let yourself feel what you feel, realizing that ambivalent emotions are a normal aspect of your rearranged life. All of this brings you full circle to consider new hopes that are made possible by your personal growth.

However it is that you've traversed this section of the book, take a moment to celebrate. You did it! You visited all the coping guidelines. In the heat of this moment, do you have a notion about your big-picture question: *What is the thing you aren't doing because grief has been in your way?*

Do now:

1. *Take note of anything that's been on hold while you wait for clarity or resolution related to your ambiguous losses.*

2. *What are you ready to try now that you have some coping skills?*

3. *Can new hope empower your sense of adventure, even if you don't know how things are going to go?*

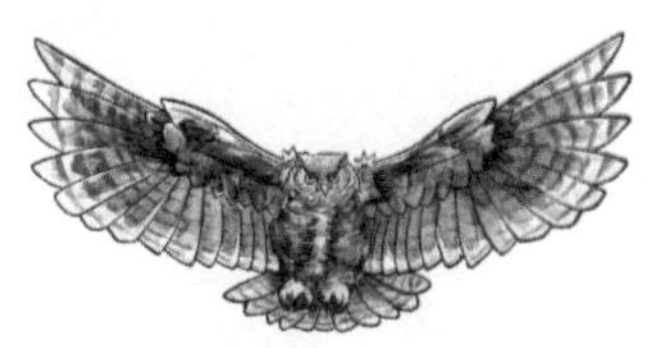

Part 4

Cultivating Community

After witnessing my son's first psychotic break, I felt loss comparable to loss from a sudden death in my closest family. It was impossible to explain this to anyone. My son was home, but he was gone! I didn't know the term ambiguous loss then, so when I tried to explain what I was feeling, the responses I got from others often made no sense and made me feel unseen and very alone with my confusing grief. I recall these comments:

- "He'll get better. He just needs the right professional help."
- "Boys will be boys. He'll grow out of it."
- "You need to take a break from the drama. I'm sure this will work out."
- "Lots of people have mental health. He just needs to take medication."
- "At least he's alive. His diagnosis isn't fatal, like cancer or something."

At some point I sought therapy. It wasn't super helpful, but at least someone was paid to listen, so I didn't feel guilty about serving up my troubles to people who found them distasteful. One paid listener suggested that I needed new friends in similar situations.

I acted on that good advice and joined a NAMI family support group. Around manila-colored conference tables pushed together to make a U, one by one we told how our lives had been so disordered by mental illness that they resembled a lousy horror movie. It never made me feel better to hear the other stories, but at least I knew I wasn't the only one trying to live that way.

At one meeting, another distraught mom got bold enough to admit this: "There's no describing the fucking layers of hell." It was the best description I'd heard of what my life had become. A longtime friend, Betsy Sunada, made me a subversive cross stitch featuring that phrase amid a pretty pastel arrangement of hearts and flowers. You have to look closely to appreciate the irony; it brings a macabre grin to my face each time I pass it in the downstairs hallway.

My American dream life had become a nightmare, but at least I was lucid enough to speak truth about what was happening in real time. And I'd found some of my people.

Still, NAMI volunteers and others kept telling me to "hold onto hope." That made no sense. What I wanted for my son was never going to happen. My old hope felt like a meaningless act of rainbow chasing. For a while, I tried to keep up appearances that I "hoped" my son might get better, return to college, and do all the things. Pretending was exhausting.

When people want to talk about hope now, I explain the value of new hope versus old hope, and I always include the term agency. Hope with agency in the form of purposeful direction is engaging and interesting, and much more helpful than strapping on my old fake smile to say I'm sure things will all work out. If you feel an "ugh" coming on every time someone encourages you to hold onto hope, you might try in your own way to start a dialogue about new versus old hope.

It's also helpful to have answers ready to roll when people use platitudes to say what they don't know how to say. Here's one that used to make me really mad: "Everything happens for a reason." No, not everything. Entropy is real. Random terribleness happens. Families like mine know how horrible it feels to hear that.

Instead of cussing people out or just avoiding human contact, I've come up with some things to say. For example, this: "Please don't say that. I cannot see that as true. My son's struggle with mental illness had no reason to it. I'm trying to find meaning in what's left of my life, but that doesn't mean his pain was something the world needed."

We can help people see things differently without being cruel. Everyone feels better when we do. Like it or not, we have hard-earned authority that we need to assert. We have learned things because we had no other choice, and now others can learn from us.

> ***Do now:***
>
> 1. *Make note of unhelpful comments you've heard.*
>
> 2. *Write down any ideas for responses if you hear similar comments again, knowing that this chapter is about to share additional ideas.*

Welcome to Our Club:
So Sorry You Are Here

Years into this strange SMI journey, I met Linda. We bonded instantly when she came to the King County Courthouse in Seattle to support me during one of my son's hearings. It took very few words for us to know that we understood one another. We knew we were members of this club no one joins by choice. Knowing her has changed my life. If you don't have a Linda yet in your life, please keep looking. You don't need to feel so alone! It's common for family members like ours to greet one another with sad solidarity, something like this: "I'm so glad to know you but so sorry that we get one another for the reasons that we do."

That day at the courthouse, when I met Linda, my son appeared before a judge whose job it was to decide whether to order a mental health evaluation to figure out if he was out of his mind enough that the thing he probably did wasn't something he did with his head on straight. That's plain speak for this: The judge was deciding fitness for trial and whether a competency evaluation would be ordered. It's illegal to try someone for a crime if they are unfit to proceed.

If you know you know. We don't come out of grammar school speaking like lawyers, but we learn this lingo over time. Speaking fancy always feels a bit like gaslighting. We family members want to scream from our guttural guts in those courts: "This is a waste of money and everybody's time! My loved one is not a criminal and needs a hospital, not this stinking jail!!!" Over time, I learned to save my rants for my pillow and talk like the people I was trying to convince so they might listen and choose a good next step or maybe do the least wrong thing.

My new friend Linda knew. We kept our composure while watching my son strut into the courtroom, his head held at an odd tilt, his hair unkempt and his eyes ablaze. His hands were shackled but holding a Bible. "Oh dear," I whispered. "He's definitely in psychosis."

His publicly appointed defense attorney, whom I had just met, was seated nearby. He quietly remarked, "Well that's good, right? He's got his Bible with him." My eyes were blurred by instant tears. "No," I explained. "He picks up the Bible when he's manic and delusional."

Boom! My emotions exploded. Another loss, another moment of watching my son die in plain sight. I had hoped to catch his eye that day, make a connection: "I see you, son. I got your back. We will get you out of this mess and back into your worthy life again."

No such luck. With his arrogant head tilt and stiff walk, my son displayed what I knew were symptoms of his illness. He was lost in his psychosis, answering the judge's basic questions with automatic intelligence that masked symptoms well enough to mislead strangers. I could see in his eyes that his mind was wandering in an entirely different reality. He was there but not there. Linda knew, but I'm fairly certain no one else in the chambers that day saw what I saw.

The wisdom of families has been degraded for decades in places where decisions get made about our loved ones with SMI. Although we are often the ones most committed to the lifelong health and well-being of those we care for, we are handcuffed by misuse of privacy laws and a general bias that families are probably part of the problem and not the solution. Family engagement is a topic that I've spoken about at state and national conferences, and I will keep sharing my truth to influence change in that arena. Join me if you are called.

In the meantime, I'll get back to the point of this chapter: Members of our SMI community need to unite in solidarity to support one another. We can teach one another about SMI, tricks to bypass barriers within the disjointed treatment system, and ambiguous loss. We can remind one another what it feels like to be treated with kindness—and how we might adjust the way we treat ourselves.

Along the way, we can also get better at recruiting people outside the SMI community to understand what we're going through and become better listeners and helpers. Because of stigma, discrimination, confusion, fear, and other complicated SMI issues, it's often difficult for outsiders to advocate alongside us.

You can help by sharing what you know. You might start by talking with someone you trust about ambiguous loss. Here are a few key phrases you might adapt and practice until they feel natural to say:

- There's a name for what I'm going through. It's called ambiguous loss.
- An ambiguous loss doesn't have clarity or resolution. That means I can't ever get closure. It's not possible because everything about this situation is ambiguous and I can't fix that.
- It's okay if you don't know what to say. I don't expect you to. I'm just learning all of this. I appreciate having someone to talk to.
- Ambiguous loss causes the same type of grief I would have if someone very close to me died (*if your person is alive but changed*).
- There's no death certificate, so it's confusing. This might sound weird, but it's like they're gone but not gone.
- Ambiguous loss means that it's really hard for me to make sense of what's happened and move on in my life. My grief is sort of frozen. (*May be true if the person with SMI is alive, missing, or has died.*)
- I'm trying to work on coping, and it's helpful if I can talk about it with someone who can listen and try to understand.
- Do you understand what I mean? Can you be that friend for me?

Do now:

1. *Look over the bulleted list above and copy down or highlight any phrases you want to practice or adjust to say out loud in your own words.*

2. *Write down any other approaches that occur to you right now.*

What to Say When You Don't Want to Say How You're Doing

A question that comes up in every ambiguous loss seminar is this: "What can I say when someone asks how I'm doing?" Consensus is strong that this question from friend, family, or stranger can be triggering, overwhelming, confusing, anger-inducing, and more. If you see a counselor or therapist, absolutely ask what techniques might help you manage your issues related to communication and friendship, especially if you find yourself lashing out or avoiding the company of others from fear of being asked.

In an email thread, one participant wrote, "If they are going to ask the question, then I feel they should brace themself for the answer. I often reply with the truth, like 'things suck' or some sarcastic remark, like 'dandy.' I can't seem to just say 'okay,' as I feel it is such a huge lie." She shared more wistfully later that she craves empathy: "It would be nice if someone would say something simple, like, 'I'm sorry you're going through tough times.' "

Another participant said her response depends on how well she knows somebody, but most friends struggle if she answers with honest details about the SMI circumstances of her loved one. "The ones that care will stand by and let me talk," she said. "Others usually run very quickly or back away slowly. I used to feel bad, but now I think, 'Hey, they asked!' "

One mom said, "Deflection is an art, and I depend on it." She went on to explain how she answers casually that she's "hanging in there," or that "life is a mixed bag, having children that really aren't doing very well." She often follows those remarks with a quick pivot: "How are YOU?" Her vague responses, she says, are partly to protect the privacy of her son with SMI and partly to reserve her own emotional energy when she cannot be sure of a friend's invest-ment in listening.

"It has been disappointing to me that some of the people I thought would show up for me have not," she says. "Others have unexpectedly stepped up. It has been very strange and kind of disorienting and sweet. I have to remind myself that not everyone has the capacity for this level of darkness. That has made me damn mad at times! Some friendships have faded, and that is another layer of loss I didn't expect. I have made new friendships and strengthened some older ones."

In truth, sharing and listening are exhausting, so be judicious about how and when you engage in difficult conversations. The brain uses almost a quarter of a person's calories, with the frontal cortex burning fuel the fastest. That's the part of the brain we use for problem-solving, so it's no wonder we get weary from trying to explain things.

Still, you need empathetic support and won't get it by avoiding people or shutting them down. Our seminar groups brainstormed a range of responses that might help you too. Try these:

How are you doing?

1. If the person asking is a stranger, such as a grocery clerk, or someone you won't deepen a friendship with:
   "That's a tough question for me right now but thanks a bunch for asking. I'm glad to be buying these lovely apples today." Include any truth to match the moment, with weather as a good fallback. You never know, but your answer might help another person see their own "both, and . . . " reality. Maybe they will think or say, "You and I are both having a rough day, and you are right that these apples are lovely." What they think or say doesn't matter. You've made a healthy human connection, and that matters for both of you.

2. If the person is not someone you trust with your deeper feelings, but you still enjoy one another and want to stay friends:
   "I appreciate you asking. It's not something I can talk about right now. I appreciate this chance to talk about lighter things."

3. If the person is someone you trust, but you don't want to overshare in a way that might feel like dumping:

"That's a tough question for me right now. Is this a good time for me to share an honest answer with you, or would you prefer to save it for another day?"

4. If the person you trust says they don't want to talk in depth in the moment:

   "I love that we're such good friends that we can be honest about our boundaries. Do you want to set a date to talk through things another time? I could really use a chance to talk out loud about what's going on."

5. If the person you trust says they want to hear more, test the water and adjust the temperature before jumping straight into the deep end of your emotions:

   "I'm feeling a lot right now. I'm not asking for your advice, and you don't need to know what to say back to me. It would be really helpful for me if you could just listen. I don't have many people I can share this with. Are you okay with this?"

Do now:

1. *As you consider the role-play examples above, make any notes about approaches you want to try.*

2. *Who do you want to practice with? Write it down.*

How are the Kids?

One participant noted that "people seem to ALWAYS want to ask about the kids. It's a cringey topic for me." Another said talking honestly about her twenty-something son would require disclosing the cognitive decline that goes with his schizophrenia—something that's difficult for others with adult children of similar ages to understand. "My son is stuck developmentally at around fifteen or sixteen," she shared. "Right around that age is when I started to notice something wasn't right. It's like I have a lifelong teenager as a son. I am working on loving him right where he is, but not many people can understand that."

In our seminars, participants relish having new friends who understand their positions. Below are sample questions and answers to consider when speaking with friends outside the SMI community, to spread understanding more broadly while protecting your own boundaries and honoring your stamina. Remember that revenge and hate are barriers to healing (refer to the chapter on how to make meaning). Spreading authentic kindness helps everyone and is possible, even when grief runs deep.

Q: How are the kids?
A: Thank you for caring about our family. It means a lot to me that you want to ask. The short answer is that times are really difficult right now. *Perhaps follow that with:*
- I don't have the energy today to give a longer answer, but I will let you know when I want to talk about it. Would that be okay with you?
- I've been reading about (SMI, psychosis, ambiguous loss) and learning a lot. Do you have the time or energy to (read a book or article/watch a video) before we talk so we can use some of the same words and share some understanding about what I want to talk about the most?

- I feel like talking about some of it today. Do you have the energy to listen now? I'm not asking for advice, but it would ease my heart a little to share some of this.

Q: How is [name]?

A: I really appreciate you wondering and caring about [name]. Sometimes it feels like my friends are afraid to ask because, as you know, it's a difficult subject. Sometimes it helps to talk about it and sometimes I have a really hard time knowing what to say. *Follow that with:*

- Today I just don't have the energy to go there but thank you again for asking because I do love [name] so much and I wish it was not so hard and painful. I appreciate you. Please give my love to [the name of someone you know in their family, as a reciprocal gesture of caring].
- Today is actually a good day for me to talk about something specific that's going on. Can I talk with you about . . . (Make it clear that you're not expecting them to listen to a long timeline and every single thing that's bothering you.)

Q: How's the fam? (Heads up! The casualness of this ask is a cue to keep it light.)

A: Well, that's a tricky question for me. *Follow that with:*

- I'd rather talk about something else, like where we might have lunch.
- I appreciate that as a topic of casual conversation for many people, but it gets heavy fast for me. We can talk about it sometimes, but not today.
- Is there something you want to share about your family? I'm happy to hear a highlight or two.
- Keep in mind that talking about families is hard right now because our crisis never seems to let up.

> ***Do now:***
>
> 1. *Consider if there was ever a time when a friend asked about your loved one and you responded in a way you weren't happy about later.*
>
> 2. *What might you plan to say in a similar situation next time? Is there anything in the chapter above to help you plan ahead?*

When Friends Who Don't Understand
Keep Talking and Talking . . .

A seminar participant whose young adult child is not doing well has struggled while friends of the same generation become grandparents. "I want to cry inside when my friends go on and on about the joys of being a grandparent," she said. "It's the kind of loss you can't really talk about." In our group, we brainstormed approaches. Here's one:

"I'm sorry to interrupt, but I need to share something. It sounds like you are finding a lot of joy in your grandchildren. That's wonderful for you. I'm having a hard time listening to all of this because our family is in crisis right now. Of course, I wish you well, but sometimes it's hard to hear about other people's happiness when joy is just not making its way to me right now. Does that make sense to you? When we share updates, would it be okay to focus on just a couple of your favorite moments? I'd love to celebrate those highlights with you, but hearing all the details pulls me toward feeling pretty depressed. I appreciate our friendship. Thank you for letting me be honest with you."

As ideas like this flowed through our group, all acknowledged how important this type of role-playing can be. A few suggested they might practice with each other. I encourage that!

Remember to adjust mastery here. Give up perfectionism in relationships. Instead, practice speaking with integrity. If you know that what you said was honest and kind, you can accept an outcome that might not be ideal but isn't because of your wrongdoing. If you make a mistake and blow your top or overshare, apologize! Explain that you're still practicing how to show up in a life that's been rearranged by ambiguous loss.

Sometimes our best intentions don't land like we wanted. When that happens, it helps to have a strategy, especially if the unwanted response triggers frustration or anger. Here are some role-playing examples that might help under certain circumstances:

- I'm sorry but I'm not sure you heard me. I really mean that I don't want advice.
- Let me say again that this is hard for me right now.
- I'm sorry, but I guess I just need some "me time" today. I'll see you soon. Take care.

If the frustrating conversation is SMI-related and shows that the person you're speaking with is uneducated about symptoms and behaviors related to psychosis, do your best to share information while honoring your emotional boundaries and your friendship. Here are some examples:

- Please don't speak about [name] that way. It's hurtful. Nonadherence to medication is related to symptoms. The brain is a complicated organ, and we cannot possibly know what it's like to be [name]. Not being able to see your own mental illness must be really confusing. There's a name for that symptom of illness. It's called anosognosia. Would you like to know more about what that means?
- I'm doing my best, but it's super hard. I hope you can understand that comments like that make everything feel worse. I don't expect everyone to be an expert about schizophrenia, but I'm grateful to anyone willing to learn enough to be helpful and supportive. Thank you for letting me say that, and please let me know if I can share more information about schizophrenia with you. I'm still learning too.

One participant on that email thread responded with this: "I love that—using people's questions as an opportunity for a brief public education about SMI. I'll think of it as a brief soundbite coming from me to someone who has the courage to ask about my family."

Do now:

1. *Make some notes about how you explain the condition affecting your loved one and/or how you defend them when needed.*

2. *Do you need to practice saying this, so you don't get frustrated and tongue-tied? If yes, do that now (out loud or silently, in your head, if necessary).*

Let's Teach Everyone What Ambiguous Loss Means!

Back on that day at the courthouse in Seattle, a friendship was forged that ultimately led to this book. My friend Linda taught me the term ambiguous loss, which she knew from her professional career as a social worker supporting those impacted by dementia. Loss is ambiguous for everyone involved, whether you're losing your memory or you're watching a person you love slowly slip away.

Linda and I saw parallels between ambiguous losses related to dementia and those related to mental illness. We had an interesting conversation, but it would be years before I remembered to apply knowledge of ambiguous loss to my own situation. I authored this book because it's the book I needed. I hope it's just what you needed and that you feel equipped to use what you've learned.

Please spread the learning! Too few people know about these concepts or how to apply them. In 2023, when my brain was first stirring around the concepts for my ambiguous loss project, I wrote to Dr. Boss. I told her about losing my son three times: to his illness, to the ineffective treatment system, and to suicide.

She wrote back promptly, urging me to take her online course and become a teacher on this topic. "I am about to be eighty-nine and need others to teach about ambiguous loss," she wrote. "Let me know how you feel about doing this." She also shared personal guidance. "I am so sorry that you lost your son. As you say, more than once. . . . Instead of 'moving on' or 'seeking closure,' I recommend moving forward and learning to do 'both, and . . . ' thinking: *He is both gone and here in my heart.*"

Indeed. From that first personalized lesson from the ambiguous loss expert herself, I found a pathway to healing. Calvin has been here all along. Because of him, you have also found your way to these important teachings. I hope you find that meaningful because it means everything to me.

Calvin's death, March 18, 2019, dovetailed with early spring. Daylight saving time had recently extended our days, so a longtime friend strolled with me one mild evening. Just past twilight, we both felt something unusual. With a nearly silent swoosh but airflow we felt in our hair, a great-horned owl swooped from behind us to land in a red alder tree in early bud. The spindly tree was right next to us, barely twenty-five feet tall. The owl's golden eyes peered into mine, an experience I've otherwise never had. It's hard to explain why, but I felt like Calvin was communicating with me through that owl. My friend felt it too. The moment lasted maybe a minute, while the world otherwise stopped around us.

I didn't speak, but I recall thinking, "Thank you, Calvin. I miss you. You were always so wise, so this makes sense. I'm so sorry it was hard for you. I will always love you. I will make sure your life continues to matter down here."

After the owl flew away, my friend and I were quiet. We knew something special had occurred. After a celebration of life to honor my son a few weeks later, I shared that story with cousins who were with me in the backyard, which is on the other side of a creek from where I'd seen the owl. They were both fascinated and one asked, "But how do you know it was Calvin?" As I opened my mouth to respond, a great-horned owl flew low and fast across the entire backyard.

"Because," I said aloud, while pointing to the flying form, "he's right there!"

Do now:

1. *Whether the loved one related to your ambiguous loss is still alive, missing, or has died, consider if there is a symbol of them that is useful to you. If not, is there something logical that you might choose as a symbol?*

2. *How might that symbol help you remember what you will always love about that person, even when times are tough?*

Final Words

My son's way-too-short life has left forever unanswerable questions. Still, with intentional coping I've uncovered meaning in my losses. I've done some of the work to get better at adjusting what I think I ought to master. Who I am is forever changing, but I've worked pretty hard to insert myself into places where I feel a sense of purpose. I definitely think about the ongoing reconstruction of my sense of identity.

I've stopped begging the universe to reverse time and give my old life back, choosing the more practical path of letting go while remembering, a revised attachment. I've learned that ambivalence is normal, although it took a long time to feel normal. I'm even open to new hope, as long as what I'm hoping for comes with agency toward a realistic goal. Despite not getting what I originally wanted—a life of laughter and fun with my whole family intact and well—I get out of bed most mornings with relative enthusiasm.

Surrounding myself with owls has helped me stay connected to Calvin. They are everywhere, actually—on walls, shelves, jewelry. Whenever I see an owl in public, I call it a "Calvin sighting." I love it when friends and family let me know about their "Calvin sightings" also. I tease my grandsons when they're bored by suggesting they count owls in my home.

Other families take comfort from similar rituals and symbols. One mom has a son who is "gone but not gone" while locked in his psychosis within a state hospital. She and her husband got matching necklaces engraved with their son's initials. "We had a little ritual and put the necklaces on each other's necks," she says. "We debated for so long about how to honor him and felt the need to do something. My husband (a quiet griever) said, 'I want a necklace, where I can have him on my heart.' This gives us a little peace. He is not forgotten!"

The journey is ongoing for all of us. I'm still losing things ambiguously and grief gets me good sometimes. After the worst of the pandemic had settled, my husband Matt got laid off from a twenty-eight-year career at the same company. In a tough job market, he's been unable to secure a new opportunity after more than two years of looking. That ambiguous loss brings disappointment mixed with new desires. As this book heads toward publication, we plan to sell this home we bought when Calvin was six and downsize, preferably in a place closer to the coast.

National events test my sense of general safety. The world is alive with ambiguity about what might happen next in health care, housing, insurance, retirement, courts, and other arenas that have direct impact on all of us but could especially harm those with SMI. My son is gone, but these are my people, and I care deeply.

My seminar participants have taken strides toward self-directed healing, and we keep in touch through a monthly alumni meeting online. One said, "I was greatly helped. I had been frozen with grief and I'm trying to thaw. The 'both, and . . . ' concept has been especially helpful in real, raw everyday life. I can now allow myself to feel joy in certain areas in life and also deal with my grief regarding my son's SMI challenges."

Another said simply, "The ambiguous loss workshop is one of the most helpful things I have done for myself."

Emotional setbacks are common. Another mom shared that she passed out when someone rang the doorbell fairly late one night. Her constant fear that her son might turn up dead got the best of her, even though that visitor wasn't bringing bad news. "You're on a path to healing," she says, "but you're constantly looking over your shoulder waiting and watching for the next crisis. It's never gone. I hate hearing the phone ring. I hate getting a text message because I never know what it's going to be."

When I started to draft this book, I invited seminar graduates to contribute. One disclosed that the seminar homework made her anxious. "I haven't wanted to face some of the feelings that would come up if I were to write," she said. "Writing prompts help, but I often even resist those!"

In further explaining her struggle with the self-directed work, she described how she eventually blended what she learned with help from a professional. Hers is a good example of what might be possible.

"I often use the excuse of being busy, but it's really more like not knowing how much of my mental energy and attention I can devote to the quiet rage I feel at my life being dominated by SMI," she said. "If I tell myself that it's safe to feel these feelings and I really believe it, maybe that means I have to dedicate some time to giving in to them, like spending a few hours in nature or with loud music, old photos, and nobody around for a few hours.

"I've been afraid of getting swallowed up and incapacitated by trying to feel my feelings and go through regular daily life at the same time. Speaking to a compassionate therapist has greatly helped. When I took ideas from the seminar to her, it made a big difference. It helped her see the framework I'm trying to work with and live in, especially the 'both, and . . . ' integration of feelings that can be so painful to coexist peacefully with. I was wishing and willing them away to the detriment of my health and other relationships."

Finishing this book, you may feel empowered, or you may feel overwhelmed. If you feel both, that makes sense! Set a kind pace for yourself as you continue onward in using these guidelines as part of your daily life. Always remember that you are not alone in living with ambiguous loss caused by SMI. Thank you for wanting to heal and shine your important light both inward and outward. You can do this. I believe in you, and I wish you well.

What is the thing that you aren't doing? Now is the time to start doing it!

Do now:

1. *Write a note in your journal to congratulate yourself for finishing this book.*

2. *Find a way to celebrate you, just you!*

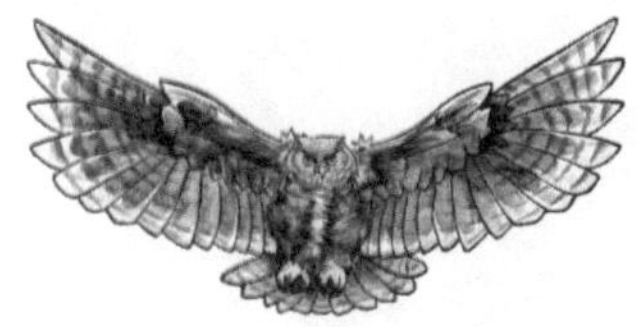

Appendices

Study Group Guidance

Coping with ambiguous loss is an activity that requires commitment, consistency, and community. You might use this guidance to start an ambiguous loss study group, which is like a mash-up between a book club and a support group. You may already have friends ready to meet up and get going. If not, the Resources and Networking section of these appendices might help you locate people with similar goals. You could meet in a quiet public place, in one another's homes, or online.

You may be the natural leader for your group or ask everyone to take turns hosting. The host makes sure everyone is heard, and group norms are upheld. Although it's wonderful to be friendly and spontaneous, meetings with a gentle structure provide comfort. I hope these adjustable guidelines and prompts help you help one another on this ambiguous loss coping journey.

Introductions: As appropriate, bring a photo (can be your background if online) of a loved one connected to your ambiguous loss. Share only the essence of your story to keep focus on your personal experiences with loss and grief:

- Your name, location, primary occupation, and one thing: I want you to know that I . . .
- Introduce the person in your picture with a brief update: This is [name], my [son, spouse, sister . . .], who has a diagnosis of . . . and is now . . .
- Your ambiguous challenge related to the situation: This is hard for me because . . .
- Your coping status: I feel . . . today, and I'm currently working on . . .

Group norms: Agree to group norms and review them at each meeting. It can be difficult for people impacted by SMI to focus on themselves. Many will want to use any group to immediately start seeking answers and resources to help their loved one who is unwell. To focus on ambiguous loss and coping with this unique and complex grief, the group can write its own norms or agree to these:

- We are here for our own growth and learning, not to retell the narrative of our unwell loved ones.
- Lessons learned here go with us into the world, but the private stories shared by others are kept confidential.
- We have been hurt by things that are not our fault. We agree to treat ourselves and one another with patience and grace.

Self-validating statements: In Part 1 of this book I encourage you to begin coping by trying on your emotions. Your group might say these statements out loud and/or discuss what feelings they bring up:

- There will never be closure because my losses are ambiguous.
- Grief and loss are not everything that I am and do.
- I can feel many things at once.

Discussion guidance: Any of the "do now" exercises in this book might provide a starting point for the conversation. Whoever is hosting can manage the prompts and make sure everyone shares the air. As host, you may need to gently interrupt someone who is talking a lot to remind them that some people haven't spoken yet. You can say, "Let's make sure everyone hears from everyone."

Ending the meeting: Finish each meeting with a simple breath practice guided by a group leader or just a pause to take three long breaths in silence. The host might say these statements in line with each breath:

- Inhale and direct compassion inward. Exhale love for yourself.
- Inhale acceptance that ambiguous losses have hurt you. Exhale love for yourself.

- Inhale gratitude for everyone here today. Exhale love for yourself.

Exploring Opposites: A thought experiment

This thought experiment helps you work with the coping guideline of normalizing ambivalence. You might take turns reading it with any friend, in a quiet and comfortable place. You can also record yourself and then listen to the recording. Be sure to speak slowly. There are ellipses to remind you to pause. Afterward, you might want to talk about your experience or write some notes.

You can stand, sit in any comfortable position, or lie down. Your eyes can be open or closed. Soft ambient music is optional. Where you go with this is up to you, so don't feel pressured to enter places you aren't ready to visit. The first time you do this, you may want to choose simple opposite feelings, such as warm and cool or darkness and lightness. After more practice, you might feel ready to explore tougher emotions, such as sorrow and joy or grief and relief.

The first part is a body scan. You can follow this script or make up your own. This version starts with the feet and moves toward the head, which tends to support relaxation. If you fall asleep, that's because you are tired; relish the rest! If you prefer, you can make up your own body scan that starts with your head and moves down to end at the feet. That might help you stay more alert, if that's what you want to feel. If you try both, notice the different effects. If you don't have some of these body parts, please adjust accordingly. The important thing is to scan the body you have to become present inside. Here we go:

> *Notice the room that you're in, the lighting . . . the temperature . . . any sounds in the distance . . . or closer to you. . . . Notice the position of your body and if there's anything you might shift to be even just a little bit more comfortable. . . . Feel free to keep your eyes open or close them at any time. Make any adjustments, at any time, to keep yourself as comfortable as you can.*

Notice your feet and what they are touching. Is it hard or soft? Notice the toes on each foot and wiggle them if you want to. . . . Notice that each foot has a bottom part and a top part. Your legs have a lower part, and you have two knees. Your legs have an upper part, and you have two hips. Notice what your hips are touching. Feel your hips, legs, and feet, noticing what it feels like to pay attention to your body. . . .

Above your hips is your waist. As you breathe, air moves into and out of your belly. Your ribs move too, in front of your body, on your two sides, and maybe even in your back. Notice what it's like to watch your body breathing in all of these directions. . . .

Above your ribs in the front is your chest. In your back are your two shoulder blades. Your outer shoulders are connected to your arms, which have an upper part, elbows, and a lower part. Your two wrists are connected to your two hands. Each hand has a thumb and four fingers. Wiggle them if you want to. Notice what your hands are touching and if they are relaxed or clenched. There is no wrong way to be. We're just taking a look around and noticing what it's like to be in our bodies. . . . Notice that right now you are safe. You are safe and breathing.

Above your shoulders is your neck, which connects your torso to your head. Your head has a top part, a back part, and two sides, with ears. On the front of your head is your face. You have a forehead and two eyes. Between your two eyes is your nose. Below that is your mouth. Notice your teeth and the tongue inside your mouth and whether you might let your mouth relax for right now. . . .

Notice the breath as it starts by coming in through your nostrils and traveling down your throat and body into your belly. As your belly relaxes, the breath moves back up to exit through your nose. Notice what it's like to watch your breath travel the full distance between your nostrils and your belly, back and forth. . . . Your body breathes itself all day, keeping you alive. What's it like to pay attention to your breath?

Begin to scan through your body, feet to head and head to feet, noticing your felt experience in each section of the body and what your body parts are touching. Keep noticing your breath. As you look around inside yourself, notice now if there is a feeling or an emotion

*calling out for attention. For example, you might feel warmth . . .
pain . . . anxiety . . . curiosity . . . serenity . . . grief . . . or something
else. Take your time to discover what's true for you, right now. . . .*

*Once you've identified something that is coming up for you, give
it a name and say that word inside your own mind. . . . Now, notice
where that feeling or emotion is strongest inside your body. . . . If it's
not clear to you where this feeling or emotion lives, then assign it a
location. Spend some time there, just noticing your experience, not
judging. . . . What do you feel, and where do you feel it?*

*Now, consider if your emotion has an opposite. Give the opposite
a name. . . . Notice if there's an obvious location for that opposite
emotion to live inside your body. If nothing comes up, then assign a
location. . . . Spend some time there, just noticing, not judging.*

*Begin to toggle between the two emotions, using their physical
locations in your body to support your experience of feeling into
them. . . . Notice what happens as you toggle back and forth between
these two feelings, in their different locations, without requiring your
experience to be anything in particular. . . .*

*Notice your breath, and let your breath join your mind in visiting
these two places inside of you. What is it like to notice and feel all of
this at once? . . .*

*Let the toggling between those two places slowly end. . . . Now
return to the experience of being in your body. Notice your feet, legs,
and torso, your shoulders, arms, hands, head. Notice any furniture
you are touching, and the air around you. The lighting. Any feelings of
coolness or warmth. If your eyes have been closed, you can open them
now or in a few moments.*

*As we finish our thought experiment, please take three conscious
breaths, bringing awareness to the experience of breathing with
intention. . . .*

Coping Guidelines and Questions to Explore

Find meaning
- What have I lost?
- What does this loss mean to me?
- Are there "both, and . . . " emotions?

Adjust mastery
- When do I struggle for control?
- What can I do instead to foster feelings of strength/resilience?
- What helps me let go of idealized relationships?

Reconstruct identity
- Who am I now that I have experienced these losses?
- Where do I belong and find purpose?
- Can I let go of wanting or needing an absolute identity?

Revise attachment
- Can I accept that someone may be gone but not gone?
- What helps me accept that what is real may not be ideal?
- How do I let go while remembering?

Normalize ambivalence
- What mixed emotions do I feel?
- Can I give myself grace to feel what I feel?

- Can I sit with strong emotions to avoid explosive, unintended actions?

Find new hope
- Am I ready to let go of old hope?
- How can I play with ambiguity to increase my tolerance for it?
- What is still possible, despite not getting the outcome I originally wanted?

Acknowledgments

I must start by thanking my consistently loving husband, Matt, who brought me coffee and rubbed my shoulders after I woke at 4 a.m. to weep and write. My mom, Judy Niebaum, was my first and most devoted reader, encouraging me onward with each new draft. My daughter, Michelle, and my grandsons, Cole and Cam, bring ongoing joy and help me see brightness into the future.

Huge thanks to my dear friend, Linda Wiley, who was the first person to explain ambiguous loss to me. She held my hand through the worst of my son's struggles and offered solidarity when no one else knew what I needed.

I am incredibly grateful to Dr. Pauline Boss, who coined the useful term "ambiguous loss" and brought coping options into the light. Each time I reached out to her, Dr. Boss personally encouraged me to keep learning and teaching these important concepts. When I shared an early draft, she lit me up by praising my writing. She also offered gentle, wise words to help me tend my own heart.

I want to thank Ashlee Reyes, my Treatment Advocacy Center (TAC) co-worker who has supported my online seminars with helpfulness and grace. I'm grateful to Nina Richtmann, Lisa Dailey, Lindsay Moran, and TAC for supporting my professional and personal growth, including through this book project. Thank you to E. Fuller Torrey, MD, for founding TAC and creating an organization focused on the unmet needs of people with the most severe mental illness conditions.

Author Pete Earley offered early editorial support to help me go deeper into the heartbreak of ambiguous loss and show how I found my way up from a deep well of grief. Without his guidance, my project might still just be a word file in my laptop. His connection to Mike Sager gave me a practical publishing path, and I'm intensely grateful to Mike for immediately understanding the value of my work and transforming my manuscript into a beautiful book.

Thank you to artist Todd Fischer for the beautiful owl painting that I commissioned years ago to commemorate my son's death. A fellow surfer, Todd understood the depths of my despair and brought to his canvas the story I shared about how I felt my son's presence after his death. Thank you to my cousin, Holly Hess, who saw the great-horned owl with me in real time and has been a cheerleader for my book since it was just an idea in my head.

I was finishing my manuscript as Gail Freedman debuted her documentary film, *No One Cares About Crazy People*. She generously read enough to know she wanted to endorse my book, which serves the very people that her film documents—families whose loved ones with severe mental illness live and die without proper care. Pulitzer Prize–winning author Ron Powers, who wrote the book that inspired Freedman's film (based on his own heartbreaking personal story) also generously read what I had written in order to endorse my book.

To Jennifer Jackson Sanner, my lifelong friend and former editor of *Kansas Alumni* magazine, and to her editorial team, I offer thanks for encouraging my book project from its earliest incarnations. I'm also grateful to my dear friend Debby Bettinger, who has truly seen me during all of my life's biggest moments and gave early important feedback and encouragement.

I also want to thank Dr. Jürgen Unützer at the University of Washington for cheering me on and offering his endorsement after reading early draft chapters. Thank you to Randye Kaye, Mimi Feldman, and Mindy Greiling for helping me share my story and information about ambiguous loss on their important podcast, *Schizophrenia: Three Moms in the Trenches*. Thank you also to Tony Mantor for including my story on his podcast *Why Not Me?*

I'm grateful to Hailey Tortora for social media guidance and to Kim and Andrew Audova for their unprecedented encouragement and support, including when I needed a log cabin in the woods to work in peace. Thanks to Stephanie Chandler and Nicole Drapeau Gillen for guidance and support as I began to navigate the confusing world of publishing.

Early readers Susan Hasselle and George Harris offered professional discernment to inform early improvements. Author Todd Brown provided invaluable feedback to improve the book's self-help structure. Reader Sherri Wittwer helped me know I was on the right track by writing immediately about her "ugly cry" upon finishing my manuscript on a plane. I also offer heartfelt gratitude to Susan Russo, Roberta Pietrok, Kimberly Starr, Tara Rolstad, Barbara Gates, Debra Lewis, Chelsey Clammer, Meghan J. M. Caughey, and Kerry Martin.

Paula Smith, you have helped me align, settle, and find my strength over and again: Thank you also for loving Calvin and offering him healing even when he was hard to reach. So many friends and family helped me honor Calvin's too-short life when his death was most raw. Special gratitude to my brother Rich Niebuam and to Heidi O'Connor, Jacki Elsom, Tomi Blackledge, and Angela Fadlovich with the swim team yard crew. Jewels Campbell, Teresa Embree, and Christina White: Matt and I are forever grateful for your friendship and generosity when our lives couldn't have been more confusing.

Thank you to co-workers from my yoga years, including Sundari SitaRam, Julie McCoy Cox, and Heather Jolma Fray. You all helped me grow and learn to guide others toward healing. Julie, when the Earth stood still and the veil was still thin, you and I knew we were seeing something extraordinary. Thank you for bearing witness with me and the wise one who visited us in the twilight.

I'm grateful to every person who has had the courage to address their ambiguous losses through my seminars. You are all so dear to me. Special gratitude to those who shared insights for this book, including Rania Dima, Marilyn King, Ellen F., and others who chose anonymity.

Thank you, Hunter Graham, for being a strong example of how to use personal tragedy to inform needed change. Thank you, Teresa Graham, for inviting me to witness tragedy as it unfolded in your family. May every reader of this book find empowerment to encourage a better world for all of us and our unwell loved ones.

Resources and Networking

In addition to the resources listed here, there are dozens of support networks on social media. Try typing schizophrenia, bipolar, family support, SMI, mental health, depression or other keywords into the browser within the platform to look around for a group that fits your needs.

Treatment Advocacy Center (tac.org)
- Schizophrenia and Psychosis Resource Center: Articles and tools to support understanding of key SMI topics for personal and systems change advocacy.
- Advocacy Navigator: YouTube videos on TAC's channel that support basic knowledge on key SMI topics impacting families and individuals.
- Advocacy Bootcamp: TAC's training program for grassroots advocates sharing their stories to impact systemwide changes. Email advocacy@tac.org for more information.
- TAC Family Support Group: Private Facebook community of people caring for loved ones with SMI.

National Alliance on Mental Illness (nami.org)
- Family to Family: Free psychoeducation training for family caregivers. Find a local affiliate for support group options.
- Peer-to-Peer: Free educational program for adults with mental health conditions. Find a local affiliate for support group options.

Team Daniel Running for Recovery (teamdanielrunningforrecovery.org)
- Individual and family support related to use of clozapine, an atypical antipsychotic that helps many people with conditions that don't respond well to other medications.
- Sponsored film, *Into the Light: Meaningful Recovery from Psychosis.*

The LEAP Institute (leapinstitute.org)

- Videos, books, and training about a specific motivational interviewing strategy called LEAP® (listen, empathize, agree, partner), designed by Dr. Xaviar Amador.
- Amador's book *I Am Not Sick I Don't Need Help!* demystifies anosognosia, a symptom that prevents self-awareness of illness, and provides practical communication tools.

Cognitive Behavioral Therapy (CBT) Informed Caring for Families

- NAMI Marin County (namimarin.org) provides free online training videos featuring Dr. Douglas Turkington, a fellow of the Royal College of Psychiatrists and founding fellow of the Faculty of Cognitive Therapy in Philadelphia. Turkington has published numerous articles and books about the use of CBT for psychosis (CBT-p).
- Turkington partners with the University of Washington Spirit Lab (uwspiritcenter.org), which offers CBT-p training for caregivers.

American Foundation for Suicide Prevention (afsp.org)

- Online resources support honest conversations with someone you love who may be suicidal.
- Spreads awareness about the nationwide 988 Suicide & Crisis Lifeline.

Schizophrenia & Psychosis Action Alliance (sczaction.org)

- Offers in-person and virtual support, in addition to engaging care partners in advocacy work to impact system change.

CureSZ Foundation (curesz.org)

- Friendsz program pairs caregivers of those newly diagnosed with schizophrenia with others who have walked a similar journey.
- Sponsors "Ask the Doctor" to provide online guidance to small groups.

National Shattering Silence Coalition (nationalshatteringsilencecoalition.org)
- NSSC provides a variety of guidebooks, including those specifically for caregivers, in addition to its advocacy work.

Mental Health America (mhanational.org)
- In addition to its policy work and community education programs, MHA offers peer training and support for people in recovery to walk alongside those still seeking recovery.

Depression and Bipolar Support Alliance (dbsalliance.org)
- Wellness tools and educational resources are offered alongside options for virtual and in person support groups.

Books, Films, Podcasts and Poems

Amador, Dr. Xavier. *I Am Not Sick, I Don't Need Help!* 20th anniversary ed. Vida Press, 2020.

Berry, Wendell. "The Peace of Wild Things." https://www.scottishpoetrylibrary.org.uk/poem/peace-wild-things-0/

Boss, Pauline. *Learning to Live with Unresolved Grief,* Harvard University Press, 1999.

Boss, Pauline. *Loss, Trauma, and Resilience: Therapeutic Work with Ambiguous Loss.* W. W. Norton and Company, Inc., 2006.

Boss, Pauline. *Loving Someone Who Has Dementia: How to Find Hope While Coping with Stress and Grief,* Jossey-Bass, 2011.

Boss, Pauline. *The Myth of Closure: Ambiguous Loss in a Time of Pandemic and Change.* W. W. Norton and Company, Inc., 2021.

Caughey, Meghan J. M. *Mud Flower.* Luminare Press, 2021.

Chodron, Pema. *When Things Fall Apart: Heart Advice for Difficult Times.* Shambhala, 2016.

Earley, Pete. *Crazy: A Father's Search Through America's Mental Health Madness.* Berkley, 2007.

Feldman, Miriam. *He Came in with It: A Portrait of Motherhood and Madness.* Turner, 2020.

Frank, Anne. *The Diary of a Young Girl.* Bantam, 1993.

Freedman, Gail. *No One Cares About Crazy People.* https://noonecares-film.com

Gillen, Nicole Drapeau. *Schizophrenia & Related Disorders: A Handbook for Caregivers,* 2023.

Greiling, Mindy. *Fix What You Can: Schizophrenia and a Lawmaker's Fight for Her Son.* University of Minnesota Press, 2020.

Jaffe, D. J. *Insane Consequences: How the Mental Health Industry Fails the Mentally Ill.* Prometheus, 2017.

Jamison, Kay Redfield. *An Unquiet Mind*. Vintage, 1996.

Jimenez, Juan. "I Am Not I." https://allpoetry.com/I-Am-Not-I

Kaye, Randye. *Ben Behind His Voices: One Family's Journey from the Chaos of Schizophrenia to Hope*. Rowman and Littlefield, 2011.

Kaye, Randye, Mindy Greiling, and Miriam Feldman. *Schizophrenia: Three Moms in the Trenches* podcast. https://www.randyekaye.com/schizophrenia-three-moms-in-the-trenches

KUOW, The Seattle Times and NPR Network. *Lost Patients* podcast. https://www.kuow.org/podcasts/lost-patients

Laitman, Dr. Robert S., Dr. Lewis A. Opler, Dr. Ann Mandel Laitman, and Daniel Laitman. *Meaningful Recovery from Schizophrenia and Serious Mental Illness with Clozapine: Hope & Help*, 4th ed. CreateSpace Independent Publishing Platform, 2017.

Lieberman, Jeffrey A., MD. *Shrinks: The Untold Story of Psychiatry*. Little, Brown Spark, 2016.

Mantor, Tony. *Why Not Me?* podcast. https://tonymantor.com/why-not-me

Miller, Richard, PhD. *Yoga Nidra: A Meditative Practice for Deep Relaxation and Healing*. Sounds True, Inc., 2010.

Oliver, Mary. "The Journey." https://hellopoetry.com/poem/5249/the-journey/

Powers, Ron. *No One Cares About Crazy People: The Chaos and Heartbreak of Mental Health in America*. Grand Central Publishing, 2017.

Silver, Shanti, and Elizabeth Sinclair Hancq. *Prevention Over Punishment: Finding the Right Balance of Civil and Forensic State Psychiatric Hospital Beds*. Treatment Advocacy Center. 2024. https://www.tac.org/reports_publications/state-psychiatric-hospital-beds/

Torrey, E. Fuller. *American Psychosis: How the Federal Government Destroyed the Mental Illness Treatment System*. Oxford University, 2013.

Torrey, E. Fuller. *Surviving Schizophrenia, 7th Edition: A Family Manual*. Harper Perennial, 2019.

Torrey, E. Fuller, and Michael B. Knable. *Surviving Manic Depression: A Manual on Bipolar Disorder for Patients, Families, and Providers*. Basic Books, 2005.

About the Author

Jerri Clark is a resource and advocacy manager at the nonprofit Treatment Advocacy Center (TAC), where she supports a national helpline for people attempting to navigate treatment and legal systems. She writes content for TAC's Schizophrenia and Psychosis Resource Center and supports national training programs for grassroots advocates and families attempting to support loved ones with severe mental illness (SMI), which means illnesses that are life-altering and usually include psychosis.

As TAC's D. J. Jaffe Advocate, she developed online resources and a training program for family members coping with ambiguous losses related to SMI. Her work was featured on podcast 85 of "Schizophrenia: Three Moms in the Trenches."

A journalism graduate with highest distinction from the University of Kansas, she spent her early career as an assistant editor for *Kansas Alumni Magazine*, earning national writing awards from the Council for the Advancement and Support of Education (CASE). She reprised her *Kansas Alumni* byline in Summer 2021 with "My Son's Story."

She has shared her story and advocacy points on PBS News Hour (*Brief but Spectacular*, January 10, 2019) as well as local news and radio stations, including KING 5, KGW, KOIN 6, NWPB, and KUOW. *The Seattle Times* has featured her family story and also published her opinion piece, "The Mental Health System that Failed My Son Is Fixable" (July 1, 2023). During a special series, "Humanity over Handcuffs," by popular podcaster Tony Mantor (*Why Not Me?*) on May 27, 2025, Clark shared her personal story and key advocacy points.

A yoga teacher for more than twenty years, she sees her ambiguous loss work as a coalescence of the self-discoveries from those practices alongside her journalism, advocacy, and lived experience as a mom stretching to survive a loss beyond human expectation.

About the Publisher

The Sager Group was founded in 1984. In 2012 it was chartered as a multimedia content brand, with the intent of empowering those who create art—an umbrella beneath which makers can pursue, and profit from, their craft directly, without gatekeepers. TSG publishes books; ministers to artists and provides modest grants; and produces documentary, feature, and commercial films. By harnessing the means of production, The Sager Group helps artists help themselves. For more information, please see TheSagerGroup.net.

More Books from The Sager Group

Miss Havilland: A Novel
by Gay Daly

The Orphan's Daughter: A Novel
by Jan Cherubin

Lifeboat No. 8: Surviving the Titanic
by Elizabeth Kaye

Into the River of Angels: A Novel
by George R. Wolfe

Who She Was: My Search for My Mother's Life
Samuel G. Freedman

The Stories We Tell: Classic True Tales
by America's Greatest Women Journalists

New Stories We Tell: True Tales by America's New
Generation of Great Women Journalists

Newswomen: Twenty-five Years of Front-Page Journalism

*The Someone You're Not: True Stories of Sports, Celebrity,
Politics & Pornography* by Mike Sager

What Makes Sammy Jr. Run?: Classic Celebrity Journalism Volume 1
(1960s and 1970s) edited by Alex Belth

Our Washington, DC: America's Hometown in Transition
edited by Susan Sheehan

The Dreyfus Collection: A Novel
by Estelle Rubin Brager

See our entire library at TheSagerGroup.net

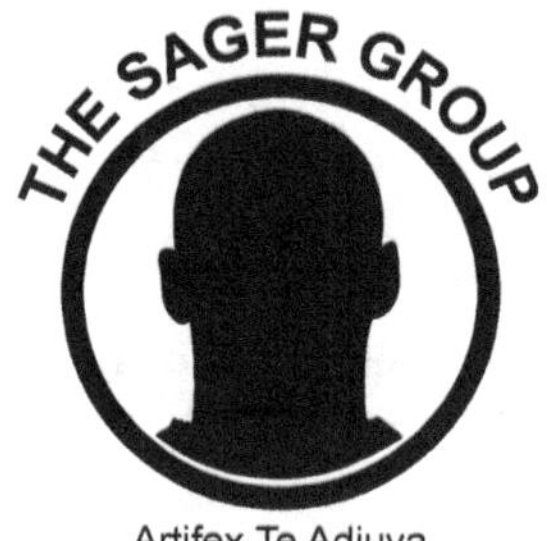

THE SAGER GROUP
Artifex Te Adiuva